Praise for
Escape from Davao

"Lukacs readily evokes the high tension and strenuous travails of the fugitives' evasion of enemy patrols en route to evacuations by American submarines. . . . Built from every available research source, Lukacs's diligent, impassioned history will aid and abet the ever-growing interest in WWII fighting experience."
—*Booklist*

"Effectively conveys the horrors of life for American POWs in the Philippines . . . a fast moving, real-life escape story, and an unexpected chronicle of a fight against censorship."
—*Kirkus Reviews*

"Like the event it covers, *Escape from Davao* is unique. Many World War II books chronicle American POWs escaping from German camps. You are holding in your hands the story of the only successful American group escape from a Japanese camp."
—James Bradley, #1 *New York Times* bestselling author of
Flags of Our Fathers, *Flyboys*, and *The Imperial Cruise*

"A remarkable story that explores the heights of human courage and compassion even as it reveals the depths of brutality that one set of human beings is capable of inflicting on another. Exhaustively researched and superbly written, the book incorporates many elements of a well-crafted suspense novel. Indeed, readers may wish at times that it were fiction rather than cruel, distressing fact."
—Bill Sloan, author of *Brotherhood of Heroes*,
The Ultimate Battle, and *The Darkest Summer*

"John Lukacs has justifiably brought attention to one of the Pacific War's most overlooked stories in his riveting book about the escape from Davao. Lukacs so breathes life into the tale that readers feel the drama and suspense as if they were present."
—John Wukovits, author of *Admiral "Bull" Halsey: The Life and
Wars of the Navy's Most Controversial Commander*

continued . . .

"In this . . . exceptional account . . . of individual triumph and collective failure, Lukacs's supple style must be noted. He writes vibrant prose and creates powerful action scenes. . . . Lukacs's skill as a storyteller makes this book very rewarding." —Thomas Mullen, *America in World War II*

"*Escape from Davao* . . . is a story unequaled among all the detailed books written about the war in the Pacific . . . a tale filled with insurmountable courage and the ultimate victory of the human soul."
—Regis Schilken, Blogcritics Magazine

"Lukacs is a gifted stylist and storyteller . . . and he knows how to build suspense. . . . At bottom, *Escape from Davao* is a morality tale, not unlike the war movies of the 1940s and '50, about pluck, luck, courage, comradeship, Yankee humor, ingenuity, and religious faith, featuring easy-to-identify heroes (the Americans) and villains (the Japanese)."
—Glenn C. Altschuler, *Pittsburgh Post-Gazette*

"A most impressive authorial debut. Lukacs manages to re-create the drama of the escape with a richness not often found in historical works. . . . Lukacs does full justice to this complex, inspiring, but also heartbreaking story."
—Richard R. Muller, *World War II*

"*Escape from Davao* is an outstanding story, framed by superb cultural and historical analysis, recommended for an audience beyond World War II buffs." —Raymond Leach, *The Virginian–Pilot*

"[Lukacs]'s careful and detailed research plus his personalization of those directly involved provided creditability that captures the attention."
—Admiral Ronald J. Hays, USN (Ret.), Former Commander-in-Chief, U.S. Pacific Fleet and Chairman, Pacific Aviation Museum, Honolulu, HI

"[*Escape from Davao*] is a gripping, gruesome, yet heroic story of inhumanity, survival, and sheer courage. . . . I read the book in two days but had to put it down every so often and catch my breath, the descriptions were so powerful."—Glenn Dromgoole, *San Angelo Standard-Times* (TX)

ESCAPE

from

DAVAO

**The Forgotten Story of the Most Daring
Prison Break of the Pacific War**

———◆———

John D. Lukacs

NAL
CALIBER

NAL Caliber
Published by New American Library, a division of
Penguin Group (USA) Inc., 375 Hudson Street,
New York, New York 10014, USA
Penguin Group (Canada), 90 Eglinton Avenue East, Suite 700, Toronto,
Ontario M4P 2Y3, Canada (a division of Pearson Penguin Canada Inc.)
Penguin Books Ltd., 80 Strand, London WC2R 0RL, England
Penguin Ireland, 25 St. Stephen's Green, Dublin 2,
Ireland (a division of Penguin Books Ltd.)
Penguin Group (Australia), 250 Camberwell Road, Camberwell, Victoria 3124,
Australia (a division of Pearson Australia Group Pty. Ltd.)
Penguin Books India Pvt. Ltd., 11 Community Centre, Panchsheel Park,
New Delhi - 110 017, India
Penguin Group (NZ), 67 Apollo Drive, Rosedale, North Shore 0632,
New Zealand (a division of Pearson New Zealand Ltd.)
Penguin Books (South Africa) (Pty.) Ltd., 24 Sturdee Avenue,
Rosebank, Johannesburg 2196, South Africa

Penguin Books Ltd., Registered Offices:
80 Strand, London WC2R 0RL, England

Published by NAL Caliber, a division of Penguin Group (USA) Inc. Previously published in a
Simon & Schuster hardcover edition. For information contact Simon & Schuster,
1230 Avenue of the Americas, New York, New York 10020.

First NAL Caliber Trade Paperback Printing, May 2011
10   9   8   7   6   5   4   3   2   1

New American Library Trade Paperback ISBN: 978-0-451-23410-0

The Library of Congress has cataloged the hardcover edition of this title as follows:

Lukacs, John D.
Escape from Davao: the forgotten story of the most daring prison break of the Pacific War/
John D. Lukacs
p. cm.
ISBN 978-0-7432-6278-1
1. World War, 1939–1945—Prisoners and prisons, Japanese 2. World War, 1939–1945—Philippines—Davao
City. 3. Prisoner-of-war escapes—Philippines—Davao City—History—20th century. 4. Escaped prisoners of
war—United States—Biography. 5. Escaped prisoners of war—Philippines—Davao City—Biography.
6. Davao City (Philippines)—History, Military—20th century. 7. Philippines—History—Japanese occupation,
1942–1945. 8. World War, 1939–1945—Underground movements—Philippines. 9. Guerrillas—Philippines—
History—20th century. 10. Soldiers—United States—Biography. I. Title.
D805.P6L85 2010
940.54'7252095997—dc22   201003238

Designed by Paul Dippolito

Printed in the United States of America

To the memory
of my father,
John F. Lukacs

Contents

I had tried to put into words some of the things that I have experienced and observed during these past months, but I fail to find words adequate to an accurate portrayal. If any American could sit down and conjure before his mind the most diabolical of nightmares, he might perhaps come close to it, but none who have not gone [through] it could possibly have any idea of the tortures and the horror that these men are going through.

—MAJ. WILLIAM EDWIN DYESS, AUGUST 16, 1943

ESCAPE
from
DAVAO

Author's Note

A verse from a poem written by Lt. Henry G. Lee, a junior officer in the Philippine Scouts, precedes each chapter. Lee, a native of Pasadena, California, was captured by the Japanese after the fall of Bataan in April 1942 and endured the infamous Bataan Death March.

Throughout the ordeal of his captivity, Lee wrote approximately thirty poems in two canvas-wrapped notebooks. These notebooks were unearthed beneath the site of the Japanese prison camp called Cabanatuan in 1945. Lee had buried his works before departing the Philippines on an unmarked prison ship that was sunk by U.S. warplanes in December 1944. Lee was killed when the second hellship he was aboard, the *Enoura Maru*, was also bombed and sunk in Takao Harbor, Formosa, on January 9, 1945.

Several of Lee's poems appeared in *The Saturday Evening Post* in November 1945 and all were later published in their entirety in a compilation entitled *Nothing but Praise*.

Throughout the book I refer to geographical locations by the name by which they were known at the time. Thus, the island of Taiwan is called Formosa, its Japanese name.

Prologue

Maj. William Edwin Dyess, U.S. Army Air Forces, serial number 0-22526, was not officially here. Not in Washington. Not seated in one of the innumerable offices catacombed inside the vast reinforced-concrete bowels of the brand-new Pentagon building. For all intents and purposes Dyess's presence in the United States was classified. Yet the dark cloak of secrecy, wartime protocol though it was, was perhaps unnecessary. After all, the mere supposition that Dyess was alive was almost unbelievable.

An exhausted apparition in loose, ill-fitting khaki, Dyess did not look very much like the dashing hero the newspapers had described him to be, a decorated pilot who wore some of his nation's highest honors—including both the Distinguished Service Cross and the Distinguished Flying Cross—among the multicolored ribbons pinned to his lean chest. Right now he looked like a man who had been through hell and back, in his case a terrifying real place with a real name—the Japanese-occupied Philippine Islands.

The tall Texan's classically handsome face was sunken and weathered, a bronzed mask drained of its youthful vivacity. Withered muscles and wispy, thinning locks of amber hair bore witness to months of malnutrition, grueling slave labor, and the insidious form of torture that he and his comrades called "the sun treatment."

A literal barefoot prophet, the erstwhile prisoner of war had carried with him throughout his odyssey few possessions: a Half and Half tobacco tin that was his billfold; a creased Mobil Oil map of the Philippines;

1

his rusty wings and captain's bars. The Presbyterian also wore a crucifix and a medal of Saint Christopher—the martyred soldier and patron saint of travelers who, in the mythos of the Catholic church, was the bearer of Christ and heavy burdens—with his dog tags. The holy objects had been given him by a dying pilot from his shattered squadron, the 21st Pursuit. Dyess had knelt by Lt. James May as he choked out his final words: "Ed, take these and wear them. Take them back to the United States when you go." It was as if May had somehow known that Dyess, unlike so many others on Bataan, would one day return home. Thus far, the items had proved a fitting bequest.

These items were not all that Dyess carried. Frozen in his crystalline, ice-blue eyes was a catalog of countless, soul-searing images, images that Dyess had purposefully and painfully carried through his waking hours and fitful dreams, images that could never be permanently laid to rest— images that no eyes should see.

Dyess had returned to the States exactly one week earlier, on Monday, August 9, his twenty-seventh birthday. But there were no throngs of relatives and well-wishers to welcome him, no popping flashbulbs and reporters waiting to chronicle the pilot's first triumphant steps on American soil in nearly two years. Instead, he arrived anonymously in Washington, the only news of his arrival a telegram he had somehow secretly conspired with Western Union to send to his wife in Champaign, Illinois, a few days before.

WILL ARRIVE CHICAGO VIA UNITED AIR LINE 2:30 PM AUG 13. REMAIN 30 MINUTES. MY PRESENCE IN US SECRET TELL NO ONE NOT EVEN FOLKS.

According to a newspaper account published months later, Marajen Stevick Dyess received "little more than a glimpse of her young husband" that day. And only later, "from a certain room in a certain hotel at a certain time [Dyess] was able to talk to his parents in Albany [Texas] by phone." It was perhaps the most bizarre, guarded homecoming ever afforded an American war hero.

But mystery had surrounded Dyess since the fall of the Philippines in early 1942. The last word anyone had received from him had been an Easter telegram sent from an overseas wireless station on the Philippine island of Cebu. In the succeeding months, as tales of Dyess's battlefield bravery began to appear in publications small and large—from his home-town *Albany News* to the *Fort Worth Star-Telegram* to *Esquire* magazine—Dyess's legend grew. A correspondent from the *New York Times*, in an article detailing Dyess's intrepid leadership and battlefield exploits on Bataan, referred to him as the "One-Man Scourge of the Japs."

But since 1942 no one knew whether Dyess was even alive, not until a few weeks earlier, when a brief, cryptic message sent from a U.S. Navy overseas station arrived unexpectedly at the Dyess home in Albany on the 23rd of July to let his parents know that their son was safe. The message, however, revealed nothing of his whereabouts, nor the manner in which he had been returned to U.S. military control. Only a handful of men, some of the most important in the American military, were privy to such details, among them Gen. Douglas MacArthur; Gen. Henry "Hap" Arnold, chief of the Army Air Forces; and Gen. George V. Strong, head of the ultrasecret Military Intelligence Service, who reported directly—and only—to the Joint Chiefs of Staff and the White House.

MacArthur, the first to hear Dyess's story in detail in Brisbane, Australia, just weeks earlier, had been so moved that his chop was immediately affixed to the freshly typed transcripts of Dyess's debriefing, thereby assuring that the documents would be sent via special air dispatch to Washington. Strong, in turn, arranged for two stenographers and an officer from the adjutant general's office to take an official statement from the pilot for the eyes of his superiors. And that was why Dyess, though weary, now sat in the inner sanctum of the War Department. As the stenographers readied to record Dyess's words, the foundation of what the War Department would later call "the greatest story of the war in the Pacific," Dyess exhumed the images—as well as the names, dates, sounds, smells, places, and faces that had been buried with them—and prepared to revisit the nightmare.

It was finally time to tell the story, the whole story, of everything that he and his eleven extraordinary comrades who had escaped with him had been through.

PART I

WAR

Lingayen
Gulf

South
China
Sea

LUZON

Philippine
Sea

PHILIPPINES

LUZON

MINDORO
SAMAR
PANAY
LEYTE
CEBU
PALAWAN
NEGROS
Sulu Sea
MINDANAO
Celebes Sea

Bataan Death March

——— Travel by foot
+++++ Travel by railroad

■ Cabanatuan
(prison camp)

Camp O'Donnell ■ ———► ● Capas
(prison camp)

Clark Field ■

San Fernando ●

Lubao ●

South
China
Sea

Hermosa ●
Orani ●

Abucay ●
▲ Mt. Natib

Morong ●

Balanga ●
Pilar ●
Orion ●

Manila
Bay

Bagac ●

Bataan
Peninsula

Limay ●
Lamao ●

Manila ●

Little Baguio
Mariveles ●

Cabcaben ●

Cavite ●

Corregidor

N
W   E
S

0   10 miles
0   12 kilometers

CHAPTER 1

Ten Pesos

. . . Soldierman, sailorman and pioneer
Get yourself a girl and a bottle too,
Blind yourself, hide yourself, the storm is near.

SATURDAY, DECEMBER 6–MONDAY, DECEMBER 8, 1941
Nichols Field, Luzon, Philippine Islands

It was late morning on Saturday, December 6, when they began filing into the post theater at Nichols Field, an American procession of sunglasses, swagger, Vitalis, and lit cigarettes with the brass insignia of Army Air Forces pilots, winged propellers, pinned to their collars.

An assortment of accents, body types, and backgrounds, the fifty-odd pilots of the 17th and 21st Pursuit Squadrons assembled in uniform fashion: clean khaki, college rings, and lieutenant's bars, with overseas and crush caps perched rakishly on their heads. They carried photographs of their wives and sweethearts in their wallets, but each shared the same seductive mistress: a love of flying. That love, as well as an appetite for adventure and a sense of duty, had brought them from all corners of the United States to this USAAF base in the Philippines. The 1939 Hollywood blockbuster *Gone With the Wind* was currently playing in the theater, but the lights did not dim on this warm, peaceful Philippine morning. These pilots were not here to see Clark Gable and Vivien Leigh.

With crossed arms, Col. Harold H. "Pursuit" George waited for stragglers to take seats. George, the forty-nine-year-old chief of staff of the Far East Air Force's 5th Interceptor Command, was a short, bespectacled, and brilliant officer with a magnetic personality. A decorated pilot in the Great War, he had piercing black eyes. Through the lazy gray haze of curling cigarette smoke, George made a sweeping reconnaissance of the room. Chatter ceased. Zippo lighters snapped shut with a clink. Pursuit George, as was his way, got to the point.

"Men, you are not a suicide squadron yet, but you're damned close to it," he said. "There will be war with Japan in a very few days. It may come in a matter of hours."

George paused. The monotonous drone of airplane motors on testing blocks filled the dewy tropical air. Leather soles nervously scraped the floor.

"The Japs have a minimum of 3,000 planes they can send down on us from Formosa and from aircraft carriers. They know the way already. When they come again, they will be tossing something."

There was church silence. None of the pilots, most of whom were rookies in their early twenties, had seen aerial combat. But George's bombshell had not caught 1st Lt. Ed Dyess by surprise. Dyess, the twenty-five-year-old commanding officer of the 21st Pursuit, had watched the winds of war whip the wind sock at San Francisco's Hamilton Field and for months had worked and prayed that his raw outfit would be ready. The odds, however, had been stacked against him long before he had descended the gangplank from the *President Coolidge* to Pier 7 in Manila back on November 20, 1941.

According to Japan's militarists, the rising sun of Amaterasu, the ancient goddess of creation, was waking the Yamato race to its destiny. The annexations of Formosa, Korea, and Manchuria, followed by an invasion of China in 1937, signaled Japan's desire to resurrect the holy mission of Jimmu Tenno—Japan's first emperor circa 660 B.C.—called *hakko ichiu*, meaning to forcefully bring "the eight corners of the world under one roof."

By the summer of 1941, the United States could no longer ignore the gathering Pacific storm. President Franklin D. Roosevelt commenced a diplomatic chess game with Japan, halting exports of American oil, iron, and rubber, freezing Japanese assets in the United States, and closing the Panama Canal to Nippon's merchant vessels. Roosevelt then looked to America's most distant ward and its most powerful overseas base, the Philippine Islands, which had been ceded to the United States by Spain after the Spanish-American War. He recalled to active duty sixty-one-year-old Gen. Douglas MacArthur, the former chief of staff, who since 1935 had lived in Manila while serving as military adviser to President Manuel Quezon's nascent commonwealth government. MacArthur was given command of all forces in the islands, designated USAFFE—United States Army Forces, Far East—but before he could build a Pacific bulwark, he first had to reinvigorate a slumbering command and repair decades of neglect.

The relentless climate—MacArthur called it an "unchanging cocoon of tropical heat"—had gradually suffused the U.S. Army's Philippine Department in a universal lethargy. There was a five-hour workday, from 0700 to noon. As the mercury rose, men retreated to their billets and barracks, tuned their radios to Stations KZRH, "the Voice of the Orient," for news and KZRM for big band hits, and took siestas while the blades of electric fans moiled the languorous air. An exchange rate of two Philippine pesos per U.S. dollar ensured that Filipino houseboys kept their bunks neat and their shoes shined, that *lavanderas* kept their custommade uniforms and sharkskin suits pressed, and that they could send a few dollars home. Though the islands were rumored to contain a collection of aging and incompetent officers and enlisted eight balls, most were energetic young officers and soldiers using the assignment as either a career springboard or a means to escape the Great Depression.

Poker, baseball, and air-conditioned double features were pastimes for enlisted men; officers golfed or rode their ponies across the Manila Polo Club. At night men from Clark Field and Fort Stotsenburg, the sprawling 150,000-acre U.S. Army complex seventy miles north of Manila in the foothills of the Zambales Mountains, slugged ice-cold bottles of San Miguel beer at the Star Bar while airmen at Nichols Field haunted joints like the Chicago Bar in nearby Parañaque. The real action, however, was found in Manila, a lively hive of culture and commerce abuzz with music from the nightclubs lining Rizal Avenue and the Escolta and aglow with the romantic incandescence of the neon signs advertising the Alhambra Cigar Company and La Insular Cigarettes. Soldiers caught furtive glances from raven-haired Filipinas, drank Tanduay rum, and danced at the Santa Ana Cabaret while sailors drank at the Silver Dollar and staggered out into the sultry night air redolent of jasmine, sewage, and burning incense. Officers mingled with Manila's social elite in the Jai Alai Building's Sky Room and debated the football fortunes of West Point and Annapolis at the Army-Navy Club. Any way one looked at it, from an officer's privileged view or from the vantage point of those in the enlisted ranks, the Philippines seemed a serviceman's Shangri-la.

But the combat prowess of U.S. troops was unknown. MacArthur also suffered a severe numerical disadvantage: he could oppose Japan's military might with only the 22,000 troops comprising the U.S. Army's Philippine Division: the all-American 31st Infantry and two regiments of Philippine Scouts, crack Filipino soldiers serving under U.S. officers. Ten Philippine Army reserve divisions would soon be available, but these troops, noted one observer, knew how to do little else but salute and line up for chow.

The American and Filipino soldiers thus far mustered drilled with brimmed model M1917A1 "doughboy" steel helmets and coconut fiber pith helmets and old Springfield 1903 and Enfield rifles. Glaringly, there were no tanks or armored vehicles in the Philippines. Two years after the bloody slaughter of Polish lancers by German tanks, anachronistic cavalry troops still galloped across the immaculate grounds of Fort Stotsenburg. Hangars throughout the archipelago housed mostly observation planes, obsolete bombers, and pursuit planes. The Asiatic Fleet was still anchored in the past at Cavite, near where Commodore George Dewey's squadron had sunk the Spanish fleet in 1898, a skeleton force of cruisers, old flush-deck destroyers, submarines, tankers, and PT boats, "a little stick which the United States carried while talking loudly in the Far East," remarked an Associated Press correspondent.

Inside USAFFE headquarters at No. 1 Callé Victoria in Intramuros, the old Spanish fortress city at the mouth of the Pasig River, MacArthur went to work. He deemed War Plan Orange—a contingency plan developed in the 1920s that called for American forces to withdraw to the Bataan Peninsula and the fortified islands of Manila Bay and wait for the Navy to dispatch the Japanese fleet—"defeatist." Instead he argued for an aggressive defense of the Philippines. Such a plan, taking into account the sheer size of the Philippines—the archipelago was composed of 7,107 islands and nearly 100,000 square miles of shoreline segmented into the three main island groups: Luzon, the Visayas, and Mindanao—was impractical. Envisioning the Philippines—and himself—as the nexus of America's military presence in the Pacific, the egotistical commander requested an expansion of his mission in late 1941.

The War Department, viewing the Philippines as, in the words of Sec-

retary of War Henry Stimson, a "strategic opportunity of utmost importance," would accommodate MacArthur. Stimson and Chief of Staff Gen.
George C. Marshall had convinced FDR that with enough time, the islands could become an impregnable stronghold—America's Singapore.
The advent of Rainbow 5, the War Department's newest plan for a global,
multi-theater conflict, illustrated Washington's commitment. The AAF
agreed to ferry thirty-five new B-17 Flying Fortresses, one-third of its
existing bomber strength, to the islands, and promised ninety-five more
B-17s and B-24 Liberators and 195 brand-new Curtiss P-40B and P-40E
Warhawk pursuit planes, as well as fifty-two Douglas A-24 dive-bombers,
by October 1942. Three radar units were scheduled to be operational by
early December. The 4th Marine Regiment would depart Shanghai—
where it had been buffering the International Settlement from the Sino-
Japanese War—to join antiaircraft, engineer, and tank elements, mostly
National Guard units, earmarked for the Philippines. MacArthur was
also promised 50,000 Army regulars by February 1942.

Ships were hurriedly discharging their cargoes onto Manila's crowded
wharves, but much of the matériel would never arrive. A shortage of
transports had created a backlog of nearly one million tons in U.S. ports
by November 1941. The eleventh-hour buildup had accelerated beyond
the logistical capacity of America's war machine, resulting in an epidemic
of snafus and shortages that would plague USAFFE throughout the coming campaign. The fledgling Far East Air Force would be affected. Lieutenant Dyess, for example, had arrived with only his crew and thirteen
pilots—half of a squadron's regular complement—and no planes. His
first batch of P-40s had finally arrived, unassembled, on December 4, but
making the planes combat-ready was another matter. There was hardly
any engine coolant or any oxygen for the planes' high-altitude compres-
sors. Because of a scarcity of ammunition, the wing-mounted .50 caliber
machine guns could not be boresighted, despite the hard work crews had
put into cleaning the barrels of the greasy, anticorrosive substance called
Cosmoline.

Perhaps the most acute shortage affecting USAFFE in late 1941 was
that of time. MacArthur thought the chance of offensive action by the
Japanese before early 1942 highly unlikely. Not only did he exaggeratedly
assure Washington that the training of his Filipino recruits was proceed-
ing ahead of schedule, he also thought that the B-17s would prove an effective deterrent. "The inability of an enemy to launch his air attack on

these islands is our greatest security," he told British Admiral Sir Thomas Phillips during a conference in Manila.

Imperial General Headquarters in Tokyo, however, had its own time-table. An unidentified plane had been discovered over Luzon in the early morning hours of December 4. Throughout the next two days, the oscilloscope of the Air Warning Service's new SCR-270B radar unit at Iba Field had registered additional blips, bogeys thought to be enemy reconnaissance planes. Since the blips meshed with intelligence reports of Japanese fleet movements, a state of alert was declared. Leaves were suspended and MacArthur ordered his B-17s to the distant safety of Mindanao, but less than half had gone south. The remaining bombers, unpainted, gleaming metallic silver, were scattered about Clark Field.

In the eerie, blacked-out quiet of Manila, tropical trade winds sighed through palms, diffused fleeting scents of hibiscus and sampaguita across Luneta Park, and fluttered American flags. Months earlier, the "Pearl of the Orient" had been a bustling, multicultural historical intersection where Pan American's Clipper flying boats skipped across the harbor while the calesa ponies and carabao carts symbolic of a colonial past still traversed the streets. Now, as searchlight beams swept the skies, the city seemed almost devoid of its soul, its future in doubt.

As George's briefing continued, Ed Dyess surely sensed that war was on the way. It was something for which he had rehearsed his entire young life.

It was hardly a surprise that Ed Dyess chose to fly. A lust for adventure and mobility seemed to be a hereditary trait in the Dyess clan. John Dyess, a Welshman who crossed the Atlantic to stake out land in Georgia in 1733, was the pacesetter for two centuries of westward migration. Dyess's father, Richard, son of a Confederate Civil War veteran, landed in Albany, Texas. Two years after the August 9, 1916, birth of his son, he took an oath as the judge of Shackelford County, a position he would hold until 1928. Thereafter, in various roles as a public servant, he would continue to be known as Judge Dyess.

Hallie and Richard Dyess raised Edwin and his sister, Elizabeth Nell, in a yellow and white house on Jacobs Street, a long block from the same Main Street that Doc Holliday and Wyatt Earp had tramped only a few decades earlier. Father and son were inseparable, sharing a love of hunting and sports and also a fascination with flight that began with a ride on a rickety de Havilland biplane when Edwin was four years old. The allure continued with news of Charles Lindbergh's transatlantic crossing in 1927. As a teenager, Dyess starred on the Albany High football and track teams, but his love for flying flourished and he worked several jobs to pay for secret lessons from barnstorming pilots.

At John Tarleton Agricultural College in Stephenville, Dyess was the school's ranking ROTC officer, student president, and one of the most talented actors in the campus theater troupe. He graduated in the spring of 1936, intending to enroll in the law school at the University of Texas. But while working on the Humble Oil pipeline that summer he thumbed a ride with a wash-out from San Antonio's Randolph Field. He became entranced with the idea of becoming an Army pilot and all but guaranteed his father that he could succeed at Randolph, the "West Point of the air." All he needed was an appointment. "Son," Judge Dyess promised, "if she can be got, we'll get her."

Dyess graduated from the advanced school at Kelly Field in 1937. He was a gifted pilot. Hallie Dyess, however, did not share her husband's enthusiasm and chided Edwin each time he buzzed Albany. But Dyess shrugged off her concerns. A Presbyterian who had embraced the church's doctrine of predestination, Dyess had developed a keen awareness of what he felt was his destiny, a decision from God that had led him to flight school. "Mother," he would reply after each admonition, "if I only have so long to live I'd rather spend that time in the air."

Tall and lean, he stood six foot one and was proud of that last inch. With recruiting poster good looks, Dyess was a young comet in the AAF. One of the service's youngest squadron commanders, he married Marajen Stevick, a pretty socialite whose family owned several Illinois newspapers and radio stations. But the couple's plans for children were put on hold because Dyess felt immediately responsible to his surrogate family of pilots.

He preferred to lead by example, and in the air the daring pilot was tough to keep up with. At Hamilton Field, he was frequently observed slow-rolling his P-40 just above the ground, banking between trees, his trademark burnt orange flying scarf flapping from his cockpit. As his pilots flew through the dust clouds and dancing leaves in his wake, he exhorted them to tighten their formations. "You look like an old maid's sewing circle," he howled over the radio. It was a combination of that folksy sense of humor and his talent with the stick that made Dyess's pilots—most were recent flight school graduates—regard him like a beloved older brother. According to 2nd Lt. Sam Grashio, who knew Dyess as well as anyone, Dyess possessed a magical aura and a mesmeric hold over people he encountered. "He was intelligent, magnetic, and fearless," said Grashio. "A natural leader who commanded respect without being intimidating . . . but you knew he was the leader. It was something you felt in your bones . . . his pilots and enlisted personnel revered him and would have followed him anywhere."

On the starlit evening of November 1, 1941, the *President Coolidge*, a 21,936-ton American President liner, passed beneath the Golden Gate Bridge. Dyess, like many of those gathered on the ship's afterdeck watching the ocean darkness swallow San Francisco, had no idea where he was leading his squadron. His orders gave his destination as "PLUM." Some pilots were certain that the *Coolidge* would drop anchor in Trinidad. Jack Donohoe, a mechanic in the 21st Pursuit, firmly believed that the squadron was headed to Jamaica. At Pearl Harbor, the *Coolidge* coupled with another transport and a Navy cruiser escort to resume its journey. The blacked-out convoy had wended along its westward course for several days when the men finally learned their secret destination; someone had correctly deciphered PLUM as an acronym for Philippines-Luzon-Manila.

As the *Coolidge*'s smokestacks poured smoke into the air across the Pacific, several pilots, Sam Grashio included, sat in on discussions headed by recent graduates of the National War College. The Japanese, declared the officers, would not be so stupid as to start a war they would surely lose within a few weeks. The pilots were convinced that the Japanese were Lilliputians who could not hope to prevail over the industrial might of the United States.

The reasons by which Americans had assured themselves of a quick victory were numerous and absurd: Japanese pilots possessed poor eyesight and could not fly their shoddy planes proficiently; the Japanese soldier's standard-issue .25 caliber rifle couldn't stop an American adversary; Japanese ships, with their pagoda superstructures, could barely float. A victory in the Russo-Japanese War of 1904–1905 had heralded Japan's arrival as a world power, but the U.S. military establishment, as well as Americans in general, remained unimpressed. Few knew that

Japan had never lost a war and that the sacred home islands had not been threatened since a pair of failed invasions in the late thirteenth century by Kublai Khan's Mongol hordes.

As Colonel George explained in his Nichols Field briefing, the AAF pilots were in peril. He concluded with an estimate of the number of planes that would be necessary to defend the Philippines—five to eight pursuit *groups*, of which Nichols Field had only one. "We were shocked," Dyess would say. Everyone, that is, except for Sam Grashio. Grashio sidled up to Dyess as the latter strode urgently toward the hangars. He had a mischievous smile on his face and a betting proposition for his commanding officer.

"I'll bet you five pesos that there will be no war with Japan," said Grashio, echoing the smug words of the officers he had listened to traveling on the *Coolidge*. "What do you say, Lieutenant?"

"I say you're on, Sam, and I'll lay another five down that the war will begin within a week."

At 0445 on Monday morning, Grashio had just fallen back asleep when he heard the officer of the day banging on the doors again. The pilots of the 21st Pursuit had been roused from their bunks a little more than two hours earlier, only to rush to Nichols Field where an enigmatic Ed Dyess spoke of an emergency, then ordered them back to their quarters. This time, the knocks were followed by a command: "Get dressed! Pearl Harbor has been attacked!"

Within minutes, Grashio and the other groggy, half-dressed pilots assembled in the operations tent at Nichols Field. Silhouetted by the glow of a blacked-out gas lantern, Dyess confirmed the sensational news of Japan's surprise attack on the other side of the International Dateline and then ordered them into their new P-40Es—so new that none of the eighteen planes had logged more than two hours of flying time. Four, in fact, had never even been in the air.

With throbbing hearts and dry mouths, they clambered into their cockpits. As the sounds of whirring propellers and clicking parachute harnesses floated along the flight line in the predawn darkness, Grashio somberly reflected on the gravity of the situation.

Strangely, no orders from Far East Air Force Headquarters were forthcoming. After several tense minutes, the pilots cut their idling engines, vacated their cockpits, and sat, stunned and bleary-eyed, beneath the wings of their planes as the first spokes of sunlight poked over the horizon. The standard operating procedure of the U.S. military, noted Grashio, remained the same. The 21st Pursuit Squadron had no choice but to hurry up and wait.

For the ABCD powers—America, Britain, China, and the Dutch East Indies—confusion reigned supreme as Imperial forces struck simultaneously at Hawaii, Guam, Wake Island, British Malaya, Singapore, Thailand, and Hong Kong. Yet nowhere was this confusion more devastating than in the Philippines. Unbeknownst to the pilots at Nichols Field, a historic series of events was transpiring in the higher echelons of the USAFFE command, a blur of blunders, poor decisions, and bad luck that would yield terrible results in the Philippines.

Word of the Pearl Harbor attack first reached the Philippines at 0230 hours on Monday, December 8 (approximately 0800, December 7, on Oahu), when a Navy radioman at Asiatic Fleet Headquarters in Manila's Marsman Building picked up a startling message: "Air Raid on Pearl Harbor. This is no drill!" One hour later, MacArthur's chief of staff, Lt. Gen. Richard Sutherland, woke the USAFFE commander in his Manila Hotel penthouse. By 0500, FEAF chief Maj. Gen. Lewis Brereton was in MacArthur's office seeking permission to launch a retaliatory raid on Formosa at first light, but the autocratic Sutherland refused Brereton's request for an audience with MacArthur. Brereton was given permission to prepare his bombers for offensive action—nothing more.

At 0715, Brereton returned to Intramuros and was again ordered to stand by. It has been speculated that during these crucial hours, an overwhelmed MacArthur, much like Napoleon at Waterloo, had lapsed into a semi-catatonic state, unable to command. As Brereton's car navigated Manila's empty streets—it was the Feast of the Immaculate Conception and many Filipinos, devout Roman Catholics, would be attending mass and fiestas—back to FEAF Headquarters at Nielson Field in Makati, the storm clouds darkened.

Shortly after receiving a transoceanic telephone call from Air Force chief Gen. Hap Arnold at 0800, Brereton hurriedly ordered his B-17s aloft, bombless, to keep them out of harm's way. As the morning progressed, Japanese planes raided Baguio, the summer capital in northern Luzon, and American installations near Davao City, on Mindanao. But these were merely feints. At 1015 Formosa time (0915 Manila time), the main strike force of the Japanese navy's 11th Air Fleet, 108 twin-engine bombers and eighty-four Zeros, after waiting for a thick fog to lift—the Japanese had feared the fog would leave them susceptible to an American attack, the attack Brereton had wanted to launch at dawn—took off from their bases. Their mission: to destroy the largest concentration of American airpower in the Far East. Their primary target: Clark Field.

At 1145, the phone rang in Dyess's operations tent. Enemy planes had been detected and the 3rd and 21st Pursuits were being scrambled for interception. Dyess eagerly relayed the message: "Tally ho, Clark Field!" Within minutes, the P-40s' supercharged 1,150-horsepower engines hurtled the olive-drab Warhawks—which Dyess had divided into three six-plane flights, A, B, and C—into the sky.

While Dyess led A and B flights in a climb for higher altitude, some planes from C Flight discovered that they were unable to locate Dyess and, perhaps because of atmospheric conditions, were out of radio contact. Therefore, when Dyess received a message advising him of a change in orders—the planes were to assemble at a point above Manila Bay to intercept Japanese bombers en route to Manila—the C Flight pilots were unaware. When engine trouble forced two pilots to abort the mission, the remaining pilots, Lts. Joe Cole, Gus Williams, and Johnny McCown, turned to the next-senior pilot for leadership.

That individual, Lt. Sam Grashio, all of twenty-three years old, regrouped the lost squadron into formation and shepherded it north toward Clark Field, sixty miles distant, the assigned objective and, in Grashio's estimation, the most logical location for action.

Almost from the beginning—he was born on April Fool's Day 1918, in Spokane, Washington, to be precise—action, in one form or another, had been the main objective of Samuel Charles Grashio. The sixth of seven children, he was short and thin. With fair skin, blue eyes, and ringlets of light brown hair, he possessed a disarming physical appearance.

Growing up, Grashio was competitive and impetuous, and deeply religious—a holy terror. The wiry altar boy could usually be found in railyards hopping freight cars and fighting. As he matured, Grashio—described as "119 pounds of condensed dynamite" in one newspaper—boxed in smokers and quarterbacked his high school football team at Gonzaga Prep to three straight championships, but shortfalls in the classroom precluded a chance at college. As the shadow of the Great Depression eclipsed the country, Grashio's career choices dwindled. He had no desire to take over his father's barbershop, so he approached the Jesuits of Gonzaga University about joining the priesthood. They told him to wait and see if his interest waned. It did.

Grashio had rekindled two old flames, one of which was his high school sweetheart, a big-eyed blonde named Devonia Carolus. The other was Grashio's longtime love affair with airplanes, which showed considerably less promise. Nevertheless, much like his father—who in 1902 had traded his likely future as a goatherder in Calabria, Italy, for a ticket on a New York–bound steamer—he took a chance and enrolled in Gonzaga's federal flight training program in 1938. With hard work, newfound focus, and the practical experience he had gained with the Washington Air National Guard, Grashio earned his pilot's license in 1940. He navigated the rigorous cadet programs at Randolph and Kelly Fields and was assigned to Ed Dyess's 21st Pursuit in 1941, a break Grashio would later consider the biggest of his life. "Ed . . . took me right under his wing. He was only two years older than I—he was twenty-five—but he was like a father to me at first," said Grashio. "Then, when I became more assured, he was like a pal." At the time, Grashio could not have known how strong that friendship would become, nor could he have known how much action was in store for him.

Despite the heavy fog of war settling over Luzon, the skies were clear and the air, recalled Grashio, was "as smooth as glass." The P-40s of C Flight passed over 3,000-foot Mount Arayat until 1220 hours, when Grashio surveyed Clark Field from 10,000 feet. Seeing nothing unusual, he decided to wing westward to join up with a formation of P-40s. Ten fateful minutes later, his radio crackled to life. "All P-40s return to Clark Field," shouted the tower operator there, his voice muted by exploding bombs. "Enemy bombers overhead!"

There were fifty-three Japanese navy Type 96 and Type 1—known as "Nell" and "Betty"—twin-engine bombers in two V formations blackening the skies at Clark Field. It was about 1230 when the first wave of Nells, like bursting storm clouds, began to rain destruction from their bomb bays. The shrill whine of an air raid siren sent men pouring from crowded mess halls. They dove into slit trenches and scrambled to their battle stations as bomb concussions rocked the ground beneath them.

The Japanese bombardiers possessed uncanny aim. Direct hits obliterated hangars, barracks, and communications stations and felled radio towers and telephone poles in showers of sparks. Fragmentation bombs ignited ammunition dumps and oil tanks, and fuel trucks exploded in orange fireballs. Shrapnel, giant sheets of aluminum, corrugated iron, and whipping propellers slashed through the air, striking men indiscriminately. Strings of bombs smacked the flight line, blowing apart dozens of new P-40s. The flames hungrily spread to tufts of cogon grass and thickets of dry bamboo. Towering plumes of dark, oily smoke billowed skyward. After the second wave of bombers had passed, dozens of gray Zeros streaked down through the smoke blanket, their blazing guns shredding the silver steel skins of the just refueled B-17s.

Antiaircraft gunners frantically fired their 3-inch guns, but most of the corroded fuses—much of their ammunition was World War I surplus—were duds and those shells that did explode did so in harmless smoke puffs well beneath their targets. Others peppered the sky with fire from old water-cooled Brownings, rifles, and .45s. Though heroic, their efforts were largely in vain; by the time Grashio had boomeranged his P-40 back to Clark, he found a broiling holocaust.

Shaken out of his dreamlike trance, Grashio reflected on "how utterly and abysmally wrong" the officers on the *Coolidge* had been and prayed for those on the ground. He then spied a handful of Zeros, the blood-red *hinomaru*, or rising sun emblems, visible on their wings. Drawing a deep breath, he motioned for his wingmen to follow, but McCown and Cole were already engaged. Suddenly, a lone Zero darted out of the swirling smoke below his ship, apparently circling around for another strafing run. His heart pounding, Grashio steadied his P-40 and the plane shuddered as he let fly a barrage of bullets. The Zero slid out of the sky leaking smoke, but Grashio would not have time to celebrate his first victory.

Wingman Williams had spotted nine Zeros preparing to dive, but before they could complete their turn, the two lead planes completed a climbing turn of their own and were now on the tails of the Americans. In seconds, the hunters had become the hunted. Grashio did not know it, but one of the pilots chasing him was Imperial Navy Chief Petty Officer Saburo Sakai. Sakai, the leading Japanese air ace to survive the war, would shoot down more than sixty Allied aircraft before being grounded by wounds and failing eyesight in 1945. After the war, Sakai would become a Buddhist and renounce all violence, but on this day he was eagerly pursuing his first American victories.

As Grashio veered left, Sakai fired a ribbon of explosive shells from his 20-millimeter nose cannon and ripped a gaping hole into the left wing of Grashio's plane. Grashio's sweaty hands white-knuckled the stick. Instinctively, he turned to his faith. As his lips trembled in fervent prayer, the three planes sliced through the sky, molten lead pouring from the Zeros' guns. "I was sure I was going to die on the first day of the war," said Grashio. Suddenly, his prayers were answered. Grashio remembered Dyess's lectures: "Never try to outmaneuver a Zero; go into a steep dive and try to outrace it." Indeed, the P-40 was much heavier—one pilot had called the armor-plated plane "a streamlined safe"—so he pointed its nose to the ground and pushed the throttle wide open. The needle in his altimeter spun wildly as the earth flashed upward at breakneck speed. Attempting such a maneuver in a new plane was "courting suicide," said Grashio, "but with two Zeros on your tail, the admonitions in technical manuals are not the first things you think about."

Grashio's luck, as well as the plane's virgin engine, held. He pulled up, skimming the treetops as the Japanese pursuers receded into the distance. When Grashio touched down at Nichols at 0130, Dyess greeted him—he had led the other flights on an uneventful patrol over Cavite—and together they inspected the damaged plane. Grashio shook his head, remarking excitedly between breaths, "By God, they ain't shootin' spitballs, are they?"

A few hours later, after the order came in to abandon Nichols Field, Dyess, Grashio, and the rest of the 21st Pursuit Squadron landed at cratered Clark Field amid clouds of pumice and dust. Guided by the "eerie glow cast by the smoldering hangars," they weaved around fire-gutted wrecks and opened their cockpits to a stinging stench of cordite, burnt flesh, and gasoline fumes. Lt. Joe Moore, whose 20th Pursuit had been decimated, summed up the damage tally in one terse sentence: "We got kicked in the teeth." Despite sufficient advance warning—nearly ten hours had elapsed between the attacks on Pearl Harbor and the Philippines—MacArthur's air force had suffered a death blow. Twelve of the nineteen B-17s at Clark Field were now charred wreckage and thirty-four of the 5th Interceptor Command's ninety-one P-40s—two entire squadrons—were destroyed. The lone radar station at Iba Field was damaged beyond repair and the one-sided onslaught (Japanese losses totaled seven planes) had also destroyed precious stocks of fuel and parts.

Two days later, with Japanese planes streaking over Manila and the port area unopposed, MacArthur and Adm. Thomas Hart would be over-heard discussing the disastrous calamity that had been delivered upon USAFFE, as well as all American forces in the Pacific.

"Oh, God help us," one of them had reportedly exclaimed, "if Clark Field can't now."

CHAPTER 2

A Long War

No time to falter or catch a breath
For thought of future, for fear of death . . .

It was one of those rare instances in the life of Lt. Cmdr. Melvyn McCoy when the correct solution was not immediately visible. As the Japanese surged toward Manila, McCoy stalked about his quarters in Cañacao, near the three silver towers of the Cavite radio station, methodically packing his seabag with the essentials he would take to the fortress island of Corregidor. Two items remained: a portrait photograph of his wife, Betty Anne, and a set of used golf clubs that he had purchased in a Manila pawnshop. He could not take both.

The thirty-four-year-old radio matériel officer for the 16th Naval District, McCoy had graduated from Annapolis with one of the highest averages in mathematics ever attained by a midshipman. He lived to discover solutions to problems, usually much more complex ones than this. Others, after all, had recently proved less vexing. Through orders and scuttlebutt, McCoy had deduced that MacArthur, awakening to the reality of the tenuous tactical situation, would order War Plan Orange into effect on the evening of Dec. 23. With no air force, no navy and no prospect of Allied assistance, MacArthur had no other recourse. Japanese warplanes had destroyed Cavite Navy Yard on December 10, forcing the bulk of the Asiatic Fleet to pull up anchor for the Netherlands East Indies, while the simultaneous sinkings of the capital ships *Repulse* and *Prince of Wales* near Malaya on December 10 had essentially eliminated Britain's strategic military presence in the Far East. The landing of General Masaharu Homma's 14th Army, 43,000 troops, plus artillery and tanks, at Lingayen Gulf in northern Luzon on December 22 had effectively sealed the decision. These units, acting in concert with landing forces advancing from Lamon Bay in southern Luzon, were racing toward Manila in a pincer movement. Just barely ahead of them were MacArthur's forces, stampeding back in a frantic double retrograde because most of the green, untrained Filipinos had thrown away their rifles upon encountering Homma's armor and airpower, commencing the rout.

McCoy also figured that as the ranking communications officer in the Philippines he would be staying behind with the small Navy contingent of ships and personnel. All around him, the demolition of equipment and stores continued in earnest. Warehouses were opened to mobs and Clark, Nichols, and other airfields were stripped, fired, and abandoned, as were Forts Stotsenburg and McKinley. Tankers, ammunition magazines, and shore installations at Cavite and Sangley Point, just south of Manila, were scuttled in brilliant, rocking blasts. Fired tanks containing millions of gallons of fuel—the Asiatic Fleet had left behind a two-year supply and the reserves of Caltex, Shell, Standard Oil, and others in Pandacan were extensive—would send orange flames and a furling pall of smoke skyward for days.

A rising tide of terror, fueled by the rumors of the proximity and reputation of the Japanese army, was sweeping panicked civilians out of Manila. Save for drunken looters, it seemed as though everyone was in flight. Everyone but McCoy. Despite the sounds of war filling his ears, the lanky naval officer with coal black hair stood resolutely, his mechanical mind clicking and turning, stroking his Errol Flynn mustache.

McCoy had spent most of his life ahead of the pack. Born January 1, 1907, a gifted prodigy, McCoy was graduated from Arsenal Technical High School in Indianapolis in 1922 at the age of fifteen and secured an appointment to the U.S. Naval Academy from Indiana's 7th Congressional

District the following year. He left with a commission and a burgeoning reputation in 1927. "It was as the Czar of Math that he shone," certified the *Lucky Bag*, the Annapolis annual.

McCoy's personality did not add up. Though he could be coldly cerebral—a disciple of the sanctity of logic and efficiency, he did not suffer fools and had little patience for incompetence—he also had a warm, vibrant verve about him. People gravitated to him, trusted him. That's because with the exception of chess and cards (he was virtually unbeatable at poker and bridge), he rarely flaunted his intelligence, choosing instead to radiate a subtle, yet mesmerizing sense of self-assurance—the hallmark of a true officer, gentleman, and genius.

After assignments in Nicaragua and aboard the battleship *West Virginia* and two destroyers, McCoy earned a master's degree in electrical engineering from the University of California–Berkeley before his transfer to the Philippines in 1940. His last peacetime mission, undertaken upon the evacuation of his family with the other dependents in early 1941, was to install battery-powered radios in lighthouses, on hilltops, and at other vantage points throughout the islands. These lonely forays to Luzon, Palawan, Leyte, and Jolo provided him with plenty of material for his travelogues, but the work was largely devoid of problems to solve— McCoy's true raison d'être. The war, however, was already changing that. And the new problems would prove an unusual and difficult calculus, even for a man of McCoy's talents.

Flame-lit Cavite shuddered with clattering explosions. McCoy, his mind now racing at flank speed, looked at his wife's picture. *It doesn't do her much justice,* he thought. And Corregidor did have, in the midst of all those guns and tunnels, a nine-hole golf course. The calculating pragmatist slung the clubs over his shoulder and headed for Corregidor. It was the logical decision. McCoy, like everyone else, expected his navy to smash through the Pacific to rescue the Philippines. Until then, he might as well work on his swing.

MONDAY, DECEMBER 29, 1941
Corregidor, Manila Bay, Philippine Islands

The hands of 1st Lt. Austin Shofner's wristwatch, like anything else moving in the malevolent midday heat, ticked lazily toward noon. Shofner, sitting in an office on the third floor of Middleside Barracks, shook a smoke from a pack of cigarettes. Ordinarily, the Marine did not smoke. These, however, were not ordinary times. An oak of a man standing more than six feet tall and accustomed to carrying 200 pounds, Shofner was miserably hungry. With each pull he subdued his rioting hunger pangs. But that other feeling, the queasy sensation in his empty gut telling him that his days as a combatant were numbered, would not go away.

It was unfamiliar territory for Shofner. In his twenty-five years, the gung ho Marine had yet to drink from a half-empty glass. He had brought that infectious optimism with him to Corregidor's North Dock less than thirty-six hours earlier when the 4th Marine Regiment had arrived to assume beach defense duties. It was not long after that he discovered the famed fortress island was not all it had been built up to be—both literally and figuratively.

Located at the maw of Manila Bay, the tadpole-shaped island—though officially designated Fort Mills and known the world over as the "Gibraltar of the East"—was affectionately called "the Rock" by American troops. Hundreds of mines sat in the water, just off a perimeter of rocky beaches, vertical limestone cliffs, and the jaws of deep ravines. Craggy hills swathed in high talahib grass were stratified into three terraces of elevation: Topside, Middleside, and Bottomside. With its own airstrip, Kindley Field, and power plant, the Rock was practically self-sustaining. The island bristled with dens of artillery, mortars, and fixed seacoast guns—the largest of which were the 12-inch cannons of batteries Smith and Hearn, which could hurl a 1,000-pound armor-piercing shell seventeen miles. Its most notable feature, however, was the bombproof Malinta Tunnel and its honeycombed maze of reinforced concrete laterals, cavernous 400-foot ventilated shafts used for hospital wards, offices, and storage. "Corregidor was indeed a mighty fortress," decided Associated Press correspondent Clark Lee. "Doubtless it would have been impregnable—if the airplane had never been invented."

A jarring duet of sirens and clanging brass shell casings sounded across the hills at 1140. Most of the Marines who had been unloading supplies and digging positions casually looked skyward—the Japanese, their Army comrades had told them, didn't dare challenge Corregidor's defenses. Lieutenant Shofner jumped to his feet. After talking a colonel into the barracks basement, Shofner also headed for the exit. Though admittedly discouraged after having seen Corregidor's "antiquity" up close, he had no intentions of waiting out the raid. The soles of his spit-shined cordovan shoes clacked down the stairs. He pulled his helmet over his closely cropped chestnut hair, ripped a final drag from his cigarette, and flicked the butt, contemptuously, to the ground. "I wanted to go out and see these planes get knocked down," he said.

Eighteen bombers, flying in a V formation at 15,000 feet, arrived to a raucous reception of hundreds of smoke puffs bursting upon the pale blue sky. Hunched behind sandbags, men and machine guns chattered away in separate, frantic staccatos. The twinkling of the metal bombs in the sunlight jolted Shofner to his senses. "I couldn't tell what their targets were," he said, "but I hoped it wasn't me." He did not wait to find out.

Just as the first bombs slammed into the Rock, Shofner dove into the barracks, buffeted by blast concussions. It was a close call, the first of many face-to-face encounters with the specter of death in this war, but luck had been on his side. His father had always told him, if you can't be smart, be lucky.

During his formative years in Shelbyville, Tennessee, a bucolic town about fifty miles southeast of Nashville, Shofner learned the values of a strong work ethic and self-sufficiency from his father, a schoolteacher and part-time farmer. When his schoolwork and chores were completed—he drove cattle and hauled buckets of springwater on a 200-acre ancestral farmstead—Shofner could be found hunting squirrels and rabbits amid the tulip poplars and hickories in the hollows along the Duck River, or else on a baseball diamond or football field demonstrating the talents that would earn him a reputation as one of the best athletes in Bedford County history.

His gridiron prowess merited a partial football scholarship to the University of Tennessee, where he met the second greatest influence on his life, Coach Robert Neyland, West Point graduate and onetime aide to then-Commandant Douglas MacArthur. Shofner saw a recipe for success, not just in football, but for life, encoded in Neyland's famous "Football Maxims." "There aren't many like Neyland in this world. He was a winner," he explained, "and he taught me mind over matter."

He took Neyland's teachings and a football nickname—"Shifty"—with him when he reported to Marine basic school in Philadelphia in August 1937. For Shofner and the Corps, it was love at first salute. With his syrupy Southern voice, powerful parade ground timbre, and chameleon personality—he could be caustically abrasive or irresistibly glib—he possessed a natural command presence. His uncanny ability to motivate was his greatest strength. Whether his modus operandi was fear or encouragement, cajolery or coercion, Shofner knew how to get the job done. And the job now facing him looked to be the most challenging task of his life.

The whirr of the bombers' radial engines receded into the distance and Shofner emerged, brushing off dirt, to survey the damage. One of the bombs had struck the supposedly bombproof Middleside Barracks, a hit that wounded some Marines in the galley. Nurses darted through the film of smoke and dust. As best as he could hear through the shouts and wailing of wounded, they needed a doctor. Shofner ordered a dentist, the closest thing to a medic within his reach, to assist with the injured.

"Suddenly," Shofner would say, "I had the feeling this would be a long war."

If ever there was a perfect place for a desperate last stand, it was the Bataan Peninsula. Twenty-five miles in length, and spanning at its widest twenty miles from the South China Sea to the upper reaches of Manila Bay, Bataan was a spine of ancient volcanic rock dominated by two colossal peaks—Mount Natib and Mount Bataan. A southern extension of the Zambales Mountains, the thumb-shaped isthmus was carpeted by virgin jungle and studded with giant coconut palms, mahogany, narra, camagong, and mayapis trees festooned with creeping vines. A menagerie of monkeys, lawin, mynah birds, and wild carabao, lizards, pythons, and boars lived in the undergrowth. On the saw-toothed west coast, rocky promontories and forbidding cliff walls painted with the fiery orange and red blooms of talisay trees and hanging pandanus fronted the South China Sea. Most of the inhabitants of Bataan lived on the eastern coastal plain, in the clusters of bamboo, thatched nipa, and clapboard houses lining the paved all-weather East Road, which hugged the shores of Manila Bay.

It was into these hostile environs that nearly 80,000 American and Filipino troops retreated during the final, humiliating days of 1941 and the first, uncertain hours of 1942. They came from all corners of Luzon, from Lingayen, from the Agno River, from the foothills of Mount Banahao, from Manila. They dribbled down the tributaries of rural roads and footpaths, eventually merging into the swollen cataracts of men, animals, and machines flooding National Highways 3, 5, 7, and, finally, 110. Sluggishly, they crossed the Pampanga River on the Calumpit Bridge, filtered through San Fernando and struggled into Bataan through the bottleneck of Layac Junction. The stink of burning rubber, infected flesh, and gunpowder, mixed with fragrant frangipani, wafted through the humid air. Fat black flies buzzed over corpses, animal carcasses, and empty ration tins, the detritus of an army under constant attack. The sounds of screeching brakes, backfiring engines, clanging metal canteens, and leather and rubber soles crushing pavement mingled with the unintelligible bits of English, Spanish, Tagalog, Visayan and Ilocano conversations, arguments, and orders. For days, the narrow roads to Bataan were clotted with trucks, staff cars, jeeps, ambulances, tanks, carts and civilian buses. Following closely behind, a handful of USAFFE tanks, infantry, ack-ack gunners, and cavalrymen—the latter armed with pistols and soda bottles filled with gasoline—gallantly held off the Japanese while engineers dynamited bridges.

Despite the lack of road signs, military police, and air cover, the plodding exodus was a chaotic success, a "small Dunkirk," one Air Corps pilot called it. Much of MacArthur's army had been able to slip into Bataan intact, carrying with it large stores of ammunition, mostly World War I surplus ordnance, but ammunition nonetheless. The exigencies of the hastily ordered retreat and the tangled bureaucracy of the Filipino government, however, had ensured that stores of clothing, medicine, fuel, and, most important, food were left behind. The abandonment of 5,000 tons of rice at the Government Rice Central warehouse, in Luzon's Nueva Ecija Province, enough to feed USAFFE troops for at least one year, was one glaring example. As per MacArthur's original defense strategy, most of the supply depots and reserves had been set up near the beaches, and were now deep inside Japanese-held territory after their landing of December 22. MacArthur had also ordered that Corregidor be stocked first with enough supplies to last the 10,000-man garrison for six months. By the time the door to the Bataan Peninsula was barred, only a few thousand tons of foodstuffs would be secured there.

The madness of the retreat had scarcely subsided when MacArthur learned that an estimated 26,000 civilian refugees had drained into the peninsula with the retreating troops. Faced with slow starvation or immediate defeat, MacArthur chose to give his forces a fighting chance.

On January 5, 1942, in one of the first orders issued from his new head-quarters located inside Malinta Tunnel on Corregidor, MacArthur put all USAFFE troops on half-rations.

And so the epic fight for the Philippines, America's first major land battle of the Second World War, began with ill-equipped American and Filipino troops burrowed into defensive positions, their weapons loaded with suspect ammunition and their stomachs empty, waiting for the Japanese to attack and for help from the States.

CHAPTER 3

The Raid

And we were sacrificed—perhaps to gain
That little time that warded off defeat
In those first awful months of swift retreat.

With the Allies in full, humiliating retreat throughout the globe in early 1942, the defenders of the Philippines looked to be waiting a long time. German forces controlled territory from the steppes of Russia to the sands of North Africa to the icy Atlantic. The Stars and Stripes no longer flew over Guam and Wake Island, nor did the Union Jack fly over the British crown colony of Hong Kong. Singapore would fall in February; the Dutch East Indies in March. Japanese forces would close the Burma Road in April, severing the supply link to Generalissimo Chiang Kai-shek's Chinese Nationalist forces. The rays of the Rising Sun shone across the Pacific Rim, to the Solomon Islands and through the Malay Barrier. And should Australia and New Zealand crumble—Australia was virtually undefended because most of the continent's troops were fighting in North Africa—it was feared that only Hawaii would stand between the Japanese and the United States.

The numbing disbelief and national outrage that followed Pearl Harbor gave way to mass hysteria. Japanese submarines sank merchant vessels within sight of coastal residents, fueling the invasion paranoia. One elected official, believing the West Coast to be indefensible, demanded that U.S. forces prepare defensive positions in the Rocky Mountains. The original copies of the Constitution and the Declaration of Independence were removed from display and shipped to vaults at Fort Knox, Kentucky. Even the Rose Bowl football game was moved from Pasadena, California, to the perceived safety of the East Coast. By February, the situation had reached such a fever pitch that President Roosevelt signed Executive Order 9066, forcing thousands of West Coast Japanese, full-fledged citizens born on American soil among them, into internment camps.

The nation desperately needed heroes, and it found them in the defenders of the Philippines. America's romantic fascination with extraordinary struggles against long odds conjured comparisons with the siege of the Alamo mission and the legendary last stand of George Custer's 7th Cavalry. In an April panegyric, *Life* magazine called the battle an "American Thermopylae" and equated MacArthur's men with the stalwart Spartans who endeavored to halt an overwhelming Persian invasion in 480 B.C. Bataan and Corregidor, names of distant places previously unheard of and locations heretofore unknown, had become in America's darkest hour rays of hope. With each passing day, the battle assumed an almost mythical significance on the home front. Atop San Francisco's Fairmont Hotel, William Winter of shortwave station KGEI beamed his "Freedom for the Philippines" news program across the Pacific and dared the Japanese to attack. As the nation mobilized, screen stars, radio personalities, and athletes gave way to war celebrities, men like Lt. Alexander R. Nininger, Jr., the war's first recipient of the Congressional Medal of Honor, and Capt. Arthur W. Wermuth, the "One-Man Army of Bataan," whose exploits were celebrated in wire stories and comic books. Capt. Colin P. Kelly, Jr., earned instant, though posthumous, fame when, after his B-17 sank a Japanese cruiser near Lingayen Gulf, he stayed at the controls of the mortally wounded bomber so that his crew could bail out.

Yet no stars gleamed as bright as those pinned to the collar of Gen. Douglas MacArthur. His élan, his corncob pipe, and his carefully cultivated intrepid persona seemed heaven-sent to a nation praying for a martial messiah. Figuratively welcomed back from his self-imposed Philippine exile, he was feted and honored in absentia across the country. Streets in large cities and small towns bore his name, as did infants. A cottage industry of MacArthur buttons, songs, and books capitalized on the general's burgeoning celebrity. But defeating the Japanese in the Philippines would prove to be an impossible challenge.

MacArthur's troops wondered where the convoys they had been promised were. Buoyed by messages from Washington that suggested aid was

forthcoming, MacArthur had reassured them that they had not been forgotten: "Help is on the way from the United States. Thousands of troops
and hundreds of planes are being dispatched," read a grandiloquent January communiqué. "It is imperative that our troops hold until these
reinforcements arrive. . . . It is a question now of courage and of determination. . . . If we fight, we will win; if we retreat, we will be destroyed." And
so the defenders dutifully scanned the horizon for the ships. FDR had cabled President Quezon in December and assured him "that every vessel
available is bearing . . . the strength that will eventually crush the enemy
and liberate your native land." But in the wake of the Japanese attack on
the Philippines, Washington concluded that it could not reinforce the
islands.

With the German and Italian declarations of war, the United States
had found itself at war with three nations, yet having been attacked by
and engaged in hostilities with only one of the belligerents. America's
ill-prepared military—budget cuts and isolationist sentiments during
the Depression had decimated the armed forces—precluded simultaneous offensive action against all three enemies. (As of November 1, 1938,
only ten months before Germany's invasion of Poland, the United States
ranked nineteenth globally in the size of its total air and land forces, just
behind Portugal and slightly ahead of neutral Switzerland.) According
to Field Marshal Sir John Dill, Britain's senior military liaison in Washington, the United States was "more unready for war than it is possible
to imagine . . . the whole military organization belongs to the days of
George Washington."

At the end of the three-week Arcadia Conference in Washington in
mid-January, the United States and Britain concluded that Nazi Germany posed the greater threat to the Allies. Anglo-American strategists
believed that should Soviet Russia be knocked out of the war, Germany
would then have inexhaustible resources with which to invade the British
Isles and perhaps even march on Central Asia to link up with Japanese
forces. A strategic defense would therefore be maintained in the Pacific
until Germany was defeated.

In his fireside chat with Americans on the night of February 23, Roosevelt intimated that the Philippines campaign would be abandoned: "We
knew that to obtain our objective, many varieties of operations would be
necessary in areas other than the Philippines." But word never reached
the men fighting there. The cables transmitted to the Philippines were

purposely enigmatic. Early in the fighting, MacArthur received messages informing him that relief shipments were being dispatched. He was not told, however, that the convoys were not intended for the Philippines. The misleading statements, which compounded in the ensuing weeks, stemmed from strategic and political necessity. The messages were designed to keep the Fil-American forces fighting—fighting long enough to save Australia and to save face. In the Far East, where shame was a cultural bedrock, a pullout from the Philippines would further damage the remnants of American prestige and the morale of the peoples of the Far East who looked to the United States as their liberator from the Japanese yoke. It would also damage the sagging spirits of the American people. The Philippines defenders had to be kept fighting at all costs. "There are times," Henry Stimson would write in his diary, "when men have to die."

As mechanics on Bataan scrounged spare parts, five brand-new planes were earmarked for Cuba. Wounded men suffered in Malinta Tunnel while bureaucrats debated a requistion to send 500 railroad picks to Nigeria because of the African nation's "strategic importance." In March, exports to the Soviet Union more than doubled—aid to the communist nation would total $346 million by May. Conversely, as the forces on Bataan were being starved into submission, not a single ship cleared for the Philippines, though FDR insisted that the Navy was "following an intensive and well-planned campaign which will result in positive assistance to the defense of the Philippine Islands." There was no such campaign.

Perhaps the biggest blow delivered by the Japanese at Pearl Harbor was a psychological one. On Christmas Day 1941, the new commander-in-chief of the Pacific Fleet, Adm. Chester Nimitz, arrived on Oahu to find morale at "rock bottom" and members of his new staff taking sedatives. The shock of the December 7 attack had even turned some senior officers' hair white. Despite the fact that its flotilla of aircraft carriers had escaped the attack unscathed and shore installations in Hawaii were relatively unharmed, a crisis of confidence had led the Pacific Fleet to assume a triangular defensive posture from the Aleutian Islands to Hawaii and down into the Panama Canal Zone.

Because of the decision to put Europe first, as "American war supplies were speeded" around the globe, revealed the *Chicago Tribune* in a 1944 exposé, the Philippines "virtually became a forgotten theater of war."

A vociferous campaign for a greater effort in the Pacific reached its apex between late January and April. Segments of the press and members of Congress blasted both the Roosevelt administration and the War Department for the perceived inability to aid MacArthur. In January, Senator James E. Murray, a liberal Montana Democrat, was unhappy to learn that a convoy had recently landed in Northern Ireland, commenting that "it would seem to me that if the expedition had been sent across the Pacific, it would have been much better." Ohio Republican senator Robert A. Taft concurred: "I am sincerely hopeful that someone is thinking of getting assistance to the forces fighting in the Far East."

That someone was an obscure, chain-smoking Army brigadier general who months earlier had been misidentified in a newspaper caption as "Lt. Col. D. D. Ersenbeing." Army Chief of Staff George C. Marshall had summoned General Dwight D. Eisenhower, a former MacArthur aide, to Washington for the purpose of resupplying the Philippines. The two men met on December 14, 1941, in the War Department offices at the old Munitions Building on Constitution Avenue. Eisenhower realized the hopeless situation, but argued that "we must do everything for [the Fil-American forces] that is humanly possible."

"I agree with you," replied Marshall. "Do your best to save them."

Eisenhower's first major assignment of the war was, in his own words, "a problem that defied solution." Submarines brought in some supplies, but trepid Navy brass thwarted plans to use aircraft carriers to ferry planes to Bataan. A blockade-running scheme was a dismal failure. Eisenhower grew discouraged, noting in January 1942, "I've been insisting that the Far East is critical—and no sideshows should be undertaken until air and ground there are in satisfactory state." Instead, the Army was undertaking other strategic operations. Within a few weeks, Eisenhower would skyrocket through the Army command hierarchy and soon be immersed in these other plans.

Initially, it seemed as though the Fil-American defenders needed little aid. One Japanese general described the retreat of USAFFE troops into Bataan as a "cat entering a sack," but the events of January and February proved the defenders' resolve. The Filipino troops who had fled the battlefields of Luzon in December had become, in one officer's estimation, "battle-hardened, vicious, disease-ridden, jungle-fighting experts." Pilots, bluejackets, clerks, and cooks were turned into infantry. The once maligned "dogfaces" of the 31st Infantry Regiment—American soldiers would not call themselves "GIs" or be popularly referred to as such until later in the war—were proving themselves to be USAFFE's backbone. So high was their morale that after learning that a Japanese submarine had shelled a refinery near Santa Barbara, California, some considered sending a radiogram: "Hold out for thirty days and WE will send you reinforcements." They took immense pride in what Lt. Henry Lee called "Our war—our own little rat trap, the hopeless defense of Bataan, a rear guard with no main body, but a thorn in the flesh of Japan."

A thorn indeed. When General Homma attempted to land 2,500 troops on Bataan's western coast in an effort to break the stalemate in late January—the crucial struggle known as the Battle of the Points—he was repulsed by Philippine Scouts and an improvised army of airmen, sailors, and engineers. An attempt to break through the II Corps sector in eastern Bataan resulted in another Japanese setback, the Battle of Trail 2. And even when Homma's troops managed to puncture USAFFE's lines, they were quickly isolated and destroyed in the Battle of the Pockets. The defenders' efforts would save Australia from invasion and perhaps Hawaii, but they would not be able to save themselves. Shamefully behind schedule, Homma would request reinforcements. As the Japanese prepared for a campaign-deciding offensive in April, an unnerving lull swept over the war-torn Philippines.

As MacArthur would later exclaim, "no troops have ever done so much with so little." USAFFE's food reserves, further drained by thousands of civilian refugees, vanished at an astounding rate. Unscrupulous quartermasters, rear echelon officers, and a battlefield black market—where cans of food and packs of cigarettes went for between $5 and $20 apiece—exacerbated the situation. As the daily ration dwindled to 1000 calories, less than one-third of the intake required by combat soldiers, men collapsed in chow lines. In March, Wainwright, when informed that the horses of the 26th Cavalry were out of fodder, ordered them slaughtered to provide his men with meat. It was a sad reward for such loyal, heroic animals: in mid-January, the 26th Cavalry had made the last mounted charge in U.S. history. The ravenous troops not only picked the jungle clean of all edible vegetation, including bananas, breadfruit, papayas, mangoes, and wild Philippine sweet potatoes called camotes, but also resorted to previously spurned species to supplement their rations of canned salmon and worm-ridden rice. They ate dogs, cats, grasshoppers, monkeys, iguanas, python eggs, and carabao, the ubiquitous Philippine water buffalo. Anything, it seemed, was fair game.

Doctors, nurses, and medics were doing their best to fight the tropical diseases endemic to the jungle, but the swarms of insects and parasites were as relentless as the Japanese. In mid-February, with most of the troops suffering from a miscellany of tropical maladies, the USAFFE surgeon general estimated the combat efficiency of the defenders of Bataan at a startling 55 percent. Most Filipino troops, fighting shoeless, were ravaged with hookworm. The hospital laterals in Corregidor's Malinta Tunnel and the two field hospitals on Bataan, where thousands of patients lay in rows of cots and triple-stacked iron beds scattered among bamboo and palm groves, bulged to capacity, supplies of quinine, sulfa drugs, morphine, blood plasma, and anesthetic having long been exhausted. Between bombings—Japanese pilots often ignored the red crosses on the roofs of the field hospitals—surgeons worked in primitive operating shacks. Upon the gory piles of gangrenous limbs they tossed metal pieces of shrapnel extracted from soldiers' bodies—the results of America's prewar scrap metal sales to Japan.

Between artillery barrages and bombing raids, the beleaguered troops wrote poems, diary entries, and letters. One note—an attempt at alleviating the gnawing fears of loved ones—written by Ed Dyess was one of the lucky ones to breach the Japanese blockade.

Bataan
Mar. 10, 1942

Dear Folks—

In just a few minutes this note is to be put in the hands of chance, & I hope it gets home by the time I do (which might not be to long)

Everything is o.k. here & not as bad as it might be pictured. The food could be better as well as living conditions, but nobody gives a damn because the moral is high.

As soon as we kick the nips off the island, we take a short trip to Tokyo for a little clean up job, & board a boat for good Old U.S.A., & to you, maybe too many days will not have passed.

All my love,
Edwin

They also tuned in music from Manila, the "Voice of Freedom"—the USAFFE radio station originating from Malinta Tunnel—shortwave broadcasts from the States, and, in the absence of celebrity-filled USO shows, performed their own skits and musicals. Chaplains offered field masses, and their sermons, as could be expected, preached the merits of hope, prayer, and patience. It was on Bataan that the famous battlefield declaration "there are no atheists in foxholes" was rumored to have been uttered by a Catholic priest, Father William T. Cummings. The rumor mill operated around the clock. The thunder bursts of sea storms were believed to be the guns of the approaching "Victory" convoy blasting its way through the blockade bringing planes and food.

The forces on Corregidor and Bataan believed implicitly that their moment of redemption was at hand, despite the best Japanese efforts to dissuade them. Enemy planes dropped menus from the Manila Hotel; sound trucks alternated bloodcurdling shrieks with songs and stilted commentary. During the nightly show on Manila's Japanese-controlled station KZRH, a seductive female voice purred propaganda. Few took the messages seriously, but it was nevertheless difficult to ignore the show's haunting theme song: "I'm Waiting for Ships That Never Come In." After reporting on the losing battle for several months, United Press International correspondent Frank Hewlett wrote the doggerel that would forever be linked with the Philippines campaign:

> We're the Battling Bastards of Bataan,
> No mama, No papa, No Uncle Sam,
> No aunts, no uncles, no cousins, no nieces,
> No pills, no planes, no artillery pieces
> And nobody gives a damn.

MacArthur's pleas for aid fell on deaf ears. "The truth," wrote historian John Hersey, came to the troops in the Philippines "in mean little doses." Morale tumbled. Soldiers resented officers or, more precisely, those that took advantage of the privilege of rank. Edgy troops on Bataan envied their counterparts on Corregidor, whom they believed had plenty of food, coffee, and smokes. Many were displeased with what they believed to be an apathetic America. "Where the devil are those planes that Henry Ford is turning out, and the rest of them?" confounded soldiers asked the war correspondents. Lt. John Burns of the 21st Pursuit captured the prevalent feelings in a diary entry: "I can't see what they are thinking of in the states, they surely could have gotten some help in here, both troops and planes, U.S. aid for every place but the P.I.'s."

While they never completely gave up hope in America, some came to resent Roosevelt, whose speeches focused on the European war. On Corregidor, Quezon became combustible after one such speech. "I cannot stand this constant reference to England, to Europe," shouted the terminally ill Filipino leader. "America writhes in anguish at the fate of a distant cousin, Europe, while a daughter, the Philippines, is being raped in the back room."

They also resented MacArthur, though he had been deceived, too. He was a persistent and eloquent champion of their cause, and worshipped by many Filipinos, but was conspicuously absent from the Bataan Peninsula, making only one trip in January. Rumors circulated that he was afraid to leave Malinta Tunnel, and "Dugout Doug" soon joined FDR and Stimson as the subject of many deprecating barbs, jokes, and songs.

Their gallows humor eventually betrayed their defenders' true fears and feelings. After the arrival of a newborn in a field hospital, one soldier cracked that if America "won't send reinforcements, we'll make our own." Some soldiers attempted to raise money in order to purchase a bomber from their own government. "Better buy one bomber than be buried on Bataan" was the slogan of the "Bomber for Bataan Fund." The optimism of January was rapidly replaced by the bitter reality of March. Months earlier, some soldiers had chalked a "V" onto their helmets, but the letter, many thought, no longer stood for "Victory" but for "Victims."

MONDAY, MARCH 2, 1942
Bataan Field, Bataan, Philippine Islands

At 1125 hours, a mysterious voice cut into the "Red Net"—the telephone circuit that connected the various USAFFE synapses and commands with MacArthur's Corregidor nerve center—at Gen. Hal "Pursuit" George's headquarters at Bataan Field, which, along with Mariveles and Cabcaben Fields, was one of the three airfields serving the remnant of the Far East Air Force. George's intelligence officer, Capt. Allison Ind, believing the call to be from USAFFE, immediately called George to the line. A brief, yet fatefully mysterious conversation ensued.

"Two large tankers, three supply ships, and an airplane in attendance are entering Subic Bay," said the voice.

George hesitated momentarily to digest the statement. "And what action does the Chief of Staff desire me to take?"

"Why, he says you are to use your own judgment, sir," the voice replied.

The call was freighted with great significance. The presence of such a large concentration of enemy ships suggested another landing attempt in western Bataan. The weakened defenders would have little chance of repelling an invasion, and any attempt to contest a landing with airpower would be a dangerous gamble. Only five battle-battered P-40s, each badly in need of engine overhauls, remained in the ragtag Bataan air force. George drew a few puffs from his pipe and then ordered Ind to raise Mariveles Field and order the 20th Pursuit Squadron's two P-40s loaded with fragmentation bombs. George paused, then issued another crisp command: "Ask Captain Dyess to come here at once."

While en route to George's quarters, Dyess ran into his operations officer, Lt. Ben Brown. "Well, Ed," said Brown, "we're putting the big shoes on Joe. Everything'll be ready when you get there." Brown's update was veiled in the same code that the pilots used on their radios to confuse Japanese interlopers. Dyess knew what Brown meant. A day earlier, a makeshift bomb rack—the fruit of Dyess's imagination, the labors of the Bataan Field Flying Detachment, and some coil springs from jettisoned Japanese fuel tanks and automobile spare parts—had been affixed to the fuselage of the battered olive drab P-40 Dyess had named *Kibosh*. The "big shoes" referred to 500-pound, high-explosive bombs.

Dyess bounded up onto the porch of George's headquarters building. Ind noticed that the pilot's eyes "gleamed." George, a smile hidden beneath his shaggy beard, asked if Dyess's bomb rack was ready for a practical test. "There never was a better day, General," answered Dyess.

"Be careful, Ed," George replied.

The fact that George was willing to commit the last few planes to such a gamble was not lost on Dyess. He had been pressing George for permission to strike back for both strategic and morale purposes, but the planes had been limited to mostly reconnaissance missions. Dyess knew that he and his pilots had to make the most of this opportunity, an opportunity to take the offensive, even if just temporarily, and win a victory for themselves.

Lt. John Posten commenced the mission, taking off at 1300 hours from Bataan Field with, in the pilots' parlance, "little shoes," six 30-pound fragmentation bombs. Minutes later, Lts. Kiefer White and Erwin Crellin, their P-40s similarly armed, lifted off from Mariveles Field. An hour later Posten returned, reporting that he had bombed a tanker, but could not verify any hits; White said that he and Crellin had gone after a cruiser that was "really throwing lead" and concluded that his wingman was shot down. It was an inauspicious beginning.

On the flight line at Bataan Field, *Kibosh* had been fueled and armed. But a successful conclusion to this mission, Dyess realized, would require something more than high-explosives. Dangling from a chain around his neck alongside his dog tags was a metal crucifix and a Saint Christopher medal he had been given by one of his pilots who had died on Bataan in February. Dyess taxied *Kibosh* into position.

At 1350, a crowd gathered to watch Dyess's heavily loaded P-40 loft out of sight. Many thought that the plane, struggling under the weight, had crashed. Suddenly, *Kibosh* appeared just above the waters of Manila Bay. "There it is!" someone shouted as Dyess lumbered off toward his rendezvous with Lt. Donald "Shorty" Crosland. Crosland was Dyess's "weaver," the pilot assigned to watch Dyess's tail. George and Ind listened with hand-wringing anticipation to the traffic crackling over the Red Net and the monotonous, even-pitched voices of the radar spotters coldly clicking off the ranges and azimuths of the planes as they circled to gain altitude.

Thirty air miles and several tension-filled minutes later, Dyess looked down from his cockpit at Subic Bay and Grande Island, the small, brown-green landmass in the mouth of the bay. The sea was rippling blue, marred only by small furrows of dissipating white foam, the watery tracks of chugging Japanese vessels. "The scene below me was like a brilliant lithograph, the colors almost too real," he remembered. With the dazzling sun at his back, he headed into his dive. Docks, piers, and warehouses bustling with activity materialized. Seeing that the heaviest concentration of Japanese ships was not along the western shores of Olongapo as he had been told, but instead near Grande Island, he descended toward the latter. He looked for a large tanker—his primary target—but could not locate the vessel. While cataloguing his options, he spied a medium-sized transport steaming between Grande Island and the western shore and swooped down for the attack.

Gunning *Kibosh*'s throttle wide open at 5,000 feet, he flew into a storm of fire opening up from ship and shore. His eyes riveted on the transport, he plunged the P-40 to 2,000 feet and ripped the release handle, letting loose the 500-pound bomb. He pulled back on the stick, and while looking over his shoulder saw the bomb splash about forty feet from its target—a close miss. Angered, he swung *Kibosh* back around, almost down to water level, and "gave the Jap the .50 caliber treatment," sweeping up and down the decks in three, blistering strafing runs before focusing his guns on the bridge. Mortally wounded, the ship stopped dead in the water.

Crosland charged down to join Dyess and the two planes tore off to engage other targets. Dyess blasted four small warehouses on the north side of the island and sent swarms of Japanese stevedores and soldiers scurrying for cover as strips of bullets splintered piers and buildings. He then turned his attention to two 100-ton motor vessels chugging between the island and the Bataan shore. Dyess caught one of the boats in the open and sprayed fire at the ship's forward guns before aiming at the hull and the engine room. Crosland, following Dyess's lead, ripped into the other side of the vessel with his .50 caliber guns. Dyess was sweeping around for another run and came in low, his plane just skimming the surface of the water. "The Japs aboard her were putting on quite an act," he later wrote. "Those astern were rushing forward and those forward were rushing astern. They couldn't have done better for my purpose. They met amidships where my bullets were striking." Seeing the ship list and then begin sinking, he clicked off the last of his ammunition into the other launch. Then both pilots winged home.

Safely on the ground at Bataan Field at 1415, Dyess entered the operations shack and called George. "I had me a field day," he said. He then provided an out-of-breath, play-by-play description of his successes—as well as his failure with the "big egg"—supplemented with commentary characteristic of his sense of humor. When asked to elaborate on the fate of one of his targets, he replied, laconically, "I'm afraid the boat leaks." Yet Dyess was hardly content. "I want to try again right away," his voice begged. "May I?"

Twilight was fast approaching and Dyess was running out of time—and chances. His crew moved about *Kibosh*, feeding fuel and a steady meal of .50 caliber cartridges into the tanks and magazines. Dyess was intent on making this mission—his third and final venture—count. On his second sortie, he had again missed one of the large freighters with his 500-pound bomb, but the miss was so close that bomb fragments had punctured the ship's superstructure and also damaged some nearby barges and lighters. Upon returning, Dyess pleaded with George for one more opportunity. George was hesitant; approaching nightfall and tropical winds stirring the airfields gave him reason to pause. But the old ace "eventually granted permission," said Dyess. "If he hadn't, I'd have missed the best shooting of the day."

Entering his dive at sundown, Dyess noticed that the freighters he had seen that afternoon had left the Grande Island docks and were "running around like mad." But he instead veered toward the north shore and its supply dumps and warehouses. At 1,800 feet, he loosed his final "egg." His aim was true; fire, smoke, and debris exploded into the air. Dyess and his new weaver, Lt. John Burns, swept the docks with their guns, adding to the conflagration before arcing skyward with a ferocious hail of tracer bullets, antiaircraft, and small arms fire on their tails.

Just as the pilots began their homeward journey, their radios informed them that observers on Mariveles Mountain had spotted a large transport, with landing barges in tow, trying to slip out of the bay. Dyess immediately veered into an interception course. Illuminated by the glow of the fires in the west, the vessel made an inviting target. He could see the six streams of his wing guns spitting shells from amidships to the stern, sparking several fires.

Burns followed Dyess and pumped additional fire into the vessel. Gunning *Kibosh*'s engine, Dyess climbed to 4,000 feet before screaming down on another strafing run. With *Kibosh*'s nose pointed at a 45-degree angle, he mashed down the trigger and stitched several deadly rows of .50 caliber bullets across the ship's bow and bridge. The vessel then exploded in a blinding flash. Dyess jerked the plane's stick to avoid being caught in the thick wash of black smoke and debris. The move was so sudden, he blacked out for a few seconds. "Colder than a pair of ice tongs," he later wrote. When Dyess came to at 4,000 feet, he saw the boiling, blue-black waves below him cresting with orange flames.

Dyess sighted another ship silhouetted in the fiery glow and, despite the large volume of antiaircraft fire it was throwing up, swooped down for another kill. In his report, Burns would identify the ship as a cruiser. Dyess made three passes, raking the vessel with fire from his .50 cals until his trigger clicked unresponsively. Mortally wounded, the ship lunged for the shore, beaching on the sand. Dyess could see the effects of the damage he had wrought through several large bullet holes in the underside of the plane. After giving Burns the high sign, the signal to disengage, he set a course for Bataan Field.

He thoughtlessly cruised over Japanese lines at 1,000 feet, "the stupidest thing of my flying career," he later admitted. Flak sent the plane quivering into a turbulent fit of exploding shells and tracer streams. "It was like flying down Broadway," said Dyess. He survived. Climbing from the cockpit back at Bataan Field, he pressed into the excited crowd gathering in wonderment around *Kibosh*'s sievelike fuselage. "We got one that time," exclaimed a shaken Dyess. They got more than one. As the excited reports of the observers crackled in and the damage estimates climbed, Captain Ind raced outside the operations shack to relay the news. The defenders of the Philippines finally had a reason to celebrate. Bataan Field erupted in joy. "It was stuff much too strong to be taken with calm and reserve," he explained. "The lid blew off our long jammed-down feelings. Restraint went to the winds, and the jungle resounded to our whoops."

Nine pilots contributed to the success of the raid—including Lt. Sam Grashio, who, after a locked release handle prevented him from dropping his bombs, skillfully landed with the bombs dangling from his wings, thus saving his P-40 for another mission. But Dyess's individual exploits were staggering. His score included one 12,000-ton transport destroyed, one 5,000- or 6,000-ton vessel burned, at least two 100-ton motor launches, and a handful of smaller barges and lighters sunk. It was impossible to estimate the full extent of the dockside damages, but the cumulative Japanese losses were so severe that Radio Tokyo reported that fifty-four American four-engined bombers and swarms of fighter planes were responsible. One can only imagine what George and his pilots could have done with such a force.

This soon-to-be-famous raid on Subic Bay would cement Dyess's legend—one that had been created by his leadership of a landing party of twenty airmen on the beach at Agloloma Bay to root out unsurrendered Japanese and finish the Battle of the Points in February—among all troops and commands in the Philippines. The price of the victory, however, was steep. Only Dyess's P-40, *Kibosh*, remained operational. Crellin's death and the wrecked planes left George without an air force, but he rallied his men with a quart of whiskey. "At least the death of our little air force was one of unmitigated glory," Ind would write. It was later discovered that George had not been speaking to Sutherland, or to a representative of USAFFE that morning, but a messenger from 5th Interceptor Command headquarters relaying intelligence. The whole conversation, said Ind, had been a quirk, "one of those impossible coincidences which led to a series of impossible coincidences."

George wasted little time assigning Dyess a new mission: he wanted the pilots to invite the nurses from nearby Field Hospital No. 2 to a party. "If this war is going to be fought by our boys and girls, Ed," he said, "they might as well have what little good times they can."

That evening, a silvery tropical moon bathed the jungle in a soft, blue light. Nervous pilots in wrinkled uniforms squired a dozen nurses wearing dresses and rationed cosmetics through the entrance to their clubhouse—a bamboo shack on stilts decorated with Japanese helmets and swords—under a set of mounted carabao horns and a placard that read: "THE DYSENTERY CROSS, Awarded to the Quartermaster by THE MEN OF BATAAN FIELD."

It must have been some sight. "Had forgotten what a white woman looked like," wrote Lieutenant Burns. Aided by some libations—medicinal alcohol mixed with lemon powder and juice—and boogie-woogie played by Cpl. Robert L. Greenman, an accomplished concert pianist banging on an upright rescued from the ruins of a bombed-out barrio, the pilots loosened up. With each dance, they temporarily escaped the war in a catharsis of candy, alcohol, and conversation.

As Greenman pounded the keys and the accompaniment of female voices and laughs filtered into the Bataan night, mechanics and repair specialists in a revetment on the other side of the field slapped patches of sheet metal onto *Kibosh*'s bullet-riddled fuselage. Cut from glistening slabs that had been treated with a violet-hued, anticorrosive paint, the patches contrasted noticeably with the plane's olive drab skin. By Dyess's accounting, there were perhaps seventy of them. "Jesus Christ," he said with a laugh, "my airplane has the measles!"

Surveying the scene, UPI's Frank Hewlett got an idea. He tore a piece of paper from his notepad, and grimy, callused hands passed it around the revetment to a chorus of laughter. Written as a faux telegram from the defenders of the Philippines to the White House, Hewlett's terse words found their way onto a bulletin board and, eventually, into campaign lore:

TO THE PRESIDENT OF THE UNITED STATES.
DEAR MR. PRESIDENT:
PLEASE SEND US ANOTHER P-40. OURS IS FULL OF HOLES.

CHAPTER 4

God Help Them

I felt my way with weary stumbling feet,
Between the broken fragments of defeat
There was a home-made flag of dirty white.

MONDAY, APRIL 6, 1942
Corregidor, Philippine Islands

Amid the twilit comfort of the cool tropic winds blowing in from the South China Sea, 1st Lts. Jack Hawkins and Mike Dobervich, USMC, sat in Hawkins's command post, a dugout chiseled into a chalk cliff near Corregidor's south shore, full mess kits of chow in their laps. After a few bites, Hawkins decided to break the pregnant silence and pose the question to his best friend. And, for better or worse, put the rumors to rest.

"How are things going over there?"

Unlike most of the 4th Marines, Dobervich had been on Bataan since mid-January with the Marine detachment guarding the forward USAFFE headquarters. His appetite had bridged their friendship across the North Channel—this was his third visit to Hawkins's mess in as many months. Mashing his rice and corned beef hash, he did not mince words with his reply.

"It looks kind of bad, Jack. The Nips are pushing hard."

"How much longer do you think Bataan can hold out?"

"Not long. Seems to me the folks at home would get something out here to us. I don't believe they realize what's going on."

"Guess not," mused Hawkins, a twenty-five-year-old, straight-shooting Texan barely three years out of Annapolis, now in command of a reinforced platoon of four dozen machine gunners. "Looks like we're the lost sheep. . . . I wonder if all these boys here realize what they're up against. I know mine do. I don't try to kid 'em along."

"I think most of them do, Jack," said Dobervich. "I suppose a few believe in that bum headquarters dope about 'Help is on the way,' but not many."

"These boys out here deserve plenty of credit, don't they?" said Hawkins. "To go on scrapping when they're up against a stacked deck like this."

"You bet they do," concurred Dobervich.

Having reached their consensus, they returned to their mess kits.

For an Annapolis plebe, deciding that he did not like ships or the sea—anything Navy, really—during his first summer cruise is quite a revelation. Such was the dilemma of Jack Hawkins in July 1936. Following the outbreak of the Spanish Civil War, Hawkins's ship, the USS *Oklahoma*, was ordered to Bilbao, Spain, to pick up American citizens. The student crew was transferred to the *Wyoming*, and it would take only a few days of rolling across the choppy Atlantic on the cramped older battleship for Hawkins to change his mind about the Navy. Nevertheless he was perhaps destined for a military career.

While growing up in the northeastern Texas farm town of Roxton, then nearby Paris and later Fort Worth—like his English ancestors who arrived in Virginia circa 1707 and drifted west, Hawkins's family relocated several times—Hawkins had several role models to emulate, including his future brother-in-law, a cadet at the Virginia Military Institute, and his Civil War veteran grandfathers. He was, after all, named for Andrew Jackson Hawkins, a relative who had served in the Louisiana Cavalry. He was also a descendant of one of Queen Elizabeth's famed Seadogs, Admiral Sir John Hawkins, the commander of the *Victory* in the sixteenth-century defeat of the Spanish Armada. Regardless of that portion of his pedigree, Hawkins knew that he did not have the salty sea air and cannon smoke in his blood. He also knew that he could not leave Annapolis, his chance at an education and a future. There was only one answer: the

Marine Corps. With just twenty-five slots for Marine placement per class, it would take four years of dedicated scholarship and subterfuge—to mask his poor eyesight he memorized the eye charts used in physical inspections—but Hawkins earned a slot.

For Mike Dobervich, the decision was equally simple: the military or the ore mines. In the early 1900s, many immigrants mined hematite and manganese from the northeastern Minnesota earth, sent for their families, and settled in the mining town melting pots of the Minnesota Iron Range. One of them, Obrad Dobervich, a Serb, settled in Ironton, where he and his wife Mara brought up eight children. All six of the Dobervich boys boxed; all would fight in World War II. They also learned the value of an education—five, Michiel included, would attend North Dakota Agricultural College in Fargo. Resourceful and hardworking—Austin Shofner would christen him "Beaver"—Dobervich lived with the mayor of Fargo while earning a reputation as an accomplished Golden Gloves boxer, honors as a four-year ROTC officer, and a bachelor's degree in agriculture in 1939.

The "Minnesota Yankee" and the "Texas Rebel," as Hawkins described them, would become best friends upon meeting at the Philadelphia Navy Yard in the summer of 1939. Standing at attention, they were a study in physical contrasts. Hawkins was six foot one and weighed 165 pounds, with wavy blond hair, blue eyes, and a fair complexion that amplified his boyish looks. A short shock of coffee-colored hair framed Dobervich's ruggedly handsome face and flint-gray eyes, while his crooked nose and burly build betrayed his pugilist past. Gentle and generous to a fault, Dobervich did not fit the profile of the archetypical Marine officer. Hawkins also remembered a distinct language barrier: "He talked in the rapid staccato of the busy North, and I—well, it always did take me all day to say anything. We weren't much alike," he concluded, "but we looked at things the same way."

They would be roommates throughout basic school and their first overseas assignment in Shanghai. The 4th Marine Regiment—located in Shanghai since the late 1920s—had lately been charged with protecting American interests and buffering the city's International Settlement from the encroaching Sino-Japanese War. The two junior officers would spend seventeen months in the wild, decadent city. By late 1941, the Japanese had encircled the city, and since the prevailing, yet impractical war contingency plan called for the understrength Marines to break for far-off

Chungking and align with Nationalist forces, Col. Samuel L. Howard successfully lobbied to evacuate the regiment in late November. Though Dobervich had contracted cerebral meningitis, he, Hawkins, and Shofner would travel together to the Philippines aboard the *President Madison*.

Now, as they finished their meals, Hawkins sensed that Dobervich was not fully recovered.

"Gee, that was good," said Dobervich. "I'll have to come back over to see you again soon, if you'll promise to feed me like that."

"Sure we'll feed you," Hawkins said laughing. "When do you think you'll be back again?"

"Oh, I don't know. Maybe in a few weeks . . . maybe never."

"Don't talk like that."

A few minutes later, a gunnysack filled with cans and cartons of cigarettes was placed in the truck that Dobervich had driven up from the North Dock. It was a generous gift, "but we gave gladly, knowing that the boys in Bataan were suffering more than we," said Hawkins.

"Take care of yourself," Hawkins called over the growl of the truck's engine.

"Okay. You do the same," yelled Dobervich. "So long."

Hawkins watched Dobervich head down the dusty jungle alley toward the North Dock and the gray unknown beyond. After lingering for a moment in ruminative silence, he pivoted and began the walk back to his dugout.

WEDNESDAY, APRIL 8, 1942
Bataan, Philippine Islands

Cabcaben Field, 2215 hours. The thunderclaps of a nearby 155 millimeter gun muffled the sounds of mechanics and pilots ratcheting the grease-slathered, metallic viscera of a single-engine Navy biplane known as a Grumman J2F Duck. The men had been working in around-the-clock shifts for the past forty-eight hours. As the chief mechanic, 2nd Lt. Leo Boelens had scribbled in his diary, "We must stay—get duck out."

It would not be Boelens's first mechanical miracle. Since his reassignment from the 27th Material Squadron, the imaginative Boelens had not only kept the few remaining planes flying, he had also endeavored to create reinforcements, scavenging parts from cracked-up P-40Bs and P-40Es to build a hybrid Warhawk known to the pilots as the "P-40 Something."

Tonight, however, he would be working against more than a shortage of parts. During trips to requisition tools, the twenty-seven-year-old had encountered columns of troops straggling back from the front. "I predict the beginning of the end," he jotted in his crude diary on April 7.

Sunk in January off Mariveles, the Duck had been refloated, repaired, and returned to service with Bataan's "Bamboo Fleet," a motley air force including the two surviving P-40s, a 1933 Bellanca Skyrocket, a Beechcraft Staggerwing, and a 1934 Waco bi-wing that the pilots flew to the Visayas and Mindanao on evacuation missions. On their return flights, the planes' fuselages were crammed with everything from batteries and quinine pills to cigarettes, cognac, candy—and the scarcest commodity of all, news from home. Capt. Joe Moore had discovered an RCA overseas wireless office on the unoccupied island of Cebu, 365 miles south, capable of communicating with California. If not for Moore, Sam Grashio would not have received the cablegram containing news that his wife had given birth to a baby girl.

The Duck, though, had delivered little good news in the past two days. Following Moore's mission on April 6, the plane had blown a cylinder. Boelens's crew was now attempting an emergency transplant with parts from another sunken amphibian.

The earsplitting explosions seemed to amplify with each turn of a socket wrench, each bolt and screw tightened. Enveloped by the tumult, the mechanics continued to work as the concussions rattled their tools and their confidence. The battle for Bataan was hurtling inexorably to its terminus. Most certainly, the "pickens," as Boelens and Dyess used to say, were not good.

Leo Boelens, the youngest of eleven children born to an immigrant Belgian farmer, possessed an energy and ingenuity acquired in part from his environment. Historically, the inhabitants of northern Wyoming's Big Horn basin—from Native Americans and frontier trappers to contemporary farmers and ranchers—were good with their hands. Centuries of evidence ranged from tribal petroglyphs pecked on sandstone walls to symmetrical rows of irrigated crops to the tanks and smokestacks of the Standard Oil refinery puncturing the big Western sky.

At five foot seven and a half, 155 pounds, Boelens was an average-sized farm boy. He would never forget his agricultural roots—he humbly referred to himself in correspondence as "a farmer, L.A.B."—but Leo Arthur Boelens's hands were not meant to till the Wyoming soil. He dropped out of the University of Wyoming and joined the Army Air Corps in late 1940. Nine months of dissecting engines and learning airplane design, construction, and maintenance in the Air Corps Technical School's aeronautical engineering program at Chanute Field near Rantoul, Illinois, awakened a latent talent. "I'm sold on this branch," he wrote his kin.

Boelens was commissioned in September 1941 and returned home just before shipping out. As a car waited to take him to Billings, Montana, and the transport that would fly him to San Francisco, shutters clicked, freezing the farewell in time, locking a smiling, broad-shouldered Boelens in his uniform, in his youth, in the permanence of black and white.

No sooner had Boelens ducked into the car than an uncomfortable feeling swept over his older sister, Christina Snyder, who had raised him following the death of their mother in 1928. They shared a unique familial bond and at that moment she was overwhelmed with a sudden premonition. As the car carrying Leo Boelens motored toward Billings, an emotional Snyder turned to the rest of her family.

"We will never see him again," she announced.

Boelens and his crew were just finishing repairs on the Duck when Ed Dyess's Ford sedan arrived. Dyess, fresh from supervising the evacuation of Bataan Field, was leading a convoy of men to Mariveles Field. There was a rumor that B-17s would be arriving there to evacuate pilots, but Dyess had stopped to inform Lt. Roland Barnick, the pilot assigned to fly the Duck, that he was to wait until the last possible minute for a special passenger from Corregidor, Col. Carlos Romulo, MacArthur's press officer and the man behind the Voice of Freedom radio broadcasts. The orders, Dyess said, came straight from MacArthur himself.

Dyess then continued his own personal mission—the evacuation of all flight personnel other than himself from the peninsula—in complete disregard of an official mandate from his superiors. Dyess had earlier objected to his inclusion on a list of pilots cleared for evacuation. "We haven't surrendered yet; I can't leave my men," he protested. Unwilling to leave, but unable to disobey a direct order, Dyess was now stalling for time for his pilots. He sent Lt. I. B. "Jack" Donalson out on Kibosh; four other pilots on two old P-35s flown up from Mindanao. And, at midnight, Dyess issued one final, surprising order: that Leo Boelens take his seat on the Duck. When Boelens mentioned Dyess's well-known departure order, Dyess balked. Boelens "was to go and *that* was an order."

Not long after Dyess's convoy resumed its trek to Mariveles, a relieved Carlos Romulo arrived at Cabcaben. He had spent hours fighting through the "mad stampede" of vehicles and defeated soldiers. Romulo's excitement, however, dimmed when he caught a glimpse of the Duck by the flickering light of the fires now engulfing Bataan. "It was the funniest-looking plane I had ever seen," he later wrote. "It looked like something reclaimed from a city dump." Romulo watched anxiously as the crew spun the propeller. There was a loud popping sound, a shower of sparks. "The engine choked and snarled, snorted and started," remembered Romulo. The revetment erupted into cheers—Boelens had done it again.

At 0118, gloomy clouds drew back to reveal a platinum moon. No sooner had the passengers boarded than a minor earthquake lasting approximately one minute rippled Bataan, the death rattle of the peninsula. The overloaded Duck waddled down the quaking strip, spluttered skyward, and struggled for altitude, hovering precariously about seventy feet above Manila Bay in the glaring streaks of searchlights. As flak bracketed the ship, the crew lightened the load, tossing out parachutes, pistols, and life preservers. The plane finally slipped the searchlights' grip and lumbered away from the embattled peninsula.

THURSDAY, APRIL 9, 1942
Bataan, Philippine Islands

An aurora swirled in the night skies above Bataan, radiating around the smoke-shrouded peaks of the Mariveles Mountains. Intermittent flashes from phosphorus bombs and incendiary shells bathed the jungle in blinding bursts of white light. The rumbling, subterranean tremors had scarcely subsided when American stockpiles of TNT and ammunition dumps were detonated, causing the peninsula to convulse. Thousands of rounds of projectiles, from artillery and mortar shells to rifle bullets, streaked across the sky in arcing rainbows. "Never did a 4th of July display equal it in noise, lights, colors or cost," observed one officer.

Surrender orders had begun to trickle down from command posts to foxholes, and so across Bataan the implements of war were euthanized. Field pieces were double-loaded and fired, blowing the breech blocks and splaying the barrels. The engines of tanks, half-tracks, and trucks were sabotaged. Codebooks, maps, and cash were buried. The Navy scuttled the sub tender *Canopus*, the largest vessel remaining in Philippine waters, and its shore installations. The bulging mushroom clouds and ghastly ruby glow of burning fuel tanks were visible for miles.

Lt. Sam Grashio had never seen anything like it. As the convoy rumbled through the "Dantesque" landscape toward Mariveles in the early morning hours, it seemed as though "the end of the world had come." Surrender, though no one could actually utter the word, was no longer a rumor, but a reality. Had he been a fool not to leave Bataan? Less than twenty-four hours ago, Dyess had ordered Grashio to fly a reconnaissance mission for the purpose of establishing safe routes of transit for evacuated VIPs. As he had drowsily strolled to the revetment, a family of monkeys that had eluded the mess cooks skittered out and disappeared single file into the brush. Everybody, it seemed, was bugging out of Bataan. But the jungle omen was lost on Grashio.

Once airborne, he disconnected from the conflict. "The sky was clear and blue and the air was balmy," Grashio noted. "No bombs were falling, no artillery shells were bursting overhead. . . . Nobody, racked with awful cramps of dysentery was racing or crawling for a vacant space at a latrine." Grashio spied several ships and recorded the data before glancing at his fuel gauge. With exactly one-half tank remaining, he could have returned to Bataan or continued south, to safety. Pulled between an instinctive desire for self-preservation and his devotion to duty, Grashio thought about what Dyess would have done. The decision made itself.

Dyess had created a cult of personality during the last days on Bataan, but his actions were not contrived; he was simply trying to fill a giant void. When MacArthur left on March 11 by way of an executive order issued by FDR, he was rumored to have taken with him—in addition to his wife, son, and Chinese amah—valuables ranging from a cash-stuffed mattress to a refrigerator. Although MacArthur did not take any such items, he did take General Hal George. After a harrowing journey, MacArthur's party arrived in Australia six days later. At a remote rail station, MacArthur would announce famously that Roosevelt "ordered me to break through the Japanese lines and proceed from Corregidor to Australia for the purpose, as I understand it, of organizing the American offensive against Japan, a primary objective of which is the relief of the Philippines. I came through and I shall return."

But whereas MacArthur's pledge was largely met with derision—the standing joke, at least among American troops on Bataan, was that upon leaving his foxhole for the latrine one soldier would dutifully inform his comrade that he was going to the head and "shall return"—George's commitment to return with planes "even if he had to go all the way to the States to get them" was taken at face value. But he was also a realist. "Tell the boys," he told Dyess privately, "that if I'm not back pretty soon it will not be because I don't want to come back." (George would not survive the first full year of the war. The brigadier was killed in a freak accident when an American plane attempting to take off crashed into George's parked C-40 transport on April 29, 1942, at an airport in Darwin, Australia.)

Though outranked by several remaining officers, Dyess essentially became George's successor. It was a daunting task. His pilots barely had enough strength to climb in and out of their cockpits, which, because of dysentery, often had to be cleaned of human waste after flights. Dyess exhausted himself by remaining conspicuously in command. And he expected no special treatment. In late March, the brass had decided to increase the rations of the pilots—and not the enlisted men—to build their strength. Dyess told his sergeants that he would not accept the food unless it was okay with the men. Though resentful of officer's privilege, they assented because it wasn't just any officer asking them—it was Dyess.

Dyess's convoy motored into Mariveles at dawn and found no B-17s. Patching in to FEAF headquarters at Little Baguio on the Mariveles radio net, Dyess discovered that a boat would take the pilots to Corregidor, from where a submarine would spirit them from the Philippines. But by the time they reached the chaotic dock area, it was too late. Their boat had been filled with nurses and the men had no choice but to wave to them, stoically and gallantly, as if watching loved ones row away from a sinking ship in the last lifeboat. At that moment, Sam Grashio and the other pilots turned to look at their commanding officer, in hopes that he would do what he always did: come up with a solution to their problem.

• • •

As his two-jeep caravan, adorned with flapping white bedsheets, crept through the battle-scarred jungle and past the foxholes and bivouacs of his weary men, the charred metal skeletons of vehicles, the mountains of stacked arms, and weaponry, Maj. Gen. Edward Postell King, Jr., could not help but think how familiar it all seemed.

On April 3, Japanese guns had boomed a barrage of high-explosive shells into the center of the skeletal Fil-American lines, and the shells, coupled with incendiaries dropped by bombers, cut a flaming swath nearly two miles beyond the southern slopes of Mount Samat, the anchor of the main line of resistance. Through this gate, thousands of fresh troops—Imperial GHQ had reinforced Homma with air reinforcements from Malaya and also several detachments of men and artillery from China—sluiced into Bataan. By April 7, Homma had cleaved the Fil-American forces. The entire Japanese 14th Army was racing toward Mariveles and there was nothing Ned King could do about it—not even surrender.

King, a former lawyer in his late fifties with a bushy auburn mustache, had been USAFFE's chief artillery officer. After MacArthur's exit, Gen. Jonathan M. "Skinny" Wainwright, a lean, leathery and unpretentious old cavalryman, was promoted to commander of USFIP—the newly designated United States Forces in the Philippines. King, in turn, inherited the troops on Bataan, now known as Luzon Force—and a no-surrender mandate from FDR and MacArthur. Ignorant of the miserable state of the Allied war effort, MacArthur intended to immediately return to the Philippines with reinforcements and wanted an army there when he did. Accordingly, though thousands of miles removed from the reality of the situation, earlier he had ordered a breakout operation to secure supplies from the Japanese base at Olongapo. To order weak men who could barely walk to disengage from a fight, march several dozen miles, and take a fortified supply depot was lunacy; King rightfully ignored the order.

As the embers of April 8 crumbled into the ashes of morning, King's agonizing dilemma remained. He could destroy his distintegrating command in a bloody last stand or else entreat with the enemy in the hope of saving his men, though at the likely cost of a disgraceful court-martial. King chose the latter option. That, after all, was what Lee had done. A descendant of Confederate officers, King was acutely aware of the significance of the date. Exactly seventy-seven years to the day earlier, on April

9, 1865, General Robert E. Lee had surrendered his starving Army of Northern Virginia to General Ulysses S. Grant at the town of Appomattox Court House, Virginia, effectively ending the Civil War. Lee's words haunted King: "Then there is nothing left to do but to go and see General Grant, and I would rather die a thousand deaths."

King arrived at the town of Lamao and, at 1200 hours, sat down at a table to surrender the largest force in American military history. Seated across from him was Homma's senior operations officer, Col. Motoo Nakayama. Nakayama, angered that King did not have the authority to surrender all of the Fil-American forces in the Philippines, was truculent and condescending. He was further insulted when, after demanding King's sword, he learned that the general had left his saber in Manila. King convinced Nakayama to accept his pistol instead, but was unable to convince the Japanese to agree to his plan to use USFIP trucks to transport the surrendered troops to a place of Homma's choosing. Nakayama refused to address King's concerns about Japan's treatment of prisoners, instead issuing only a brief, nebulous reply.

"The Imperial Japanese Army are not barbarians."

Ed Dyess was seeing otherwise. He had been resigned to gather his squadron and surrender in an orderly fashion, but that was before he watched enemy planes strafe the unarmed troops waggling bedsheets, towels, and other makeshift surrender flags. The piercing, frightened cries of civilians and children, heard above the thunder of shellfire and bombs, rang his ears in a "symphony of despair." Dyess first considered joining the guerrillas rumored to be operating in Luzon, but the distance was too great. He also knew that Americans could not take to the hills without quinine to protect themselves from malaria. Peering through the smoke-filled haze suspended above Mariveles Bay, he saw hundreds of desperate men—some swimming, others paddling on rafts or clinging to oil drums, crates, and various pieces of debris—struggling toward Corregidor, but he could not, in good conscience, order his men into the oil-slicked, shark-infested waters.

Time, however, ran out on Dyess and his men. The Japanese army had metastasized across Bataan, closing all possible escape routes. Near Little Baguio, Dyess's car found three enemy tanks blocking the road. Nervously, the pilots thrust their hands into the air, waving white handkerchiefs. A Japanese soldier motioned them forward, but, noticing their sidearms, quickly halted them. Frantically unholstering their .45s, the Americans again raised their arms. As the ranking officer, Dyess was punished for the transgression in a torrent of scalding Japanese and blows to his face. "The jig certainly was up," wrote Dyess.

Luckily for the passengers of the Duck, now skidding across Manduriao Field with an empty gas tank, Carlos Romulo's briefcase had not been a casualty of the airborne purge. Searchlights from Japanese ships had sparkled the sky above Cebu Harbor, forcing Romulo to produce a map of secret airfields, thus landing them here, two miles northwest of Iloilo, at dawn. They blinked in disbelief while gazing upon the flowers, green rice fields, and efflorescent splendor of an Iloilo untouched by war. And then the Victory Restaurant, a tiny shack on the field just opened for breakfast, came into focus.

While downing eight fried eggs and six cups of coffee, Romulo watched Barnick finish eleven eggs, bacon, and biscuits. Boelens ate four orders of ham and eggs. One passenger guzzled ten cups of fresh hot coffee. With each guilty bite, they saw the gaunt faces of friends left behind on Bataan.

Not long after the sumptuous breakfast, they gathered around a radio. Romulo recognized the voice as that of one of his assistants with the Voice of Freedom, Philippine Army 3rd Lt. Norman Reyes. Reyes's voice quivered amid the crackling static:

> Good evening everyone, everywhere. This is the Voice of Freedom broadcasting from somewhere in the Philippines. Bataan has fallen. The Philippine-American troops on this war-ravaged and blood-stained peninsula have laid down their arms. With heads bloodied but unbowed, they have yielded to the superior force and numbers of the enemy. . . . All the world will testify to the almost superhuman endurance with which they stood up until the last in the face of overwhelming odds. . . . Men hedging under the banner of unshakable faith are made of something more than flesh, but they are not made of impervious steel. The flesh must yield at last, endurance melts away and the end of the battle must come. Bataan has

fallen, but the spirit that made it stand, a beacon to all the liberty loving peoples of the world, cannot fail.

With tears in his eyes, Romulo looked away. Though a quiet man who favored an economy of words, Leo Boelens was the only one in the group capable of a response.

"God help them."

PART II

HELL

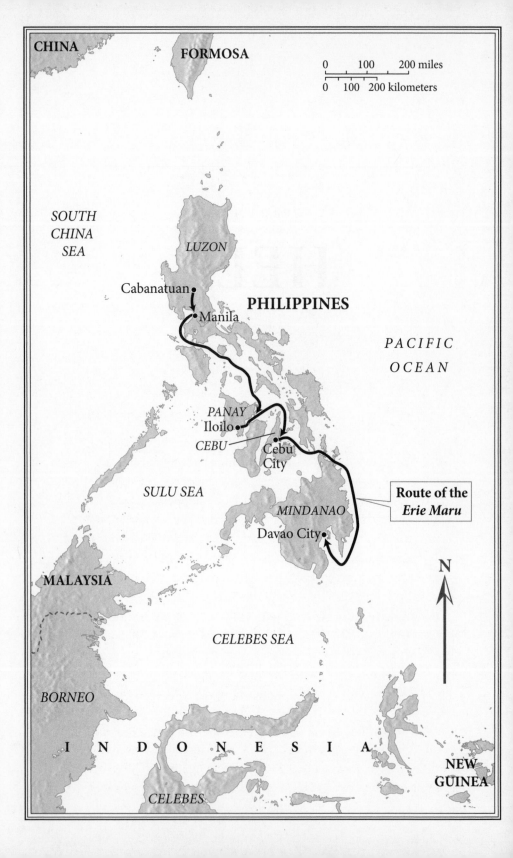

CHAPTER 5

The Hike

There was a blazing road that had no end
Eight thousand captives—not a single friend . . .

FRIDAY, APRIL 10, 1942
East Road, Bataan Province, Philippine Islands

The story seemed too far-fetched, too irrational—too disquieting—to be true. According to a witness recounting the story in savage detail for Ed Dyess, an American officer was being searched by a Japanese three-star private. "All at once he stopped and sucked in his breath with a hissing sound," Dyess was told. The soldier had found a crumpled wad of yen, a seemingly trifling offense. But Japanese logic dictated that a prisoner in possession of currency, Rising Sun flags, or any Japanese objects must have taken the items from the body of a dead Japanese. The price for such dishonorable behavior, Dyess learned, was steep.

The Japanese officer supervising the shakedown forced the American to his knees, unsheathed his sword and raised it above his head. "There was a swish and a kind of chopping thud, like a cleaver going through beef," said the witness. "The captain's head seemed to jump off his shoulders. It hit the ground in front of him and went rolling crazily from side to side between the lines of prisoners." The headless body, spurting blood, flopped forward and the dust at the prisoners' feet coagulated into scarlet mud. The dead man's hands opened and closed "spasmodically." The executioner then hovered over the body, wiping his sword clean, before strutting off. The private, after collecting the deceased's possessions, continued down the line. "Now, as never before," seethed Dyess, "I wanted to kill Japs for the pleasure of it."

Dyess had been simmering ever since his first, foreboding encounter with the Japanese near Little Baguio, but his blood had really begun to boil when he and the remnants of the 21st Pursuit were assembled near Mariveles the following morning. The sun had burned off the dawn mist, revealing a mob scene of vehicles, refugees, surrendered American and Filipino soldiers, and swaggering Japanese troops. "A Philippines Times Square," recalled one American. The POWs were corralled in sun-splashed staging areas and forced to stand at attention. Some Japanese soldiers, similarly exhausted and hungry, offered cigarettes or food from their *bento* boxes. But few were in a magnanimous mood. They had not conquered Bataan quickly or with impunity; by late April, roughly 40,000 patients suffering from everything from malaria to combat wounds would fill Japanese hospitals. And though they despised their adversaries taking so long to surrender, their full fury was reserved for a greater affront: the fact that the Americans and Filipinos had allowed themselves to be captured at all.

According to the code of Bushido—"The Way of the Warrior"—in which all Japanese personnel had been indoctrinated, the paradoxical, paramount goal of life was death in all its glorious fealty and finality. One who surrendered, therefore, defied his destiny of death, betrayed his emperor, his country, his family, and his comrades. In essence, he betrayed *yamato damashii*—the very soul of Japan.

In the oppressive heat, the Japanese had searched the POWs, ostensibly for weapons or items of military intelligence value, but really for loot. They worked efficiently and forcibly, taking jewelry, Parker ballpoint pens, Zippo lighters, and American cigarettes. The Japanese had a fancy for wristwatches—many strutted around, their forearms decorated with a half-dozen Timexes, Hamiltons, and Elgins. Malicious guards shredded photographs of prisoners' loved ones. One seized a pair of eyeglasses, smashed the lenses, and walked away, leaving the prisoner to grope around. Another furiously tugged at a West Point ring on an officer's swollen finger. Undaunted, he held the man's hand to the trunk of a tree and, with one, swift slice from a bolo—a Philippine machete—separated both the ring and the finger from the American. Determined not to let his Randolph Field ring become a Japanese souvenir, Dyess defiantly hurled it into Manila Bay. Sam Grashio, taking his cue, tore up a photograph of his wife before the Japanese could do so. "There still was plenty of fight left in us," said Dyess. "We were prisoners, but we didn't feel licked." Their fighting days were finished but, as time would tell, they could ill afford to surrender their fighting spirit.

Flanked by soldiers wearing tropic field caps with cloth sun flaps, prisoners began marching out of Mariveles, three or four abreast, in long mosaic columns of blue, khaki, and olive drab. They moved up the steep grade of the serpentine East Road, its white partial-asphalt surface cratered and shimmering with heat waves, their eyes widened to a bewildering panorama. Guided by rays of sparkling sunlight filtering down through the jungle canopy, they passed twisted old banyan trees grotesquely splintered by shrapnel. The mangled metal hulks of fire-gutted vehicles, some licked by dying flames, littered the battle-scarred landscape. Swarming with hordes of insects, decaying bodies clogged ditches and thickets of bamboo and ipil-ipil. The impenetrable walls of steamy emerald jungle receded, revealing a hissing, crackling funeral pyre of corpses, timber, and cogon grass. Clouds of acrid, brooding smoke, mixed with the pungent perfumes of cordite and rotting flesh, wafted across the peninsula.

But it was no sightseeing tour—the pace was maddening. Successive sets of impatient, time-conscious guards incessantly spurred the prisoners forward with unintelligible Japanese and commands of "Speedo! Speedo!" Growing progressively more frustrated, they breached the language barrier with pricks and puncture wounds from their bayonets. Prisoners were also punished for their lethargy with fists, clubs, and rifle butts, and had no choice but to absorb the blows and trudge on in silent misery. Talking consumed energy, of which they had little. It also produced a need for water, of which they had even less, despite the artesian wells scattered about the war-torn jungle wasteland.

Even rest breaks, which were few and far between, sapped vital energy. With a flash of their steel bayonets, the guards would occasionally prod the columns of gaunt, stubble-bearded prisoners off the East Road, usually to make room for the never-ending convoy of Imperial Army tanks, trucks, and troops slithering through the smoldering jungle. As if by design, the Japanese chose canebrakes, fields, or vacant lots that offered little or no protection from the searing rays of the soul-scorching sun. There the men would sit, sometimes for hours, and for seemingly no good reason, enduring what they would call the sun treatment—brutal sessions of prolonged exposure that left them mentally, physically, and spiritually drained.

The passing motorized processions stirred ashen clouds of powder, which settled upon the prisoners, lending a spectral appearance to the shuffling masses. Near Little Baguio, Dyess and Grashio watched in horror as the Japanese swept sick and wounded prisoners from Field Hospital No. 1 into the march. For nearly a mile, these men—some of whom were amputees—hobbled along, their bloody field dressings unraveling with each excruciating step. Grashio saw one legless Filipino dragging himself forward with his arms. "I can never forget the hopelessness in their eyes," Dyess would write.

While most of these hapless prisoners inevitably and perhaps mercifully fell victim to bullets and bayonets—groups of guards called "buzzard" or "clean-up" squads trailed the columns—some met more gruesome fates. One wobbly, disoriented patient, flung into an onrushing column by a cruel guard, was struck down in a grotesque crush of metal, rubber, bones, and flesh. In the subsequent procession of squealing steel treads and tires, his clothes—all that remained of the man's existence—were embedded into the oil-slicked thoroughfare. One prisoner, Sgt. Mario "Motts" Tonelli of the 200th Coast Artillery, a former standout football player at the University of Notre Dame and with pro football's Chicago Cardinals, recalled the sound of hundreds of hooves rumbling the ground like an earthquake. A raucous troop of cavalrymen soon galloped past, a Rising Sun flag flapping in their midst. Tonelli spied a barely discernible object bobbing above the ensign and the loud, jumbled mass of horses and humanity. Abruptly, it came into full, horrific view: a mutilated human head, skewered atop a pike and veiled with a swarm of fat black blowflies and maggots crawling from vacant eye sockets and nostrils. "We're in trouble," Tonelli would say.

While their minds struggled to process the macabre, waking nightmare, Japanese soldiers leaned from trucks to spit on them or clobber them with rifles and bamboo poles. Others mockingly threw up their arms in imitation of the surrender motion. For Dyess, the ultimate insult was seeing hundreds of Fords and Chevrolets idling on the congested road. "It is hard to describe what we felt at seeing these familiar American machines, filled with jeering, snarling Japs," he wrote. "It was a sort of super-sinking feeling. We had become accustomed to having American iron thrown at us by the Japs, but this was a little too much."

The demoralized, dehydrated prisoners, further weakened by hunger and disease—each prisoner was estimated to have carried between one and four diseases on the march—predictably began to stumble. Temperatures soared and discipline all but evaporated. Men slipped from the columns and lunged for the artesian wells, others for roadside carabao wallows, the scum-covered puddles of brackish, bacteria-laden water in which floated the carcasses of dead animals and bloated corpses. Few reached either. Fusillades of gunfire reverberated, and, with measured proficiency, guards slashed stomachs with a sequence of Z-shaped cuts. After jerking their dripping bayonets from the slashed bowels, the guards wiped the instruments clean of the fresh blood.

As morning melted into afternoon and the fabric of reality unraveled before his eyes, Dyess could not shake the story of the beheaded Air Corps captain—he had known the man personally. Dyess's own head whirled in delirium and throbbed with splitting headaches. With each step, the normally cool, collected Texan grew dangerously more flammable. He longed to strike out against his captors, but quickly pulled himself out of the emotional nosedive. "By going berserk now," he understood, "I would only lose my own life without hope of ever helping to even the score." Until the situation improved, Dyess could only ball his fists and continue along the East Road, all the while making a vow to live—and fight—another day.

In either direction, as far as Sam Grashio could see, the sad columns of shadows stretched along the East Road and vanished into the coppery twilight. Grashio prayed that one of those shadows was Dyess; they had been separated hours earlier when Dyess was beaten into a ditch by a hysterical Japanese soldier. Now he had only the charismatic officer's words to sustain him. "Dyess . . . told me we had to survive if only to someday gain revenge on our torturers. As always when I was around Ed, some of his spirit rubbed off onto me."

Though there was no logical explanation for the madness Grashio had witnessed, some predictable patterns and concrete constants were revealed. The earliest lesson involved the frequent inspections: the tremulous chorus of whispers that floated through the ranks—"Get rid of your Jap stuff, quick!"—would have to be acted upon immediately. And Grashio's separation from Dyess revealed the guards' penchant for committing acts of violence against tall prisoners. Insignias of rank also made inviting targets for torment: officers were forced to bow before Japanese privates. And Americans were often humiliated in front of Filipinos.

Grashio could see that in the eyes of the Japanese, stragglers were viewed not as sick, starving men who needed assistance, but as noncompliants and weaklings. Because of a scarcity of oil (most fuel was usurped by the Imperial Navy for its ships and planes), Japanese soldiers were conditioned to march long distances, and therefore few had sympathy for an enemy they regarded as lazy and decadent.

Since it certainly seemed as though the Japanese had no intention of providing food or water, the POWs would have to fend for themselves. Jack Donohoe of the 21st Pursuit, for instance, found a moldy, weevil-infested sack of horse feed that he and another POW devoured. They would attempt to eat at their own risk. Grashio remembered seeing a case of PET evaporated milk fall off a passing truck. "Prisoners swarmed over it like ants," he said. "The Japanese leaped in among them, swinging their fists, kicking and flailing with rifle butts until all the parched and famished wretches had been pounded back into line."

There were, however, no absolute certainties when it came to the mercurial Japanese. No two guards seemed or acted alike. An incident that might drive one into a rage could simply amuse another. To Grashio, there seemed to be only one plan of action: "Realists learned early . . . that it was essential to be obedient and submissive. . . . Any captive who was undisciplined, uncooperative or rebellious rarely survived to boast about it."

The POWs themselves were even less predictable. Out of the fiery Philippine blast furnace came the worst by-products of humanity. Before the Japanese segregated the prisoners, they marched together, Yank and Filipino, officer and enlisted man, dogface and bluejacket, pilot and Philippine Scout. When permitted, stronger prisoners bore wounded on their shoulders or on litters. Water and food were shared. But as the hours and days dragged on, an "every man for himself" attitude gradually prevailed. The command structure—the cornerstone of military discipline—crumbled. In some cases, it took days. Others, merely hours. Homogeneous groups fared best; individuals separated from their units and friends struggled to survive. As the mercury rose, the situation worsened. Some officers shirked their leadership responsibilities. Enlisted men, blaming officers for their current predicament, refused to obey orders. Canteens were stolen. Food was hoarded. Tempers flared. Pickpockets prospered.

At least they could count on the Filipino civilians, most of whom were Catholic and for whom the march seemed a horrifically real *senakulo*, a passion play depicting the Stations of the Cross, the sufferings endured by Christ before Crucifixion. Civilians hid cans of water in clumps of cogon and flung rice balls, cookies, and cigarettes into the columns. Children bounded alongside, pressing fruit, sugarcane, and cassava cakes, as well as bottles of water, into prisoners' hands. Women shuttled fish, chicken, and rice wrapped in banana leaves and merchants opened their *carinderias*, refusing payment. Others discreetly called to the prisoners—"Hey, Joe"—and flashed their index and middle fingers in the universal "V for Victory" sign.

Often, the aid came with consequences. At Limay, a farmer and his wife were burned at the stake for aiding the POWs. Elsewhere, a pregnant Filipina who had thrown food to the Americans was bayoneted through her womb. Though Homma had advocated a policy of rapprochement with the estimated seventeen million Filipinos, there were some members of the Japanese military who felt that the Filipinos should be punished for their desertion of the Asian cause and their loyalty to the United States. As those sentiments became reality, the Filipinos saw that for them, Japan's Greater East Asia Co-Prosperity Sphere meant anything but prosperity. They had heard stories of Japanese brutality in Manila and now saw their fathers, sons, and brothers bayoneted and left to slow deaths writhing in the Bataan dust. Until the day MacArthur made good on his promise—and they believed firmly that he would—they were determined to share with their allies the burdens of occupation and captivity in the best spirit of *balikatan*, a Tagalog word meaning "shoulder to shoulder."

But for men hoping and praying just to survive another minute, or another hour, to make it to the next rest stop, the next town, even the next palm tree, that day seemed hopelessly distant. At midnight, after an exhausting, circuitous march, Grashio's group was herded back into a rice paddy not far from Cabcaben Field. He collapsed onto the ground and fell asleep. If he was lucky, another day—and more survival lessons— would greet him in the morning.

• • •

Contrary to popular belief, the evacuation of Filipino and American prisoners of war from the Bataan Peninsula was not an atrocity of deliberate design. Based on poor intelligence, plagued with breakdowns in leadership and discipline, and launched in a chaotic environment made combustible by a broiling tropic sun, cultural clashes, and ethnic enmity, the operation was, quite simply, a catastrophic *masakozi*—the Japanese equivalent of an American snafu.

As a military plan, the Bataan Death March was conceived in 14th Army operations tents in March at the order of Gen. Masaharu Homma. On paper, the plan to evacuate the prisoners from Bataan to a prison camp in central Luzon appeared humane and logistically sound. The majority of the prisoners would march up the East Road, but vehicles would convey sick and wounded incapable of making the roughly sixty-five-mile journey on foot. Food was to be distributed and medical aid stations would be set up along the route. At the town of San Fernando, the prisoners would board railcars for a twenty-four mile train ride to Capas, in Tarlac. Homma even requested that his men treat the POWs with a "friendly spirit," in loose accordance with the Geneva Convention articles that Japan never officially agreed to observe. (Japanese delegates to the Geneva conference had signed the document standardizing the treatment of prisoners of war in 1929, but Tokyo never ratified the pact.) The directive was no surprise, considering that at the outbreak of hostilities, the emperor himself had decreed that enemy POWs were to be handled "with utmost kindness and benevolence."

Homma's intentions were most likely sincere. The tall, powerfully built fifty-four-year-old officer was considered one of the most principled strategists in the Imperial Army. His foreign postings included duty as an observer with the British Expeditionary Force during World War I and later as a military attaché in London. The pro-Western officer had suppressed a pamphlet accusing America of exploiting the Philippines while head of the army's propaganda corps in the 1930s. Even as the ultranationalists swept to power, Homma never embraced their beliefs, reportedly even criticizing Japanese atrocities in China. Called the "Poet General" because of his habit of composing verse to ease the tension of battle, Homma was a "brilliant, passionate, unpredictable, and slightly unstable" fantasist given to flights of whimsy, who, according to British historian Arthur Swinson, was straitjacketed by "the iron discipline of the Japanese army." Homma's weaknesses included egotism and acute affections for drink and women, but his tendency to become immersed in strategy and delegate details to subordinates was perhaps his greatest flaw.

That flaw, combined with one fatal miscalculation, a change in Homma's chronology of conquest and subsequent breakdowns in communications and discipline, would doom the evacuation operation to complete, calamitous failure. Homma's command had underestimated the number of prisoners it would become responsible for by nearly half. Though Tokyo's Domei news agency announced the capture of 60,000 Fil-American troops, the actual number was closer to 70,000; Homma's staff had expected and made provisions for only 40,000 prisoners. Compounding the problem, the 14th Army had these additional prisoners on its hands three weeks earlier than anticipated—Homma had not expected Bataan to fall until late April. Instead of modifying the plan, Homma characteristically became engrossed with the details of the planned invasion of Corregidor and the conclusion of the Philippines campaign.

And despite the vaunted Japanese notions of Bushido discipline and obedience, most commanders were unable to restrain their men. Consequently, the official orders and instructions, as prescribed by Emperor Hirohito and General Homma, never filtered down to the junior officers and foot soldiers who actually carried out the evacuation. These men instead resorted to their own brand of discipline to complete the task, a system of corporal punishment unique to the Japanese military hierarchy in which officers and soldiers could strike subordinates. So it was only natural that when the long-abused Japanese foot soldier finally had a chance to inflict blows on disgraceful POWs, the succession of institutionalized violence would continue.

Certainly, beheading and running over men with tanks had nothing to do with disciplinary failures or administrative incompetence. Instead, virulent ultranationalism and racial hatred helped spiral the situation out of control. No doubt a direct malignant influence was the fanatical Col. Masanobu Tsuji, an iniquitous figure who reportedly dined on the liver of a dead Allied pilot in Burma and was responsible for myriad massacres and war crimes in Singapore and China. Lurking in the shadowy chaos following the surrender, Tsuji commenced a personal terror campaign, issuing false orders for mass executions and reportedly conducting demonstrations on the disposal of enemy POWs for Japanese troops.

A final rationalization for the Death March holds that many Japanese, intoxicated with the speed and scope of their early conquests, believed that it was impossible to lose the war. The "victory disease" was pandemic. And whether by impulse or design, retribution was becoming the victors' policy. On April 24, a rancorous editorial appeared in the *Japan Times & Advertiser*: "They cannot be treated as ordinary prisoners of war. . . . To show them mercy is to prolong the war. . . . An eye for an eye, a tooth for a tooth. The Japanese Forces are crusaders in a holy war. Hesitation is uncalled for, and the wrongdoers must be wiped out."

SUNDAY, APRIL 12, 1942
East Road, Bataan Province, Philippine Islands

For hours, Ed Dyess had stumbled along in the turbid darkness, mechanically placing one foot in front of the other, step after step, mile after torturous mile, somehow keeping the grueling pace while many, unable to will another step, dropped around him. Their groans and screams were layered with the ripping sounds of bayonets piercing flesh, a contrast to the peaceful rustling of palm fronds in the night air. Muzzle blasts of orange flame ended the misery of countless others.

Those that continued on did so in a half-conscious daze. They had seen comrades tied to trees and used as targets for bayonet practice. One American had started counting the decapitated corpses he had seen littering the road, but stopped at twenty-seven for fear of going out of his mind. "The bloodthirsty devils now were killing us for diversion," said Dyess.

The POWs were expected to maintain the relentless pace, regardless of whether the guards were on foot or bicycles, resulting in excruciating cramps. Many prisoners were forced to defecate in motion, further soiling their grimy bodies. Said Sam Grashio, who was marching in another column further north, "the imaginations of our captors were inexhaustible when it came to devising ways to increase our suffering."

For Dyess, the worst part of the ordeal began at sundown of the previous evening, when the prisoners were herded into the courtyard of a Spanish mission near Balanga. They had watched Japanese cooks dump soy sauce and cans of Vienna sausage into bubbling cauldrons of rice, but after the prisoners were searched they were marched away from the tantalizing food. "When you came here you were told you would eat and be let to sleep. Now that has changed," bellowed a Japanese officer in English. "We have found pistols concealed among three American officers.

In punishment for these offenses you will not be given food. You will march to Orani before you sleep." Dyess saw through the thinly veiled ruse: "The Japs were simply adding mental torture to the physical."

After twenty-one hours and nearly thirty miles on their feet, they were prodded into a barbed wire compound at three o'clock in the morning. The enclosure, built to hold perhaps 500 men, immediately became a polluted prison yard filled with more than 2,000 POWs. They collapsed in an orgy of aching muscles; blistered feet; empty, growling stomachs.

At dawn on April 13, the first rays of the sun began to incubate the distended cesspool, intensifying the stench. Feces, urine, and legions of gray, squirming maggots from the overflowing straddle trench that served as the prisoners' latrine spilled across the ground. The shouts of starved, hallucinating prisoners filled the compound. Feverish POWs screaming obscenities at the Japanese had to be subdued. Many dehydrated men, their eyes sunk deep into their sockets and their lips blue, lapsed into comas. The Japanese ordered the prisoners to carry the dead outside the wire and bury them in shallow graves. "The strain was telling even on the strongest men, or rather we ceased to be men—more like filthy, starving rabble," said Dyess.

Finally, after being fed a small ball of sticky gray rice, the prisoners resumed the march at dusk the next day. It was about midnight when the rain first started falling—solitary droplets pattering into the dust. It soon fell in wet, chilling, God-sent sheets, cleansing the crust of blood, human waste, and grit from the prisoners' bodies. With trembling hands, men clanged canteen cups, mess kits, and cupped hands into the air. Though the downpour lasted only fifteen minutes, it provided many weary prisoners with the strength to continue. "I felt like a fighter," Dyess would write, "who has been saved by the bell."

WEDNESDAY, APRIL 15, 1942
San Fernando, Bataan Province

The march would proceed north from Orion to Abucay and then on to Highway 7, which funneled the filthy, starving prisoners into the sugar mill town of San Fernando. There, the train depot buzzed with insects and rumors, the latter, of course, regarding the POW's ultimate destination. Sam Grashio did not have enough energy to mull over the future. Only a few hours removed from a terrifying nightmare spent with

1,500 other prisoners in a squalid, sheet iron warehouse near Lubao, he was chiefly concerned with getting his bearings. "I was so close to total physical and mental collapse during the latter part of the march that half the time I did not know where I was," he admitted. As he understood it, the prisoners were supposedly headed via train to a prison camp somewhere in central Luzon. Regardless of the destination, most were relieved to know that they would not have to walk. They believed that the worst was behind them.

Then several ramshackle, steel-sided boxcars began reeling down the narrow-gauge tracks. Most were World War I–era "Forty and Eights," so nicknamed because they were designed to ferry forty soldiers or eight horses. But the Japanese jolted open the cars' rusty doors and prodded the prisoners inside with bayonets and rifle butts, sadistically forcing in dozens of men until movement was virtually impossible. The doors then slammed shut in a series of concurrent, metallic shrieks. Latches clanged. Padlocks clicked.

Temperatures in the poorly ventilated cars reached in excess of 100 degrees Fahrenheit, and a dreadful odor quickly filled the rolling kilns. The POWs had not bathed in weeks and their bodies stank. Floorboards were soon smeared with urine, feces, and vomit. "The stink was so overpowering, I feared I would suffocate," said Grashio. Soon after the cars lurched forward, some men fainted. In some cars, men died upright, unable to slump to the floor.

The door to Grashio's boxcar had not been completely closed and, unlike in other crammed cars where the strongest prisoners or those nearest the door refused to budge, men rotated positions for fresh air. As the cars clicked and crawled through the sugarcane fields, dried-up dikes, and sunken rice paddies of Pampanga Province into the great, flat emptiness of central Luzon, Grashio contemplated both his future and his destination. A desperate man in a nearby car, however, had already given thought to his next stop: Grashio watched him commit suicide by jumping from the train as it crossed a trestle.

The train panted to a stop as the doors of the sweltering, swollen railcars screeched open. Prisoners gasping for air tumbled out of their shadowy stupor into the blinding sun.

Having not eaten in two days, Ed Dyess emerged disoriented and weak. The days had melted together, grisly atrocities fused by the stultifying heat. His only recollections of the past seventy-two hours were a handful of haunting images: a Filipino hanging on a fence, his entrails hanging from his slashed abdomen like "great, grayish purple ropes" . . . three Americans savagely lashed with a horsewhip . . . six thirst-mad prisoners dashing for an artesian well as guards raised their rifles and in a hailstorm of bullets two men, fatally wounded, crawled determinedly toward the water until additional volleys stopped them.

Unbeknownst to Dyess, he had endured the most infamous war crime in the annals of American military history, a survivor not a statistic. Others were not so lucky; nearly 700 Americans and perhaps as many as 10,000 Filipinos were believed to have died throughout the three-week-long nightmare that they would call, simply, "the Hike."

Upon regaining consciousness, he learned that the three-hour trip had brought him to Capas, in Tarlac Province, the location of a prison camp named O'Donnell. After a requisite session of the sun treatment, the prisoners were rousted to their feet for the final leg of their journey. Soon after reaching the crest of a small knoll, Dyess squinted through the dazzling glare to spy clusters of squatty shacks and tumbledown buildings teeming with what looked like thousands of people. The enclosure was ringed with silvery strands of barbed wire and cornered by guard towers that loomed out of the thick rug of cogon grass. Atop each of the crude timber parapets was a large Rising Sun flag. The real sun plunged behind the craggy peaks of the Zambales Mountains, bathing the bleak, rambling plain in a foreboding shadow. Dyess shuddered.

"As we stood, staring dazedly, there came to me a premonition that hundreds about to enter O'Donnell prison this April day never would leave it alive," he said. "If I could have known what lay in store for us all, I think I would have given up the ghost then and there."

CHAPTER 6

Goodbye and Good Luck

Then came the bitter days when those alive
Fought in a vicious struggle to survive
When we begrudged the little strength we gave
To dig our withered dead a shallow grave.

WEDNESDAY, APRIL 15, 1942
Corregidor, Manila Bay

Our flag still flies on this beleaguered island fortress," General Wainwright had reassured President Roosevelt from Corregidor after Bataan's surrender. But not for much longer, thought 1st Lt. Jack Hawkins. Through his field glasses, Hawkins had seen the enemy columns snaking into southern Bataan and knew that the Japanese would now focus their attention—as well as their full arsenal—on the Rock. And, as Hawkins had also seen, the notion of defeat was a distasteful one. Hundreds of Bataan refugees had washed up on Corregidor, including three haggard, half-drowned soldiers he provided with coffee, food, and medical attention. "They were soon revived enough to talk, but still they were hesitant," he recalled. "A dreadful haunted look was in their darkly circled eyes." Eventually, one managed a whisper: "It's awful to be licked."

Yet Hawkins was confident that Corregidor would not go without one helluva fight. The resilient garrison had adopted a molelike routine of repairing and rebuilding at night. Ammunition was plentiful and there was enough food, theoretically, to last through June. Though they had no radar, they had Private Soochow, the Marines' Shanghai mascot mutt. Whenever he tore across the beach for cover, the Marines wisely followed the canine's lead because Japanese bombers were certain to appear. Many "shelter-shocked" soldiers, however, avoided the relentless bombardments by refusing to leave the island's tunnels and bunkers. Recognizable by their pallor, they were disparagingly diagnosed with "tunnelitis."

Hawkins, who rarely left his dugout command post overlooking the foxholes in which his men were burrowed with their water-cooled Brownings, could handle the bombs and the shelling. He hated the waiting, which was reminiscent of the tension in the tinderbox of Shanghai, where the 4th Marines believed that any small spark would ignite a war. Continuing to surveil the swells of Manila Bay, Hawkins knew that the marines and the Japanese would soon finally tangle. His thoughts, as they often did, drifted to home and to his fiancée. And what of his best friend, Mike Dobervich? *Is he still alive,* Hawkins wondered, *or would he be better off dead at any rate, than alive in the hands of the Japs?*

THURSDAY, APRIL 16–THURSDAY, APRIL 23, 1942
Capas, Tarlac Province, Luzon

Not a single prisoner suffering inside Camp O'Donnell would dare consider himself lucky, but Mike Dobervich might have been the luckiest man in the whole squalid stockade. The charmed Marine had not only recovered from cerebral meningitis in time to leave Shanghai, he had also survived three months on Bataan. Providence had shined on Dobervich once more, when a Japanese officer ordered him behind the wheel of a GMC truck loaded with sugar, thus saving him from experiencing the Death March on foot.

Rumbling in a slow convoy of captured vehicles, he had watched helplessly—the guard riding next to him pointed a bayonet at his side— as the parade of beatings, torture, and death unfolded. He saw an American colonel shot down while dashing for a spring and bristled with rage seeing staff officers run through a looting gauntlet at Balanga. He, too, would lose his wristwatch, two fountain pens, 500 Philippine pesos and 40 U.S. dollars on the trek, but his uncanny good fortune had enabled him to keep his life. Yet such sights and experiences would not stay in Dobervich's rearview mirror. Nor would his incredible luck last.

Braking at the gates of O'Donnell on April 11, he must have felt like Dante entering the fiery depths of Inferno. The heat and the camp's desolate location made the comparison appropriate. "The infuriating, obtuse guards looked to us as though each had horns and a tail and was carrying a pitchfork instead of a rifle . . . it quickly became apparent to all of us that we were doomed to eternal hellfire," said one Filipino. The reception awaiting the prisoners augured as much.

Dobervich was one of the first to experience the infamous "welcome" speech of Capt. Yoshio Tsuneyoshi, the camp's commandant. "We were herded in front of the Japanese headquarters building and from general down to private, we all stood at attention and had to salute the camp commander who had us stand at attention for 16 hours in the terrific heat," wrote Dobervich, recalling his first dose of the sun treatment.

After a long wait, Tsuneyoshi, a stumpy middle-aged man wearing horn-rimmed glasses, a Hitler mustache, and a baggy uniform with a sword dangling from his belt, strutted onto a canopied platform, where he commenced a rambling tirade. Behind Tsuneyoshi was a youthful, fat Filipino-Japanese who translated the rants.

Many prisoners, too tired, too thirsty, and too miserable to listen, sat stupefied in the sun, their heads bowed, their backs turned to the unintelligible shouts. One intuitive American officer sensed that the orator "breathed the very essence of hate." Ed Dyess, who endured a similar harangue upon his arrival, speculated on Tsuneyoshi's mental competence, remarking that the disheveled would-be dictator "roared at us with a pomposity reminiscent of Mussolini's. But the loose-lipped vacuity of his expression was that of an idiot."

"The captain, he say Nippon has capture Javver, Sumatter and New Guinyah," droned the interpreter. "Captain, he say we soon have Austrayler and New Zealyer."

There were several variations of the sulfurous speech, but a gloating summary of Japanese victories was standard. Tsuneyoshi declared that he cared little whether the prisoners, whom he referred to as "dogs," lived or died. He recited a long list of regulations—from the necessity of saluting all Japanese to the prohibition of escape attempts—all of which seemed to be punishable by death. His tone, his theatrical delivery, and his message ultimately remained the same.

The interpreter continued: "The captain, he say America and Nippon enemies. Always will be enemies. If Nippon do not defeat America this time, Nippon fight again and again until America is defeated. Always will be war until America is Nippon's."

Reaching a crescendo of hysterics, Tsuneyoshi spewed forth such a volume of verbal venom that even the most exhausted prisoner was forced to lift his head and take notice.

"Captain, he say you are not prisoners of war. You are sworn enemies of Japan. Therefore, you will not be treated like prisoners of honorable war. Captain, he say you will be treated like captives." The interpreter, himself worked into a frenzy, spit a final promise: "Captain, he say you will have trouble from him."

Satisfied with his performance, Tsuneyoshi clicked his spurred boot heels and stomped off the stage. Many things could and would be said about the diminutive Japanese despot, but it could not be said that he was not a man of his word.

Although most prisoners would spend less than two months in O'Donnell, the experience would provide a lifetime of horrors. "Words cannot describe the conditions," Dobervich would later say. "Only the eye could appreciate the seriousness of it all."

The Japanese would attempt to cram 50,000 prisoners into the half-finished Philippine Army recruit depot originally intended to house 9,000 men, to catastrophic results. Roughly 600 acres, or just under one mile square in total area, with no electricity or sanitation, the enclosure was nothing more than an ever-expanding coop of men. Subject to the temperamental whims of an asthmatic gasoline pump that broke down every few hours and sadistic guards that shut off the water main at irregular intervals, the parched prisoners waited around the clock in meandering lines at two small spigots to fill their canteens with tepid water. Bathing was possible only when it rained. The prisoners were fed tiny portions of lugao, a pasty rice gruel full of floor sweepings and weevils that tasted like glue, plus occasional helpings of rotten camotes, mango beans, and other cast-off vegetables. Ravenous men were soon reduced to stealing food, scheming other prisoners for their rations, and scrambling to catch grasshoppers, rats, and stray dogs. Many traded or deferred their rice rations for cigarettes, transactions that the Grim Reaper would ultimately collect on.

The starvation diet, begun on Bataan and continued into captivity, ushered in a slew of vitamin deficiency diseases. The worst was wet beri-beri, a ruthless illness that shut down a man's kidneys, causing body tissues to become repulsively engorged with fluids until the ballooned skin cracked into fissures oozing with yellow pus and the overtaxed heart failed. Slit trenches overflowing with excrement spawned swarms of green and bluebottle flies, humming airborne agents of contagion that flew from fecal matter to festering sores to rice, spreading a vicious cycle of diarrhea, amoebic dysentery, and death throughout the compound. The entire camp, lacking mosquito nets and blankets, convulsed with the spiking, sweat-drenched fevers and teeth-chattering chills of malaria. A hospital was set up, but without medicine, doctors were powerless to stop the plagues visited upon the POWs. Hopeless cases were sent to a ghastly vestibule to the hereafter known to the prisoners as "St. Peter's Ward."

Not content to let starvation and disease thin the prisoners' ranks, the Japanese were responsible for additional deaths through abuse, torture, and outright execution. Those barely able to walk were forced into gangs for labor outside the camp. "Many came back and had to be carried to the hospital only to die in a few days," said Dobervich. The Japanese dispensed brutal beatings for minor infractions and shot or beheaded those deemed guilty of more serious transgressions. They specialized in cruel and unusual punishments. Some prisoners were leashed to stakes like animals and left to die in the blistering heat. Another pitiless pastime was to place a hose into a victim's throat or rectum and pump water until the entrails ruptured. One POW who escaped the barbed wire perimeter was immediately apprehended, flogged, and strung up in front of the Japanese headquarters. Amazingly, the delirious man escaped once more, only to be recaptured and whipped into a bloody, unrecognizable heap of shredded skin. "We never saw him again," said Ed Dyess, "but we know he didn't escape." The message was delivered with terrifying, unmistakable clarity: there was only one way to truly escape O'Donnell.

It was not long before the corpses began to appear everywhere. Stripped of their tattered uniforms—to be recycled for use by needy prisoners—the naked, emaciated bodies were informally stacked like cordwood. Sometimes, they blackened and bloated in the sun for days until men strong enough to dig graves could be found.

The burial details were hard, morbid, mind-numbing work. On average, it took four men to carry one corpse; more were required to haul the distended bodies of those who died of wet beriberi, which often weighed in excess of 300 pounds and were liable to burst if mishandled. Guided by guards, they trudged outside the wire and ascended a rise to a crude cemetery—"Boot Hill," some called it—carrying the corpses by their bony arms and legs or else in litters, to the yawning mouths of mass graves. "Then you would take the dog tag, if they had one, and put it in their mouth for burial and cover them up," said Motts Tonelli. There was no ceremony, no prayers, just corpse after corpse, sometimes twenty or thirty, little more than bones and skulls, the remnants of men who had fought for a common cause thrown together in a common pit.

As the deaths continued, the work became increasingly more macabre. Tales of men being buried alive were commonplace, including one told to Dobervich by a fellow Marine. "Before the covering process started one of the dead bodies began to move and there was a feeble effort to raise its head. The Jap guard ordered this Marine of mine to strike the head with a shovel," wrote Dobervich. "He hesitated and that angered the guard so that the bayonet was thrust at him, so he was forced to obey."

Because of the high water table, which filled the pits with seepage, floating corpses often had to be pinned with bamboo poles while weak men tossed weighty shovelfuls of dirt. Dogs and buzzards gnawed on the arms and legs, stiffened with rigor mortis and silhouetted in the milky moonlight, that poked through the thin blanket of dirt. Worse yet, the arrival of the rainy season in May caused corpses to rise from their shallow graves and float back to the camp in canals of blood-tinged water.

The whole affair looked to be part of some sinister plan; the prisoners had watched, dejectedly, as Red Cross trucks carrying food and medical supplies were turned away at the gates. The death rate would peak at fifty corpses every twenty-four hours; nearly 2,000 of the 9,000 Americans that had crossed O'Donnell's infernal threshold in April would be dead by June. Segregated in another compound, the Filipinos fared worse. Endless, dawn-to-dusk funeral processions would ultimately bury 20,000 men, or half of the Filipino contingent. "Many Nippon die Bataan," the guards told prisoners, "we let just as many prisoner die here."

Starving, surrounded and stalked by death, the prisoners congregated in forlorn clusters, suffering through their surreal existence in a somnolent, hunger-induced daze. Men became so lethargic and pulse rates dropped so precipitously that it was hard to tell who was dead and who was merely asleep. Inanition, the word scrawled on so many makeshift death certificates, was the biggest killer. Many despondent prisoners, unable to stomach the nauseating rice ration or endure the omnipresent stench of pestilence and human waste any longer, simply gave up the will to live. "A person had to keep his hope and courage up," said Dobervich, "for to lose hope was a way of signing your own death warrant." Dobervich spoke from experience; if not for his attitude and some quinine given to him by some Czechoslovakian civilian prisoners, the former boxer would not have survived a brutal bout with malaria.

The Japanese had mostly forbidden religious services. Many men recalled long-dormant faiths and personal prayer. Older men with families endured in the hope of seeing loved ones again. Others, like Tonelli, engaged in symbols and ritual. Once finished with his grisly burial labors, Tonelli would dig up his Notre Dame class ring, which he buried in a metal soap dish beneath his barracks to confound would-be thieves. After having been stolen by a guard during the march, it had been miraculously returned by an English-speaking Japanese officer who had been educated at the University of Southern California and had seen Tonelli score the winning touchdown in the 1937 game between the two schools. The ring momentarily transported Tonelli far from O'Donnell, to a stadium full of cheering people, reminding him of better days. Complementing his strong Catholic faith, the ring became an existential talisman. Perhaps never would the school's Latin motto—*Vita Dulcedo Spes*, "Our Life, Our Sweetness, Our Hope"—which was inscribed on the ring, mean so much to one alumnus.

Each night, as the searchlights swept the dark compound and the mournful, tinny clinking of the canteens of men waiting in the water lines sounded through the rows of shabby barracks, many struggled to find something similarly worthwhile to hold on to. And for an explanation. "We used to lay in the bunks and guys would say, 'God, why are You doing this? I never did anything wrong.' These young guys would be praying to God *out loud*," said Tonelli.

Many prisoners, likewise whirling in emotional and spiritual vertigo, had other troubling questions. "Where was America?" asked Capt. Bert Bank. "America's abandoning us. We live in the greatest country in the world and here we are, prisoners of the Japanese." The myth of American invincibility had been shattered. Bataan "was one time," commented one American officer, "that the cavalry didn't come over the hill to the rescue."

As the reality of the surrender sank in, the prisoners' morale plummeted. Fear and doubt permeated the camp. Tsuneyoshi had boasted to Sam Grashio's group that Japanese forces had bombed California and even Chicago. Though skeptical, their spirits were so low that they half-believed the bombast. "We had heard no war news for so many days so we feared that the whole tale might be true," said Grashio.

It had once been inconceivable to think that in this epic conflict of contrasting cultures Japan could ever, even temporarily, hold the upper hand. But now it did. The taunts of English-speaking guards communicated that notion. "The Japs kept asking us where the wonderful American Army and Navy were and where was the Air Corps about which we boasted so much," wrote Bank. Numbed by the trauma of their defeat, the prisoners had no reply.

Bert Bank's enlistment in the Army ROTC battalion at the University of Alabama in the mid-1930s, he would claim, was attributable to friends who thought he looked good in uniform. But it was no secret that Bank, intensely patriotic, possessed a deep love of country. He also needed a way to pay for college. The son of Russian Jewish immigrants, Bank grew up in the coalfields of Tuscaloosa County near the mining town of Searles. Jovial and dynamic, he possessed the makings of a successful lawyer—a friendly face with a permanent smile, a politician's handshake, and the chatty charisma of a Southern raconteur from the pages of Twain or Faulkner. But after enrolling in law school, Bank was called up to the AAF's 27th Light Bombardment Group and assigned to Savannah, Georgia, where he drilled by day and romanced his share of Georgia belles—including Miss Georgia, 1939—by night.

Just as he would never work a courtroom, Bank would never sit in a cockpit. The ship carrying the unit's A-24 dive-bombers was rerouted to Australia, and Bank, forced to join the ranks of planeless pilots, received a rifle and infantry training. The twenty-seven-year-old's most valuable contribution to the war effort was his contagious sense of humor. While bathing in a jungle stream, he amused his comrades by posing for a photograph wearing nothing but a palm frond. Nothing bothered the affable Alabaman. Not the lack of food—Bank's nickname was "Garbage Mouth" because he ate everything—nor the wound he received from a strafing Japanese plane. Every war cloud over Bataan had a silver lining. "If this damn war keeps going on," he told his comrades after a promotion, "I am going to be a general pretty soon."

All Bank had now was his sense of humor and his fellow prisoners. Thankfully, making friends had always been easy. He had had no shortage of friends in college, including one notable classmate, a gangly football player named Paul Bryant who would become the celebrated coach of the Crimson Tide. Bank had befriended Ed Dyess on the third day of the march, when both had attempted to drink from an artesian well and were almost killed for their temerity. Dyess and Bank navigated the remainder of the march together, during which time Bank procured a piece of sugarcane that Dyess later credited as having energized him to finish the ordeal. They would continue their friendship in captivity.

The Death March had proven the necessity of solidarity, a message Dyess intended to convey to the men of the 21st Pursuit—if he could find them in the chaos of O'Donnell. Other than segregating the Americans and Filipinos, the Japanese had made no attempt to identify or group the prisoners according to their units or ranks, toppling the hierarchy so essential to order and discipline and thus eroding conditions even further. Although he was near a state of collapse, Dyess's sense of military propriety stirred him to shepherd his squadron. He and Grashio had been fortuitously reunited not long after their respective arrivals and the two officers, with Bank's help, attacked the task together. Sadly, their efforts would be too late for many.

One man had been discovered, his naked skin yellow with jaundice and covered with sores and fecal matter, dying beneath a barracks. Dyess had the man cleaned up and installed inside. Procuring a tin of sardines, he plotted with Grashio to feed the man. "That our squadron leader would give away such a rare and precious commodity when he needed food badly himself, and would trust me, also half-starved, to deliver the can intact, show what kind of man Ed Dyess was," said Grashio. The man later died, but "the whole episode," Grashio noted, "bolstered my own faith in humanity at a crucial time in my life."

Though more dark days undoubtedly lay ahead, Grashio and a handful of others had begun to harness the powers of faith, solidarity, and hope, guiding forces that would mean the difference between life and death in Camp O'Donnell—and conceivably beyond. "It may seem ridiculous, but in the face of all our adversities, we continued hopeful and optimistic during the first month of our captivity," said Dyess. "Indeed, there were many of us who never despaired of regaining our freedom."

Their compatriots on Corregidor, however, had yet to experience the crucible of captivity. If the distant rumble of artillery and the formations of bombers above O'Donnell each day were any indication, their time was near.

SUNDAY, MAY 3, 1942
Corregidor

The concussions rocked the reinforced concrete recesses of Malinta Tunnel in mad, seismic tremors. Flickering lights splashed shadows across the shuddering walls as pieces of concrete fell to the floor. Choking dust wafted through the crowded laterals fetid with the odor of gangrenous flesh and gasoline fumes. Men and women rushed about the steamy subterranean maze, shouting above the din of diesel generators and the beeping and gear grinding of the jeeps and ambulances crawling through the crowded corridor. Such distractions, compounded by a pounding heart and trembling hands, made even simple tasks—like writing a letter—difficult. Strangely, Maj. Steve Mellnik, struggling with a letter to his wife, Thelma, was not preoccupied with his present surroundings. It was his future that concerned him.

Mellnik, a onetime USAFFE staffer, was used to being in the know. Though currently a member of the Harbor Defenses staff, he continued his conversations and chess matches with high-ranking friends who had convinced him of the hopelessness of the situation. His own inspections of the island, as well as other ominous events—he had recently helped dispose of several million dollars of U.S. paper currency in an incinerator—served as additional proof. Corregidor's "clock," Mellnik realized, "was approaching midnight."

As Corregidor's fate went, so went that of Mellnik. Realizing that this letter was perhaps his last message to his wife and two young daughters, the thirty-four-year-old labored to camouflage his dread thoughts. But he did not have much time: a submarine was scheduled to dock at Corregidor shortly to evacuate VIPs and nurses, as well as important documents and a few sacks of mail. All he could do was steady his heart and his hand.

3 May, 1942

Hello, darling—

Won't have a chance to get another one of these very soon dear—so, I just want to remind you that I love you just heaps & heaps, and that the past year has seemed like ten years. . . . The radio has kept you in touch with what is going on here, so there is little I need say.

Corregidor's defenders had been living on a six-square-mile bull's-eye since Bataan's fall. The daily attacks resembled a weather pattern: clouds of Japanese bombers hovered out of the reach of the Rock's antiaircraft guns to loose torrents of bombs; thunderous hailstorms of mammoth artillery shells whooshed across the sky like roaring freight trains before gouging the island and tossing hunks of concrete and the barrels of Corregidor's giant cannons about like toys. An estimated 1.8 million pounds of shells, not to mention countless bombs dropped during thirteen separate air raids, had fallen the day before. In the next twenty-four hours, 16,000 shells would flay the Rock in what would ultimately be the heaviest bombardment of the campaign and, in some experts' estimation, the most vicious concentrated artillery barrage of the entire war. The bombardments had decapitated hills and denuded Corregidor of its lush vegetation, turning the green island into a smoky landscape of craters and charred trees, and its once proud structures into knots of rebar and piles of pulverized cement.

Yet Mellnik was still there. He had been aboard the *Don Esteban* with MacArthur and his family as the steamer churned away from war-ravaged Manila en route to Corregidor on Christmas Eve 1941. And nearly two months ago, on a gloomy night in March, he was one of several men to shake MacArthur's hand before the general departed for Australia.

There would be no dramatic flight from Corregidor for Mellnik. If anything, the percussion of armor-piercing shells echoing outside Malinta Tunnel likely persuaded him that his own life's journey was nearing its end. He could not possibly have known that his personal Philippine epic had barely begun.

The ship carrying Tekla Mellnick and her two young sons docked in New York harbor in 1911, four long years after her husband, Maxim, a tenant farmer, had left the Ukrainian village of Nevir to cultivate a better life for his family in America. The family reunited in Dunmore, Pennsylvania, a town of smokestacks, company houses, and church steeples built above thick seams of hard anthracite coal in the foothills of the Poconos. Their American dream was painfully short-lived. The influenza epidemic of 1918 took Tekla Melnick's life, spurring both sons to strike out on their own after receiving U.S. citizenship. Changing the spelling of his last name, eighteen-year-old Stephen Mellnik joined the Army in 1925.

An ambitious private in the 12th Coast Artillery Regiment, Mellnik watched his sergeant on the gunnery range and set his sights on stripes of his own. Upon gaining the promotion, he then coveted a commission, a distant dream for a noncom with a faint Ukrainian accent who had not even finished high school. The five foot seven Mellnik did not possess an intimidating command presence either, save for a scar on his left cheek from a childhood accident. West Point is your only chance, his comrades told him, half in jest. But it was Mellnik who got the last laugh. After persevering through pounding migraine headaches at the U.S. Military Academy Preparatory School at Fort Monmouth, New Jersey, to win a competitive appointment, Mellnik graduated from West Point in 1932.

It was during difficult times that he fondly remembered his family's arrival in the islands in 1939, the excitement of his first command, the festive gaiety of dances, and teaming with his wife to win Corregidor's 1940 mixed doubles tennis championship. But those halcyon days were gone. And so was the confidence and buoyant banter of previous letters and cables he had sent home. Distracted and unable to continue, Mellnik signed off.

> *Don't feel like concentrating on writing sweet—just feel a bit too far away from you. Do take care of yourself & the children. I'd just about cry to think about anything happening to them.*
>
> *By the time you get this, we will either be relieved or prisoners— or—. . . .*
>
> *Steve*

WEDNESDAY, MAY 6, 1942
Corregidor

As noon approached, news of the surrender reached the Rock's defenders in a variety of ways. Yet no matter whether one got the word from a battalion commander or a battery mate, through the Voice of Freedom or observation of the white flags that popped up across the fire-blackened island, it hit with instant, devastating ferocity.

It took General Wainwright less than twelve hours from the moment the Japanese landed on Corregidor just before midnight on May 5 to reach the heart-wrenching decision. Though the Marines of the 1st Battalion had destroyed many landing barges and fought valiantly with a largely punchless arsenal of 37- and 75-millimeter guns, machine guns, grenades, and Molotov cocktails, they could not stem the overwhelming enemy tide. As Japanese infantry determinedly clawed toward Malinta Hill with the aid of air and artillery support, daylight revealed a hopeless tactical situation: three enemy tanks had also rumbled off the beach and were clanking toward Malinta Tunnel. Fearing for the safety of the 1,000 patients in the hospital laterals—his troops had no antitank weapons—Wainwright realized the futility of further resistance.

The Marines, upon hearing the code phrase "Execute Pontiac," which instructed them to destroy their guns and surrender, took the news the hardest. One tried to shoot a runner who delivered the order to his gun position. Marines in the 2nd and 3rd Battalions, having watched the tracer bullets and shell bursts of the previous night's fighting with great anticipation and now denied the chance to prove their mettle, were especially distraught. After recovering from the initial shock, Lt. Jack Hawkins and his men channeled their roiling emotions into bending rifle barrels, throwing pieces of weapons into the surf, and rolling ammunition boxes over cliffs.

The surrender was doubly painful for Capt. Austin Shofner. A few days earlier, Shofner had suffered burns on his face and hands while rescuing survivors after a Japanese shell exploded the powder magazines at Battery Geary. After breaking his Marine sword over his knee, he watched as men "wept like children. Stern, hard-bitten commanders threw their arms around private soldiers and bawled. The tears streamed down my own face and mingled with the grime and sweat and stubble of beard."

• • •

History, as well as the U.S. Navy's new listening post at Wahiawa, Hawaii, some twenty miles north of Pearl Harbor, would record the last official message from American forces in the Philippines as having originated on Corregidor at 11:55 A.M., local time. The author of the message, Lt. Cmdr. Melvyn McCoy, probably should not even have been there.

McCoy had had several opportunities to flee Corregidor. A place had been reserved for him aboard the *Lanakai*, a 120-foot sailing schooner that had been used in the 1940 Hollywood film *Typhoon*, starring Dorothy Lamour, but the duty-bound officer was not aboard the two-master when it departed on December 26. Weeks earlier McCoy and several colleagues had begun outfitting a small sloop, the *Southern Seas*, for a last-minute flight from the Rock. The boat, however, was stolen from its moorings on May 4, thus marooning McCoy on Corregidor.

Having already supervised the destruction of all codes and equipment, McCoy concluded his last duty as radio matériel officer for the 16th Naval District by handing the simple written message, prepared on behalf of both himself and a fellow communications officer, to a radioman waiting at the last functioning transmitter.

"Beam it to Radio Honolulu," said McCoy. "Don't bother with code." The clock in the Navy tunnel ticked toward noon as a series of electronic clicks and beeps sent McCoy's words out into the ether:

GOING OFF AIR NOW. GOODBYE AND GOOD LUCK. CALLAHAN AND MCCOY.

And then, as in all other places to have fallen under the dominion of Imperial Japan, there was nothing but stark silence.

SATURDAY, MAY 23, 1942
Corregidor

The misty morning air, fragrant with the smell of smoke, wet blankets, and coffee, was also tinged with excitement. Three transports were anchored off the South Dock, presumably waiting to remove the prisoners, Jack Hawkins recalled, "to what we hoped would be better conditions."

Any place would seem to be better than the 92nd Garage Area. The defenders of Corregidor had spent the first weeks of their captivity suffering on what was essentially a concrete skillet. Water was the biggest problem: Hawkins and several other men slaked their thirst with water drained from the radiator of a destroyed truck. Delirious from sunstroke and dehydration, many men were dragged to the surf, in which corpses floated, to be revived. The monsoon season had arrived late, but now Mother Nature had slapped them with sheets of stinging rain, turning makeshift shelters into a muddy, miserable mess. And only recently had the Japanese provided food, giving credence to the rumors heard by Melvyn McCoy that they were being held as living collateral until the remaining USFIP forces in the Visayas and Mindanao surrendered.

The conquerors had enlisted work parties, mainly for the gruesome task of burying and cremating the thousands of corpses that littered the island, and many prisoners, Austin Shofner among them, jumped at the opportunity because it enabled them to escape the crowded compound to forage for food. Shofner did not find much food during his forays outside the wire, but he did find a new pair of shoes, perhaps an omen. Both Shofner and Hawkins had considered escaping from Corregidor. Shofner had been approached by Edgar Whitcomb, a B-17 navigator and Bataan refugee, but Shofner did not feel confident in his swimming skills. Hawkins, too, felt that the time was not right, so he wished Marine Lt. Bill Harris, a former Annapolis classmate, good luck in the endeavor. Drying their blankets near a fire, both pondered the progress of Whitcomb and Harris as well as their own future. (Whitcomb and Harris had joined forces in fleeing Corregidor on May 22, but separated shortly after reaching Bataan. In one of the war's strangest adventures, Whitcomb was recaptured by the Japanese, and, after enduring extreme mental and physical torture, was repatriated to the United State in a civilian exchange by pretending to be a mining engineer. He rejoined the fighting in the Philippines in early 1945. Harris made it to Borneo before his recapture in 1943. He spent the rest of the war in a POW camp in Japan.)

"Where do you think they will send us, Shof?" asked Hawkins.

"Don't know," replied Shofner, "but I hope I never see this rock again. Maybe they will put us in some decent camp somewhere now, like Fort McKinley."

"You expect more than I do, if you expect anything decent from these Japs."

Hawkins was hardly surprised when he and Shofner were shoved into one of the overcrowded holds of the *Hoku Maru* later in the afternoon. As if the superheated congestion belowdecks—each of the 7,000-ton ships was packed with more than 3,500 men—was not bad enough, the vessel had been used to transport horses, as evidenced by the piles of manure on deck. "This was in keeping with the general Japanese attitude toward American prisoners," noted Hawkins. "They persisted in treating us like animals." The real humiliation, Hawkins and Shofner would soon learn, was still to come.

SUNDAY, MAY 24, 1942
Manila, Luzon

A modern-day Jonah trapped inside the steamy, steel bowels of a freighter, Steve Mellnik had been both figuratively and literally in the dark for hours. The only clues to his whereabouts had been the sounds: an anchor chain winding around a capstan; the steady, laborious pulsing of the ship's engines. And then, in mid-morning, the propellers suddenly stopped churning.

Crewmen entered the hold and funneled the POWs toward the lower deck entranceway where a gangplank reached to a refuse barge. Mellnik, squinting at the sun rays glittering off the water, recognized the far-off silhouette of the Manila Polo Club. Strangely, instead of tying up in the dock area, the ship had laid anchor about a mile offshore.

To Melvyn McCoy, the Japanese plan became obvious when the barges stopped short of the beach and the prisoners were ordered into the chest-high water. "The Japanese wanted to be sure we made the march through Manila in wet clothes and with wet equipment," explained McCoy. Accordingly, the Americans floundered ashore, holding their musette bags and bedrolls above their heads. They were prodded onto Dewey Boulevard and commenced marching through the debris-strewn streets to Bilibid Prison, the high-walled penitentiary that would serve as a way station to another place of incarceration. Jack Hawkins, ever inquisitive, turned to Shofner, sloshing alongside him.

"Shof, I wonder if we will ever find old Mike again. Do you think he is still alive?"

"I'll bet he is alive somewhere," answered Shofner, who was usually as optimistic as he was opinionated. "They couldn't get the 'little beaver' down."

The march soon proved a major Japanese miscalculation. The Filipinos lining the streets—the Japanese had ordered all Manilans to watch the spectacle—were appalled by the condition of the prisoners. "Many of them were openly crying and sometimes they would furtively give us the 'V for Victory' sign," recalled Hawkins. "They tried to give us water and bits of food as we passed, at the risk of being clubbed by a Jap rifle butt."

Nonplussed, the Japanese endeavored to end the movement quickly. Troops on horseback harried the prisoners with their mounts while foot soldiers motivated malingerers with bayonets. The column, which coiled for nearly a mile around buildings and down rubble-strewn streets, crossed over Quezon Bridge to Azcarraga Street, the prisoners supporting and carrying one another to keep the pace. Several were roughed up, but there would be no executions or outright atrocities on this march; perhaps the presence of several thousand civilian onlookers restrained the Japanese from exhibiting the bloodthirsty behavior they had shown on Bataan.

One spectator in particular wanted to do more than provide food, water and support. But for now, this man—one of their own, yet a captive of another sort—was taking notes.

In so many ways, it was excruciatingly difficult for Charles "Chick" Parsons to stand there helplessly and watch as the parade of prisoners passed by his home at 1925 Calle Roberts in Pasay. As a man, it was painful to watch his mother-in-law and wife try to come to the aid of the POWs with a glass *garapon* filled with water, only to be driven off by Japanese bayonets. Parsons could not make an attempt, not for any lack of guts—before war's end, MacArthur would call Parsons "the bravest man I know." At this moment, he could not risk being recognized. His heart pounded inside his barrel chest—which was covered with a tattoo of an eagle and a battleship surrounded by American flags—at the sight of his countrymen being so humiliated. After all, he should have been marching with them.

Officially, Parsons was not a civilian. Robust and handsome, the forty-two-year-old businessman was also a Navy Reserve officer who had been called to active duty in December. The chaos of the Christmas retreat had trapped Parsons in Manila, forcing him to burn his uniforms and devise a contingency plan. But it did not take him, a man who would develop a reputation for thinking on his feet, long to do so. And it was perhaps no coincidence that Parsons, an amateur magician who possessed an uncanny skill for card tricks and other sleight-of-hand maneuvers, would attempt to solve his problem with an illusion.

Parsons's partner in the Luzon Stevedoring Company, away at the start of the war, had been named the honorary Panamanian ambassador to the Philippines due to the fact that their company handled a significant amount of shipping under that country's registry. So, in his partner's absence, the engaging entrepreneur ceased being Lt. Charles Parsons, and assumed, not entirely fraudulently, the identity of the *consul de Panama*, a neutral nation. (It was a common practice in the prewar era for small nations with limited resources to enlist the heads of companies as envoys to represent their diplomatic interests in distant countries.)

With his jet-black hair and bronzed skin, the result of his two decades in the islands, Parsons looked the part of a South American diplomat. He embellished the ruse by unfurling a Panamanian flag outside his house and speaking only Spanish. It was the only choice. Other American civilians and their families were carted off to the internment camp at Santo Tomas University on Calle España; a repatriation of diplomats was likely his only chance to escape the Philippines, save his family, and rejoin the war. But Parsons did not intend merely to survive.

Parsons used the freedom afforded by his counterfeit diplomatic privileges and his extensive array of contacts to cast a wide-ranging intelligence net. It started with cocktail parties with neutral friends and expanded to clandestine conversations and conferences with priests and business associates. Soon, peddlers stopped at his back door, ostensibly to sell their wares, but instead to perform a transaction of information. He reportedly even ventured outside the city, canvassing outlying areas in disguise to gain more information.

With the help of his wife, Katrushka, called Katsy, Parsons began to collate his gathered information: issues of the Japanese-run *Manila Tribune*; the estimated size and disposition of enemy military units in the islands; the prices of foodstuffs; the mood of the people; the sight of Filipinos he had seen strung up in trees near Rizal Stadium; the stories he had heard of government officials, civilian nationals, and regular Filipino citizens being rounded up by the dreaded Japanese secret police, the Kempeitai, and never seen again; the names and numbers of individuals, as well as conditions, inside the various internment and POW camps. The murmurings of the Death March and other atrocities committed against

American military personnel were of particular interest. "Eyewitnesses, with whom I talked later, shuddered when recalling the sight of the prisoners of war on their trek from Bataan," he would write.

The deception worked—for a time. In late April, he was arrested and taken to Fort Santiago, the old Spanish citadel in Intramuros, which the Kempeitai had transformed into a dank dungeon where enemies of the emperor could be interrogated, tortured, and, if necessary, executed. Parsons endured whatever the Japanese could dish out, but the threat of death was never relaxed. One day during his confinement, several Chinese consular officials were led away and beheaded. "Look out," sneered a Kempeitai officer, "the same may happen to you." Through it all, Parsons did not talk. After several agony-filled days, he was released to the commonwealth prison at Muntinlupa and, later, to Santo Tomas.

Parsons had been temporarily furloughed in order to recuperate from his ordeal at Fort Santiago—he was inordinately pale and his wife noticed that the fingernails on his right hand were just beginning to grow back—and was present at his home the day the Japanese paraded the American POWs through Manila. Luckily for the dehydrated prisoners lying in Parsons's front yard, the third attempt by the Parsons family to come to their aid proved the charm. Six-year-old Peter, the middle of Parsons's three young sons, successfully reached the POWs with a water jug with the assistance of the Japanese soldier-sentries who had been assigned to guard the compound of the suspicious Panamanian consul on Manila Bay.

Staying inconspicuously in the background, Chick Parsons was cataloguing the scene, adding it to the other intelligence items he had painstakingly gathered over the past few months. But before he could share that information, before he could become one of the most important yet little-known espionage legends of the Pacific war, and before he could aid his captive countrymen, he first somehow had to engineer his own escape from the occupied Philippines. It would require his greatest trick yet—a disappearing act for the ages.

CHAPTER 7

A Rumor

We saw an open grave, waiting for him.
We watched him from our fence, in silent throng
Each with the fervent prayer, "God make him strong."

TUESDAY, JUNE 2–THURSDAY, JUNE 4, 1942
Cabanatuan, Nueva Ecija Province, Luzon

S teve Mellnik thought that he had seen the worst of it during his two weeks in the 92nd Garage Area. That optimism disappeared when the trucks carrying the survivors of Camp O'Donnell growled into Cabanatuan.

The Americans climbing and tumbling from the trucks—the Japanese, alarmed by the staggering death rate of the Filipinos, had issued a mass pardon and sent them home to die—presented a pitiful spectacle. They were little more than sunburnt scarecrows with scraggly beards, sunken faces, and chopstick arms and legs. "An icy shiver of fear went through me," recalled Mellnik. He identified a former enlisted orderly who tottered up and feebly grasped his shoulders. "Sir," he asked, "is it different here—will they treat us like humans?"

Jack Hawkins, unable to find Mike Dobervich in the wobbly mob, launched an exhaustive search the next morning. Invariably, his queries met with the same laconic reply: "Never heard of him." Finally, a corporal from the 31st Infantry referred Hawkins to the hospital, where he believed Dobervich was fighting "the bad sick," or malaria. After waiting for the gate sentry to turn his back, Hawkins slid beneath the barbed wire fence and skulked across the road separating the main compound from the hospital. In a dysentery ward, he scanned the sorrowful faces of the living skeletons lying on the excrement-covered floor. *"My God,"* he whispered to himself, *"I hope Mike is not here."* He wasn't. Nor was Dobervich found elsewhere. Renegotiating the wire at sunset, Hawkins raced to his barracks and, out of breath, fell into line for *tenko*, the Japanese word for roll call. That night, Hawkins resigned himself to the fact that his best friend was, in all likelihood, dead.

Morning found Hawkins on the ground outside his barracks, absorbed in his miserable breakfast of watery lugao. He did not even look up when a pair of army shoes stepped directly into his line of vision, engulfing him in a sizeable shadow. "Give me some of that," demanded a voice. It was a voice Hawkins had never expected to hear again.

He was severely underweight, but it was no ghost—standing in front of Hawkins was Mike Dobervich, bare-chested and wearing a broad-brimmed straw sombrero. Hawkins was flabbergasted, but it was, after all, mealtime. Springing to his feet, he embraced Dobervich with a flurry of questions. Dobervich, producing a coconut, nodded. It was his turn to share some food.

"It's a long story," said Dobervich.

Dobervich provided a full account of his ordeal. He told of driving the truck out of Bataan and the terror he had witnessed through the dusty windshield; Captain Tsuneyoshi's welcome speech; the burial details. "I did not interrupt him often as he spoke," said Hawkins. "But sat in rapt attention, picturing in my mind the horror he was describing."

"That two months in O'Donnell was the worst nightmare I ever went through," continued a shaken Dobervich, pausing to throw pieces of the coconut shell at a rock. "The men were dying off like flies."

"That's the most awful thing I ever heard of in all my life," responded Hawkins. "What do you suppose the people back home will think when they hear about it?"

"Oh, they won't believe it. The American people never believe anything terrible. They will probably stop up their ears and say, 'Oh, this is too terrible. It must be propaganda.'"

"I wish every American could have a chance to see what we've seen, and then they could realize they've got to be tough in dealing with these Japs. They're not human beings."

"Mike, the American people have got to completely crush Japan—

destroy their cities, beat their Armies, sink their Navy, and put dough-boys into what used to be Tokyo."

Dobervich's appalling tale had awakened them to two complementary truths: that America must somehow learn of the prisoners' plight and, once sufficiently roused, strive for total victory. Just who would be responsible for that revelation, though, was beyond their ken. At Cabanatuan, more basic concerns, like surviving to see the next sunrise, would require their attention.

TUESDAY, JULY 7–SATURDAY, SEPTEMBER 26, 1942
Cabanatuan, Nueva Ecija Province, Luzon

"You won't like it here," the officer, a prewar acquaintance who had survived the savage aftermath of Bataan, told Melvyn McCoy. McCoy, just arrived from Manila, was beginning to understand why. The awful stench had hit him even before he had set foot inside Cabanatuan.

"Good God," he gasped, pointing to the rows of fly-covered corpses awaiting burial.

"You'll get used to that," replied the officer, casually, continuing his rote summary of the events that transpired on the Death March and in O'Donnell as he moved McCoy along.

Only after reliving the macabre litany of atrocities did McCoy's docent offer some animated, and astute, commentary.

"Those things don't happen to Americans, McCoy. I know we've heard of Hitler starving and killing people by the thousands; and we've heard of the Japs using living Chinese for bayonet practice. But we're Americans, McCoy! Nobody ever taught us about that."

That much was true. They had not had any formal survival training. Boot camp had taught men how to dig foxholes and clean rifles and about venereal disease. Officers had been taught to fly planes, to range artillery, and to lead troops in battle—but not what to do in prison camp. They had no idea how to conduct themselves while being starved, tortured, or while facing a firing squad. Not only had they not been given the means to achieve victory, they had not been prepared for losing. Of course, nothing could have prepared one for Cabanatuan.

Located seventy-five miles north of Manila in Nueva Ecija Province, Cabanatuan was composed of three separate sites, Camps One, Two, and

Three, situated six, twelve, and eighteen miles north of Cabanatuan City, respectively. Some 9,000 Americans, which included all of the Bataan POWs, as well as most of the officers and some men from Corregidor, called Camp One home. (All of the participants in this story were confined in Camp One. In future references, the terms "Cabanatuan" and "Camp One" will be used interchangeably.) The former Philippine Army cantonment was parceled into four compounds, three of which were heavily guarded and contained the prisoners' barracks. It was fitting that the Japanese had planted Cabanatuan in the midst of neglected rice fields that were overgrown with weeds; nothing but the hardiest, most resilient of men would survive the inhospitable conditions.

"We used to say in Shanghai that we may be eating fish heads and rice one of these days," said Jack Hawkins. "The whole trouble is [in Cabanatuan], we didn't even get the fishheads." Some prisoners augmented their diets with lizards, frogs, and dogs. The Marines, however, made it known that they would skewer any man who dared look at their mascot, Private Soochow, with hungry eyes. Watching the dog share the Marines' meager chow pained many of the more commonsensical prisoners, but the protein-poor menu at Cabanatuan, tasteless, soggy rice, served thrice daily and infrequently flavored with wormy camotes or tiny bits of dried fish, was in itself another form of torture. "The artful Japs," said Ed Dyess, "gave us just enough food to keep us in agony of hunger at all times." Food thus became an obsession that dominated their thoughts, their conversations, and even their dreams. Each night, Hawkins dreamed of fried eggs, crisp bacon, and buttered toast. And each morning, he woke "with a drooling mouth and a pain in my empty stomach." While Dyess's cravings made a circuit, from Hereford steaks to eggs and chocolate milk shakes, Sam Grashio remained fixated on ice cream and lemonade.

Dysentery prevented them from keeping what little food they did get in their systems: the buildup of gas caused them to prematurely expel their bowels before their bodies could collect vital nutrients. Avitaminotic diseases like scurvy and pellagra tormented the men, the former characterized by painful, bleeding gums and the latter by scaly sores and hallucinatory delusions. Elephantiasis, encephalitis, and tuberculosis, sicknesses that most medical personnel had only read about, appeared. Mosquitoes were responsible for the exponential increase in cases of malaria, the bane of every prisoner, and dengue fever, known as "break-bone fever" because one felt as though his bones were being pounded by a hammer. It was therefore hardly any great surprise then that at any one time, one-fourth to more than one-third of the camp's population was crowded into the sawali-sided nipa shacks that masqueraded as a hospital. "The hospital was a place without beds, the men lying on raised bamboo shelves," said Dyess. "There was a primitive operating room that almost never was in operation and a dispensary that seldom dispensed anything."

Many ultimately ended up in "Zero Ward"—so named because should one land there, his chances of leaving alive were zero—a larger version of O'Donnell's St. Peter's Ward. The Japanese did issue some antitoxin when a diphtheria epidemic threatened their own personnel, but they remained largely indifferent to the prisoners' suffering. "Buried 52 today," read one of Mellnik's late-June diary entries. "Camp is gloomy morgue. Dead men lie on streets until noon." Hawkins recalled bulldozers aiding in the disposal of the corpses, but most of the details remained dependent on human labor. Likewise, the dwindling number of living prisoners relied on the only individuals that they been able to count on since the war began: each other.

When Hawkins was stricken with acute diarrhea and began to lose the will to eat, Dobervich waited in line for hours to fill Hawkins's canteen and forced rice, as well as a bitter black charcoal paste, a homemade remedy that produced positive results for some dysentery patients, down Hawkins's throat. He also resisted efforts to admit Hawkins to the so-called hospital. Hawkins turned the corner after ten touch-and-go days.

Not long after Hawkins's recovery, it was Shifty Shofner's turn. A gruesome tropical ulcer in one of his feet had bored its way to the bone, becoming so painful that he could not walk. Hawkins and Dobervich dutifully served as human crutches, helping their buddy to the latrine until some salicylic crystals and rest healed the sore.

Ed Dyess felt he had someone looking out for him, too, after jaundice and dengue fever had rendered him almost bedridden. Bank and Grashio helped nurse Dyess back to health—or what passed for health at Cabanatuan. After six weeks, Dyess emerged from his ordeal weighing only 120 pounds, nearly one-third under his normal weight of 175. He explained how his unique perception of God had kept him alive: "I never thought of God or addressed Him as a distant, awesome being somewhere in the sky. I felt much closer to Him than that. . . . I thought of Him as 'The Old Man'—the affectionate, respectful title soldiers apply to a commanding officer. . . . I would say to myself: 'I have nothing to worry about. The Old Man will see me through.' "

Dyess's understanding of predestination and fatalism had been formed during his youth, but "it was a Jap bullet that crystallized these teachings into belief." He had been flying over enemy lines on Bataan when a slug ripped into his P-40. Had he not been leaning to one side, the bullet would have plowed into his brain, killing him instantly. His recent illness, therefore, was no different from the bullet incident: it simply had not been his time.

Mellnik noticed that the prisoners reacted to their predicaments in various ways. Heavier men, he observed, were unable to endure the starvation diet and succumbed to death earlier than smaller prisoners. "Those who had imbibed a great deal and exercised rarely did not survive either," he said. Others convinced themselves that it was their time, demonstrating that survival was as much a mental and spiritual battle as it was a physical one. Shofner learned a valuable lesson in motivation when a fellow Marine entered his bay for a chat.

"Shof," the officer told him, quietly, "it's easy to die."

"What do you mean, easy?"

"Last night I was awake when Joe died. It was real peaceful. No struggle, no pain . . ."

"Hey," replied Shofner, angrily. "Knock it off. That's no way to talk. You got to live, boy, live. Think about your wife and kids. This won't last forever; and remember, you're not alone here, not by a long shot."

"Shof, we're not going to get out of this, you know that. Every day just prolongs the agony. It's senseless, Shof. I'm going to die."

And he did; Shofner helped bury the Marine four days later. Sam Grashio had made up his mind, too—he was not giving up. "It is hard to kill a man by mere ill treatment if he is determined to live, and I was . . . I wanted to see my wife, family and friends again. I wanted to let the American people know what we and the Filipinos had endured."

Grashio credited his reflexive retreat into his Catholic faith for his outlook. He had developed a strong conviction that he had no explanation for, a powerful belief welling inside of him that "somehow, God would not let me die in a Japanese prison."

• • •

War had, at the very least, kept them busy. Weapons needed to be cleaned; paperwork shuffled. But prison camp was different. There were few distractions from their dull, miserable existence. Making matters worse, the forced intimacy that accompanied sharing a crowded prison camp with thousands of other sick, smelly, and disgruntled men, oddly juxtaposed with feelings of loneliness and abandonment, frayed nerves. "The strain of captivity and prison life can snap the tiny threads of reason," noted Shofner. To preserve their sanity and to prevent menticide—the death of the mind—those that chose to live became combatants once more.

Their Yankee humor and ingenuity proved powerful weapons. Inspired by the omnipresent mud—the ruthless sun might have taken a sabbatical, but the rains of the monsoon season had mired Cabanatuan into a giant bog—the rank stench, the swarms of flies, and their inability to bathe, the Marines founded a fraternity of filth called "Skunk Patrol, Alpha Chapter." They greeted each other with a sign and countersign ritual: a lifted leg was acknowledged by a handclasp of the nose. Because Shofner possessed a notebook, he held the office of "stinkitary."

The mucky roads and alleys that connected Camp One's compounds soon had familiar names like Main Street, Michigan Avenue, and Broadway. "A Milwaukee man had named a path for himself," noted Dyess. "It was Buboltz boulevard and led to the latrines." And there was a hustler on every corner. Since many guards suffered from venereal disease and were willing to trade anything for sulfa tablets, some resourceful POWs took Japanese-issued tooth powder, formed it into tablets with a spent cartridge, stamped the pills with a "W," the trademark symbol of the Winthrop Company, which made the drugs, and then sold the product back to their unwitting captors. Their racket did not last long, but the sight of a wretched guard slinking off to take a dose of phony pills was more enjoyable than the cigarettes the men received in payment.

Prisoners produced shows and musical performances, or focused on practical pursuits such as fly-killing contests or compiling rosters and death lists. Some signed up for labor details to escape the drudgery of the camp, but they soon learned to avoid anything that involved close contact with the Japanese, namely to avoid contact *from* the Japanese. Language courses were popular, too; Steve Mellnik, for example, practiced his Russian with other officers. In a bizarre act of benevolence, the Japanese issued, of all things, softball equipment. It was an absurd gesture. "I couldn't have run around a baseball diamond if the devil himself had been chasing me," said Hawkins.

Some prisoners taught classes in subjects relating to their civilian careers or special interests. Hawkins remembered seeing Melvyn McCoy sitting on the ground, twitching his mustache while reciting logarithms, from memory, to a circle of pupils. But Hawkins skipped McCoy's lectures to sit in on the ubiquitous card games. Gambling was the favorite prison camp pastime. Prisoners bet on everything, from whether a POW rushing to the latrines in a broken gait would make it in time, to the number of worms in their rice. The stakes usually involved cash or cigarettes, the latter an emergent form of camp currency. Many bet their rice rations, mortgaging their meals and their futures. Outside of food wagers, most bets were made on the cuff—if a man died, his debts were forgiven. That was good for Shofner, a regular in the camp's high-limit poker game—a regular loser. "That guy McCoy is a shark," he often complained, disgustedly, to Hawkins. There also was the matter of the bet that he had made with a friend on Corregidor in February, for $10, that the United States would recapture Manila by the Fourth of July. Marking the date in Cabanatuan, Shofner had to settle the wager, scoring it as "Lost. (Pd)." Nevertheless, he continued making bets and the prisoners refused to snuff their few flickering flames of hope, for which rumors served as so much emotional kindling.

Germany's surrender was among the first rumors "reported" at Cabanatuan, but the most popular ones naturally revolved around phony tales of America's great Pacific offensive. Considering that their conversations focused on food, they hoped to eat "Thanksgiving turkey in Albuquerque." "In '43 we'll all be free," they also liked to say. Some believed that Uncle Sam was arranging a prisoner exchange; Dyess had heard that a steamer in Manila Bay was being readied to transfer the prisoners to Ecuador. According to another universally accepted rumor, FDR had deposited $50 million in Swiss banks to help the Red Cross care for American prisoners. One officer kept track of all the rumors to have circulated Cabanatuan, reportedly collecting more than 2,000. None was ever confirmed.

Since Cabanatuan was almost hermetically sealed off from the outside world, they had no way of separating fact from fiction. Most of the rumors had come from the guards or from hurried conversations with

Filipinos during a work detail. Some, no doubt, had been invented by well-meaning men who simply wanted to boost camp morale. There was, in fact, a secret homemade radio that picked up station KGEI in San Francisco, but possession of a radio was so risky that its existence, as well as the news it supplied, was not widely known. The Marines, however, were treated to their own nightly "broadcasts" courtesy of Lt. Leon Chabot. Though Chabot's broadcasts usually possessed more style than certifiable substance, the 4th Marines' very own Walter Winchell (Chabot often waited at the gates to speak with truck drivers returning from Manila) occasionally landed a scoop. "Well, gentlemen, this is the latest from Manila," Chabot declared one memorable summer night before humming his own sound effects, a few bars of "The Marine Hymn." "The United States Marines have landed on Guadalcanal!" The skeptics in his audience shrugged off the news, but Chabot was vindicated a few weeks later when they read between the lines of an article in the *Manila Tribune*, a pro-Japanese propaganda organ, that claimed the Japanese were mopping up remnants of the U.S. Marine Corps at a place called Guadalcanal.

It was heartening to know that their countrymen were fighting somewhere, but after learning that Guadalcanal was nearly 3,000 nautical miles from the Philippines, "we could judge that the United States truly was making little or no progress in the Pacific war," said Hawkins. As the rains muddied the weeks into months, new rallying cries revealed their sagging spirits: " '45 if you're still alive"; " '47 if you're not in heaven." For the canteen half-empty crowd, "the Golden Gate in '48" seemed more accurate.

One sure sign of the war's progress was the arrival of the Iwanaka Educational Unit on August 14. Named for the unit's commanding officer, Maj. Yasuaki Iwanaka, the unit's mission was to train 600 Formosan conscripts for guard duty, a significant development in that it betrayed the fact that Japanese combat troops were needed elsewhere.

The Americans observed the recruits drilling in the adjacent compound. "All day long they would march up and down, goose-stepping, and practicing with the bayonet, to the accompaniment of their weird marching chants, which they howled at the tops of their voices," recalled Dyess. Unaware that these browbeaten recruits were being trained as their overseers, the prisoners found the exercises humorous. "The bayonet practice put us in stitches," added Dyess, "those of us who were strong enough to laugh, that is." These laughs were much-needed morale boosters, but at Cabanatuan it was the Japanese who most often enjoyed themselves at the Americans' expense.

Guarding prisoners was not honorable or coveted duty. The assignment usually fell to the dregs of the Imperial Army, xenophobic alcoholics, sadists, and mentally unstable soldiers—and now, colonial conscripts considered social inferiors—deemed unfit for combat. Consumed with venomous hatred, they rejoiced in reminding the prisoners of their pitiful station. Dyess could not forget the "futile rage" the prisoners felt upon seeing an American flag used as a rag or mop in the Japanese kitchen.

The guards beat the prisoners at the slightest provocation—for failing to salute, for presenting a poor appearance at inspections, and sometimes just on a whim. One POW was ordered to masturbate by a guard. When he refused, remembered Sam Grashio, he was beaten "so mercilessly he went mad and died two or three days later." On one occasion, Bert Bank and several others were lined up face-to-face and ordered to slap each other. "[The guards] were mean, really mean," said Motts Tonelli. "Another thing they'd do is come up behind you and slap your ears, you know, and you'd get dizzy. They'd step on your feet; we didn't have shoes." One guard, described by Dyess as "a stocky, evil caricature on the human race," gained infamy for brutalizing prisoners on a building-moving detail. As laborers slid poles under a nipa structure and struggled to raise it to their shoulders, the guard ran alongside, screaming maniacally and beating them with the shaft of a golf club. Fighting back or resistance of any kind meant certain death, so the prisoners had no choice but to absorb both the blows and the humiliation.

For the Americans watching through the barbed wire, one of the new arrivals stood out, a veritable Japanese giant with a muscular, six-foot, 190-pound frame. Handsome and immaculately attired in clean, sharply creased uniforms and shiny leather boots, this towering officer was a noticeable contrast to the sloppy guards whose fatigues, observed Grashio, "usually looked slept in." "He looked more like an Occidental than an Oriental," commented another prisoner. His adamantine luster, noble presentation, and tyrannical parade ground demeanor suggested that impressions were important to 1st Lt. Yoshimasa Hozumi. It would take but a few weeks for him to make an indelible impression on the prisoners.

After a guard had been killed, presumably by local guerrillas, Hozumi led a punitive expedition to a nearby barrio. The prisoners heard the echo of gunfire and saw plumes of smoke laze across the sky. The detail returned later that day, several hundred soldiers singing and shouting while triumphantly parading through the gates in a display, according to one witness, reminiscent of a "college snake dance after a football victory." One could call it a victory: the barrio had been razed and fifty of its inhabitants, including women and children, were rumored to have been killed. Hozumi rode at the head of the riotous procession on horseback, followed by two soldiers who carried aloft a severed Filipino head, which, according to the same startled witness, "stared wildly in transfixed and sightless terror as its murky juices oozed down the pike on which it was impaled." The grisly trophy was transferred to a fence post near the gate and a sign affixed, an inscription in English and Japanese, which read, "A Very Bad Man."

As if the wanton cruelty of their captors was not enough, the men were also forced to deal, in the operative sense of the word, with the greed of their own countrymen. Even as prisoners were dying by the dozens on a daily basis, there were some Americans trying to turn a profit in the camp's burgeoning black market. It was a strange partnership, yet a highly lucrative one. The Japanese bought canned goods, cigarettes, and candy bars from Filipinos and then distributed the items to the Americans to peddle around the camp. The exorbitant prices—a can of corned beef purchased for 80 centavos, or 40 cents, for example, sold for 10 pesos, or 5 U.S. dollars—separated many prisoners from what little money they had. A few frugal, future-minded individuals held on to their money. Hawkins remained relatively affluent because of his foresight to sew $200 in cash, along with his Annapolis ring and his watch, into the seams of his uniform. Dyess secreted his cash between his toes. "While it rubbed blisters and sometimes made walking painful, I held on to it," he said. The alternative—poverty—was potentially much more painful.

Nearly everything in the prison camp had its price. Just about the only thing that no amount of cash, rank, or influence could purchase, however, was freedom. Some would pay the ultimate price making that discovery.

SUNDAY, SEPTEMBER 27–FRIDAY, OCTOBER 2, 1942
Cabanatuan, Nueva Ecija Province, Luzon

Though the entertainment value was admittedly low, Steve Mellnik was curious to learn the reason for the cancellation of the evening's prisoner production. "Our three escapees are back," a passing prisoner informed him. "The Japanese are making them put on a show."

The three escapees were Naval Reserve ensigns who had fled from Cabanatuan before the five-strand barbed wire fences and four-story guard towers had sprouted from the abandoned paddies. After more than three months on the lam, the fugitives had turned themselves in, for reasons no one yet knew. "We did not know what turn this 'show' would take, and we looked forward to it with foreboding," said Mellnik.

A hush fell over the audience as an odd procession mounted the outdoor stage later that afternoon. Leading the way was the camp commandant, Lt. Col. Shigeji Mori, followed by bodyguards and an interpreter. To some, Mori was faintly recognizable; he had reportedly owned a bicycle shop in Manila before the war. Next came the escapees, their hands bound behind their backs. Another failed escapee, a prisoner of Hispanic or Native American descent who had attempted to pass himself off as a Filipino, was led to the stage with a rope. "He had been kept in solitary confinement for months now and he was always led like a dog on a leash when he made his infrequent walks from his cage," said Hawkins. The "show" commenced with Lt. Col. Mori's words, followed by those of his interpreter.

"Colonel Mori, he say, escape is a crime," crooned the interpreter, accenting the word "crime" with an excited inflection. "Colonel Mori, he say, Japanese are kind to you. Japanese give you food and mediseen. When war over, we friends."

A low grumble rippled the audience, but the "show"—and the interpreter—went on.

"Colonel Mori, he say, you not escape. Japanese keep you good, after war send you back to wife. Colonel Mori, he say, if you escape, you will die. Then wife have many tears. Colonel Mori, he say, escape is a crime."

Finally, the three ensigns were summoned to the dais. They spoke, each in turn, of their failed attempt to survive in the wilds, of being beset by starvation, sickness, and poisonous snakes and of the hostility of the Filipino populace. They concluded that they were blessed to be back inside the camp where they could receive the "benevolent kindness of the Japanese."

"We were both amused and disgusted at their speeches," said Hawkins. From the cuts and bruises exhibited by the prisoners, it was obvious that the statements had been composed under duress. But the men in the audience also saw that the escapees were otherwise in good physical shape.

"That gives me a laugh," said Dobervich as the Marines walked back to their barracks. "Starvation outside! Why those boys are as fat as pigs."

The true story, the prisoners discovered, was that the escapees had lived comfortably as free men, and had turned themselves in only to prevent the executions of their benefactor, a *teniente del barrio*, or Filipino mayor, and his family. "Colonel Mori understood little of American psychology or he would never have staged the show," said Hawkins.

Escape may not have been the most discussed topic in prison camp (food was), but it was the most contemplated and controversial of subjects. Some prisoners, mostly officers, held a vague belief that escape was their sworn duty. For most, the desire to escape was a simple matter of self-preservation, even in light of the infamous Japanese directive that surfaced as a result of the flight of the Navy ensigns. The edict, dated July 10, 1942, grouped the prisoners in "shooting squads" of ten men. It threatened that if any one prisoner escaped or attempted escape, the remaining nine men were liable to be executed. To the Americans, this was a clear violation of Article 51 of the Geneva Convention, which stated that, "after an attempted or accomplished escape, the comrades of the person escaping, who assisted the escape, may incur only disciplinary punishment on this account." But to the Japanese, it was a method of deterrence that ingeniously joined the Americans' burden of conscience with Japanese partiality to mass punishment.

Nevertheless, there were escapes. And after each incident, the prisoners waited with trepidation. Eighteen men from the shooting squads of two hospital patients were collected for execution, but the delirious, terminally ill patients had merely wandered off and were found nearby, dead. After a prisoner escaped from a work detail, the Japanese decided to execute five prisoners, picked at random from a group of 100 men, in retaliation. One soldier, recounting the incident for Dobervich, told how he watched, powerlessly, while his brother was selected. Then there was the case of the five American black marketeers who had temporarily escaped and were caught sneaking back in with sacks of canned goods. The members of their shooting squads were pardoned, but the five were punished for their recklessness with a firing squad.

The inconsistency with which the Japanese dealt with these incidents was maddening, but with escape no longer an individual risk, the American camp administration was forced to take preventive measures. Escape attempts were expressly forbidden and, to enforce the ban, POWs were assigned to patrol the inner perimeter. It was a divisive decision.

Rain-laced winds rifled the camp on the impenetrably dark night of September 30. It was so dark that one of the perimeter guards, Motts Tonelli, could not see the three men crawling through the drainage ditch that bisected the camp's inner and outer fences. It was a perverse quirk of fate that one of the men passed directly beneath Tonelli as he stood, yawning, at the lip of the trench answering nature's call. What happened next was a blur.

Cursing loudly, the angry man leapt out of the shadows and lunged for Tonelli. Stunned, Tonelli screamed for help. Shots fired by a tower sentry ripped through the mist as prisoners rushed from a nearby barracks to help the American guards subdue Tonelli's attackers, Army Lt. Cols. Lloyd Biggs and Howard Breitung and Navy Lt. Roy Gilbert. The scuffle was short-lived, but Biggs hotly denounced the perimeter guards, saying that it was the duty of the Americans to assist him in his escape, not stop him. Biggs refused to calm down, even as a searchlight illuminated the mob for the squad of Japanese guards arriving on the scene.

Remanded to the American headquarters, Biggs continued to rail against the American administration and the perimeter guards. Tonelli denied the accusation that there had been a deliberate attempt to prevent his escape. The noncom was not a member of the officers' shooting squad and had no stake in the group's escape. At any rate, Biggs had used the word "escape" so often in his recriminations that the eavesdropping Japanese stepped in. At 2300 hours, he was marched to Lieutenant Colonel Mori's headquarters. There, Biggs lost both his temper and his mind. He threatened Mori that he would personally see to it that the Japanese officer himself was punished after the war. It was a fatal blunder. Just hours removed from his speech and now insulted in front of his men, Mori had no choice but to make an example of these men. Tonelli's involvement was inconsequential. "There is but little doubt that had it not been for Biggs' loud voice and arrogant attitude, the affair never would have come to the attention of the Japanese authorities," said McCoy.

The next morning, Hawkins found a modern Golgotha atop the hill near the Japanese headquarters. The three would-be escapees had their hands bound behind their backs, and ropes leading through pulleys affixed to a crude scaffolding above their heads had hoisted their arms behind them at such an angle as to make standing normally impossible. They were forced to lean forward, balancing on their toes, to relieve the agonizing pressure on their arms. Yet it was likely that the battered men, hanging quietly cataleptic amid the sounds of creaking wood and twisting rope, were beyond feeling any pain. Hawkins saw that their arms and legs had been savagely bashed and broken and their faces beaten beyond recognition, "to a bloody pulp hardly resembling anything human." He watched in horror as the prisoners were doused with water and summoned back from unconsciousness. Unable to stomach anymore, Hawkins retreated to his barracks.

Beatings of the three men continued, growing with ferocity as the day went on. Japanese sentries forced Filipinos passing along the road to pay a cruel toll: those that refused to beat the prisoners were beaten themselves. "The Japanese never missed a chance to try to drive wedges between the Filipinos and Americans," noted Grashio, watching the sordid scene from his barracks. Each blow, each thud of timber on bone and flesh, resounded throughout the compound. Despite the cold, wailing wind, Dyess could hear the beatings, occasionally varied with the "slither and slash" of a whip. Hawkins covered himself with a blanket in an attempt to muffle the sounds. The noon sky turned dark. "The tropical typhoon which had been gathering," said Hawkins, "broke in all its fury."

"I think I prayed that night that those men could die soon," recalled Dyess. "I had no hope that they would survive. Yet, when morning came—after I had had an hour or so of tormented sleep—they were still there." In a supernatural display of stamina, they remained for two more days, weathering the typhoon and the barbarous beatings. Naked and shivering, they leaned defiantly into the chilling downpours, half-erect and half-alive, while the typhoon blew buildings down around them. The rains cleansed the bloody gashes that had clotted on their bruised, purplish bodies "like clumps of tar," but the Japanese quickly opened new ones. Sopping and awestruck, the POWs watched silently through the barbed wire. It was almost as if their own emotions, which had long ago been cauterized in order to survive, were being ripped open once again. "No one spoke," said Dyess. "We watched these men . . . and could find no words." The Japanese were equally incredulous—and impatient.

On the third morning, the rains finally let up and commands set Japanese noncoms in motion. After a final flogging saw a hissing whip sever the ears of one of the colonels, suspending it on his shoulder by a long thread of skin, soldiers emerged from the guardhouse carrying rifles, shovels, and picks. The escapes were cut down and their lacerated bodies loaded onto a truck. A sword-carrying Japanese officer climbed into the cab and the truck rolled away in the direction of a nearby schoolhouse. Soon, the sound of two volleys of gunfire snapped across the paddies, shattering the silence in the camp.

Twenty-four hours would pass before the men of the officers' shooting squads learned their fates. Their lives were spared, but they were forbidden from leaving their barracks, except to use the latrine, for one month. Later, Dyess was told that a Japanese officer had done one of the Army colonels, presumably Biggs, the "honor of beheading him personally."

SATURDAY, OCTOBER 3–THURSDAY, OCTOBER 22, 1942
Cabanatuan, Nueva Ecija Province, Luzon

After the storm of the preceding week, the news that the Japanese were offering a ticket out of Cabanatuan was a ray of sunshine streaming into the prisoners' bleak world. Remembered Shofner, "It began, as all big things do in prison, with a rumor."

It was twilight and Shofner was lying on the barracks floor, his head propped on his scarlet and gold football jacket—a relic of his playing days with the Marines' football team in San Diego in the late 1930s—reading a medical text when Hawkins and Dobervich came in.

"Come outside and get some fresh air, Shof," suggested Dobervich, wary of eavesdroppers. "I've got some hot dope for you."

Dobervich revealed that 1,000 men—healthy, "literate laborers"—were being transferred to a new camp. This time, there was a precedent; the Japanese had issued a call for 400 POWs with technical skills weeks earlier. It was unknown, however, whether the new detail was destined for Japan, China, or Mindanao, the southernmost island of the Philippines.

"Any place would be an improvement on this hole," said Dobervich.

Hawkins and Shofner agreed. The three Marines were the first to submit their names.

Though they were wary of being shipped to Japan, where there would be no chance of escape or recapture by friendly forces, many POWs felt that signing up was a necessary risk. In less than six months, nearly 3,000 of their comrades had died. But some prisoners were having difficulty making up their minds. Steve Mellnik waited for reasonably solid information from his high-ranking friends that the detail was headed to Mindanao before signing up.

Dyess decided to put his fate in a deck of cards. He dealt himself two poker hands, the north hand representing Cabanatuan and the south hand the blind possibility of Mindanao. He laid the cards flat in front of him; north lost to a pair of aces. "My own choice was simpler," said Grashio. "When Ed told me he had signed up, I did too." Though his health was failing, Bert Bank could not resist the gravitational pull of Dyess's personality, either. "Where he goes," Bank explained, "I was going."

Examining the manifest, Hawkins noticed Melvyn McCoy's name. He was not yet acquainted with McCoy, but he was well enough acquainted with the officer's reputation to feel confident in his own decision. As Hawkins would learn, McCoy had his reasons for signing up. The promise of more food and the opportunity to escape Cabanatuan certainly were influencing factors, but for the shrewd logician, the decision was almost purely, and appropriately, a numerical one.

"I was interested in Mindanao because, although I had had no news for some time, I knew that island to be just 600 miles closer to the Netherlands Indies, New Guinea and Australia," McCoy later explained. "All areas in which I presumed United States forces to be operating."

CHAPTER 8

The *Erie Maru*

Life is a morning breeze, cool in the hair;
Death is an aged crone whose life is done,
Life is a laughing girl, nude in the sun;
Death gives release from barbs that fate may hurl—
I'll take the barbs, the breeze, the laughing girl.

MONDAY, OCTOBER 26–TUESDAY, OCTOBER 27, 1942
Cabanatuan

They had converged into Cabanatuan individually, by chance, and now they were leaving together, by choice. But the sight of Lieutenant Hozumi, standing imperiously at the gate with a jewel-encrusted sword at his side, caused many to have second thoughts. "We thought it a bad omen that Lieutenant Hozumi should be in command of the operation," said Sam Grashio.

Under a steady gray drizzle and Hozumi's watchful glare, the Iwanaka Unit's 3rd Company marched the 969-man detail out of Cabanatuan. Among the anonymous "good lucks" and "goodbyes," a familiar voice called out to Dobervich, Hawkins, and Shofner. It was that of a sergeant who had taken the young officers, as many seasoned noncoms often did, under his wing in Shanghai. "You three stick together now," he said. "It's three musketeers, you know, all for one and one for all."

The movement was a reverse of the route the prisoners from Corregidor had taken to Cabanatuan nearly five months earlier: they traveled by foot to Cabanatuan City and by rail to Manila, where they slept on the concrete floor of Bilibid Prison. But the Japanese had no parade planned for the following morning. Manila was a ghost town. There were more Japanese flags, which were displayed on nearly every building, than people. There were underfed calesa ponies clopping the empty streets, and gaping holes where lampposts once stood; every scrap of metal, as well as other valuables, had been carted off to Japan. "I can't see much of this 'Greater East Asia Co-prosperity' here, can you?" crowed Dobervich.

Prodded into the port area to Pier 7, they sat amid piles of rubble and waited as their ship—identifiable to most by only the number 684 painted on its side—was loaded with cargo. Only a few months earlier, the *Erie Maru*, a decrepit, coal-burning tub with a displacement of 7,000 tons, would have seemed out of place at this mooring, a long, expensive quay built to accommodate luxury liners and thus nicknamed the "Million Dollar Pier." Now in October 1942, the bay was filled with sunken ships whose rusting superstructures and masts protruded up through the surface like so many crooked tombstones in a watery graveyard.

Sam Grashio had not expected first-class accommodations, but he had been optimistic when boarding the ship. "It seemed wonderfully refreshing just to be out of camp and on a ship of any kind," he said. "I should have known better. Anything connected with the Japanese that was half-pleasant or promising always had a catch in it somewhere."

TUESDAY, OCTOBER 27–THURSDAY, NOVEMBER 5, 1942
At sea aboard the Erie Maru, *Philippine Islands*

There were several catches. First of all, the vessel was carrying countless drums of aviation gasoline, meaning that one torpedo could turn the ship into a floating funeral pyre. The chance of such an attack was high because the Japanese had neglected to mark the ship as a prisoner of war transport. Viewed through the periscope of an American submarine, it would look like just another Japanese merchant vessel, an inviting target.

The environment belowdecks was more immediately troubling. The prisoners were crammed into two sweltering, poorly ventilated holds, which had been partitioned into sleeping compartments, ten feet deep, five feet wide, and three feet high, along the bulkheads. The Japanese endeavored to fit twelve men into these berths, which more closely resembled those on the African slave ships than anything offered by modern vessels. Similar, and, in most cases worse, conditions would cause their comrades on other voyages throughout the Far East to refer to these vessels as hellships.

While most prisoners were forced to remain in this malodorous tangle of limbs and filth, some managed to sneak topside and escape the noxious gasoline fumes and colonies of bedbugs and lice. The Marines milled about the ship's afterdeck with hundreds of other prisoners before spying a platform, twelve feet in height, of rice sacks. They scaled the canvas-covered mountain and, finding that there was enough room to lie down, claimed the high ground with nary a complaint from the guards. It was atop this perch that Jack Hawkins caught his first glimpse of Corregidor in nearly six months. The recuperative powers of time had all but healed the Rock's war wounds. Hawkins hardly recognized the island, astonishingly verdant in the fading daylight.

Corregidor, like the prison camps and their collective experiences since December 1941, slid behind them as the ship churned through Manila Bay. On the horizon was the South China Sea, the crossroads of their future. If the ship continued its westerly course, they were headed north, for Japan. South meant Mindanao. Shifty Shofner couldn't resist the opportunity.

"Which one of you boys would like to make a little bet on which way we turn?"

"How are you betting?" asked Hawkins.

"I say we turn south."

Hawkins declined the offer; he, too, thought they were destined for Mindanao. Dobervich, however, was willing to indulge Shofner. After pondering the stakes, Shofner suggested a steak dinner, payable in San Francisco.

"You're on!" agreed Dobervich.

"I hope you win, Shof," said Hawkins, remembering the "four coats cold" winters the Marines had shivered through in China. "In Mindanao, at least, it would be warm."

"Yes, and don't forget, old buddy," Shofner reminded him, "Mindanao is closer to friendly territory."

Hawkins noticed that Shofner's face "turned suddenly thoughtful." Shofner's grin widened much more noticeably when the bow of the *Erie*

Maru plunged due south. It was with great ceremony that he took out his tattered notebook and recorded the victory: "Beaver owes me one steak dinner—Frisco."

The bet and the corresponding discourse lightened a tension-racked moment, but Shofner, competitive even in captivity, kept track of his wagers for a reason—he planned one day to collect.

The *Erie Maru* certainly was no American President liner, but compared to the conditions they had endured throughout the previous half-year, remarked Steve Mellnik, "life aboard ship was sheer luxury." Hoses provided saltwater showers and fresh sea breezes carried off much of the odor emanating from the crude trough latrine, as well as the all-pervading gasoline reek. They were fed clean rice, squash, spinach, dried fish, pork, and chunks of corned beef from cans labeled "Cavite Navy Yard." Some prisoners belowdecks broke into a storeroom and gorged themselves on sardines, pork and beans, and condensed milk.

The generous portions and their captors' relative kindness proved a long-standing theory of Jack Hawkins's: "The reason for this lavish treatment, we learned, was that for the duration of the voyage we were being fed by the Japanese Navy and not by the Army. This confirmed the belief that I had maintained since Shanghai days, that the Japanese Navy was a superior organization in every way to the Japanese Army."

Other than the guards arrayed around the deck, Hozumi's men stayed out of sight, making the actions of the ship's crew more conspicuous. One example was the compassion shown a POW who had been stricken with a strange paralysis. He was carried up from the fetid hold and placed beneath a veranda outside the captain's quarters. He received frequent visits from the captain and gifts of fruit, cigarettes, and vitamin pills from concerned crew members. One shy sailor placed a vase of flowers next to the ill American.

This officer regained use of his legs and would be able to walk off the ship in Mindanao, but two others who had fallen ill in mid-voyage would not be so fortunate. Yet they, too, were shown extreme courtesy and buried with military honors—one at sea and one on land—by the Japanese. This first burial took place after the ship had emerged from the Sibuyan Sea and stopped at the port of Iloilo on the island of Panay to unload some cargo. Dyess and the rest of the prisoners watched solemnly from the deck as the body was lowered into a seaside grave. "The burial scene reminded us that we too probably were destined to fill nameless graves, far from home," said Dyess. Dyess was then suddenly distracted by the sight of two planes on the flight line of an airfield near the dock area. The engines were idling and there were no pilots or ground crewmen within sight. *If only I could reach one of the planes,* he thought. His mind shifted gears from the funeral and the forecasted finite ending to the potential, indeed the possibility, that their temporarily improved position afforded. He wasn't the only one entertaining such a notion.

The three Marines had little to do but talk—to prevent trespassers from seizing their nest atop the rice sacks, they rarely descended to the deck or left their perch unguarded—so escape became a frequent topic of conversation. Emboldened by their full stomachs and beset with boredom, they first considered jumping overboard and simply swimming for the shore. None, however, was willing to put their beliefs in the poor marksmanship of their enemies to the test. That left only one remaining option. That was what Shofner and his new friend wanted to discuss when they climbed up onto the Marines' pallet of rice sacks late one morning.

"I want you to meet Ed Dyess," Shofner said to Hawkins and Dobervich.

"I'm glad to know you both," said Dyess, offering his right hand.

Hawkins could tell Dyess was a fellow Texan by the drawl from his bloody, blistered lips.

"Ed is the one who made that bombing raid with the P-40 on the Japs in Subic Bay," added Shofner.

Hawkins had figured that out, too. The rusty wings pinned on the pilot's tattered shirt had given away his identity; he was *that* Dyess, a semi-celebrity among the POWs.

"That was really a fine piece of work," said Hawkins.

As the four prisoners leaned in their heads, Dyess told the Marines in hushed tones that he was considering launching a mutiny and sailing the ship to Australia. Dyess planned to simultaneously strike the engine room, the radio room, and the bridge. He had already organized a contingent of pilots and airmen and he needed to bring more conspirators into the fold.

"There ought to be enough Naval people on board to run the ship, if we could take her over," said Dyess. "The question is whether or not we could get this gang organized well enough to overpower the Japs on board."

Though the prisoners outnumbered the Japanese nearly five to one, the Marines were skeptical. "They were armed and we were not. We were sick and weak and they were not," said Hawkins. Still, the plan was intriguing enough that they decided to consult with a Navy officer.

"How about McCoy?" suggested Shofner. "He's one of the smartest navigators I know."

Later that afternoon, Dyess pulled the Navy commander aside. McCoy advised Dyess to scuttle the idea immediately. Even if the prisoners were successful in taking control of the ship, he argued, the crew would likely get off a message to the Japanese base at Davao City, ensuring that planes and patrol ships would scramble to intercept the prison barge. The ship was an 8-knotter, he added, too slow to evade any pursuers.

The reality that the timing was simply not right was difficult for Dyess to swallow, but he deferred to McCoy's experience and aborted the plan. "There was always something convincing and compelling in McCoy's advice," Hawkins would note. "It was easy to trust his judgment." Giving up on the concept of escape, however, would not be easy for Dyess. Or the Marines. Nor would it be any easier for McCoy. Unable to forecast their immediate future, they hoped that the rare opportunity provided by the *Erie Maru* would not be their last.

FRIDAY, NOVEMBER 6–SATURDAY, NOVEMBER 7, 1942
Davao, Davao Province, Mindanao

Much to the prisoners' dismay, the *Erie Maru* had not been built for speed. Leaving idyllic islets and a gurgling, foamy wake in the receding distance, the ship had sauntered out of the lower Visayas and through the Surigao Strait into the Pacific, sluggishly skirting the famed Mindanao Deep before its agonizingly slow stretch run down the east coast of Mindanao into Davao Gulf.

The vessel had unloaded some cargo at Davao City the previous day, but the ship then steamed back along the palm-fringed coastline for approximately fifty miles before dropping anchor. Increasingly restless, the prisoners began to wonder if they were ever going to disembark the steamy, rusty tub. Mercifully, at 0800 hours, the ship's public address system crackled to life. "Now hear this, hear this," announced an American voice. "We are at Barrio Lasang on Davao Gulf. We'll disembark and march to Davao Penal Colony twenty-seven kilometers away. Supper will be served at the end of the gangplank. When you leave the ship, form a column at the far end of the pier. That is all."

The announcement came not a moment too soon. Despite the surfeit of food and humane treatment, eleven days had proven the threshold of their endurance. The vessel had become a floating pigsty, a fact not solely attributable to the sow the Japanese had penned on the deck. Motorboats shuttled the prisoners to the pier of the Lasang Lumber Company, where a session of the sun treatment awaited them. "There were trees nearby where we could have waited more comfortably in the shade," said Hawkins, "but this was not Hozumi's way of doing things."

After several hours, they took their lunch of cold, glutinous rice balls and pickled cherries and were ordered to their feet. Waiting at the end of a jungle road was the place about which they had heard so much, yet knew so very little. "As we marched, there was a single question in our minds," said McCoy. "Will this be better than Cabanatuan, where starvation, brutality and death had been our ever-present companions?"

The light of civilization dimmed behind them as they marched deeper into the heart of the jungle, a murky labyrinth of stagnant swamps, decaying vegetation, thickets of bamboo and thick cogon. Their arrival was heralded by a concert of chattering monkeys and cawing green parrots. Immense black pillars of mahogany yawned up through dangling vines to the sky; fat banana leaves and the green, feathery fronds of squat nipa palms formed a canopy that obscured the sun. Night fell quickly, amplifying the cacophony. "Mile after mile the corridor wound on, its walls unbroken by crossroads or clearings," said Dyess. "They really were putting us away this time."

A brief pelting of raindrops soaked their ragged garments and dampened their spirits. The march, difficult in daylight, became nearly impossible in the pitch-black darkness. They groped along, tripping over boulders and stumbling into the potholes that marred the slippery road. Though several rest breaks had been staggered along the route, men began to fall out. Yet surprisingly, there were no "buzzard" squads waiting to bayonet stragglers. Instead, these men were picked up by trucks and driven the rest of the way. Somewhere between the main gate at Cabanatuan and the pilings of the Lasang pier, their miserable lives had accumulated value.

Hawkins and Dobervich hobbled as far as they could until cramps and blistered feet forced them to ride. Only 300 prisoners would finish the hike on foot, but Shofner was one of them—the bullheaded Marine was not giving the Japanese the satisfaction of picking him up.

The trucks rolled beneath an arch made of gargantuan mahogany logs—on which the words "Davao Penal Colony, Established 1932" had been carved, visible in the moonlight—and into a barbed wire compound. It was around 0200 when the prisoners drowsily disembarked and joined the milling throng assembled before a row of long, low-slung buildings wrapped in gray, weathered clapboard surrounded by barbed wire.

Locked into a half-crouch with cramps in his legs, Hawkins saw a stumpy, black-bearded Japanese standing next to Lieutenant Hozumi. Judging by his clothing, a uniform similar to those worn by Japanese soldiers sans insignia, Hawkins presumed that he was a civilian interpreter.

"Well, what are you standing there for?" the man screamed in near-perfect English. "God damn! Crazy Americans! Get inside the buildings."

He then strode over and slapped the nearest prisoner, Dobervich, for emphasis.

"Who the hell does he think he is, Simon Legree?" said Dobervich, rolling his sore jaw.

This behavior was too much for Hozumi, likely exasperated from supervising the movement. He pounced upon the interpreter and delivered a powerful blow that sent the little man staggering backward into a whispering apology. Evidently, slapping prisoners was a prerogative exclusive to Hozumi. Hawkins nudged Dobervich.

"C'mon," he whispered, "let's get in there before somebody gets cracked again."

Illuminated by the weak glow from low-wattage, insect-covered electric bulbs, they staggered along a narrow, sunken aisle of wooden planks before crashing onto the floor in a heap of sodden clothing and sore muscles.

Hawkins soon heard Dobervich's snores, as well as the faint hum of hordes of mosquitoes descending upon them. Soon these sounds were replaced by hacking coughs and shuffling feet, signals that the building was steadily filling with occupants. With dozy eyes, Hawkins saw a large, hungry-looking rat scramble along the rafters and disappear under the eaves of the rusty corrugated-iron roof. He stayed awake just long enough to see Shofner crumple to the floor beside him. And then the faint light radiating from the dim bulbs swinging above them in the cool, whistling night wind flickered out.

CHAPTER 9

A Christmas Dream

Across one brutal, endless year
We with our battle done,
Send you our hearts through time and space
A Christmas gift—our war cleansed souls—

SATURDAY, NOVEMBER 7–THURSDAY, DECEMBER 24, 1942
Davao Penal Colony

Though more than six months and 600 miles removed from the battlefield, embattled bastards they remained. "Nobody was glad to see us," said Sam Grashio.

Not Maj. Kazuo Maeda, the commandant of "Dapecol," the abbreviated name for the Davao Penal Colony. "He stormed about, declaring that he had asked for prisoners capable of doing hard labor," said Steve Mellnik. "Instead, he shouted, he had been sent a batch of walking corpses." Maeda announced that they would receive food to strengthen their weak bodies—but there was, of course, the requisite catch. "Here you will learn about hard labor," Maeda thundered through an interpreter. "Every prisoner will work until he is actually hospitalized. Punishment for malingerers will be severe."

The welcome from the 1,000 Americans already present at Dapecol was cold, too. "To them," observed Grashio, "we seemed like poor relations." Having arrived from the prison camp at Malaybalay in Bukidnon Province comparatively clean and well clothed, with food, footlockers, and even a library, these POWs had experienced none of the cruelty and deprivations that the Luzon POWs had. Eventually, the "country club

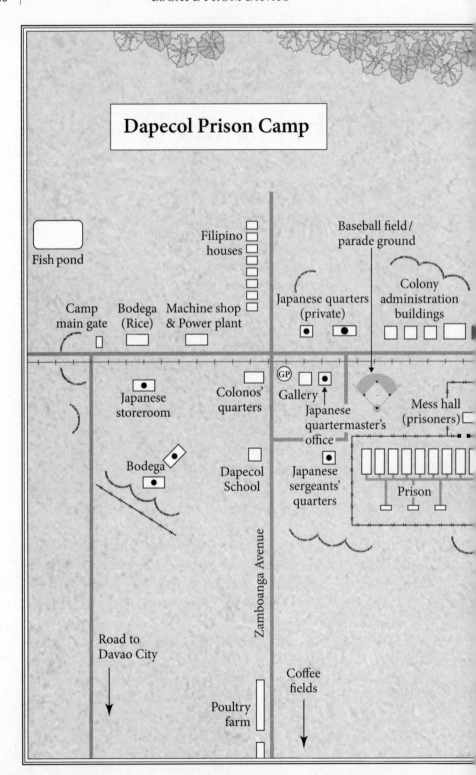

Dapecol Prison Camp

Fish pond

Filipino houses

Baseball field / parade ground

Colony administration buildings

Japanese quarters (private)

Camp main gate

Bodega (Rice)

Machine shop & Power plant

Japanese storeroom

Colonos' quarters

GP Gallery

Mess hall (prisoners)

Japanese quartermaster's office

Bodega

Dapecol School

Japanese sergeants' quarters

Prison

Zamboanga Avenue

Road to Davao City

Poultry farm

Coffee fields

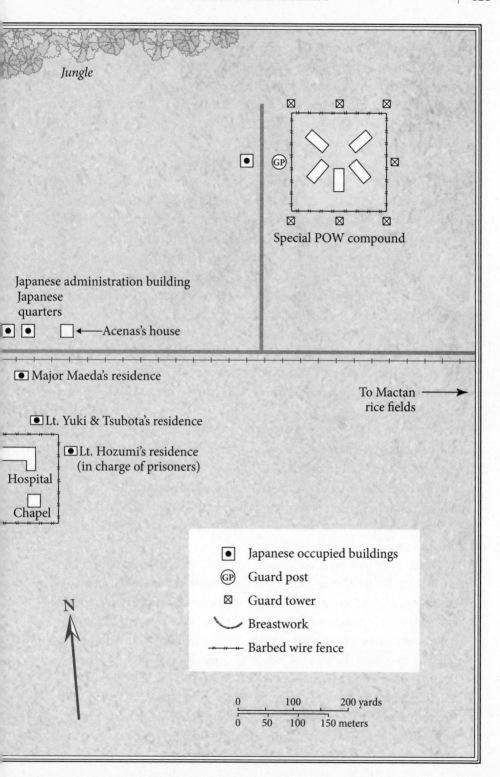

Jungle

Special POW compound

Japanese administration building
Japanese quarters
←——Acenas's house

Major Maeda's residence

To Mactan →
rice fields

Lt. Yuki & Tsubota's residence

Lt. Hozumi's residence
(in charge of prisoners)

Hospital

Chapel

N

Japanese occupied buildings
GP   Guard post
Guard tower
Breastwork
Barbed wire fence

0   100   200 yards
0   50   100   150 meters

boys" from Mindanao extended compassion to their countrymen—with curious results. One gave a tin of sardines to a skeletal newcomer only to watch him turn and sell it. They could not understand what primitive survival instincts their country cousins from Cabanatuan had resorted to.

Only a man who had been through what they had—or one who had been on Bataan—could have understood. Marooned on Mindanao, Leo Boelens had spent the past six months at Malaybalay trying to fix the problem of boredom. He played poker, wrote poetry, repaired cigarette lighters, and read voraciously, taking a particular interest in titles such as Dumas's *The Count of Monte Cristo*. Unlike many of his complacent comrades, Boelens had begun arranging a mental schematic for movement months earlier. "[Fili]Pinos going over hill," he wrote in his diary on May 13. "I think over plans of going." But he stayed, and was reunited with Dyess and Grashio in Dapecol. While giving Dyess a shave, he learned what had transpired in his absence: "The tales they tell about the Death March from Bataan to O'Donnell," Boelens recalled.

Though their current predicament seemed to be more hopeless than the last, Boelens was glad to be among friends. Abandoned by their government, a source of embarrassment for their countrymen, and unwanted by the Japanese, these bastards had no choice but to stick together.

The benefits of hewing a penal colony out of the wilds of Mindanao, as Paulino Santos saw it in the early 1930s, were many. Santos, the pioneering director of the insular government's Bureau of Prisons, believed that not only would a prison plantation reduce overcrowding at Manila's Bilibid Prison, it would also check the suspicious expansion of the Japanese in Mindanao.

Davao City had been occupied, economically speaking, by the Japanese long before the arrival of the Imperial military, ever since Issei entrepreneurs had bought out coconut plantations built by American ex-servicemen—veterans of the Spanish-American War and the Philippine Insurrection—to grow abaca, the fibrous hemp plant used to make rope. By the eve of the war, the Japanese, comprising nearly 20 percent of the total population of Davao Province, controlled the hemp industry—and consequently the local economy—and were poised for a wider invasion. Success of the Greater East Asia Co-Prosperity Sphere, after all, depended on access to the resource-rich hinterlands of Mindanao and all the gold, chrome, manganese, iron, oil, lumber, copra, and fruit contained there. So it was Santos's prescient desire for a large physical barrier that precipitated the creation of the Davao Penal Colony thirty miles north of "Davaokuo" in 1932. With its own hospital, railroad, and power plant, as well as living quarters for 1,000 inmates and a staff of administrators and their families, Dapecol was essentially a self-sustaining city some 140 square miles in size.

Much of the colony's substantial acreage consisted of fields and paddies tended by colonos, as inmates were known. But regardless of their penitential labors, few colonos entertained hope of leaving Dapecol. Since their ranks included some of the commonwealth's most violent criminals—most were serving life sentences for murder—Dapecol was designed as an ultra-maximum-security prison along the lines of Devil's Island, the infamous, reputedly escape-proof colonial jail in French Guiana, and Alcatraz.

Dapecol was surrounded by an impenetrable swamp that served as an intimidating deterrent to any escape plan. Stretching for nearly twenty miles in all directions, the swamp was a mosquito-infested miasma. Although tribes of headhunters reportedly frequented the area, little else but giant insects, poisonous snakes, and Philippine crocodiles lived in the swamp. The colonos and inhabitants of fringe barrios who combined Spanish Catholicism with indigenous beliefs perpetuated the myth that the bog was an evil, supernatural entity. Myth or not, despite the fact that there was no fence ringing the colony's outer perimeter, not a single colono was believed to have escaped from Dapecol in the camp's ten-year existence.

The war, however, brought about a unique, converse phenomenon: fleeing what was essentially a Japanese prefecture, thousands of Davaoeños seeking food and shelter broke *into* Dapecol. While the Japanese army later evicted most of the evacuees, as well as nearly 800 inmates (who were transferred to Iwahig Penal Colony on the island of Palawan), a skeleton crew of agricultural agents and 150 colonos was left behind and tasked, according to the orders of Gen. Hideki Tojo, with teaching 2,000 American POWs how to work the colony.

Forcing POWs to labor for the benefit of an enemy's war effort was forbidden by the Geneva Convention, but Tojo had deemed POW labor essential to the Greater East Asia Co-Prosperity Sphere. A telegram relayed by the Swiss government to the United States in February 1942 stated that, "ALTHOUGH NOT BOUND BY THE CONVENTION RELATIVE TREATMENT OF PRISONERS OF WAR JAPAN WILL APPLY MUTA-TIS MUTANDIS PROVISIONS OF THAT CONVENTION TO AMER-ICAN PRISONERS OF WAR IN ITS POWER." By definition, the Latin expression *mutatis mutandis* represents a substitution of terms; the Japanese translation was that Nippon would observe the convention only insofar as it did not clash with the existing Imperial Way. Tojo had communicated this caveat to the generals who had been assigned responsibility for POW camps during a July conference in Tokyo:

> In Japan, we have our own ideology concerning prisoners of war, which should naturally make their treatment more or less different from that in Europe or America . . . you must place the prisoners under strict discipline and not allow them to lie idle doing nothing but eating freely for even a single day. Their labor and technical skill should be fully utilized . . . toward the prosecution of the Greater East Asiatic War.

There was perhaps no better place for an implementation of this ideology, no other corner of the empire where war prisoners could be more secretively hidden away and their labor more effectively exploited with such minimal investment in their welfare and supervision, than the Davao Penal Colony. In fact, Dapecol was so isolated that many POWs had no idea where on earth they were. Some, judging by what their officers and smuggled maps told them, knew their present location only as a point somewhere seven degrees north of the equator.

And yet, despite Dapecol's seclusion and reputation, the Japanese were taking no chances with their American slaves. Inspecting his surroundings, Jack Hawkins found that the prisoners were being housed inside a heavily guarded rectangular stockade sited at the epicenter of Dapecol—a prison yard within a prison. Hawkins's view, however, was limited to the 72,000-square-foot pen. If he had stood in one of the guard towers that loomed above the thirteen-foot, triple-fenced wall of barbed wire, he could have seen the entire colony in a broad, daylit panorama.

Dapecol was an open, largely treeless compound encircled by an infinite green sea of banana trees and coconut palms. A mile-long main thoroughfare stretched alongside a pair of narrow-gauge railroad tracks on a west–east course that ran parallel to the prisoners' barracks. Lining this road were a number of wooden and nipa structures, mostly warehouses called bodegas, and the colony's machine shop and diesel power plant. At the first intersection was the northern extension of Zamboanga Avenue, where the Filipino administrators' homes were located. A row of administration buildings, as well as guards' quarters, straddled the main road opposite the baseball diamond, which was adjacent to the POW compound. Giant petrified kapok trees anchored the edge of right field while a burbling stream snaked along the left field boundary and through the prisoners' mess area, separating the POW compound from the Japanese officers' billets. Further east, Dapecol's main thoroughfare abruptly ended, leaving only the steel rails, which followed a tapered furrow into the unfathomable depths of the jungle.

Conditions were spartan, but Dapecol was an improvement over Cabanatuan. Spigots and wells provided plenty of water for drinking, bathing, and laundry. There were three large, peculiarly ornate latrines. Just outside the fence, to the right front row of the barracks facing north, was a kitchen and mess hall. There were nine barnlike barracks allotted to the POWs on the basis of rank, starting with enlisted men in Barracks One and progressing to field-grade officers in Barracks Nine. In each, between 150 to 200 men were sardined into fifteen-foot intervals of space called bays. There were approximately sixteen bays per barracks, eight on each side. The Marines had laid claim to a section in the rear corner of Barracks Five called Bay Ten. Hardened by the Darwinian, dog-eat-dog existence at Cabanatuan, Hawkins was caught off guard by the friendly prisoner staring at him from across the aisle.

"How ya doin'?" inquired the stranger, extending his hand. "My name's Sam Grashio."

"Jack Hawkins," he replied, noticing Grashio's wings. "I see you're a flier."

"Yep, I was in Ed Dyess's squadron. Twenty-first Pursuit. Do you know Dyess?"

"Yes, I just met him on the ship the other day," replied Hawkins. "Fine fellow, isn't he?"

"You bet he is; finest in the world. There's nothing the boys in the Twenty-first wouldn't do for Ed."

Grashio then mentioned that he was going to fill his canteen, and offered to do the same for Hawkins. Hawkins handed his over with no hesitation—something he would not have done at Cabanatuan, a place where there was little honor even among thieves. He couldn't quite put his finger on it, but he sensed that there was something different about Grashio.

For the circumspect, close-knit Marines, only time would tell if Grashio was someone who could be trusted with more than a canteen. And time, as any colono could tell them, seemed to stand still at the Davao Penal Colony.

Before dawn, brassy bugle calls blasted across the colony, commencing a tedious routine that would be replayed nearly every morning of every day throughout the next two months. After a breakfast of rice flavored with oleomargarine and starchy, carbohydrate-rich cassava roots, the prisoners were stood at attention, forced to salute the Rising Sun flag—the "flaming asshole," it would come to be called—and counted out for work details. It was an egalitarian system; almost every POW—even the sick and near-crippled, as well as aging officers—was mustered.

Once a detail reached its manpower requirement, it joined the others marching out into the rising daylight. Prisoners went to the bodegas, and to the garage. Others were assigned latrine duty, to chop firewood, or to repair roads and fences. Many labored in the orchards—which overflowed with lemons, limes, papaya, bananas, coconuts, star apples, and jackfruit—or the south fields full of cassava, camotes, corn, peanuts, and sugarcane. Plowers were introduced to a herd of ornery Brahma steers while yet farther south thousands of clucking chickens welcomed those assigned to the poultry farm.

Most climbed aboard rickety flatcars hitched to a small diesel engine waiting on the narrow-gauge track. With a jerk, the tiny, overburdened train—it was soon christened the "Toonerville Trolley," in honor of the popular cartoon strip—rolled away, clicking past abaca and banana groves into a dank jungle where monkeys cavorted. Twenty minutes later, the passengers disembarked at the Mactan rice fields and plunged, barefoot, into the watery squares to plant, weed, or reap the rice crop. Rice was Dapecol's "cash crop" and much of the colony's labor pool and acreage—depending on the season, between 350 and 750 prisoners and as many as 600 paddies—was devoted to its cultivation. The rice detail was undoubtedly the dirtiest, most demanding, and perhaps the most dangerous. The sunken paddies were filled with cobras and rice snakes, but an invisible predator called *Schistosoma japonicum*, a parasite that penetrated sores and cuts, would prove to be their most sinister enemy.

Just beyond Mactan, POWs hauled wet gravel in five-gallon cans from a creek bed onto flatcars. Seven miles down the rail line, others grunted and pulled in two-man teams felling mahogany behemoths with long bucksaws. The trunks of these ironlike hardwoods were so wide that when lying on their sides some were taller than the lumberjacks. The giant logs were shipped by train to the Japanese outpost at Anibogan and then floated downstream on the Tuganay River to the same sawmill whose pier the *Erie Maru* had tied up to.

After spending nearly a week on a bucksaw with Mike Dobervich, Jack Hawkins noticed that Major Maeda possessed a special interest in the logging detail. Upon learning that the Lasang Lumber Company was owned by a Japanese civilian, Hawkins understood why Maeda had been so angry during that first assembly—and why he had promised the prisoners more food. What Tojo called ideology, Maeda considered income. "No doubt by utilizing the free American and Filipino labor to furnish the valuable hardwood logs to the Japanese-owned saw mill down the river, he was finding a very convenient way of augmenting his meager salary," said Hawkins.

The prisoners, in turn, exploited their jobs to supplement their rations. Although the Japanese instituted searches to prevent them from pilfering fruits and vegetables, many poured egg yolks into their canteens and used secret pockets in their uniforms and musette bags, as well as hollowed-out heels of wooden shoes, to conceal food. None of these would-be thieves and smugglers became as accomplished as the Marines, whose potluck assignments had taken them to all corners of Dapecol, enabling them to sample nearly every type of food grown there. Not only did they cure their scurvy with stolen lemons, limes, and papaya, they gained weight. Hawkins gained an incredible thirty pounds in six weeks by scarfing down contraband bananas and Dobervich gained even more, so much that his bulging waistline became a source of amusement for Shofner. Claiming that Dobervich's waist was thirty-nine inches, Shofner goaded the latter into a bet, then magically produced a measuring tape. The end result added one more "steak dinner, Frisco" to the list in his notebook. The unselfish Marines also shared the fruits of their labors with those who were less fortunate: one-fourth of their smuggled food was donated to the patients in the POW hospital who were unable to forage for themselves.

Relationships with the Filipinos, both civilian and convict, were additional fringe benefits of their labors. The Americans were understandably wary of the convicts in the bright orange fatigues, but "the gentlemen prisoners," as the colonos called the Americans, soon learned that they shared a common enemy. The colonos despised the Japanese not only as invaders of their homeland, but also because they had not fulfilled their promises of amnesty. To spite their deceitful new wardens, they taught the Americans the art of goldbricking. "They showed us how to appear very, very busy without actually doing anything," said Ed Dyess. "We mastered the trick." Grateful, Dyess would pay his new friends the highest possible compliment: "They were the grandest bunch of murderers and cutthroats I have ever known."

Though all civilians, even women and children, were subjected to beatings if they were caught aiding the POWs, many accepted the risk. Prisoners working in the jungle often found fried bananas mysteriously packed in their belongings and their canteens filled with coffee and sugar. Other civilians slipped cigarettes and rice cakes to prisoners working near their homes.

And there were special patriots like Fely Campo. Not long after the Campo clan evacuated to Dapecol, the nineteen-year-old nursing school graduate was called by the Japanese to work at the Filipino hospital. When the Americans arrived, the eye-catching, raven-tressed Campo responded to her own orders. She threw quinine pills into the wire stockade and smuggled needles to doctors by sewing them in the hemlines of her skirts. She conspired with a chaplain to clothe the prisoners, giving the priest shirts, which he layered beneath his cassock and distributed during services. Few prisoners learned her real name, but Campo's sobriquet—the "Florence Nightingale of Dapecol"—proved that her daring efforts were greatly appreciated.

Not all of the aid, however, was material. One day, a little girl and boy, only three or four years old, toddled out to the spot where Hawkins and Dobervich were cutting grass in a ditch and spontaneously broke into a rendition of "God Bless America." Their Formosan guard, a choked-up Hawkins noticed, paid no attention to the performance because he did not understand what the children were singing. "But Mike and I did," said

Hawkins. "This was the indomitable spirit of the Philippines, alive and dominant even in its tiny children."

Their itinerant labors also more closely acquainted them with their jailers. Because of rampant disease and the awful odors, the Japanese had mostly stayed on the periphery of previous camps. But at Dapecol, captors and captives regularly mixed, creating a unique new vantage point.

The prisoners rarely saw Major Maeda. And what they did see was hardly impressive. Five feet tall with horn-rimmed glasses, a single gold tooth and a double chin, Maeda "looked the nearest thing to a pig for a human being that I ever saw in my life," recalled one POW. The fifty-three-year-old officer was also reportedly a heavy drinker. A 1910 graduate of the Imperial Army Academy at Ichigaya, Maeda preferred to while away the war in a beer- and sake-soused state of seclusion, making rare public appearances clothed in rumpled fatigues or a kimono.

Maeda's nefarious subordinate, Hozumi, on the other hand, was sober and stern, obsessed with discipline and disconcertingly omnipresent; one never knew when he might strut out from the jungle for a surprise inspection. He regularly abused his guards, but there was no better indication of the terror he inspired among his own men than after one had been caught stealing a prisoner's watch—Maeda, in one of his few admirable decrees, had prohibited thievery—the man preferred suicide to facing the tempestuous officer's wrath. Just as his guards could never salute with sufficient smartness, the POWs could never work as productively as Hozumi demanded. "[Hozumi] seemed to be of the opinion that the prisoners could grow enough food for the entire Japanese Army," said one American. According to the prevailing rumor, Hozumi had shamed himself in battle, hence his current assignment. "He seemed bent on proving his bravery by smacking around every American prisoner in reach," noted McCoy.

Some Formosans shared cigarettes and pictures of girlfriends or turned their backs so that the prisoners could steal food, but they were a distinct minority; most of the "Taiwanese yardbirds" shared Hozumi's proclivity for violence and delighted in dispensing vicious beatings. "We have been waiting 100 years to do this to you," one informed a POW. The abuse became so common that prisoners asked each other, "Did you make the 'hit parade' today?" Some guards preferred psychological tools of torture, such as a form of Russian roulette. A guard would place a pistol to a prisoner's head and pull the trigger. The hammer always swung to a dead, relief-filled click and no prisoner was ever believed to have been killed by this sadistic game, but death was not the point of the exercise. "They had the power to kill you if they wanted to, and they kept your nerves on edge with all this harassing they'd do," said one POW.

The only way the prisoners could strike back was with words, so they coined nicknames based on the guards' distinctive physical traits or behavior. Hozumi's dapper dress, vanity, and violent nature earned him the monikers "Tailor's Dummy" and "The Crown Prince of Swat." Maeda's aide, Lt. Hiroshi Oura, aka "Five O'Clock Shadow," always seemed in need of a shave. The prisoners dodged mud slung by an odious guard named "Skeleton Face," and rulings from "The Judge," a corporal rumored to have been a former justice of the peace. "Big Speedo" supervised work in the fields, as well as sadistic subordinates such as "Mussolini." "Clark Gable" had big ears; "Betty Boop" plump cheeks and a bubbly demeanor. Dyess hated to admit it, but a well-built guard called "Robert Taylor," after the American actor, was "genuinely handsome." Though only four foot ten, ninety pounds, Mr. Nishamura lived up to the reputation of his namesake, "Simon Legree," the brutal slave dealer in Harriet Beecher Stowe's *Uncle Tom's Cabin*, and grew to become a giant problem for the POWs. The civilian interpreter, who had reportedly once lived in the United States, enjoyed beating the prisoners with a riding crop or an iron pipe wrapped in leather. Interpreter Shusuke Wada could not match his colleague's affinity for violence, but the bespectacled hunchback was no less animated in his hatred. Always on the move, rushing to order around POWs, he had the best epithet of them all: "Running Wada."

But the guards would be the least of their worries. Impatient with the prisoners' slow recuperation, Maeda rescinded his order for extra rations. He reduced the menu at the prisoners' mess hall—some sardonic wit placed a sign over the entrance proclaiming the building "Ye Old Rice Bowl"—to a watery soup containing kang kong, a thin green weed, and rice ladled proportionally in different-sized scoops according to the labor they performed. Those who worked at Mactan received the highest allowance, 600 grams per day. The smallest scoop, reserved for nonworkers and hospital patients, contained only 450 grams and was called "The Death Dipper." If they were lucky, the rice contained dried, wormy fish, or stringy pieces of carabao that they derisively called "NRA" meat—meaning from the neck, ribs, and anus.

To put their consumption into perspective, consider that a soldier's daily ration in the peacetime U.S. Army was four pounds, seven ounces, or 2,013 grams. At Dapecol, even the most well-fed prisoners were laboring on a fraction of the necessary nutritional requirement. And who could say what they really received since Lt. Sumio Shiraji, the corrupt, overweight quartermaster, often forced the POWs to sign for more supplies than were actually delivered.

They had lived with hunger for months, but it was not until they were literally surrounded by food at Dapecol that it became a universal psychosis. They traded recipes and arranged menus for the restaurants they were going to own at war's end. Their lust was so intense that men no longer ogled pinups and traded tales of amorous liaisons. Instead, they fantasized about food advertisements from old magazines and told lurid stories of home-cooked meals.

As the battle of nutritional attrition raged, the casualties continued to mount. The sick lay on wooden bunks or shelter halves filled with cotton-like kapok fiber, yet without medicine, the hospital staff could not stop or reverse the effects of the POWs' steady deterioration. The Marines' smuggled food and the clandestine help of Fely Campo and other Filipinos could not make enough of a difference.

Unsanitary living conditions worsened the problem. Their barracks were infested by bedbugs and rats scampered over them while they slept. Dengue fever and malaria were unremitting tropical plagues, yet it was the appearance of some bizarre new illnesses that was most alarming. Those suffering from dry beriberi, an affliction that caused excruciating joint pain, massaged their aching hands and feet for days at a time without sleeping. Some hunched for so long that their nutrient-deprived bodies locked into a grotesque state of living rigor mortis. They were also plagued with numerous skin disorders, the worst of which was "rice rash." The *Schistosoma* parasite caused men to scratch their itchy legs raw and bloody, then the parasite caused throbbing headaches and debilitating nausea.

Some men awoke to find that they had lost the use of their arms or legs. One POW suddenly and unexplainably lost the ability to speak. Those stricken with drop foot, a condition caused by paralysis of the flexor muscles of the leg, lurched around in a sad, shuffling gait. One prisoner endured a hernia operation with limited anesthetic only to have each of his 125 stitches burst open after a malaria attack. After forty-two days, the wound finally healed. Less than twenty-four hours after being discharged from the hospital, the POW was assigned to a work detail. Deferments, even for partially paralyzed men, were almost unheard of. American officers, protesting the forced inclusion of malaria patients on work details, were hushed by Maeda: "We treat you like we wish."

Such a policy looked to spell Bert Bank's doom. Bank had lost fifty-five pounds; an attack of wet beriberi had swelled his feet so badly that he had been forced to cut off his shoes; and, worse, he was slowly losing his eyesight due to vitamin deficiency. Each day, his ability to move about, to work—and thus eat—diminished. His friends began dissolving into blurry smudges, recognizable only by their voices. Nevertheless, Bank worked the fields. "Well, hell, I was cutting, instead of the weeds and vines, I was cutting the vegetable stems," he said. While most guards kept hitting him over the head, as if he were a broken machine, one perceptive guard realized Bank's blindness and he was reassigned to a rope-making detail. Other ill or elder prisoners were assigned similar less-taxing tasks such as making straw hats or weaving baskets. One aging officer became Father Time at Dapecol. Since he possessed one of the few functional timepieces, his only duty was to ring the bell that dully heralded the hours throughout the day.

Although the wanton cruelty of Cabanatuan—thus far, reportedly only six prisoners had perished and there were few incidents of outright torture—had as of yet not followed them to Mindanao, Dapecol was on the verge of becoming a death camp. Here, the Japanese seemed content to kill slowly, by starving and working their slaves to death. It was a case of simple, yet fatal, arithmetic: their forced labor burned more calories than they were consuming.

Most prisoners, feeling powerless to alter the trajectory of their fate, continued to work, to waste away, and to acquiesce to the protracted lobotomy of their spirit. But a few, sensing that each POW was only marking time to an inevitable end, were stirred to action.

Melvyn McCoy angrily plunged a handful of rice seedlings into the thigh-high mud and then wiped his furrowed brow. Each of the prisoners in the line mimicked McCoy until a signal from a Filipino adviser shifted them into a sluggish, one-foot retreat, restarting the routine. It was the same silent, choreographed misery on yet another steamy, sun-tortured afternoon in Mactan. Exasperated, McCoy turned to the sweat-drenched POW next to him, Steve Mellnik.

"Steve," whispered McCoy, "we've got to do something to get off this treadmill!"

"Step on it, Mac," warned Mellnik as a guard glanced in their direction and began tramping through the paddy. "The slave driver is coming."

The conversation would to have wait until the evening, outside Barracks Eight. After the workday ended, the two friends—they had met weeks earlier while digging a garbage pit—wandered off for some privacy.

"Did you have anything in mind about getting off this treadmill?" asked Mellnik.

"Nothing specific," answered McCoy, "just an unhappy feeling that we're marking time and getting nowhere. . . . To answer your question, step number one is to find food."

"Are you thinking of a second step?"

"Hell, yes! Escape! I want out," blared McCoy. "I've been watching the guards, I can lose them without half-trying!"

"I'm sure we could give them the slip," agreed Mellnik, but "we'd either starve in the swamp or return to . . . punishment. No, thanks."

"You've got a point," said McCoy. "I suppose the first thing is to find a path through or around that damned swamp. You're the ground soldier, what equipment would we need?"

"Food, shoes, leggings, and medicines—we couldn't move far without quinine."

Further discussion revealed another necessity: absolute secrecy. Fearing that some "hopeless and irrational" men might make their plans known to the Japanese, they decided to pursue the procurement of food and keep the larger, still abstract goal of escape to themselves.

It would not take long for the seed that McCoy had planted to sprout. Days later in the Mactan mire, they heard shouts, repetitive Japanese commands rising in volume, in a nearby paddy. Peering over the dike, they watched as an older Filipino approached an irate guard and bowed deferentially. After some brief words and gesticulations, the Filipino conferred with some Americans who had angered the guard by not gleaning some rice properly. They quickly tidied the area, mollifying the guard.

"Who's the peacemaker?" McCoy asked a nearby POW.

"That's Candido Abrina. He's an agricultural adviser and a good Joe.

Though he brags like hell, he's saved lots of us from getting punished. Everybody calls him Pop."

Impressed, Mellnik sidled up to Abrina later in the day: "This is a lousy war, Pop. When are the Americans coming?"

Abrina grabbed Mellnik's scythe and pretended to perform a demonstration.

"The biggest U.S. convoy in history arrived yesterday!" he replied in an excited tone.

"Where?" asked an incredulous Mellnik. "Lingayen Bay? Aparri? Atimonan?"

"None of those places," whispered Abrina. "In Africa . . . they landed at Oran and Casablanca. Aren't they in Africa?"

Upon spying a guard, Abrina abruptly ended the conversation and moved on.

"Pop can't be dreaming up those African names—he's hearing them over a shortwave set tuned to a U.S. station," said an excited McCoy upon hearing Mellnik's report. "We can trust a Filipino who'll listen to a U.S. broadcast. Let's cultivate him."

Getting close to Abrina was a work detail in itself. Men jostled for space next to him on the Toonerville Trolley. "O.K., gang," he began, passing around a pack of cigarettes, "what do you want to hear?"

"It was easy to see why everyone knew Pop," Mellnik would write. "He was a ham actor and born comic." The jovial, suntanned raconteur with the toothy grin regaled his audience with what Mellnik called "highly improbable" tales of his adventures in sultans' harems and scraps with Moro pirates. In reality, the fifty-five-year-old Abrina had been a cashier at the Philippine National Bank in Davao City. He had moved his family to Dapecol and had been permitted to stay on as an unpaid agricultural adviser. As he was a reservoir of morale in the midst of a severe drought, the veracity of Abrina's tales was inconsequential. The POWs knew on which side his loyalties lay. In serious moments, the fatherly Filipino counseled the prisoners that their misfortune was only temporary. "You must have faith," he would say.

Each day brought McCoy, Mellnik, and Abrina closer. During lunch, Abrina shared the latest rumors and radio news. McCoy soon felt comfortable enough to ask Abrina to assign them to a more nutritionally rewarding detail. Abrina reported that the Japanese were displeased with the poor egg production at the chicken farm. The POWs reacted with blank stares, but they brightened when Abrina added that the colony's fifty-acre cornfield, left untended for months, was ready for harvest. The hens, he explained, needed feed to lay eggs. He had figured out a way to appease both the Japanese and the assistant superintendent, Juan Acenas, while feeding the chickens at the same time. As for feeding the Americans, he had a plan for that, too.

One morning after the rice harvest had ended, two guards accompanied Abrina, McCoy, Mellnik, and fifty prisoners on a half-hour hike to the cornfield. The men faded into the stalks to begin work and Abrina called the two officers over. Mellnik, remembering his own youth as an enlisted man, tried to impress the guards by demonstrating firing positions and a snappy manual of arms; McCoy, academic subjects. There was awkward, icy silence. But the Americans did not know that they were only an opening act.

"In Davao, I sleep with *takusan* [many] girls," declared Abrina with his limited but functional command of Japanese. The guards immediately took notice, their raised eyebrows and grins evincing success where lectures in marksmanship and electrical circuitry had failed.

"Yes," added Abrina, "different girl on each day: Ilocano on Monday, Moro on Tuesday, Portuguese on Wednesday, Chinese on Thursday, Cebuano on Friday, and Russian on Saturday."

"Who on Sunday?" one asked.

Abrina shrugged, as if weary from the schedule: "Church and rest on Sunday—no girls."

Abrina held court for the rest of the day, describing seduction techniques and answering the guards' "embarrassingly probing questions in great detail, all the while strutting and posturing like a debonair but tired Don Juan," remembered Mellnik. While marching back to the camp, the Americans noticed that the guards were so enthralled with Abrina that they paid little attention to their charges. "As [the guards] embraced Pop and called him their *tomodachi* [friend]," said Mellnik, "the latter glanced at us and grinned as if to say, 'See what I did?' "

The plan had been established. But to begin liberating food, more conspirators would have to be brought into the fold, no easy task in a camp full of potential snitches, collaborators, and selfish operators. These individuals would have to be trustworthy, as well as elusive and experienced. As luck would have it, there was a surprise waiting for Mellnik in his bay.

• • •

This time, it was Paul Marshall and Bob Spielman who had arrived with impeccable timing.

"As soon as we got here," said Spielman, "we asked about old friends. It didn't take long to learn that Major Mellnik lived in barracks number eight."

Mellnik had not seen either since Cabanatuan, yet he should not have been surprised to see the two sergeants turn up in Dapecol. They had a knack for that sort of thing. As they explained, they, too, had traveled south aboard the *Erie Maru*, but upon arrival had been impressed into a salt-making detail near Lasang. But there was more to their story. Much more.

It began on Corregidor—sometime in March, in all probability—during one of the many boring lulls between attacks. Marshall's platoon leader believed there was top-quality booze aboard President Quezon's luxury yacht, the *Casiana*, which had been sunk at its moorings in January. The wreck rested in only a few feet of water and its deck was often exposed during low tide. The sergeant found a volunteer in Marshall, a well-built—he stood five foot eight, 150 lbs.—and well-rounded— he was an avid outdoorsman as well as a talented violinist—self-starter whose confident aura and dark, pencil-thin mustache made him seem much older than his twenty-four years. Marshall dove on the wreck and surfaced with two cases of liquid treasure, one each of scotch and Canadian Club whiskey. That was not all he found. Robert Blake Spielman, almost identically adventurous and mustachioed, had swum out to the *Casiana* with similar notions. From that point forward, Marshall and Spielman would become an almost inseparable, sometimes insufferable, dynamic duo destined to cause problems for friend and foe alike.

Case in point: the party thrown later that night, according to Marshall, "got a little out of hand" and landed himself, Spielman, and several other revelers in the jug. They awakened the following morning to throbbing headaches and hangovers made worse by Japanese bombers roaring over Corregidor on an early run. Their jailers ran for cover, but fortunately for Marshall and Spielman, a staff officer both men had befriended during previous duty assignments—Steve Mellnik—arrived just in time to release them.

For Marshall, it would be a temporary furlough. Weeks later, he was weathering a heavy bombardment outside Malinta Tunnel when news came in of casualties at Kindley Field. A Japanese shell had toppled an observation tower and wounded several of Marshall's buddies, but the "old colonel" in charge of the hospital had decided against sending help. "He had only two ambulances and he said that he was damned if he was going to lose them," remembered Marshall. Similarly obstinate, but possessing considerably less rank, Marshall was equally determined not to lose his friends. He "absconded" with an ambulance and barreled down the pockmarked road, weaving around hairpin turns and smoking craters amid exploding shells. After loading the wounded, he reran the mile-long gauntlet only to be greeted by MPs at the tunnel entrance. "That son-of-a-bitch was going to court-martial us," said Marshall. Marshall later admitted to being the "instigator" of perhaps the only party thrown on Corregidor during the battle, but would remain modest and unrepentant regarding the second offense. "We were just lucky, young kids that didn't know any better," he would say. "But, you know, you get a call for help, why, what are you going to do? Sit on your butt? They'd have done the same thing for me."

A static life was no life for Paul Herman Marshall. Since his birth in McCune, Kansas, in 1917, Marshall had been propelled through life by the forces of nature and fate. Much in the same way that the tornadoes of his childhood hustled him into his family's root cellar, the Depression would blow him west, across the Dust Bowl into adulthood in Pueblo, Colorado, where he graduated from high school in 1935. Marshall migrated to California to take a job as a meat salesman with Armour, but the biggest leap came when he wandered into an Army recruiting office in Los Angeles in the winter of 1941. As the potbellied sergeant told him, enlistees had their choice of domestic duty stations or overseas posts. "Where you want to go is the Philippines," he added. "I've done duty twice over there and it is really great, you will *love* it." And so Marshall, a night manager of a supermarket earning a monthly salary of $180, signed his life over to Uncle Sam for a $30-a-month Army paycheck and the promise of adventure. Before shipping out, he gave his father, then working for a Chrysler dealership in Pueblo, his Plymouth with the understanding that a vehicle of comparable value would be waiting for him after what was likely to be, at the most, a one- or two-year absence.

Like Marshall, Bob Spielman had enlisted in the Army to satisfy his hunger for adventure. A rangy, rugged latter-day frontiersman from the South Texas flyspeck of Carrizo Springs, Spielman began chasing work throughout the West at the age of sixteen. Freight trains and a strong sense of self-confidence carried him through Colorado, Wyoming, and into the Civilian Conservation Corps. The fall of 1940 found the tough, teenaged Texan in Cheyenne, breaking horses, bulldogging cattle, and trying to lasso a future. "I rode in the rodeos, but not with a lot of luck," he said. "Lost a lot of skin doing that." The weather was turning cold and Spielman's stomach was rumbling—ranchers laid off their hired hands in the winter—so he signed up at Fort Warren. The Philippines would provide all the adventure he needed.

His rackets were as numerous as they were lucrative. He ran poker and blackjack games, fished from his own sailboat, the *Sea Urchin*, sold octopus to the Chinese operator of the Corregidor PX, and taught illiterate soldiers how to write their names. "Every evening we would go down to the Spiff Bar," recalled Spielman. "They would buy the beer and I taught them to write their name. I would write it and they would trace it . . . they were happy when they were successful." And there were the women.

In Manila, while working as Mellnik's one-man administrative staff at USAFFE, Spielman "spent his spare time 'scouting and patrolling,' " as Mellnik called it. "The large number of breathless girls who called him by phone each day testified to the success of his off-duty efforts!" But Mellnik was impressed by more than just Spielman's little black book. He probably saw a lot of himself in the enterprising, hardworking sergeant. And in Paul Marshall, too. The friendship between Mellnik, Marshall, and Spielman was a rarity within the social caste system of the prewar Army—but it was real. "He could take an enlisted man and shake his hand and walk right along side of him," Marshall would say of Mellnik.

In Cabanatuan, when a malignant case of malaria had crippled Marshall, Spielman would help his enfeebled buddy outside on clear days, propping his ashen, sickly body against the barracks for some fresh air and sunlight. Twice Marshall was taken to the hospital and because staying meant certain death, twice Spielman personally discharged his friend. "We were very, very close," said Marshall. "Like brothers."

Though no stranger to rackets, Spielman was sickened that some unscrupulous men were profiting from hoarded medicine. One day, the immorality in the camp and his best friend's approaching mortality moved him to action. He cornered a known operator and requested a dozen qui-nine pills. When a price was quoted, Spielman jabbed the tip of his mess kit knife into the man's gut. "I have a pal who is about to die and you are going to help him live," said Spielman. The black marketeer, said Spiel-man, "had a change of heart."

After the brief reunion, Mellnik took his old friends to meet McCoy. The foursome exited the barracks to speak privately, which they did while circling the perimeter.

"Steve and I have learned how to amuse guards and keep them tied to one spot," said McCoy. "Meanwhile, you two will gather fruit for the whole detail. This way we reduce the number of people roaming the roads and getting caught. How does that sound?"

"That's okay by us," replied Spielman, enthusiastically. "You and the major are the old-timers. You call the signals; Paul and I will carry the ball."

"You can trust Bob and Paul," Mellnik assured Pop Abrina the following morning. "They're part of my team."

"Then now we are five!" whispered Abrina in delighted, conspirational tones.

At the cornfield, the foragers fanned into the tunnels of coconut and banana trees with burlap bags, their appetites serving as divining rods. Then Abrina went to work on the guards. When McCoy entered the act with his own lascivious litany, Mellnik slipped away to check on Marshall and Spielman. During the midday siesta, the two noncoms parceled out the contents of their bulging bag to the other prisoners. "Major," drawled Spielman, "I think we're gonna live!"

They practiced their roles to perfection over the next few weeks, ben-efiting the entire detail's health. The prisoners gained weight and their sores, depression, and fatigue disappeared. The two sergeants even brought fruit into the compound through an ingenious system in which Spielman played the role of smuggler and Marshall the decoy: the lat-ter was slapped by the guards for moving in ranks, thus drawing atten-tion away from the former as he slipped safely inside. It had been months since their meeting aboard the *Casiana*, but they still had their touch. Despite their accomplishments, late December brought about an inevi-table question.

"Say, Pop," asked McCoy, "what happens when there's no more corn to pick? Could you arrange a work detail for us near meat and vegetables?"

"You left out the pie and ice cream," said Abrina sarcastically. "But for *tomodachis* like you, I'll ask Acenas—he'll have ideas."

Unlike superintendent Pascual Robin, a Japanese collaborator, Juan Acenas had some credibility with the Americans—it was his radio that supplied the news that Abrina transmitted to McCoy. Acenas, lean, bald, and bespectacled, arrived unexpectedly in the cornfield one day. Though there was enough rice and vegetables to increase the prisoners' rations, he told Mellnik, Maeda balked at the proposal. But he did have an idea. Maeda had refused to authorize work on the experimental coffee farm, a project close to the agriculturist's heart.

"Unless we do something soon the heavy undergrowth will kill the trees and our ten years of developmental work," said Acenas.

"Let's tell [Maeda] he can sell coffee beans in Davao City and use the money to buy machinery," said Abrina, continuing Acenas's train of thought. "The old crook will probably keep the money, but who cares?"

Back in the compound that evening, the Americans sat around a fire as a pot of tea simmered. Spielman voiced the thought on each of their minds.

"I'm tired of jail. I want to walk out of here and keep on going."

McCoy agreed. Both their food supply and relative freedom would likely end with the corn detail, he said. Again the voice of reason, Mellnik objected to any rash action.

"We can't take off blindly. For all we know, Jap troops might be bivouaced around the colony! . . . What happens to Pop when four of his men don't show up? What will the Japs do to the corn detail and the men who sleep in our bays? I don't want their lives on my conscience!"

"Those are all valid objections that we should try to overcome by planning," said a partially acquiescent McCoy. "The important thing is to decide to escape. Are you with me?"

After several tense seconds, Marshall broke the silence.

"Commander," he said, "I'm with you on leaving here, and I'll go along with whatever you and the major decide. But I want a fighting chance, not a way-out gamble, for my life."

The impossible problem had been placed in front of McCoy. It was up to him to find a solution.

• • •

To celebrate the Christmas season, as well as the first year of what only the Japanese could consider co-prosperity, Major Maeda had declared a rare holiday from work. Maeda also had promised the prisoners additional food and entertainment. That was why Jack Hawkins and Mike Dobervich had dashed through a torrential downpour toward the camp chapel on a miserably wet, bone-chilling Christmas Eve.

Despite the chorus harmonizing well-known carols, the tension inside was palpable to the crowd, remembered Fely Campo. "The Japanese told us, 'You can talk, you can mix with [the Americans], but no foolish ideas.' " The tension was alleviated somewhat when the Japanese choice for master of ceremonies, 2nd Lt. Kempei Yuki, ascended a stage bedecked with shiny tinsel and opened the unforgettable Dapecol Christmas show of 1942.

Diminutive and decidedly unmilitary in his appearance and demeanor, with kind, almond eyes and a boyish face, the thirty-five-year-old Yuki appeared the antithesis of his superior, Hozumi. The English-speaking enemy officer had done his best to make their voyage on the *Erie Maru* as tolerable as possible, ordering that they receive cookies, candy, and cigarettes on a Japanese holiday. He also attended a POW funeral, bringing a bugler and some flowers he had purchased in Cebu City. When the chaplain concluded the ceremony, Yuki stood at attention with the Americans and saluted. Deemed trustworthy, Yuki would be the closest thing to a friend in a Japanese uniform the prisoners would know.

The first performance was a traditional harvest dance performed by several teenage girls and boys from the families of the colony's administrators. The prisoners were mesmerized not only by the graceful movements, but by the costumes, too; the radiant rainbow woke them from the drudgery of their dreary khaki, green, and brown existence.

As the Filipinos cleared the stage, a prisoners orchestra launched into a set of familiar pieces such as "Stardust" and "Apple Blossom Time." To the homesick POWs, the nostalgic sounds were indistinguishable from those of the big bands of Artie Shaw or Glenn Miller. "It was like a dream there in the dimly-lighted chapel," wrote Hawkins, "listening to the harmony of American dance music." One prisoner noted that the band's theme, played several times throughout the evening, must have been "consciously chosen." It was "Outside of Paradise."

After the musical interlude, there was a murmur of astonishment when the curtain was raised to reveal none other than Mr. Nishamura, the despised interpreter. But Nishamura's skillful rendition of the Charleston amended the prisoners' opinion of their loathsome adversary, if only temporarily. Next, a samurai sword dance and a frighteningly realistic depiction of hara-kiri, Japanese ritual suicide, caused the audience to shudder.

As the American portion of the program began, a wave of communal laughter, starting with the Japanese officers and guards seated in the front rows, washed over the audience. There was wild applause for the Jewish private from the Bronx and an Italian corpsman from Philadelphia who jitterbugged across the stage, for an accordion-playing officer; and, finally, for prisoners from New Mexico who donned face paint and feathers for a traditional Native American dance and contributed an uproarious impersonation of Carmen Miranda.

"The difference between friend and foe [was] forgotten, and everybody in the audience united by a common feeling of enjoyment and laughter," wrote Fely Campo's father, Anastacio. "Cigarettes and presents were passed around in the friendly atmosphere of peace and goodwill among all of us." The entire audience had just barely finished singing "Auld Lang Syne," recalled Fely Campo, when a gong abruptly ended the convivial atmosphere. "Everybody out," ordered the Japanese. "Go back to barracks."

Upon exiting, each prisoner collected a rice stick fried in coconut oil from the altruistic Filipinos. As they filed back to their barracks or to midnight mass, the music, dancing children, and laughter conjured memories of their loved ones and better times which had long been relegated to the cobwebbed corners of their minds. Misty-eyed, they did not need the sign that had been erected near the chapel—"Los Angeles City Limits. City Hall 11936 kilometers"—to remind them that they were far from home on this holiest of nights.

In Barracks Five, Jack Hawkins was lying beneath his mosquito net, wide awake. "Suddenly I was overcome by a surging desire to burst out of the nightmare life had become," he related. Impulsively, he reached under the net, tapped Dobervich, and inquired if he was awake.

"Yeah," grunted Dobervich, woozily.

"I was just thinking," said Hawkins. "I don't know how it will be, but we're not going to spend another Christmas like this."

CHAPTER 10

A Big Crowd

I probed the whirling darkness while the rain
Played on the nipa with a rhythmic stamp . . .

FRIDAY, JANUARY 29–SUNDAY, FEBRUARY 14, 1943
Davao Penal Colony

C rankcase oil and powdered lime kept the flies in check, yet nothing could stop the latrine rumors from proliferating. Some wiseacre had tacked up an appropriate sign over the latrines that read, "KGEI."

Generally, the reports just smelled funny: the Navy was operating near the Celebes Islands, just south of Mindanao; actress Deanna Durbin was dead; a new Ford awaited each prisoner at home. Other rumors, such as that yarn about the Red Cross packages, were more offensive to the ear. Most of the POWs thought the story that they would be receiving relief parcels was a cruel hoax similar to the rumors about the repatriation ships. The matter was settled on the unforgettable afternoon of January 29.

"It's Christmas, Commander McCoy!" shouted a sailor. "It's Christmas!"

McCoy, aware that the holiday had passed—and that some prisoners were going stir-crazy in captivity—requested an explanation.

"Stuff from home," came the reply. "Boxes from the States. Red Cross boxes."

Throughout the compound, prisoners could not believe their eyes— nor their fingers. "Hands trembled as they tore the boxes open," one of McCoy's POW peers would write. "Eyes sparkled as edible treasures were pulled forth and held up to public view, while hardbitten, battle-scarred soldiers and sailors, exactly like children on Christmas morning, shouted excitedly: "*Look* what *I've* got!"

Each POW received approximately two boxes, fifteen-pound cardboard cornucopias containing cans of corned beef and salmon, sardines, coffee, instant cocoa, jam, and chocolate bars, as well as butter, cheese, and powdered milk. There was even clothing and toiletries. Vitamin tablets, sulfa drugs, anesthetics, and quinine, too. From a morale standpoint, most important were the labels: Kraft cheese, Welch's Grapelade, Domino sugar, Swan Pure White Floating soap. The name brands served as familiar symbols of home, thoughtfully packed, canned, and vacuum-sealed evidence that they had not been forgotten. "As each prisoner ripped open a box, I suspect that there were many besides myself who worked with a catch in the throat," recalled McCoy.

The rejuvenating effect was almost instantaneous. Within days, bedridden men walked; mangy beards, unsightly ulcers, and rashes disappeared; spirits soared. Savoring the bliss of their sated appetites with after-dinner smokes—though the Japanese had rifled the boxes, plenty of packs of Camels and Chesterfields remained—they even began talking about sex again. And at least one of them began again to entertain thoughts of another taboo subject.

The belated Christmas gifts had arrived not a moment too soon for Ed Dyess. His legs were scarred with tropical ulcers; an infected finger had almost been amputated; and the mass of scurvy blisters in his mouth had at one time been so painful that he could hardly eat. Smuggled fruit cured his scurvy, but for every step forward Dyess invariably took two back: at Christmas, he was besieged with malaria and a nasty skin infection. "Ailments always went in pairs for me," he lamented. Fortunately for Dyess, Sam Grashio had landed a regular assignment in the Japanese kitchen, the most coveted of camp jobs. It was there that he met Abe-san, the mess sergeant, a Tokyo tailor in civilian life who had sized up Grashio and taken a liking to him. Abe-san stood up to other Japanese on his behalf and let him snitch scraps, which essentially kept Dyess alive until the timely arrival of the Red Cross packages.

On the heels of that seminal event was another surprising development: the Japanese distributed a series of postcards to the prisoners, for most the first opportunity they had had to communicate with their loved ones since before the fall of the Philippines. They were not postcards in the traditional sense, but formulaic comment cards by which a POW could complete an unfinished sentence or underscore given words—the second item, for example, "My health is—," provided four choices: "excellent; good; fair; poor"—and communicate his condition.

Predictably, the Japanese sought to censor the cards, lest a prisoner's statements cast an unfavorable light on Imperial hospitality. For the most part, the POWs were equal to the task. Some sought to communicate through codes and Bible verses. Of the latter, Second Corinthians, first chapter, eighth verse, was a favorite: "For we would not, brethren, have you ignorant of the affliction which came upon us in Asia. We were crushed beyond measure—beyond our strength, so that we were weary even of life." One POW, however, attempted to divulge his whereabouts by stating that his new home would be "built seven yards north and one-hundred and twenty-five yards east of the old one." The Japanese, recognizing the latitudinal and longitudinal coordinates for Dapecol, sentenced the offender to one month of solitary confinement.

One prisoner mentioned that he was working on a chicken farm, but when the card was returned for his signature, discovered that the words "for the use of the Americans" had been added. Suspicious of Japanese intentions, many did not take the exercise seriously. A dubious Leo Boelens bet a friend that he would arrive home before his card. Another prisoner directed his senator to oppose any attempts at reinstituting Prohibition in his absence. And, sadly, there was one POW with no one to write to. So he addressed his card to Dorothy Lamour.

Though he had no idea whether the cards would reach his wife in Illinois, a resurgent Dyess had been convinced of something else, as evinced in a prophetic postcript: "I will be home."

Nineteen forty-three, by all early indications, certainly looked to be a year of change. In addition to the arrival of the Red Cross parcels, Major Maeda had abolished the whimsical work assignment system, giving most prisoners regular jobs in an effort to improve efficiency.

While Grashio and Boelens continued in the Japanese kitchen and in the machine shop, respectively, Dyess had spent time on the plowing detail, an exercise in futility, if not hilarity. "We would go tearing around, the Americans swearing at the cattle, the Japs swearing at the Americans and the cattle bellowing at both the Americans and the Japs," he remembered. "After a day's plowing, the field looked as if it had been dive-bombed, strafed, and had been fought over by tanks in a major engagement." Nevertheless, the Japanese thought enough of Dyess's skills to put him in charge of driving the camp bull cart. It was a military demotion if there ever was one. Here was the celebrated hero who had attacked enemy ships in Subic Bay at speeds of several hundred miles per hour now creaking around the camp in a rickety cart that resembled a frontier buckboard.

Though initially indignant, Dyess warmed to the assignment. He had a good relationship with the carabao, which he named Betsy. He had no immediate overseer, either, nor did he have to work in the Mactan mud. The cart, which transported produce, tools, and supplies around the camp, was at first inspected at all checkpoints, guardhouses, and gates. Then Dyess noticed that as the guards became accustomed to his face, their attitudes grew more relaxed. Waving him along with a greeting or a light for his cigarette, they thought little of his movements.

It was about this time that the Japanese instituted English classes for the guards and Dyess became one of the instructors. Since the Japanese wanted to learn only "cursing" words, the classes deprived the prisoners of a favorite pastime—calling their captors unprintable names to their faces—but "it was the nearest we ever came to good-natured kidding with our captors," he would say.

For Dyess, though, it was all an act. Suppressing his hatred to become, in his own words, "the camp's No. 1 good will ambassador," he saw a window of opportunity opened by his new social status and improved health. "I figured it was time," he said, "to begin cashing in." He wasn't the only one.

As Pop Abrina predicted, the appeal to Major Maeda's pocketbook succeeded. Each morning, Abrina's troupe, the main ensemble of McCoy, Mellnik, Marshall, and Spielman, plus fifteen or twenty supporting cast members, formed up at the main gate. After Abrina barked the name and number of POWs in a hodgepodge of Spanish and Japanese, "*Café, ni-ju-ichi!*" (Coffee, 21), the sentry then chalked the figure on the blackboard and waved the prisoners on to the coffee fields and, unwittingly, another day of larceny and lavish feasts.

Although highly rewarding, their act had become considerably more complicated, not to mention hazardous. An early reconnaissance had revealed that the coffee patch was bordered by the colony's chicken farm. "There's our meat ration," McCoy had said, licking his lips and looking at the wire coops full of thousands of clucking hens. "All we need now is a bit of luck and guts."

"And a helluva lot more information!" added an ever-pragmatic Mellnik.

The chicken farm was almost as heavily guarded as the main POW compound. Above the barbed wire perimeter fence that surrounded the henhouses was a thirty-foot watchtower. Dense jungle bounded the pen on two sides and there were about twenty-five yards of open space separating the edge of the coffee patch and the coops, leaving only one logical approach via a foliage-lined cart trail. Additional reconnaissance revealed that the lone guard rarely appeared between noon and one o'clock, when he took his post-lunch nap.

The plan, which Mellnik named "Operation Chicken," required each man to perform a specific role. While the "snatcher" was directly responsible for entering the enclosure and retrieving the chickens, the "watcher" patrolled the access trail. The role of the "guard sitter" was to prevent any guards from wandering onto the scene. The "coordinator," stationed in a concealed position near the "snatcher" and the insertion point, a camouflaged depression beneath the fence, was the triggerman. He communicated through simple signals: raised hands indicated "all clear"; doffing a hat and wiping one's brow postponed the insertion. Once the snatcher entered the enclosure, the coordinator "talked" to him by throwing pebbles. A single pebble bouncing off the roof served as a warning; a handful was a general alarm. Once safely inside, the snatcher purloined as much poultry and as many eggs as he could. "We made it a point of honor never to take less than two [chickens] on a single raid," said McCoy.

Hardly a day passed without the sound of pebbles clanking off the galvanized iron roofs. Each successful mission seemed to raise the stakes ever higher, with freelancing guards and squawking hens breeding an increasingly disturbing amount of close calls. More than once, no small bit of luck was the difference between a last-second, feather-filled flight and capture. On one memorable mission, Marshall climbed the rafters of a bodega and hung for thirty heart-pounding minutes as a group of guards milled below him. "It was risky," Spielman admitted, "but not as risky as being too weak to actually escape."

Their synchronized stealth enabled them to liberate 133 chickens in three months. The hens were "quanned" with vegetables in five-gallon "quan" cans in the coffee fields, "quanned" meaning to clean and cook the birds. The single most important word in the prisoners' vocabulary, "quan" was derived from the Tagalog "kuwan." Although primarily used to describe anything edible, it became a "whatchamacallit," an all-purpose linguistic widget that grew to possess multiple meanings and uses.

Though they did smuggle in food for needy POWs, the chicken thieves held their quanning parties—chicken-sharing parties, that is— in the fields to avoid bringing the stolen birds inside the compound. The source of the quan had to be kept secret because the Japanese wanted desperately to solve the mystery of the missing hens. "After we had stolen 75 of these chickens the Japanese noted their losses," said McCoy. "Thereafter we had to work with infinitely more guile, for we knew that, if caught, we would be punished with a severity ranging from a mere flogging to death by torture."

Confounded, the Japanese took out their frustrations on the chickens: one POW witnessed a guard throw a hen against a wall in some strange method of interrogation; the Japanese also withheld feed as punishment for the chickens' lack of egg production or else their perceived complicity in allowing the Americans to snatch their eggs. Of course, such odd behavior was not unusual. The Americans had seen their bedeviled captors pry open the hoods of broken-down trucks and beat engines—in effect, punishing the recalcitrant motors—with sticks. Another sliced the tail off a stubborn bull on the plowing detail so that the animal would "lose face" among his peers. A nerve-racked Pop Abrina, however, did not find the Americans' antics or the responses of the bumbling Japanese entertaining. "You're taking a big gamble every day!" he told McCoy. "And one of these times you'll lose!"

The plotters decided that they had to tell their Filipino friend about their inchoate escape plan. It fell upon Mellnik to break the news one day during lunch.

"We must tell the world what the Japanese are doing in the Philippines," he declared. "We must make the horrors of O'Donnell, Cabanatuan and Davao a matter of record. And we have a once-in-a-lifetime opportunity to reach MacArthur's headquarters and influence history. We can't do it alone, Pop; we need your help!"

Abrina was not moved by Mellnik's plea. Abrina was so startled, in fact, that he avoided the conspirators, renouncing his vow of silence only to denounce McCoy several days later.

"You and the major [Mellnik] are crazy," he said to McCoy, "because you risk your lives for nothing. It's impossible to escape—no one has yet tried! How will you cross the swamp? What will you do about the head-hunters who live on the other side?"

Perhaps it was his latent patriotism, or else it was the thought of participating in a real adventure, instead of living vicariously through fabricated tales, that brought Abrina around. He approached the two officers, the raconteur's gleam evident in his eyes.

"I was thinking, Major, that a convict might lead you through that swamp! But you'd have to offer him something."

"We have influence in high places," chimed in McCoy, elatedly, before explaining that Mellnik had worked for MacArthur. They could not promise anything, but they would do everything in their power to secure a pardon for any colono who assisted them.

Abrina's support was a major coup—they would need as much help as they could get. The Second World War was filled with countless impossible missions, but perhaps none more inherently difficult to execute than escaping from a Japanese prison camp. Some Allied POWs, officers mostly, felt duty-bound to attempt to escape. A few even succeeded. Handfuls of Australians, Britons, and Dutch were able to filter from Ambon, Borneo, Burma, Hong Kong, and Thailand to friendly territory. Mostly, those rare successes were small-scale escapes, piecemeal breakouts by lone actors or pairs of POWs.

But for every success story, there were hundreds of failures, almost all of which were fatal. According to one American POW who recorded a history of escapes at Cabanatuan, it was estimated that of the twenty-three prisoners who attempted to escape, fourteen were executed outright. The fates of the others—many of those recaptured were removed to other places of incarceration or else executed elsewhere—were immediately unknown, suggesting a terrible success rate. That dismal percentage was a deterrent itself, yet there were a multitude of other reasons why the vast majority of Allied prisoners in Japanese hands did not seriously entertain thoughts of escape.

If, as the preeminent POW researcher Gavan Daws suggests that, a prisoner's white skin was a "prison uniform he could never take off," his generally poor health was a weighty ball-and-chain. Men living in a near-death state knew that they could not survive on the lam in a dense, malarial jungle. The Japanese line of thinking was clear: feeding or caring for the prisoners' medical needs might have the corollary effect that they would grow strong enough to escape or harm their captors. So, opined one Dapecol POW, "they didn't, and we didn't."

The shooting squads and the grisly public torture spectacles also curbed most prisoners' desire to stray. The kowtowing of their officers to the Japanese in some cases bordered on treason, and, in many camps, an escape attempt would require them first to elude perimeter guard details composed of their comrades.

Geography was perhaps the most formidable impediment to freedom. Nearly all Allied POWs were surrounded by Japanese troop concentrations in depth on land and by thousands of miles of water patrolled by the Imperial Navy. On Mindanao, the further the group ventured from Dapecol, the more dangerous its situation would be. The swamp that encircled the penal colony was only the first hurdle. "The question was, 'how do we rejoin the forces?' " said Spielman. "There is no point in escaping and hiding underneath a rock somewhere."

After traversing the swamp and sixty miles of jungle, their next goal would be the town of Cateel on the eastern coast of Mindanao. There they would acquire a vessel to sail to Australia, 1,300 miles distant, the closest friendly territory, according to the news reports supplied by Acenas's radio. Despite the distance, McCoy was confident that he could reach the continent by dead reckoning. What he needed was manpower, a crew of at least nine men to staff three watches. Expanding their ranks would diminish their already infinitesimal odds for success, but, as Mellnik had told Abrina, the group had higher, historically significant aspirations. They had no choice but to organize and operate on a grand scale.

Stealing chickens, however, was proving easier than recruiting an escape team. There was already a small pool of potential trustworthy candidates, and all seemed hesitant even to discuss escape, let alone participate. One evening, Mellnik approached Maurice Shoss, a young officer he had known on Corregidor. Shoss's reply was representative: "You must be joking, Steve. No one can escape from here!" Having disclosed their plans to Abrina, who was now actively seeking guides on their behalf, the plotters had passed the proverbial point of no return. A sense of urgency dictated that they move on to the next phase of planning. McCoy ordered that efforts to round out their party be redoubled.

"They must be willing to follow orders, risk their lives, and keep their mouths shut. If they have those qualities, I'll make sailors out of them. Keep your eyes open for such men."

Thanks to Shofner, the Marines had been permanently assigned to the plowing detail. During their rest period, they napped, played bridge, hunted wild pigs, and scavenged fruit for sumptuous banquets cooked in a bamboo clubhouse lodged deep in the banana groves and nearly invisible to the nearest guardhouse. This idyllic existence was made possible because many labor details at Dapecol were unsupervised. Because of Japanese combat losses elsewhere, only a fraction of the 3rd Iwanaka Unit remained to garrison Dapecol. Steadfast in their belief that the swamp made Dapecol escape-proof, Maeda and Hozumi only employed roving patrols to maintain order.

Even so, there was an ominous sign that these halcyon days would not last. Maeda had reduced the prisoners' rations following the arrival of the Red Cross packages and though these supplies were soon exhausted, the rations were not raised. Accordingly, the Marines began making contingency plans. Huddled together as cold rains drummed the tin roof of Barracks Five, they secretly pored over a map of the Pacific and charted distances and terrain. After each session, their focus returned to Australia. Like McCoy's group, this group, too, had deduced that Australia was the closest Allied-held territory. They also possessed McCoy's moxie, believing that only one portion of a sea voyage, the final 400-mile leg from Timor to Darwin, was laden with potential danger. What they did not possess, though, was McCoy's seafaring experience or the necessary Filipino contacts that could turn their plan into reality.

Reaching an impasse with their planning, they nevertheless began to squirrel away cans of food for future developments—though they never actually allowed themselves to discuss just what kind. "We avoided any actual direct conversation about escape," said Hawkins. "We did not formulate any definite plans, but we were thinking. Every night I went to sleep with escape on my mind. Once awakened, the dormant thoughts could not be quieted."

Austin Shofner was doing more than thinking about escape. It was a Thursday night in mid-February. After an hour-long talk in relative seclusion in Barracks Five, Shofner and Ed Dyess had reached an agreement on a tentative joint escape plan: that they would sleep on it. It remains lost to history just who contacted whom first, but the fact remains that both had decided that the timing was right for an escape, that the odds would likely never be more in their favor, and that they could not go it alone. "It still looked good the next night, and we decided to give it a try even if we lost our lives," said Dyess.

"When do we go? Right now? Sure!" exclaimed a breathless Sam Grashio when approached by Dyess. "If we tried to escape and were executed, so what? It would only be faster than staying on to expire of disease or starvation," he explained. "If the escape was successful, I would save my life." Escape had been a regular topic of conversation for Dyess and Boelens, so when Boelens detailed what he could contribute, it became obvious that he had only been awaiting the order to proceed.

Hawkins and Dobervich were intrigued by the proposed interservice partnership, yet characteristically apprehensive at the same time. They were well acquainted with Dyess and Grashio, but Dyess's glowing recommendation of Boelens would not suffice. Before signing on to any venture, especially one with life-or-death consequences, they would have to meet with Dyess's entire team. And the sooner the better. "I felt I was already dead," Hawkins would later say. "I felt I was living on borrowed time." With the clock ticking, a conference was scheduled.

At nightfall, the Marines left Bay 10 singly, at intervals so as not to arouse suspicion, for the rendezvous point: the shed located some fifty feet behind the barracks that served as the prisoners' barbershop. They believed that the shack's proximity to the latrines, more specifically to the odor, would give them the privacy and security they needed.

They had just pulled up three stools when Leo Boelens appeared. Perfunctory handshakes and a few minutes of small talk provided the Marines with all they needed to know. Boelens exuded a quiet confidence and his "rugged, bronzed" face, said Hawkins, revealed "depths of strength and character. . . . I liked what I saw and what I learned."

As soon as Dyess and Grashio arrived, Shofner rose to survey the surrounding area. Satisfied that there were no eavesdroppers, he returned and signaled for the meeting to proceed.

Leaning his angular frame against a post, Dyess struck a match to light a cigarette; the flame illuminated his hunger-chiseled features and serious demeanor. After a whispering sizzle of glowing red tobacco and burning paper, he exhaled his thoughts in hushed tones.

"I've always planned to get away from these little bastards, and I think the time has come to do something about it. I don't have anything definite in mind yet, but if we can get out of here we can try to get to the south by boat. I say the time will be right pretty soon, because things are going to get tougher around here. Look at the chow we're getting now—just like Cabanatuan."

"And we never know when they might start the shooting squad idea here either," interjected Hawkins. "That would stop the whole idea for good."

Dyess nodded in assent. "I've been thinking about that angle, too. We would have to give it up altogether if there was a chance of anything happening to the boys left behind."

Though there was no precedent by which to predict Maeda's response and no accounting for the mercurial Japanese temperament, they all agreed that reprisals would be unlikely.

"I don't believe Maeda would do anything serious," said Dobervich. "If Hozumi were in command, I might have a different opinion."

Their ethical reservations addressed, they next discussed the physical obstacles to an escape, namely, how to leave Mindanao. Dyess outlined two proposals, the first of which called for the escapees to steal an enemy plane, which either Dyess or Grashio could fly to freedom. Capturing a plane, concurred the Marines, was highly unlikely.

"Well, how about the boat?" asked Dyess. "Is there anyone here who could get us to Australia? How about you, Hawk? You studied navigation at the [Naval] Academy, didn't you?"

"Yes, I did, but this is a different problem," said Hawkins, explaining that not only did he have little practical experience, but that he would also be hampered by the lack of charts and instruments. "I'm willing to try, but I want you to know that I don't claim to be an expert."

They needed more than a navigational expert. They needed someone knowledgeable, experienced, and shrewd enough to shepherd the operation. It was Shofner who voiced the name on everyone's lips: McCoy.

"I guarantee he's shrewd. I've been playing poker on the cuff with that boy and I know."

Whether McCoy would throw in his lot with the group was a matter of conjecture, but their mission was clear. "We even went so far as to state exactly what our mission was," said Hawkins. "It was our intention to bring America and the whole world the awful true story of what the Japanese had done and were doing to the survivors of Bataan and Corregidor."

Though their plans were born out of an innate desire for self-preservation, there was more riding on their mission than their own lives. On Christmas Day, the Marines had prepared a huge fruit salad from their stash and taken it to the hospital. The sight of the diseased, emaciated patients had served, by Hawkins's recollections, as a "sobering" impetus to action. By February 1, more than one-third of the POWs occupied a special "sick" compound apart from the main hospital, which had long since reached capacity. They could not have known that the tide of war was slowly turning in America's favor, but they did know that if someone did not do something, the empirical evidence suggested that there would likely be no Americans left in the Philippines to greet Mac-Arthur should he ever fulfill his promise. That "someone," they realized, was them.

"There are a lot of other camps and a lot of lives that could be saved," Shofner reminded the others. "Who knows how many men are in the same rotten boat we're in right now?"

They had kin in misery all over the Far East. The same monstrous ideological momentum that had propelled them into O'Donnell, Cabanatuan, and Dapecol had driven countless Allied prisoners to other levels of hell everywhere from Borneo to mainland Japan. Thousands would continue to die on other death marches, in other camps, and on voyages undertaken in the holds of hellships inconceivably worse than that of the *Erie Maru*. And tens of thousands more had been destined to reach Japan, Manchuria, Burma, and Thailand to toil on docks and in mines and factories owned by companies such as Mitsubishi and Mitsui and on projects with ominous names like the "Death Railway."

"We hoped that by our efforts we might serve in some way to relieve the suffering of those men we left behind, and at the same time arouse the righteous fury of the American people for the punishment of Japan," Hawkins would write. At the very least, they believed that through a startling revelation "tremendous international pressure would be brought to bear on the Japanese," forcing their enemy to make some improvements in their prison camps in order "to regain some of their 'face' lost in the eyes of the civilized world."

They might not have had a complete plan, but they had a powerful purpose. As the meeting adjourned, there was one last important order of business to discuss.

"Don't forget the ball game," said Dyess, "I'm depending on you to play tomorrow, Shof, and you too, Hawk. We've got to beat those Japs if it's the last thing we ever do."

The Japanese had challenged the prisoners to a baseball game, and though few Americans were capable of strenuous activity, the challenge had been accepted. Baseball was, after all, the *American* national pastime. More important, the game was an opportunity for redemption. "This was another Bataan," noted Hawkins, "but this time we were going to be on the winning team."

By Sunday afternoon, excitement had reached a fever pitch. Punctuated by the sounds of balls popping leather, chatter rippled the standing-room-only crowd at the ball field. Hundreds of POWs, civilians, and guards milled along the crowded baselines as a five-piece Filipino prisoners' band blared "Take Me Out to the Ball Game." Hawkins, scratched from the lineup due to an upset stomach, watched with Dobervich from the rickety grandstand as Hozumi and Maeda took their seats in the front row.

Calling the teams together, the umpire, Lieutenant Yuki, tossed a silver peso into the air. Ed Dyess won the toss and elected to bat last. Dyess trotted out to left field and Yuki, his sword dangling from his side, hunched behind Lt. Col. Charles "Polly" Humber, Jr., a former West Point letterman, who sizzled warm-up pitches into Shofner's catcher's mitt. As soon as Yuki commenced the game in accented English—"Batter up!"—the pro-American crowd launched into a fusillade of applause and throaty cheers, turning the hardscrabble field into Yankee Stadium. "Geeve eet to heem, Colonel," yelled a New Mexican POW.

Humber did. Out of an elongated windup, he rifled a pitch past the ear of the first batter that sent the Japanese diving to the dirt. The crowd roared in approval. "Ball one," said Yuki, waving a finger. No sooner had the batter returned to his feet than Humber's next offering struck him in the head. Exploding with pent-up emotion, the crowd cheered lustily as Shofner, feigning concern, helped the woozy Japanese off the field. Adding to the surreal scene, the band spontaneously struck up "Stars and

Stripes Forever." "Hozumi's countenance, always forbidding, darkened like a threatening thundercloud," recalled Hawkins. Despite the overwhelming crowd support, the Americans finished the first inning down 4–0.

A few innings later, the Americans' lead-off hitter, Austin Shofner, hustled to beat out an infield hit. He attempted to steal second base on the next pitch, but malnutrition had siphoned his speed. Seeing the ball arrive before him, he lowered his shoulder and barreled into the second baseman like a freight train. When the dust settled, Shofner was standing proudly atop the base amid of cascade of "hurrays" from the raucous crowd. The Japanese fielder, having dropped the ball in the collision, was covered in dirt and bleeding profusely from the mouth.

The Japanese held a 14–10 advantage heading into the final inning. Humber beaned another enemy batter and then proceeded to strike out the next three. In the bottom half of the inning, a rally knocked in two runs and loaded the bases with just one out, launching the crowd into a frenzy. But consecutive strikeouts ended the game for the Americans. "We'll get 'em next time," promised one dejected prisoner as the crowd filed back to the barracks. There would be no rematch; the Americans had come too close to winning.

The conspirators could not dwell on the most recent Japanese conquest. As Shofner told those gathered at the barber's shed at nightfall for his report, he had spoken to McCoy and more serious matters needed their attention.

"He wants to go all right," explained Shofner, "but he has three other fellows to take along. He says the four of them have already been planning to escape for quite a while."

"Too dangerous with such a big crowd," said Grashio.

They nodded in agreement. Ten would make the group too unwieldy, their plans too vulnerable to discovery. Fast travel, too, would be difficult. Shofner was dispatched to Barracks Eight with a message: the invitation had been extended to McCoy only. He returned with McCoy minutes later.

"I can't let them down," stated McCoy. "Besides, we need more men for mutual protection in the wild country and to handle the sailboat when we put to sea."

McCoy provided some background information on Mellnik, Marshall, and Spielman, but Dyess's group told him they would need more time before they could give him a final answer. The cardsharp, his skills of evaluating and bluffing his opposition having been perfected by thousands of hands of bridge and poker, smiled as he rose to take leave of his suitors.

"Here is one point to consider," said McCoy. "Now that we have betrayed our plans to each other, it will be best to stick together. If we separate, the first group to escape would be the only one to escape. The Japs would take measures after one break to prevent another."

The Dyess group acceded to McCoy's demand. Ten it was.

McCoy, the ranking officer, was appointed their leader through mutual consent. They also decided that each individual, regardless of rank, would have a voice in planning the operation. McCoy's, at least early on, was the loudest.

"All prisoners think a good deal about escape," he said, "mostly because they have little else to do. Hundreds make some plans, but only a few make an effort. That is because the most important factor in an escape is the will to try. One has to want freedom more than anything else in the world. Only then will he calculate all the risks and still be willing to accept them."

McCoy had commenced those calculations, yet all ten men, an extraordinary fraternity united by fate and circumstance, would repeatedly have to demonstrate their determination as they entered into pursuit of their goal. The will to try would be only the first small step, in a manner of speaking, out of the Davao Penal Colony.

CHAPTER 11

The Plan

All night in endless circles that return
Each to the same beginning that I discern
The deep-grooved wheel ruts of the captive's mind
Obliterate the path I search to find.

MONDAY, FEBRUARY 15–SUNDAY, MARCH 14, 1943
Davao Penal Colony

In spite of their iron resolve, the would-be escapees were immediately overwhelmed with the magnitude of their mission. "It was one thing to decide to escape," recalled Sam Grashio, "quite another to determine when, where and how."

They soon realized the necessity of planning their large-scale escape through small-scale strategy: one move, one issue, one day at a time. The high stakes—their lives and the lives of their fellow POWs—demanded such an approach. Ghastly visions of those tortured escapees at Cabanatuan haunted their every thought and move. "We knew that a most careful escape plan, thought out to the last detail, would be required," said Jack Hawkins. "There would have to be an absolute minimum chance of failure."

They began formulating their plan in nightly, lightly attended conferences at the barber's shed (in fact, since any extended association of enlisted men with officers typically raised eyebrows, Paul Marshall and Bob Spielman did not attend a single meeting). During these clandestine gatherings, they addressed an evolving string of problems.

The first move was perhaps the biggest. Before they could think of tra-

158

versing the notorious swamp or navigating the enemy-controlled Pacific, they had to find a way out of the main compound. One by one, ideas were nixed. And then, finally, it hit them: instead of cutting barbed wire fences and eluding searchlights, why not just walk right through the main gate in broad daylight? Thinking conventionally, after all, was not going to enable them to achieve the impossible. The solution lay in their forced labor. An authorized morning exit on a work detail would be doubly advantageous, not only giving them a way out, but also a significant head start. Details were required to return to the compound by five in the afternoon and chances were good that the Japanese, wary of the jungle and its rumored cannibal inhabitants, would not launch a search party until the following morning. Their plan, however, was entirely predicated on being unchaperoned. No guards could be killed or injured in the course of their flight, in order to lessen the risk of reprisals for the POWs left behind. Compounding matters, rumors were rife that reinforcements would soon be arriving to bolster Major Maeda's garrison. As if they did not have enough considerations, an imaginary hourglass had been flipped.

A Sunday, they then decided, would be the best day to escape. The Marines had a built-in excuse to leave the compound: they changed their bulls' grazing grounds on Sundays. And since Grashio would soon be relieved from his duties in the Japanese kitchen, Shofner said that he could see that Grashio was added to the plowing detail. As for getting the others out, McCoy had presciently addressed the problem before the merger of the escape parties. He and Abrina had devised a plan weeks earlier: the coffee pickers, Abrina told Lieutenant Hozumi, wanted to build a rain shelter because many were getting sick as a result of frequent downpours. The work would take place on Sundays and could only spur production. Short-handed and stressed, Hozumi was quick to say "Ok-ka." McCoy, Mellnik, Marshall, and Spielman had been the only ones leaving the compound for the halfhearted labor, but the guards at the main gate had grown accustomed to seeing their faces the past few Sunday mornings.

Unfortunately, there was no known way through or around the swamp, nor any way to know what lay on the other side when—or if—they emerged alive. Or so they had thought. Tipped off to the embryonic escape plans by Abrina, Juan Acenas showed up in the coffee patch one day where he mused about his time in the forestry service, days of yore spent dodging poison darts fired by indigenous tribesmen while mapping the wilds of Davao Province. And then, once he was certain that no Japanese were watching, he got to the point of his visit.

"Pop said you took surveyor training at West Point," Acenas said, pressing a small package containing surveyor's tools and a pencil map of the colony area into Steve Mellnik's hands. He then winked surreptitiously before strolling off. "You might find them interesting."

The map, which charted the area around Dapecol for approximately forty miles, revealed two possible avenues of escape: the railroad cut heading north from Anibogan, and an abandoned trail that started at Dapecol's western boundary and meandered northeast before penetrating the swamp. (Due to heavy Japanese traffic, the jungle road that cut south to Davao City was eliminated from consideration.) Though likely heavily overgrown, the old trail intersected with the railroad at its end, near a barrio some twenty miles north of Dapecol called Lungaog where, according to Acenas, friendly guerrillas might render assistance. Following the rail line was the most direct route, but also the most dangerous, given the Japanese outpost at Anibogan and the fact that a search party would move rapidly along the rails in pursuit. It was an easy decision.

As plans progressed, a preemptive enlistment of heavenly aid made sense to Grashio. Having a Catholic priest along, he reasoned, might make locals more sympathetic. "Everyone accepted the idea as sound," said Grashio, "and also agreed that I had the right man in mind." That man was Father Richard E. Carberry, a thirty-eight-year-old Iowan who had been twice decorated for bravery on Bataan while serving as a chaplain in the 45th Infantry, Philippine Scouts.

They then decided that after a guide was added, membership in their exclusive group would be closed. It was a heart-wrenching decision. Shofner, for example, would have liked to invite John Winterholler, a friend who had been a star athlete at the University of Wyoming, but the debilitated Marine would likely not survive the arduous journey. And it pained Dyess and Grashio to abandon Bert Bank, but Bank's poor physical condition precluded his participation. It was equally difficult for Grashio to work with Motts Tonelli in the Japanese kitchen and not be able to tell Tonelli, "a cool, fearless man who had become a fast friend," about the escape or extend him an invitation. All but necessary accomplices were deliberately kept in the dark. "This was partially for their own protection," said Dyess. "If, after the escape, the Japs should suspect any remaining prisoner of having any advance knowledge of it, that individual's head would be as good as rolling in the sand."

They were also looking out for themselves. The rapid mental deterioration of the prisoners had left them no choice but to use extreme discretion. Stool pigeons potentially lurked behind every palm tree; one careless comment in the latrines might not only result in a miscarriage of their plans, but could conceivably cost them their lives. "PWs on the ragged edge of death would have done anything to improve their lot," explained Mellnik. "Such men came in all ages and sizes; their common denominator was despair."

After compiling a list of essential matériel, they commenced the task of outfitting their exodus. Some key items were already on hand: Dobervich had kept a compass hidden since his capture; McCoy had torn out pages from a navigational table shortly after Corregidor's surrender; Hawkins had managed to hold on to his Hamilton wristwatch. Most of their gear, however, would have to be bought, bartered for, built, or, if deemed absolutely necessary, stolen. Once acquired, the items were inventoried in Shofner's notebook. Missing from those pages, for security reasons, were the stories behind each acquisition.

When he wasn't pilfering tools from the machine shop, Boelens crafted a five-gallon gasoline can into a quan can and fashioned a homemade sextant with the help of a picture from a *Webster's* dictionary. Mellnik complemented Boelens's work by locating an astronomy book, which McCoy used to compile data on the principal stars and to compute right ascensions and declinations of the sun for navigational purposes. A formula based on observation of the pointer stars of the Big Dipper found in a yellowed copy of Ripley's *Believe It or Not!* enabled McCoy to set the accurate time and determine the variation of Hawkins's wristwatch.

While Sam Grashio snatched matches from the Japanese kitchen, Ed Dyess used his bull cart to smuggle fruit into the hospital. The doctor was called away, leaving Dyess alone long enough to grab a quart bottle of quinine pills, some water purification tablets, and a first-aid kit containing sulfa drugs, iodine, and field dressings.

The going price for tins of Spam and corned beef was five packs of cigarettes, so the conspirators parted with their smokes to augment their stocks of canned food. The procurement of food, however, was primarily charged to McCoy, Mellnik, Marshall, and Spielman. They continued Operation Chicken to build the group's collective strength and traded surplus meat for other goods. McCoy also collected socks from each POW and then, over the course of several days, slipped into a bodega near the coffee patch and filled the socks with polished rice.

Claiming that he wanted to draw plans for the home that he was going to build after the war, Hawkins borrowed an engineer's drawing set from an officer who had been captured on Mindanao. Days later he returned the set, minus the protractor and dividers needed for plotting the course of their flight. Hawkins was also charged with procuring the bolos needed to slash their path to freedom. For this difficult task, he solicited the help of an aging colono who had shown them how to build a trap for the wild pigs that rustled in the undergrowth on the colony's boundaries. Unfortunately, the foliage-covered pit netted them not a single pig, though they did snare an unwitting Japanese guard, an event that amused the entire camp. But this time the relationship produced results: the colono delivered three shiny bolos with intricately carved wooden scabbards. Hawkins tried to pay with cash, but the silver-haired Filipino would have none of it. "You kill Japs," he said.

Hawkins attempted to smuggle the long knives inside the compound wrapped in his shirt, but to his horror saw that the Japanese were searching for contraband fruit. Dobervich, thinking on his feet, snatched the bundle and fell out of line, pretending to fill his canteen at a water tank. Leaving the bolos on the ground, he nonchalantly returned to be searched. When the search was completed, the guard waved the detail through the gates, at which time Dobervich hustled over to pick up the bundle, which he carried through the gates unnoticed to several sighs of relief.

After so many other nerve-racking efforts, the list in Shofner's notebook was nearly complete by the first week of March. The whole painstaking process had proved a cathartic endeavor. "We weren't dreaming of getting out of that place," said Shofner. "We were planning it."

McCoy and Spielman were anxious to accelerate the plan. Habitually cautious, Mellnik did his best to temper their enthusiasm. After all, they still needed a competent guide and to cache their equipment and supplies outside the compound. McCoy finally erupted one evening: "What the goddamn hell are we waiting for? If we delay until everyone is well and conditions are perfect, we'll never start." McCoy was right. Each passing day gave Lieutenant Hozumi more time to bring in reinforcements and increased the chances that their plans would be discovered. "We finally resolved to make our break, guide or no guide, before the end of the month," said Hawkins. A date was circled: March 28.

Sam Grashio, always "the most steadfastly enthusiastic member of our little conspiracy," remembered Hawkins, was even more excited than usual.

"Boy, we've got our guides now," said Grashio, breathlessly. "Two of them."

The thunderstruck trio of Hawkins, McCoy, and Shofner, the only conspirators present for this early March conference, blurted questions in rapid-fire fashion.

"Two! What do we want with two, Sam?" boomed Shofner. "Isn't one enough? If we don't watch out, everyone in camp will be in on this deal, and we'll get caught for sure."

"Now don't get excited, Shifty," retorted Grashio. "Keep your shirt on. Wait 'til you have to hear what I have to tell you."

Grashio explained that while digging camotes near the dispensary he had struck up a conversation with a clean-cut, well-spoken colono who worked in the hospital. He made such a good impression that Grashio felt comfortable enough to broach the subject of escape.

"We just talked in generalities," Grashio assured the others.

"Does he want to go with us?" asked Hawkins.

"You bet he does. I began to feel him out after talking awhile, and he jumped at the idea. He's ready to go anytime."

"What's his name?" asked McCoy.

"Benigno de la Cruz. I just call him Ben. And incidentally, he's had training in first aid and pharmacy. That might come in handy."

"We could use a good first aid man," agreed Hawkins. "By the way, what's he in for?"

"Homicide—like most of the others. He says he accidentally killed a fellow in a fight over a girl when he was just a kid."

Six feet tall with dark eyes, wavy black hair, and Spanish features, Ben de la Cruz spoke English, Tagalog, and Visayan, as well as several other Filipino dialects. Born in Bulacan Province, north of Manila in central Luzon, he was raised by a series of relatives, including a doctor who trained him to deliver babies and mend wounds. This knowledge had made him a valuable assistant to Dr. Victoriano Quizon in the Filipino hospital, where he worked with Fely Campo. Even so, he was in Dapecol because of his temper—after dodging a knife thrown by the brother of his paramour, he pulled the weapon from a tree and stabbed his assailant. There was no love lost between de la Cruz and the Japanese, either: he had been attacked by a bayonet-wielding guard and was lucky to have escaped the confrontation with only a broken nose.

"What about the other one, Sam?" asked Shofner. "You said there were two."

"Yes, I'm coming to him. That's Victor—Ben's best friend here in the colony. Ben says he wouldn't want to go without him. He's an expert woodsman and knows all about living in the jungle. But here's the important thing about Victor. He knows the trail to Lungaog! He did some work clearing it before the war."

Both men were potentially invaluable assets, but McCoy remained cautious.

"I'd like to see these boys before we commit ourselves too far."

"It's all arranged," replied Grashio.

He had instructed the Filipinos to walk by the coffee patch the next day so that McCoy's group could evaluate them from afar. McCoy liked what he saw, as well as what he heard after conducting a follow-up interview. Victorio Jumarong, as it turned out, was almost the complete opposite of de la Cruz. Short, stumpy, and slightly older, the illiterate Ilocano spoke little English. Jumarong, too, had been sent to Dapecol for murder; he had killed two men, one in a bolo fencing bout. McCoy sensed that despite their youthful crimes, both were trustworthy. The Filipinos likewise trusted McCoy and they pledged their loyalty to the Americans. Thus the desperate, disparate outfit—consisting of a sailor, a mechanic, a priest, plus pilots, soldiers, Marines, and now murderers—became thirteen.

Despite the portentous significance of their number, Grashio's luck was running that week. One of the plowers had contracted malaria and Shofner arranged to substitute Grashio in his place. The impish practical joker also arranged for Grashio's initiation into the plowing fraternity. Sensing that the city-raised pilot was tentative around the balky Brahma bulls, he conspired to assign Dobervich's bull—the friendliest, but also the most lively and unpredictable of the herd—to Grashio. During the latter's first day on the job, the grinning plowers gathered to watch as Shofner led a wary Grashio toward the tethered beast.

"Now, Sam, there's nothing to be afraid of," he said, nudging Grashio.

"All you have to do is watch his horns. They take a pass at you sometimes, but just keep away from the horns."

"He'll kill me!" shouted a worried Grashio.

Shofner, of course, had neglected to tell Grashio that Dobervich usually began each day by giving the bull a small pinch of salt. The bull, desiring its treat, eagerly trotted toward Grashio, who howled as he executed an about-face and raced through a camote field with his new friend lumbering after him. The plowers convulsed on the ground in laughter.

What little free time the men had was devoted to the same leisure pursuits as in previous prison camps. When not talking about food, they held Bible classes, debates and lectures. Bridge, poker, and cribbage tournaments were popular. Chess, too. After 187 consecutive losses, Spielman finally bested a head-scratching McCoy.

The prisoners' library was off-limits to nonworkers, and since the prisoners who worked all day had no opportunity to use them, the books went largely unread. There was also a small commissary where the prisoners could purchase peanut brittle or moldy tobacco with the token pay they received for their labors. Field officers received 40 pesos; captains and lieutenants, 30 pesos; noncoms and privates received 15 and 10 centavos, respectively. Dyess recalled receiving the equivalent of $10 in occupation currency, but only after signing a statement certifying that he had received $250 in cash, plus food and clothing.

Dyess daringly exacted a small amount of revenge following an event that would be rivaled in the minds of the Dapecol POWs only by the Christmas celebration. On one memorable day, the long-abused prisoners lived vicariously through one gutsy colono, a small Igorot with a long memory who had been flogged for selling tobacco to the Americans. After brooding for several days, he nearly decapitated a napping guard with an ax. As stunned POWs watched, he then diced the body with a bolo, took the guard's rifle, and leapt into the jungle.

Following an impressive funeral, the Japanese gathered the guard's ashes in an urn, which, in keeping with their burial ritual, they placed in a shack along with some rice, meat, sweet cakes, and beer, sustenance for the departed's spiritual journey to the afterworld. When the Japanese returned, however, they were astounded to find the food gone, and empty beer bottles. "It was the first beer I had had in many a day," Dyess later confessed.

• • •

Austin Shofner was determined to execute this mission by the book, even though they were essentially writing their own escape manual. He suggested that they have what in Marine Corps terminology was called a dummy run, a rehearsal of the escape plan to verify the existence of the foot trail to Lungaog and also to see if the groups could be coordinated.

On Sunday, March 14, Boelens, Father Carberry, Marshall, and Spielman remained in the compound while the Marines went out to tend their bulls, this time with Grashio alongside. Almost simultaneously, Dyess, McCoy, and Mellnik departed for the coffee fields. Despite avoiding the main camp thoroughfares and doubling back through the banana and coconut groves to avoid roving patrols, they reached the rendezvous point—the plowers' shack on the opposite side of Dapecol—shortly after the plowers, out of breath but in high spirits, their dispositions congruent with the sunny morning.

"Well, boys, it's going to work," said McCoy. "We had no problem getting here. No trouble at all!"

Grashio and the Marines brightened when McCoy fished two chickens from his musette bag. Preparing lunch was Dobervich's responsibility. "Mike was an enthusiastic cook," said Hawkins. "In fact, enthusiasm was about his only qualification for the culinary art."

Dobervich's pots had just begun to boil when de la Cruz and Jumarong arrived. Grashio made the introductions. It was the first time that the Americans and Filipinos had a chance to become acquainted face-to-face. Their appearances, Hawkins noted, were as dissimilar as their dress. The angular, twenty-five-year-old de la Cruz "was neatly dressed in immaculate blue duck trousers and a blue poplin shirt to match. He had that appearance of utter cleanliness peculiar to the Filipino people." Jumarong stood out with his bright orange Dapecol pants and "look of serious determination in his oval Malayan face."

Leaving Dobervich to cook, the party skulked, one at a time, across the road that led to the nearby guardhouse. After wading through the thick cogon that choked the neglected banana grove bordering the jungle edge for nearly a quarter of a mile, they stood at the imaginary fence line, the invisible boundary separating them from Dapecol and freedom. It did not take Jumarong long to find the mouth of the trail.

"Have you been over this trail before?" McCoy asked.

Jumarong's response was channeled through de la Cruz: "Yes, sir. I know the way."

Wanting to be sure that there was more to the trail than just a beginning, they pressed through the undergrowth. They had penetrated only about 300 yards into the jungle, but the penal colony seemed miles—and hours—away. "Although it was a sunny morning, the darkness in the jungle gave the illusion of approaching nightfall," said Hawkins. They peered up at the dense tropical foliage and with each step, the spongy, puddled jungle floor swallowed their feet. Squadrons of mosquitoes dove upon them and squirming leeches suckled at their legs.

As the others optimistically retraced their steps back to the plowers' shack, Hawkins and Shofner lingered behind to pick the leeches from their legs. Though accustomed to long marches through difficult terrain, the Marines had not seen anything like this.

"It's going to be rough, Jack," said Shofner.

"You said it. This won't be any picnic."

CHAPTER 12

Cat-and-Mouse

All night I lie with eyes that ache to close
And fight my mind which cannot find repose . . .

MONDAY, MARCH 15–FRIDAY, MARCH 26, 1943
Davao Penal Colony

The POWs, so deeply immersed in their secret preparations—
which, up until now, had gone astoundingly well—were probably
unaware of the date. The Marines, to have so brazenly, yet unin-
tentionally, tempted fate, surely were not. They were tying up their bulls
for the evening when Mike Dobervich turned a hungry gaze toward the
onion patch.

"Go ahead, Beaver," said Jack Hawkins. "Get us a couple. There are no
Japs around."

"May as well," said Dobervich. "The Japs will eat 'em all anyway if we
don't get 'em."

Dobervich plucked a handful of green shoots and the Marines had no
sooner started down the road toward the main compound when a red-
haired American officer emerged from the coconut grove, his arms flailing as he charged toward them.

"Put those onions down, you thief. What the hell do you mean going
in my onions?"

"Whadaya mean, *your* onions?" retorted Dobervich. "They're just as
much ours as they are yours or anybody else's. After all, we've been working here all day to plant more."

"Hand 'em here, goddamn it," shouted the officer. "I'm in charge of these onions and if anybody pulls 'em, I'll pull 'em."

"Well here, take 'em," growled Dobervich defiantly, tossing them at the man's feet.

It was called chickenshit. The exchange was typical of the behavior in prison camp that sickened Hawkins. Though they were prisoners of war, Hawkins thought that men should still act like soldiers. And officers, he believed, should be held to a higher degree of accountability. In order to provide an example for the men, they needed to conduct themselves with discipline and dignity. Onion picking was not a court-martialable offense and should not be treated as such. Hawkins believed that there was a reason why the Marines had fared better in captivity than prisoners from other services. "They retained their military customs, their discipline, and their honor in dealing with each other. They tried to do the best they could, and I was proud of them," he would say. Unable to endure the absurdity any longer, Hawkins joined the argument.

"Control yourself. I don't like your language. That's no way to talk to your brother officers and you'd better calm down."

"Who's talking to you?"

At that point, before blows were exchanged, Shofner intervened.

"Come on Hawk, Mike," he reasoned, pushing his two fuming friends down the road.

"You'll hear about this," the officer shouted in the distance.

They did. That evening, they were summoned before the camp's commanding officer, Army Lt. Col. Russell J. Nelson. Finding their antagonist present, they arrived to learn that they had, for all intents and purposes, already been tried for their "crime."

"It has been reported to me that you pulled up five dozen onions from the onion field today," announced Nelson. "As you know this is against the Japanese regulations and I shall have to punish you. We cannot risk getting in trouble with the Japanese in such a way. Have you anything to say?"

"Yes, sir," replied Hawkins, scowling at the informant. "Our reporter here, in addition to being guilty of indecent language and improper conduct, seems to be unable to tell the truth. There were five onions pulled, not five dozen."

"That is immaterial," snapped Nelson. "The Japanese rules were still broken.

"I understand that you three have an enjoyable situation with your plowing—good food and so forth. Lieutenant Dobervich and Lieutenant Hawkins, you are suspended from the plowing detail until further notice. Captain Shofner, since you had nothing to do with this offense you will receive no punishment."

Realizing the consequences of the sentence, Dobervich immediately entered an appeal.

"But sir, we've taken four months to learn plowing. If you put new men in our place they won't get any work done. Why not give us some other punishment that won't interfere with the farming?"

"I realize all those things," replied Nelson. "Possibly after you have had time to redeem yourselves, you will be allowed to return to the plowing detail. This is more of a gesture to pacify the Japanese should they learn about this thing."

Nelson's words revealed that the antique command hierarchy that had been present in other prison camps, one that preferred appeasement of the Japanese to leading men and providing a strong representation for them to their captors, was in effect in Dapecol. There was nothing they could do. The incompetent "Committee of Colonels," as one Dapecol POW mockingly referred to the prisoners' leadership, was the highest court.

"At any normal time this would have been no punishment at all," Hawkins would say of those ominous events on that fateful Ides of March, "but now, when our plans were nearing their climax, it was the most undesirable blow we could have received."

Nonsense—that was Melvyn McCoy's response. They had worked too hard, for too long to see their plans ruined by such a trivial incident. McCoy promised to discuss the matter with Nelson, whom he considered a friend. The Marines also approached Lt. Col. Polly Humber, the chief American agricultural supervisor. Sympathetic, Humber promised to intercede on their behalf, too. "Just wait about a week or two," he reassured them. "I'll talk to the colonel and I'm sure he'll come around."

Two weeks would be cutting it extremely close, but that time frame would permit Dobervich and Hawkins to participate in the escape. Unfortunately, they would not be able to assist in the shuttling of equipment, a residual effect that would have major ramifications. The POWs knew that they could not expect to just walk past the sentries, their clothes bulging with gear, so they had decided to smuggle their supplies out of the compound prior to the escape and cache the items at a concealed location. After careful consideration, they settled on a dense thicket located in a neglected banana grove between the plowers' shack and the jungle. The Japanese rarely patrolled the area, so the chance of their gear being discovered was minimal.

On March 17, as Dobervich and Hawkins reported for work on a pig-pen construction project, the others commenced their clandestine labors. Each escapee was largely responsible for smuggling his own gear out of the compound, a process not too difficult, given the fact that the Japanese had become accustomed to seeing the prisoners departing for work details with musette bags, blankets, and shelter halves, which they used for comfort during rest periods. But after several days, a predictable problem surfaced: the amount of gear brought out by the coffee pickers was too great and there was no way to safely transport it to the makeshift supply depot near the plowers' shack on the other side of the camp. Too great a burden had been placed on the shoulders of Grashio and Shofner. It became apparent that they would not be able to complete the undertaking by March 28, or what Shofner had begun to refer to as "E-Day."

For McCoy and Mellnik, the problem threw a wet blanket on the party thrown by West Point graduates to celebrate Founders Day, the academy's birthday, on March 21. With Japanese permission, the West Pointers had gathered with Annapolis alums near the coffee patch to share food, songs, speeches, and memories. The highlight was the recitation of fake telegrams that had been "delivered" to Dapecol to honor the occasion. There were messages from FDR, Adm. Chester Nimitz, even Joseph Stalin. The telegram "received" from General Hap Arnold, chief of the Army Air Forces, produced the most guffaws. It read: "Have air superiority over Kansas. Don't give up. Help is on the way."

As reverent as they were to tradition, there were more pressing matters at hand; McCoy and Mellnik quietly excused themselves. After much deliberation, it was Ed Dyess, exhibiting his characteristic derring-do, who finally came up with a risky, eleventh-hour resolution.

"Shof, you and Sam just handle the equipment for yourselves, Hawk, Mike and Leo," he announced at conference on the evening of March 23. "I think I can handle it the rest of the way."

SATURDAY, MARCH 27, 1943
Davao Penal Colony

On some level, it had to feel oddly familiar. With the late morning sun reflecting a brassy shimmer off the pilot's wings pinned to his threadbare khaki shirt, Dyess climbed onto his bull cart. The only instruments to check were the crucifix and Saint Christopher medal hanging from his neck. In lieu of an ignition switch, he tugged Betsy's reins and the carabao clopped forward, pulling him once again toward great peril and what would perhaps be the most important mission of his life.

Whether he knew it or not, every act of goodwill he had performed over the previous months had been for this mission. Every cigarette, every friendly wave, every sack of star apples he had given to the guards would be redeemed in the next hour. In one bold stroke, Dyess planned to pack his bull cart with half of the escape party's gear at the coffee patch, then transport the load across the breadth of the penal colony, past numerous guardhouses and sentry posts, to the plowers' shack, where Shofner and Grashio would offload the supplies. If he was caught, there would be no bailing out, no living to fly and fight another day. Failure meant certain death.

While the coffee pickers crouched in the weeds, Steve Mellnik perspired nervously, literally sweating every facet of the mission. Finally, McCoy poked his head through the bushes: "Here he comes!"

With a "whoa, Betsy," Dyess eased the cart to a complete stop. McCoy, Mellnik, Marshall, and Spielman sprang from the brush with their gear, covering it with saplings—which would be declared as fence posts should the Japanese inquire—and fruit, which would also shield the contraband cargo from prying or alert eyes.

"Need any help?" inquired Mellnik as Dyess returned to his primitive cockpit.

"It's a lonesome mission. I'd welcome company."

Once Mellnik settled atop the heaped freight, Dyess maneuvered down a feeder path that bled into a secondary road bisecting the camp. They had bounced along for several hundred yards when the first of three sentry posts along the route appeared on the hazy, heatwave-warped horizon. Seeing the sentry stir inside his hut, Mellnik's mind raced. *Was he alert or dozing? Would he suspect two PWs riding a cart? What would he do if he discovered equipment under the fruit? What would I do?* Swiveling his neck, Dyess interrupted Mellnik's train of thought.

"I've flown this route fifty times," he explained. "Each trip is different. Some sentries always stop me for fruit; others never do. You just can't tell."

After what seemed like an eternity, the cart slowly crawled abreast of the sentry post. Mellnik made frighteningly fleeting eye contact with the guard, then quickly turned his head and swallowed a deep breath. The lethargic guard, likely recognizing Dyess, did not move. Five yards separated them from the sentry post. Then ten. Soon, the shack disappeared in the distance. "I exhaled and went limp," recalled Mellnik.

Betsy plodded forward with leisurely indifference, pulling the creaking cart and its passengers past gun emplacements and beneath guard towers in which sentries with binoculars scanned the jungle prison. The cart moved in slow motion, as if fighting against the torrid tide of heat and humidity inches at a time. For once, Mellnik welcomed the oppressive heat. "I found solace in the steam bath atmosphere," he said. "It would make the sentries less attentive."

Thankfully, that was the case with the second sentry post; the guard had fallen asleep and they passed by with ease. Dyess whistled with optimism.

"One more to go," he chirped.

Mellnik could not believe their luck when the drowsy soldier at the final sentry post waved them by without even a cursory examination—nor what transpired next. To his astonishment, Dyess jerked the cart to a stop and jumped to the ground. Mellnik watched apprehensively as Dyess "stretched luxuriously and saluted the sentry" and then pointed to the cigarette between his lips. Rummaging for matches, the guard, obviously familiar with Dyess, obliged. Dyess exchanged an *"arigato"*—"Thank you"—for a nod and slight bow.

Minutes after the surreal event, Mellnik still could not believe what he had witnessed. He stared at Dyess, puffing contentedly as he steered toward the banana groves, and remembered his Kipling, albeit in a paraphrase, *"You're a braver man than I am, Gunga Din."*

Dyess's celebratory bravado was premature. They arrived at the rendezvous point to find Grashio and Shofner waiting as planned, as well as a guard—perhaps the only one in the camp that Dyess did not know—posted only a few yards up the road. "There was nothing to do but start unloading," said Dyess. "Any funny business then would have been fatal."

Dyess maneuvered the cart between the guard's line of sight and the edge of the road. He and Mellnik unloaded the poles from the side of the cart facing the guard while Grashio and Shofner hurriedly carried the contraband cargo off the other side. In order to shield the gear from the rains and the Japanese, it would be stored in five-gallon gasoline cans that Grashio had acquired from the Japanese kitchen and covered with banana leaves.

Returning to the coffee patch as the workday drew to a close, Mellnik said "silent good-byes" to the men whom he had spent the past few months working and stealing food with, men whom he knew he might never see again. He sensed questions in one prisoner's eyes, a friend he had known since Corregidor—"I was grateful that he did not ask them."

Pop Abrina, feeling similarly sentimental, pulled both McCoy and Mellnik aside and placed some pesos in their hands, a parting gift from Juan Acenas.

"My wife and I prayed for you last night," he said, his voice almost a whisper.

"My God, Pop!" said McCoy. "Did you tell her about us going?"

"She knows I've helped you," he said, nodding. "When I couldn't sleep last night, she asked what was wrong. I told her I was afraid somebody would find your supplies in the coffee patch. So she got down on her knees and prayed!"

When the column marched back to the compound, Abrina paused at the lane leading to his house. McCoy and Mellnik turned to see the middle-aged Filipino standing in the twilight waving goodbye, his fingers forming the V for Victory sign.

As the countdown entered its final hours, the emotional, yet constrained farewells seemed to be the most difficult problems remaining. Dobervich and Hawkins were relieved to learn that their sentence had been commuted, thanks to the efforts of McCoy and their high-ranking friends. Only a few additional items—the most important of which was the quart bottle containing nearly 1,000 quinine tablets that Dyess had pilfered from the pharmacy—needed to be cached, but Shofner had presumably completed that task in the afternoon.

As the last of the conspiring POWs passed through the gates of the main compound that evening, most were confident that the only thing standing between them and their freedom was time. Yet for all their meticulous planning, they had overlooked one important thing. Incredibly, they had forgotten about their universally despised archenemy.

Visibly shaken, Shofner and Grashio returned to Bay Ten that evening and collapsed next to Hawkins.

"What's the matter?" Hawkins asked Shofner. "You look like you've seen a ghost."

Shofner, his mouth bloody and swollen, had almost seen his own. As usual, Lieutenant Hozumi's timing had been near-perfect. At noon, the officer, Simon Legree, and two guards had strutted into the plowers' shack for a surprise inspection—just barely missing Dyess's delivery.

"[Hozumi] caught us with our pants down," said Shofner.

Heavy rains the night before had postponed the plowing, so the plowers had been sitting around enjoying bananas when Hozumi surprised them. Flying into a rage, he ordered the POWs to attention and instructed his cohorts to rummage for contraband food. He then went down the line, slapping the prisoners. "Dogs!" he shrieked. "You steal fruit! Is the fruit of the Japanese empire!" Hozumi saved his full fury for Shofner, the senior officer. The Marine was powerless to do anything but absorb the blows.

"I stood like a post, staring at the horizon across the top of his head. His hand whacked across my face, bringing a trickle of blood. Anger and frustration boiled inside me, but from the corner of my eye I could see a guard with rifle ready, waiting for my slightest move. Hozumi already had his hand on that meatcleaver of his."

Hozumi continued to work Shofner over, but the latter's attention was subconsciously riveted on the guard ransacking the prisoners' belongings. He opened Shofner's musette bag, which contained the bottle of quinine pills that he had not yet stashed. "My heart took a nosedive," Shofner would say. The guard reached inside and, after several excruciating seconds, moved on. He had surely touched the bottle, but he had not been looking for medicine and likely would not have comprehended the presence of the pills anyway. "His orders had been to search for food," Shofner would later reason, and with the Japanese, "orders are orders."

"I didn't feel Hozumi's slaps anymore," he added. "Relief made me numb."

Hozumi finally stormed out with his entourage. One of the guards kicked at Shofner's bag on his way out, but providentially his foot did not hit the bottle.

"How lucky can you get?" exclaimed Grashio, who himself had been working to cover gear near the jungle's edge and had nervously watched the spectacle from afar. Father Carberry, toting two gas cans full of blankets and other supplies to the rendezvous point just as Hozumi was departing, had also been fortunate to duck into a banana grove before being spotted.

It was the closest of calls. Had Hozumi discovered the quinine, some type of severe punishment, ranging from solitary confinement to torture or death, would have been guaranteed. An extensive investigation, one that might have led Hozumi to uncover the escape plan, almost certainly would have been launched. "Once Hozumi's suspicions were aroused," theorized Hawkins, "that implacable individual could be counted upon to take relentless countermeasures." Thankfully, the only damage Hozumi had seemingly inflicted was to Shofner's face.

Once darkness fell, the escape party—minus Mellnik, Marshall, Spielman, and the Filipinos—gathered for one final, furtive meeting at the barber's shed.

"Now men," McCoy addressed the group, "tomorrow's the day, and I guess we are all set. I think we should reach an understanding right now that if any one of us becomes too weak to carry on, or is wounded, or has to fall by the wayside for any reason, the rest will have to continue on without him."

Heads nodded. McCoy then suggested that they not wear their leggings the next morning so as to not draw any undue attention when they departed the main compound. He also advised that they leave their bays looking as lived-in as possible.

"Just pretend you are going to work as usual, and we can't miss," he concluded.

At lights out, they settled into their bunks and tried to catch a few winks. In Barracks Five, Jack Hawkins's eyelids were locked open as raindrops noisily pattered the tin roof above his head. His mind was filled with "all kinds of disconnected thoughts." He thought of his fiancée, Rhea. Was his blanket in the thicket soaking wet? Was he a fool to leave the camp and risk probable death? He had lain awake with sleepless anticipation before early-morning duck hunts in the past. "Tomorrow, I would be the hunted and not the hunter," Hawkins would recall. "The stakes were high in this game. . . . To be won was freedom—a chance to live again, a chance to fight again, perhaps even a chance someday to see home again. This was a rich prize to be won, and I was staking my life on it."

There was something else gnawing at Hawkins. Hearing that Dobervich was restless, too, he reached over and tapped his friend on the shoulder.

"Whadaya say?" replied Dobervich, poking his head beneath Hawkins's mosquito net.

"Say, Mike, you know what we agreed out there tonight—about leaving anybody who falls out or gets shot? Well, as far as I'm concerned, that doesn't go for you and Shof and me."

Dobervich reached his hand under the net to clutch that of Hawkins.

"That went without saying, Jack."

While the Marines expressed their motto of *Semper Fidelis*—"Always Faithful"—a few snoring prisoners away, Ed Dyess was equally restive. He could not shake a premonition that the cool night wind had swept through the eaves and settled upon him.

"I felt something was wrong, I couldn't say what," he would write. "I just didn't believe we were going . . . that's how psychic you get in prison camp."

SUNDAY, MARCH 28–TUESDAY, MARCH 30, 1943
Davao Penal Colony

The day began like any other Sunday—just as McCoy wanted it. The plotting prisoners were clangorously bugled out of their bunks, but it was the announcement from their barracks leaders that rang in their ears: "This is a special order from Lieutenant Hozumi. As a punishment for disobeying the rules against the picking of fruits and vegetables, all hands will forfeit their recreation today and will work in the rice paddies. This means every man who is not actually hospitalized. Fall in outside the barracks after breakfast."

As curses, grumbles, and groans echoed through Barracks Five, Jack Hawkins's hands froze and dropped the shoe he was putting on. He turned to look at Mike Dobervich, who, sitting beside him, beat him to the question: "My God, what do we do now?"

"Shof joined us at this time looking as he had been shocked beyond recovery," added Hawkins. "There was a blank, dazed look on his face. His mouth was drooping."

"It's all my fault," whispered Shofner, hoarsely. "The plow detail—getting caught with the fruit. It's all my fault."

But the natural-born leader quickly snapped out of his fugue state and dashed in the direction of Barracks Eight. His gloomy mood, though, did not improve upon his return.

"McCoy can't figure a way out of this one and neither can I," he said. "How about you?"

Dobervich and Hawkins shook their heads. The Air Corps contingent could not come up with an alternate flight plan, either. After some hasty yet cautious conferencing, the escape party reluctantly decided on the only course of action available: postponement. The new E-Day, they decided, would be the following Sunday, April 4.

But what about the Filipinos? The thought of both colonos showing up at the rendezvous point and being discovered along with the stashed gear by the Japanese was chilling.

While lining up to board the Toonerville Trolley, the Marines noticed Ben de la Cruz walking down the road toward them. In all likelihood, he had heard of Hozumi's pronouncement and had come to investigate. Careful to avoid eye contact until he passed the spot directly abreast of where the Marines were standing, he shot a quick, inquisitive glance in their direction. Without speaking, Hawkins shook his head from side to side. Never breaking his stride, de la Cruz nodded receipt of the message and continued down the road. "He knew the plans were off," said Hawkins.

Toiling in the rain and mud of Mactan was miserable, yet having to endure the suspense-filled week was worse. "The strain," said Steve Mellnik, "was frightful. Problems filled my mind. Each Japanese appeared as an accuser, and each PW as an informer. I became acutely aware of evening roll calls, the searches at the gate, and the ubiquitous sentry posts. . . . Did Hozumi have more surprises?"

The nerve-racking tension notwithstanding, none of the conspirators had second thoughts about their decision to participate in the plan—or at least none intimated such thoughts to the others or later documented them—but their apprehension was nevertheless evident.

Leo Boelens's terse diary entry for March 28—"?????????"—illustrated the dark cloud of uncertainty hanging over them.

"How far is it to Australia from here, Commander?" Marshall asked McCoy one day.

"About sixteen hundred miles to one of the nearest points—Melville, for instance."

"And you mean, if we can find a sailboat, you can take us there?"

"Within ten or fifteen miles of any place on the map," replied McCoy, as reassuringly as possible. "Provided, of course, that we can rig up some halfway decent navigating equipment."

"And provided, of course, that we had a lot of luck with the weather, and the Japs didn't stop us. But I kept these thoughts to myself," McCoy later wrote.

Even Pop Abrina's faith was being tested. "What will happen next?" he asked.

The hourly bell that rang across Dapecol's fields seemed only to signal a spike in their stress levels. Mellnik noticed that the usually mischievous, energetic duo of Marshall and Spielman was quiet and moody. And that he and McCoy were prone to overreaction at the slightest incidents. All of the members of the escape party took turns badgering Shofner, asking no fewer than ten times by Mellnik's count, "How well did you hide the stuff?"

Their cached gear was the main source of their anguish. They wondered if it would be so waterlogged that it would be useless to them on their journey or, worse, that it would be discovered. The stockpile of supplies contained food, medicine, bolos, and other items that served as conclusive proof of escape preparations. And their names were written all over this escape plan—literally. Both their names and in some cases their serial numbers had been stenciled and stitched on their musette bags, blankets, and other personal belongings. The discovery of their supply depot was as good as an admission of guilt.

"As each day passed without discovery, each of us sent up a prayer of thanks," recalled McCoy. "And each of us prayed that, on the coming Sunday, we would not be punished with an order to work." Their anxiety skyrocketed with the startling midweek news flash (most likely originating with Lieutenant Yuki) that Dapecol's garrison was scheduled to be reinforced by additional troops the week of April 4. All work details would thereafter be guarded. They would have to execute their plan the next Sunday. There could be no more delays.

Dyess, Grashio, and Boelens focused their nervous energy into practical pursuits. While Boelens labored in the machine shop, the two pilots performed an exhaustive ground-level reconnaissance. They observed the tendencies and movements of tower guards. They noted the schedules of patrols, timed their own movements, and measured distances.

Hawkins coped in his own way. "I think what happened to me in the Philippines, which psychologically was a really good adjustment to make," he said, "was that I thought I probably was not going to survive at various times. And so I just resigned myself to that and didn't think about it. You just went ahead and did whatever you had to do."

But that did not mean that Hawkins had completely switched off his survival instincts. He and Dobervich were returning from the fields late one sultry afternoon when they heard rifle shots emanating from the direction of the hospital compound. Soon, bullets buzzed over their heads and they instinctively dropped to the dirt.

"What's going on?" said Hawkins, lifting his head ever so slightly from the ground.

"Don't know. But that was close!"

When the shooting had stopped, they rose to their feet and saw a congregation of prisoners and Japanese milling about the hospital compound. Getting closer, they saw the lifeless body of an American at the base of a guard tower just outside the fence line.

"What happened?" Hawkins asked one of the prisoners.

"Jap in the tower shot him. Tried to shoot another fellow inside the compound, too, but missed."

Slowly, the details were pieced together. According to eyewitness accounts, the dead prisoner, Sgt. John H. McPhee, had been digging camotes directly below the northeast corner tower just outside of the hospital stockade. McPhee had tossed his canteen back over the fence into the compound to be filled by one of his buddies. When it was returned to him, he raised it to his lips, an action that infuriated the tower guard. Unable to understand the commands being shouted at him, McPhee tilted the canteen and spilled a few drops onto the ground to show the guard that it was only water. Incensed at this innocuous gesture, the guard unshouldered his rifle and opened fire. The first bullet struck McPhee between the shoulder and the neck. He staggered forward, screaming, "My God—don't shoot me again!" The guard—Superior Private Osenaga, aka "Liver Lip"—ignored the plea and pumped several rounds into McPhee's body before turning his rifle on the POW who had tossed the canteen to

McPhee. The latter zigzagged for his life as bullets ripped through some hospital structures—thankfully, no patients were hit—and ricocheted out of the compound.

By the time the compound gates were locked for the evening, the camp was seething. Random, senseless acts of violence on the part of the guards had been on the rise in recent weeks. In February, an enlisted prisoner was struck with a hoe by the guard known as "Fishface." The attack left a deep gash in the POW's leg, necessitating a four-month hospital stay. And in March, the Army lieutenant colonel in charge of the sugar-cutting detail had attempted to bring in some cut cane for the hospital patients. The guards caught the officer and tied him to a stake, where he was severely beaten for twenty-four hours.

This latest act, however, was nothing short of cold-blooded murder. But that's not how the Japanese saw it. At evening announcement time, the barracks leaders read a message from Major Maeda: "The Japanese commander regrets that it became necessary to shoot an American prisoner today to prevent his escape. Let this be a warning to other prisoners, that any attempt to escape will meet with the same action."

"Those miserable stinking bastards," someone snarled within earshot of Hawkins in Bay Ten. "They'll pay for this someday."

Muffled by the roar of revulsion, Hawkins turned to Dobervich.

"Maybe someday before long we'll be telling the folks at home about this and all the other thousands of men murdered out here," he whispered.

Or maybe, they began to wonder, they wouldn't. Maybe McPhee's shooting had been a preemptive warning. Maybe the Japanese knew something.

"Are [the Japanese] playing cat-and-mouse?" Shofner asked himself as he lay in the darkened barracks on his crude bed, fighting insomnia and wakeful nightmares of a looming Japanese trap. *"Will it end in the thunder of machine gun fire?* I fought the visions that came rising up, of a dozen bodies flopping like dying chickens in the dirt."

PART III

FREEDOM

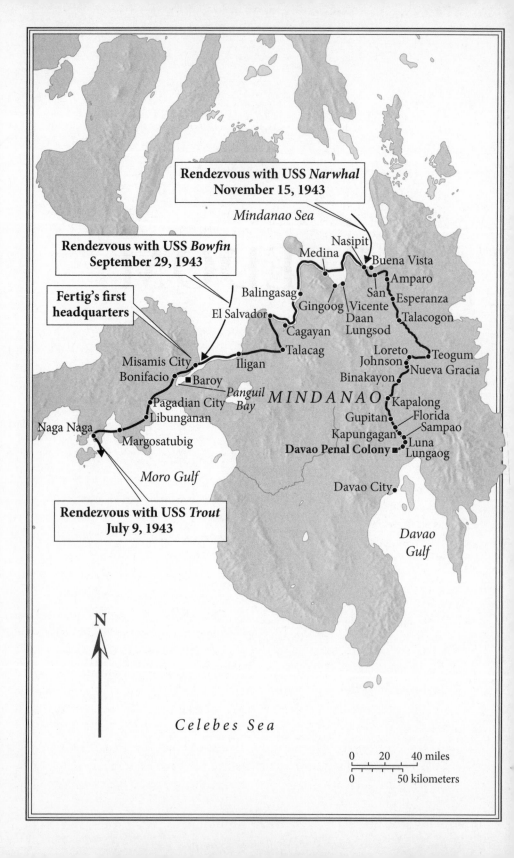

**Rendezvous with USS *Narwhal*
November 15, 1943**

Mindanao Sea

**Rendezvous with USS *Bowfin*
September 29, 1943**

**Fertig's first
headquarters**

Nasipit
Medina
Buena Vista
Balingasag
Amparo
San
Esperanza
Gingoog
Vicente
El Salvador
Daan
Talacogon
Cagayan
Lungsod
Talacag
Loreto
Teogum
Misamis City
Johnson
Nueva Gracia
Iligan
Bonifacio
Baroy
Binakayon
*Panguil
Bay*
MINDANAO
Kapalong
Pagadian City
Gupitan
Florida
Libunganan
Sampao
Naga Naga
Kapungagan
Luna
Margosatubig
Davao Penal Colony
Lungaog

Moro Gulf

*Davao
Gulf*

**Rendezvous with USS *Trout*
July 9, 1943**

Davao City

N

Celebes Sea

| 0 | 20 | 40 miles |
| 0 | 50 kilometers |

CHAPTER 13

A Miracle

I am awake. Across the prison yard . . .
The camp is deadly still
I barter choice for life, and I must pay—

SUNDAY, APRIL 4, 1943
Davao Penal Colony

Just before dawn, Steve Mellnik awakened and through a window, watched as the stars faded into a pewter, overcast sky.

The day was finally here.

Mellnik dressed, tiptoed down the aisle, shook Melvyn McCoy awake, and went to the mess hall, where he found cooks preparing rice for those scheduled for Sunday labor. Picking at his food, he asked himself, *"Would everyone appear?"*

Within a few minutes, all of the conspirators were present and accounted for, with the exception of Father Carberry. They sat at different tables, exchanging not so much as a glance. When the reveille bugle sounded, rousing the rest of the camp from its slumber, they rose from their seats. "Little did that Jap bugler realize that he was sounding our call to action," said Jack Hawkins. That was the prearranged signal; they would assemble at the main gate at 0800.

In their barracks, they dressed and packed their possessions. It would not take long. Nearly one year as prisoners of war—in the case of Dyess and Grashio, this morning marked the 361st day they had awakened in captivity—had stripped their lives down to the barest essentials. They looked like an assemblage of military misfits. While McCoy buttoned up

185

the suntans of an Army officer of MacArthur's staff, which he had found on Corregidor, Shofner packed his treasured Marine football jacket and pulled on a comical pair of red wool socks. "I had marched too many miles as a Marine to start flirting with foot problems now," he reasoned.

Thanks to Mike Dobervich, Hawkins was perhaps the best-dressed member of the escape party. Among Dobervich's many gifts to Hawkins was a shirt that had belonged to a man who had been beheaded on the Death March and a leather AAF jacket. Hawkins also had a canvas sun helmet, complete with the eagle, globe, and anchor emblem of the Marine Corps, that he had purchased in Cabanatuan for a pack of cigarettes. He wore a new pair of U.S. Navy–issue tennis shoes—a rare gift from the Japanese, recently shipped from Manila—which he had had smeared with mud to lessen their attention-grabbing whiteness.

Paul Marshall was perhaps the poorest of the prisoners. "We were going barefoot all the time in the camp," he recalled. "Most of the officers had shoes, one kind or another." Slipping on a pair of sandals made from rubber tires and throwing a small bag over his shoulder, he resembled a hobo about to hit the rails. "I had one blanket and half a pup tent. And I had a little sack with a couple of changes of underwear and socks . . . that's all I had when we went in down there [to Dapecol]. And that's all I had when we left."

In Barracks Eight, as Mellnik slid a razor and a worn toothbrush into his musette bag, McCoy covertly packed his belongings, including his maps and charts, medicines, and some delicate piña cloth handkerchiefs, gifts for his wife and daughters, under his clothes. He managed to find room in his musette bag for his most prized possession, a half-roll of toilet paper that he had kept since Corregidor. Finally, he folded his mosquito net under his bulging shirt.

"Where are you going with the mosquito netting?" asked an older Army officer.

"This net? I'm going to wash it during the noon rest hour today," said McCoy, nonchalantly. "It's full of bedbugs again."

"If he suspected anything he did not say so," McCoy later recalled.

Back in Barracks Five, Bert Bank sensed something strange was transpiring. When Bank maneuvered close enough, it looked as though Ed Dyess was rubbing a greasy substance, perhaps some kind of cooking fat, on his pants and leggings.

"Ed," asked Bank playfully, "you going to take a trip?"

Dyess shrugged and laughed a nonsensical answer: "I just found this stuff." Though his eyesight had all but vanished, Bank's other powers of perception had heightened. He now understood what was going on. Dyess, he believed, probably felt guilty about leaving him behind. Bank, not wanting to make a difficult situation any more so, decided not to press the issue.

It was almost 0800 and there was still no sign of Carberry. Grashio made some hurried inquiries. Carberry was laid up in the hospital, he was told. Malaria. "I went there at once," recalled Grashio, "and found him lying in bed. He told me that he hoped to go with us but that he was too weak to make the attempt now; that we should go without him." Carberry could not bring himself to tell Grashio the truth, that he had feigned the malaria attack because he had been forbidden to participate in the escape by Father Albert Braun, the senior chaplain. Braun was ill and short-handed—one priest had died—and feared that a priest's participation in an escape would cause Maeda to abolish religious services. Carberry's mission, as Braun saw it, was to stay and minister to the prisoners, not to save his own life. (Carberry's faithful obedience would cost him his life. After suffering through nearly two more years in Japanese prison camps, he would survive the bombing of the POW transport *Oryoku Maru* by U.S. planes, only to die in late January 1945 while en route to Japan aboard another hellship, the *Brazil Maru*.)

On his way back to the main gate, Grashio met a POW named Chuck O'Neil, a friend and flying school classmate he considered safe. Grashio confided in O'Neil that he was attempting to escape and asked him in the event that he made it home and Grashio did not, to inform Grashio's family of what had happened to him. O'Neil agreed. "He said I was crazy," said Grashio.

Pop Abrina, in all probability, had been praying. Standing in the doorway of the chapel, he watched anxiously as the escapees formed their respective groups—six coffee pickers and four plowers—and proceeded to the main gate. They had no idea that Abrina was watching them from afar, but another pair of eyes hardly mattered since it seemed as though the entire camp—or every Japanese, at least—was watching.

With McCoy out front, the first group, composed of Mellnik, Dyess, Boelens, Marshall, and Spielman, marched up to the gate.

"Detail, halt," ordered McCoy.

It had come to this. Months of planning, mounting mental strain, and hushed conferences. The enormous weight of worry that had accompanied their constant fear of discovery by the Japanese or, worse, betrayal by their own. Every surprise inspection, search, and shakedown, every stolen, borrowed, bought, and carefully concealed piece of gear, every prayer, every painstaking detail, every carefully concocted story, every angle worked, every gamble taken. It had all been for this moment.

Each single bead of sweat seemed a river coursing down their brows. They thought that they could hear the thumping of their hearts. And that the Japanese could, too. Watching from a few feet away, Jack Hawkins sucked in a deep breath and stood like a statue. Believing that each of them looked "suspiciously bulky," he wanted to remain motionless, invisible. "I don't suppose there was anything particularly unusual about my appearance," recalled Hawkins, "but I felt as conspicuous as if I were dressed in prison stripes."

"I knew that the next minute or two would bring the supreme test for us," remembered Dyess. They still had several additional sentry posts to pass, but none was more important than this one. It was the gateway to freedom, the point where all work parties leaving the main compound were required to check out.

Usually, the sleepy sentries made a swift count, chalked the number of departing POWs on the blackboard, and allowed the detail to pass. But not this time. Though McCoy had counted twice, the sentries remained curiously unimpressed. One stepped out from the guardhouse to inspect the party, doing so with what seemed to Dyess to be unusually intense scrutiny. If the Japanese knew of their plans, as Shofner had feared, now would be the time for a theatrical interception. Dyess realized that at this point the mission was in the hands of a higher power.

"If the Old Man is with us," he said to himself, *"we'll make it. If He isn't, we won't."*

As the guard strode up and down the file of prisoners with narrowed eyes, they could not blink or breathe—there was nothing left to do but believe.

Finally, after several seconds—which seemed like an eternity—the guard turned and barked his decision over his shoulder: "Okay." McCoy presented a customary salute and with a command—"Forward march"— moved the detail out. As each prisoner passed though the gate, another guard chalked up the numbers on the blackboard. *Ichi. Ni. San. Yon. Go. Roku.*

Six clear, four to go.

"Come on gang, fall in," said Shofner, moving the plowers into the spot vacated by the coffee pickers. Hawkins could tell that Shofner's voice was unusually shaky.

"Easy now, Shof," whispered Hawkins. "Just like every day."

Shofner saluted and barked the Japanese word for plowing, *"kosaku."* Unlike McCoy's group, the plowers didn't even receive a raised eyebrow. The guard wagged his finger at the Americans, counting and chalking off four men. With a salute from Shofner, they were on the way. "My feet felt light," said Hawkins, "as if they were scarcely touching the ground."

Abrina had a jaunt in his step, too, as he strolled from the chapel. Each Sunday, a truck traveled into Davao City and a handful of spots was reserved for civilians who wished to visit relatives or purchase supplies. Believing that an alibi would be highly valuable, Abrina had made plans to be absent from Dapecol during the prisoners' evening *tenko*.

Their first hurdle cleared, the two details went in different directions, ostensibly to their work assignments. As Shofner led the plowers to their shack, McCoy's men executed a sharp left outside the main gate and began marching parallel to the fence line, passing in rapid succession the row of barracks. Their path took them directly beneath the guard towers. Mellnik glanced up anxiously. "Though we were moving a regulation 128 steps per minute, I felt as though we were crawling. I had an insane desire to run."

"We walked as nonchalantly as possible," recalled Dyess, "but it seemed to me that my heart was beating my brains out. I thought I could actually feel the guards' eyes on the back of my neck."

They had almost cleared the compound area when the residents of Barracks Eight emptied toward the mess hall. That was when Frank "Siki" Carpenter, a good-humored officer and one of Mellnik's close friends, spied Mellnik—or, rather, Mellnik's musette bag.

"Hey, Steve!" Carpenter's piercingly loud voice cried out across the compound. "Your toothbrush is sticking out of the back of your musette bag. Are you planning to escape?"

If ever there was an occasion when Carpenter's brand of humor was in poor taste, this was it. And if the POWs had learned anything during their period of incarceration, it was that all Japanese knew the meaning of at least one word in English: "escape." The mere mention of the word, of course, had sealed the fate of the three would-be escapees at Cabanatuan.

But Carpenter had no inkling of what was transpiring. Luckily for the escapees, neither did the Japanese. Mellnik, pretending not to hear Carpenter, lowered his head as they double-timed it from the area. The adrenaline surge was so powerful that they were almost jogging.

"Hold it down," snapped McCoy. "The tower sentries are still watching. If they see Americans rushing to work, they'll know damn well something is wrong!"

As they decelerated, familiar sights passed in sentimental slow motion.

"Dammit," said Spielman, wistfully, while skirting the poultry farm, "I hate to leave those 2,800 plump hens. In a way, I almost gave my life for them."

Because the coffee patch was located on the far southwest quadrant of the colony, the journey of McCoy's group to the rendezvous was not only longer, but also potentially more perilous. In the process of making two left turns and doubling back via interconnecting roads, they encountered another guardhouse. Whispering last-minute instructions, McCoy warned them to be ready to jump the guard if necessary, but to otherwise proceed according to plan.

"Act military," said McCoy. "Give him one he'll always remember."

Once they got within range, McCoy bellowed the command: "Eyes left!"

As he snapped his right hand to his head, six heads jerked in unison, a show of parade-ground precision. Stiffening to attention, the guard, recalled McCoy, was "so surprised that he returned the salute and smirked toothily as we marched on past."

In the span of several minutes they skulked, singly, unseen across two heavily patrolled roads near the Japanese billet and headquarters area, depositing them into the banana groves.

"*The Old Man is with us today,*" Dyess thought to himself. "*What we're having is more than luck; a lot more than luck.*"

Though it seemed a lifetime, the entire movement took all of thirty minutes. According to McCoy's log, his group reunited with Grashio and the Marines at the plowers' shack at 0830. Locating their stashed supplies, they discovered that most of their gear was waterlogged. After wringing a week's worth of rainwater out of their blankets and wrapping the salvageable supplies in shelter halves, they tied their heavy bedrolls around their shoulders in horseshoe fashion and dispersed into the brush to wait for Ben de la Cruz and Victor Jumarong. Ten nervous minutes passed. Then twenty. The dreary sky began to spit a heavy downpour.

"Good old rain," whispered Boelens, breaking the uncomfortable silence. "It'll cover our tracks."

"Cover our tracks, hell!" retorted Shofner, gruffly. "I wish those guys would come on so we could start making some tracks."

The escapees sat silently in the rain. Had the Filipinos been waylaid? Had they gotten cold feet? Or were they conspiring at this very moment with the Japanese? They had just about decided to go on without the two guides when Jumarong finally arrived, alone, at 0900.

"Where's Ben?" asked an irate McCoy.

"Ben want to know if you ready," said Jumarong in his best broken English.

"You tell Ben come quick or we go without him."

Although the Americans were shocked, such dilatory behavior on the part of the two colonos was in fact standard operating procedure in the Philippines, where no amount of talk or planning is enough to convince one of another's sincerity or intentions. Jumarong and de la Cruz needed proof, needed to see with their own eyes the ten *gringos*, loaded down with gear, ready to go. "Apparently," wrote McCoy, "they wanted to make certain we really meant to escape."

A wolf whistle from lookout Spielman signaled Jumarong's return at 1030. This time, de la Cruz was with him. "They did not explain the tardiness," explained Mellnik. "And we were too relieved to make an issue of it."

Anxious to put distance between themselves and the Japanese, they silently formed up in a single-file line—the Filipinos at the fore, Dobervich and Hawkins bringing up the rear—to move out. One by one, with reserved exuberance, the prisoners passed through the jungle threshold.

The escape party had scarcely penetrated the fringes of the jungle, yet it seemed even more darkly foreboding than it had during the dummy run. The fugitives panted and splashed through puddles of standing water and tangles of dense foliage for nearly an hour before their exhausted lungs, unaccustomed to the musty humid air, demanded a rest.

Dobervich and Hawkins took seats on a log next to Spielman and Marshall as the latter doled out cigarettes. It was the first time that the others had had an opportunity to meet the young Army enlisted men. Hawkins studied Spielman; he knew a Texan when he saw one.

"What part of Texas are you from?" he asked.

"Carrizo Springs."

"That's down in the mesquite country, isn't it? I'm from Texas, too."

"Good. That makes three of us," said Spielman. "I hear Captain Dyess is from Texas."

The escapees were just about acquainted when McCoy ordered them to their feet. Covering their cigarette butts with mud, they returned to the trail, which grew more indistinct and overgrown with each labored step. Drenched with perspiration, they bridged gullies, crossed innumerable small streams, and stumbled over stumps, all while trying to keep from being ensnared by drooping vines. It was unlike any trail any of them had ever seen. "In fact, I could hardly believe that we were on a trail at all," said Hawkins. Neither could Mellnik.

The afternoon sun breached the gloomy skies and the ceiling of thick tropical foliage, providing enough light for Mellnik to notice that their shadows were moving in the wrong direction. He pulled McCoy aside and both officers carefully observed Jumarong. At 1400 hours, their suspicions were confirmed by a frightening discovery: their own footprints, proof that they had indeed been moving in circles. A nervous Jumarong entered into a hasty conference with de la Cruz in Tagalog.

"Victor says that he has lost the trail," reported de la Cruz. "It has been over a year since he was on it and the trail has changed."

Jumarong tried to get his bearings, but another hour of aimless wandering forced McCoy to call a halt. He pulled out Acenas's map, which the others examined over his shoulder.

"I'm afraid we've lost it for good. I imagine we are about here, but there is no way of knowing," he said, hazarding his best guess of their location with a fingertip. "I believe the best thing to do is to try to follow a course generally northeast and try to hit the end of the Japanese logging railway about here."

McCoy's finger moved to a point some ten to fifteen miles northeast of Anibogan.

"If we go that way, we'll be getting into the swamp pretty soon," said Hawkins.

"I'm afraid you're right," admitted McCoy, "but I don't know what else to suggest. If we don't head for the railroad we'll probably just wander on into the jungle indefinitely."

Following the compass, they proceeded on the new course. Predictably, the terrain became progressively more marshlike. The mud grew thicker and deeper; clumps of shrubs gave way to mangles of trees.

There was no sign of a Japanese search party, but they were hardly alone. Doves flapped away upon their advance and they heard the grunts of wild hogs. Mosquitoes invaded their nostrils and ears and attacked any exposed skin, as did the leeches. Once gorged with blood, the half-inch-long parasites were capable of doubling, even tripling in size. And for fear of infection one could not simply pull off the bloated blue blobs. During breaks, they singed the tiny parasites with lit cigarettes. The nicotine also provided a much needed spike in energy. Still, by the time they encountered their first major obstacle, a large stream, Dyess and Grashio were noticeably flagging in the oppressive late-afternoon heat.

Shofner suggested felling a tree across the stream. "Shof was always quoting the Field Manuals," said Hawkins. "As we say in the Marine Corps he knew 'the book'—or claimed he did." Thanks to Boelens's prowess with a bolo, their bridge was in place minutes later. Placing one foot carefully in front of the other, each man slowly felt his way across. The last, Grashio, was only two feet from the bank when he wobbled off and splashed into the water.

"Haw, haw, haw," laughed Shofner as he helped Grashio ashore. "Old Surefoot himself. That's the Air Corps for you. Boy, how did you ever pilot a P-40 with balance like that?"

"Oh, shut up, Shifty," was all Grashio, dripping and embarrassed, could manage in reply.

"Jeep pilots, that's what you Air Corps boys are," joked Shofner.

"Don't talk about the Air Corps," interjected Dyess. "What have the Marines done in this war anyway?"

"Ever hear about Guadalcanal?"

"Toot, toot. The Marines have landed. Why don't you quit blowing your horn."

"Okay, boys, let's knock off the Army-Navy game," said McCoy, hustling them forward.

Only later would Grashio understand that Shofner's ribbing was not without purpose. They needed to be prodded forward by any means necessary, be it the whip of Shofner's tongue or otherwise. "His judgment

was remarkable about who could profit from a few words of encouragement, who needed a few minutes' relief from carrying his pack, and what
kind of half-joking, half-jarring remark would pick us up a bit," recalled
Grashio. "Shofner knew what had to be done, how to do it and possessed
the dynamic leadership to get it done."

Hawkins, though, wasn't one to open his mouth very often. He did
not think McCoy was checking the compass often enough to maintain
an accurate course heading, but for the time being he decided to keep
his thoughts—as well as his fears that they were again covering familiar
ground—to himself.

They encountered another large stream at approximately 1745, and
with nightfall near decided to set up camp rather than attempt another
crossing. After a dinner of canned corned beef, deviled ham, and cold
rice, they drained their canteens. Ready to refill his with swamp water,
Hawkins asked de la Cruz for the water purification tablets from the first-
aid kit. Instead, the Filipinos pointed out an alternative water source: the
long, fibrous buhuka vines festooned around their bivouac. The Americans were surprised to learn that when sliced open, a six-foot length of
inch-thick rattan yielded a half-canteen's worth of sweet, pure water.

"I never knew my porch furniture was good for drinking," cracked
Hawkins.

Jumarong then demonstrated how to use strips of the vines to bind
saplings and branches into raised sleeping platforms that would keep
them out of the leech-infested mud and water, the level of which would
inevitably rise with the nightly rains.

They finished their beds in the darkness and were just about to turn
in when they heard the sound of drumbeats pulsing the jungle. "It was a
dull throb," Shofner wrote, "like the heartbeat of the primeval rain forest." Hypnotized by the ghostly cadence, they stopped slapping the persistent mosquitoes to listen. The rumors of cannibal tribes that inhabited
the swamp, previously dismissed out of hand, had suddenly become audi-
ble reality. They had heard of the Atas, Manobos, and Magahuts, but just
which, if any, of these indigenous tribes was responsible for the strange,
rhythmic beats was unknown. The message being pounded through the
jungle was equally puzzling.

"What is it?" asked one unsteady voice.

"Drums," deadpanned another. "Wild people."

"Do you think they know we're here?"

"Hard to say."

Shofner, sensing that the moment was ripe for raillery, decided to break the spell. In time with the drumbeats he chanted, "Heads are available! . . . Heads are available! . . . Heads are avai—"

"For Christ's sake, Shof, shut up!" came an interruptive reply out of the darkness.

The drums silenced just as quickly and mysteriously as they had begun, but the incessant pounding reverberated in their heads as they dozed. According to Dyess, the fugitives were jolted awake by more sounds—"a resounding crash followed by heavy splashes and the most spectacular profanity"—only to learn that they were not under attack from headhunters or the Japanese. The Marines' bed had collapsed, dunking the occupants into the watery ooze.

A steady, soaking rain, as well as their crude bunks and escalating anxiety, ensured that the night was a miserable, largely sleepless one. But there were others who were restless that night, too.

SUNDAY, APRIL 4–MONDAY, APRIL 5, 1943
Davao Penal Colony

Bert Bank had experienced many a restless night since the start of the war, but nothing quite like this. For Bank and more than 500 others, the ordeal had begun around 1800, during evening *tenko*. As per usual at day's end, the POWs were lined up and counted. But this time, they were recounted. Then counted again. No matter which way the Japanese figured it, ten American POWs and two Filipinos were unaccounted for. Word quickly spread down the lines of assembled prisoners and was transmitted across the colony: the unthinkable, the impossible—an escape—had happened.

It was a testament to the degree of secrecy with which the escapees had both planned and executed their breakout that almost nobody at Dapecol—American, Filipino, or Japanese—could believe it. At the Filipino hospital, a stunned Fely Campo remembered an innocuous conversation that she had had a few days earlier with another nurse named Maximina Orejodos. "Some things are going to happen," Orejodos had said, cryptically. Campo knew that Orejodos and Ben de la Cruz had become romantically involved, but she never for a moment considered that he would be participating in an escape attempt with American prisoners.

"The Japanese were beside themselves," remembered Carl Nordin, who, like the rest of the POWs at Dapecol, was at the same time proud, bewildered, and fearful. "They kept counting and counting and counting. Of course, they couldn't figure out how it could have happened. . . . I don't think they realized that they had let themselves in for it, that they had gotten too lax."

But the Japanese promptly and characteristically assigned responsibility for the escape to the remaining prisoners. Manny Lawton, a friend of Bank's, recalled standing at attention at sunset as the detested interpreter known as Running Wada delivered a rambling oration on behalf of Major Maeda: "For every man who escape, de other nine in his squad wirr be shoot kirred. You are arr guilty of herping them escape. De major say you wirr arr be confined to camp untir he decide what what other punishment wirr be necessary."

This revelatory pronouncement signaled either an alarmingly abrupt reversal of Japanese policy or a major miscalculation on the part of the escapees in judging Maeda's character. While some POWs maintained that the Japanese never brought up the subject of shooting squads—not upon the prisoners' arrival in November 1942, nor in the chaotic period immediately following the escape—others believed that the "ten for one" rule enacted at Cabanatuan was in use at Dapecol. A consensus was never reached and will likely forever remain a point of contention. "I never knew that there was a change in that order," said Jack Donohoe, but, because it was so difficult to predict Japanese behavior, also said, "I didn't know if 100 people would be killed or not."

Nobody knew. Bank believed that the Japanese intended to spill the prisoners' blood in retribution for their wayward comrades' indiscretion. It certainly seemed that way. The Japanese first marched the new American camp commander, Col. Kenneth Olson, as well as the leaders of the barracks where the fugitives had lived to Maeda's headquarters for questioning. The sounds of the beatings leaked out to the compound. "The Japanese worked some of them over pretty good," remembered Donohoe. The Japanese then secured the names of those who slept next to the escapees. These men, the Americans were reportedly told, were to be executed, a summary guilt-by-association judgment. "Sleeping between [Dyess and Grashio] did not make me too popular with the Japanese," said Bank.

There was plenty of blame to go around. The Japanese knew that the POWs had had help. Pop Abrina returned from Davao City that evening to find the camp in an uproar and a squad of soldiers, led by Hozumi and

Lieutenant Tsubota, waiting at his home. Feigning surprise, Abrina denied that he had anything to do with the escape. He truthfully told Hozumi that he had last seen the Americans the previous afternoon. He had been in Davao City and the driver of the Japanese truck could vouch for him. Unable immediately to implicate Abrina, Hozumi stormed out, leaving a promise. "[The Japanese] threatened me and my family to be shot to death should [they] find later on that I was responsible for the escape," Abrina would write.

While the fuming Japanese plotted to recapture the runaways, the POWs huddled together, discussing everything from the meaning of the escape to the significance of its timing. There were, of course, the unavoidable rumors: MacArthur had landed in Mindanao; Davao Province was in revolt; guerrillas were preparing to attack Dapecol and liberate the prisoners. Naturally, the prisoners debated the import of the escape as it pertained to them. Some, such as Army Lt. Col. John H. McGee, who had been organizing an escape party of his own, grudgingly admired the escapees' enterprise and courage. Yet others bitterly resented what they believed to be a selfish act because of the consequences it would bring down upon those left behind. Proof that the escape polarized the prisoners is found in a conversation overheard by Lawton that evening.

"Those dirty bastards," said one incensed POW, "don't they know they might get a bunch of us killed?"

"Wait a minute," someone replied, "the book says that it is the duty of a prisoner of war to escape if he can."

Came back another: "That's true. But the guy who wrote the book didn't consider that we might be captured by barbarians who refuse to abide by the Geneva Convention rules."

"Yeah, and another thing. He assumed the prisoners would be within a reachable distance of our lines. Those guys know damn well they can't swim to Australia."

Bert Bank had no idea how Dyess, Grashio, Shofner, and the others planned on reaching Allied territory, but he prayed that his friends would make good on their escape. As for his own fate, he knew that his slim chances for survival would be nil if there should be another escape this evening, a real likelihood with so many men like himself staring at the prospect of execution. That's why he was keeping a vigil over the others in his bay—just as they were over him.

In the wee hours of the morning, he heard some rustling noises. Bank saw the blurry outline of a man rise from a nearby bunk and begin fastening his canteen belt around his waist. Bank startled the man when he asked him if he planned to escape because, if so, Bank was going, too. No, the POW stammered, he was just trying on his canteen belt. Bank, not buying the story, groped for his own gear. "Well, I put my belt on also, explaining that I was just trying on my belt," said Bank, "and we remained up all night watching each other."

At dawn, the entire camp stood at attention before Major Maeda. For several minutes, the portly commandant blasted the POWs with incomprehensible Japanese, and, no doubt, alcohol-tinged breath. The English distillate, courtesy of the interpreters, was 100 proof: "Eleven American dogs have escaped from us. YOU must pay."

The words were followed by the sound of the boots of several squads of fully equipped soldiers, led by Lieutenant Hozumi, marching through the camp's gates. For those who had been at Cabanatuan, the movement must have seemed hauntingly familiar.

MONDAY, APRIL 5, 1943
Davao Province

Nearly two dozen trees splashed across the newly rain-swollen river, the escapees' own Rubicon, a boundary that demarcated the jungle from the swamp. Twelve pairs of feet then traversed the wet trunks, a bridge spanning their past and, they hoped, their future. Heaving the logs into the water so that the makeshift bridge could not be used by their pursuers, they pressed forward. There was no turning back.

The escapees entered what they believed to be the swamp at approximately 1000 and quickly began to understand why the tropical quagmire had such a fearsome reputation. Each step required concentrated effort—pulling one's foot out of the slimy, green-brown ooze was like walking in tar. They encountered thickets of cogon, the ubiquitous sword grass that, theorized Grashio, "must have been created by Satan personally." The cogon reached immense heights of seven to twelve feet, and each four-inch-wide, half-inch-thick blade was "covered with sharp spines that ripped clothing and flesh impartially."

Jumarong and de la Cruz, slashing a path at the vanguard of the procession, were soon bleeding profusely despite the burlap wrapped around their forearms. Shofner, Dobervich, and Boelens, the strongest members of the group, shouldered the cutters' packs so that they could hack unencumbered. Yet no matter how violently the Filipinos swung their bolos, the cogon seemed to grow taller and thicker, an intimidating illusion created by the rising water level. The stagnant swamp water crept higher each passing hour, "an especially sinister progression for me," recalled Grashio, "as I was the shortest of the whole group."

An occasional grassy hillock provided a brief opportunity for rest, but these swamp oases were few and far between. It certainly seemed that the swamp was indeed an evil entity actively conspiring against them, taunting, tripping, and entangling them with submerged logs, twisted tree roots, and thorn-studded vines. "The buhuka vine, which had quenched our thirst the day before, now seemed to regret its helpfulness and became a painful hindrance," said Dyess.

They staggered in silence. The only sounds were those of heavy, labored breathing, the burbling suction of their footsteps, and that of steel bolos slashing sword grass. The intense heat and high humidity were physically and emotionally enervating. While they looked at the map and thought in terms of kilometers, their progress, in reality, was measured in yards. Even with de la Cruz and Jumarong cutting at full capacity, they were averaging only 300 to 400 yards an hour. And Hawkins was growing increasingly worried that the tremendous output of energy was for naught. He had to speak up.

"Shof," he whispered, "McCoy might be the best ship's navigator in the Navy, but I don't believe he's doing much of a job here on the ground. I'd swear we're going in circles."

"You know, I've been thinking the same thing."

"So have I," added Dobervich, overhearing their conversation. "McCoy doesn't watch his compass close enough. Remember the night compass march we made at Basic School, Jack? I think that's the way we should do it now."

"If we are circling," said Hawkins, "it means our bones will rot here in this swamp."

Shofner called for a caucus. According to Hawkins, McCoy "frankly admitted that his Naval training had not included anything to cover a situation such as this" and gladly turned over navigation duties to the Marines. The POWs also agreed to share cutting duty. A team of two men, it was decided, would cut for ten-minute intervals. This fair rotation would enable them to operate at peak efficiency, a necessity since the Japanese search party, which surely had set out at dawn, would have the benefit of their clearance work and thus move considerably faster through the swamp in pursuit. With time their enemy, the Marines quickly applied their training to the situation.

Taking the compass, Hawkins assumed the lead position directly behind the cutters. As they hacked forward, Hawkins remained stationary, watching until they progressed to the limit of his vision, at which time he would close up behind them, take another compass reading, and restart the process. Shofner, meanwhile, was charged with shepherding the party—which was strung out in a long, serpentine fashion in the tunnel of cogon—forward while keeping an eye on Hawkins. Dobervich was tasked with keeping stragglers in front of him and also keeping himself moving, a chore with as many as three packs on his back. "We moved forward a few paces and stood, moved again and stood," said Shofner. It was slow, monotonous progress, but progress nonetheless.

Making the mission more difficult was the fact that following a straight line and adhering to the readings was practically impossible. Obstacles consistently cropped up, necessitating numerous navigational detours. "We came to places in the jungle impossible to cut through. Sometimes we climbed over, and again we crawled under, holding our noses just above the slime and expecting to meet snakes face to face," remembered Dyess.

Thankfully, they had not encountered any of the swamp's rumored inhabitants—animal or human—and there was still no sign of pursuing Japanese, but they began to encounter potentially more dangerous enemies: themselves. Shofner and Mellnik, for example, were soon at each other's throats. Shofner felt as though Mellnik was not carrying his weight, and he had evidence: Mellnik had dropped their portable stove, Boelens's quan can, and it had to be retrieved. And perhaps Mellnik simply did not appreciate Shofner's motivational methods. Whatever the case, small slights festered into major arguments. Once, when Shofner overheard Mellnik berating Dobervich, he vociferously interceded on behalf of his fellow Marine, unperturbed by the fact that Mellnik outranked him.

"I'm the senior Marine here," shouted Shofner. "Don't you ever speak to another goddamn Marine here. You speak to me, you understand that, skinhead?"

By noon, several crises had only narrowly been averted and it seemed as though the group, as well as the carefully conceived escape plan, was slowly being shredded to pieces much like their clothes, faces, arms, legs, and psyches. Although the Marines were confident that the party was now moving in a somewhat linear fashion toward its northeasternly goal, McCoy estimated that they were traveling less than fifty yards an hour. There were no visible road signs indicating positive progress, no proof that it was worth it to push oneself a little further. One by one, they began to break down physically and mentally.

"How does one die in the swamp?" Mellnik asked himself. *"From exhaustion? Drowning? Or by just quitting?"*

McCoy stumbled upon an underwater obstacle and sat down in water up to his mustache, refusing to move. He had awakened with nausea and other symptoms of a forthcoming, full-blown attack of malaria or dysentery. Finally, after a long break, he struggled back to his feet.

"We've got to go on," he mumbled, "it's only one o'clock."

It was during these desperate hours that they learned that they needed to fight the swamp, not each other. Dyess, staggering perceptibly, was just about to surrender his gear to the water—a step to sure death—when Dobervich grabbed him.

"No, don't do that, Ed," warned Dobervich, hoisting the pack on to his shoulders. "You've got to keep your gear. Here, give it to me."

After swinging a bolo with wild, blind rage for one cutting shift, Grashio reached a dangerous stage of delirium brought on by exhaustion, hunger, and dehydration.

"Tell McCoy to go on without me," he told his partner, Mellnik.

"Hell, we weren't leaving anyone," said Marshall. Mellnik had bitten his lip open, relying on the pain and salty taste of his own blood to remain conscious. From that point forward, he and Spielman shadowed Grashio closely.

It was mid-afternoon when they finally reached a point at which no words of encouragement, no physical assistance, not even Shofner's indomitable spirit, could will them any further. Marshall summoned enough energy to climb atop Spielman's shoulders. Peering over the wall of cogon, he spied a mammoth fallen tree, perhaps eight to ten feet in diameter and nearly thirty feet long, half-submerged no more than 100 yards behind their position. "Sloshing back, we hoisted ourselves onto the trunk and flopped like lizards, bellies up," said Shofner.

As they lay gulping in deep breaths, too exhausted even to wave away the whining mosquitoes, Hawkins took stock of the situation. Never, not while huddling in his dugout during the worst bombardments on Corregidor nor during the darkest days in Cabanatuan, had he allowed any negative thoughts to creep into his mind. Until now. "I was afraid that the end had come for McCoy, and possibly for all of us, and I was horrified at the thought of perishing in this God-forsaken stinking swamp. I doubted that McCoy could move on the next day and I wondered if I could last through another day myself. And what if the end of another day, and another, and another should find us still lost in that almost impenetrable prison? One by one, our food gone and strength exhausted, we would sink down into that brown slimy water and perish. I glanced downward—and shuddered."

After several hours, their bodies responded to the rest. The log stirred to life as they began to build a sleeping platform large enough for the entire party. Then someone, in the midst of chopping saplings and vines, inadvertently struck a hornet's nest. Leo Boelens was the first to sound the air-raid siren: "Duck! Duck!"

The warning came too late. What seemed like a thousand angry wasps came pouring from their disturbed hive. They were large, much larger than the yellow jackets in the States, and fanatically aggressive. "Their stings were like stabs with a hot dagger," remembered Grashio. Spielman, stung no fewer than a dozen times, was the hardest hit.

Frantically abandoning the log to yelps and profanity, they dove into the water, their only defense, and stayed there submerged for nearly thirty minutes until the brutal attack was finished. Finally, Sam Grashio angrily spluttered up out of the water.

"What next?"

"The pain of the stings took our minds temporarily off our other troubles," said Dyess. But only temporarily. After a supper of corned beef, rice, and hot tea, they stripped their saturated clothes and huddled around a small fire. Their sullen faces told a grim tale.

"We were all visibly frightened over our circumstances," remembered Hawkins. "Things looked really bad and confidence in ourselves was badly shaken . . . the swamp was proving to be an enemy more deadly than the Japanese."

Dyess concurred. "We had no way of knowing how much swamp remained to be conquered. Our shoes were falling apart. Our legs and bodies had been slashed severely by the sword grass. Infections would start swiftly. Another day like this one would finish us off."

Not stopping to eat, they agreed, had been a critical mistake. An inventory of their stocks showed that they had forty-two cans of corned beef and fish and a kilo of rice, enough food to last for at least two, perhaps even three days. "Engines won't run without fuel," said Dyess.

That, however, was where the consensus ended. Jumarong suggested returning to the vicinity of Dapecol to locate the original trail. There were murmurs of agreement, which McCoy immediately moved to silence.

"Look at the map," he reasoned, pointing out that they were only two or three miles from the railroad. "If we keep on that compass course we are bound to get out tomorrow, or the next day at the very latest."

"And if we don't get out by then, then what?" Mellnik asked.

"Let's don't even think about it."

But Mellnik had thought about it. He announced he was going back to Dapecol. He'd take his chances with the Japanese. Maybe the ruthless heat, the water, and the cogon had taken their toll. Maybe the legends were true; if the swamp did not kill you, it would drive you mad.

At first glance, Mellnik's statement suggested cowardice. But perhaps he was the only one courageous enough to voice an opinion that others might have shared but were afraid to say: that this whole quixotic emprise had been a bad idea, that they had been fools to attempt an escape.

"You know what would happen to us," said Hawkins, trying to appeal directly to Mellnik's capacity to reason. "Nobody could go back, and live."

Then, speaking like a lawyer before a jury, he made an impassioned plea to the others: "They will torture any or all of us if he does that, and kill us if we ever get there."

But Mellnik was not thinking about it. He was going. Several seconds of uncomfortable silence passed. And then that silence was broken.

"No," boomed the clearly agitated voice of Shofner, "you are not."

Until now, the escape party had operated democratically. But now, with the union dangerously close to fracturing, there were too many disparate voices. With the senior officer, McCoy, physically unable to command,

and Dyess's powerful personality drained by his dreadful condition, someone had to take charge. At this critical juncture, Shofner probably could not help but be reminded of the maxims of his coach and mentor, Robert Neyland. One, in particular: "If the line goes forward, the team wins; if the line comes backward the team loses."

Jumarong had proffered the suggestion, so his departure was probable. It was unlikely that de la Cruz would abandon his friend. Should Mellnik be permitted to leave, Marshall and Spielman would, in all likelihood, accompany him. Sapped of the manpower of their youngest and strongest members, the remainder of the escape party would certainly perish in the swamp, but recapture was a more realistic fate. Even if Mellnik should make it back to Dapecol, he would likely be tortured until he divulged the whereabouts of the others. Shofner saw the situation with unmistakable clarity: this team could not retreat. Mellnik could not be allowed to secede from the group—and thereby cause its distintegration—under any circumstances.

"You can't stop me," retorted Mellnik, defiantly.

Shofner then literally rose to the challenge, his erect posture and build, though decimated by months of disease and hunger, still quite formidable.

"The hell I can't," he bellowed. "Just give me the opportunity."

"You don't have any weapons," countered a dubious Mellnik.

"I'll kill you with my own two hands," promised Shofner, curling his giant hands into fists as if presenting weapons for inspection prior to a duel.

There was little doubt that Shofner, sufficiently riled, would have done just that—had they not at that very moment heard violent thrashing sounds coming from a thicket no more than fifty feet away. Marshall doused the fire and they jumped from the platform, half-nude, into the swamp, their bolos drawn. With bated breath, they crouched silently in the waist-high water.

"What could it be?" whispered Dobervich.

"There couldn't be any Japs in this place," reasoned Hawkins.

Jumarong leapt back onto the log, jabbering in Tagalog and motioning madly for the others to follow. Ben de la Cruz translated: "Come on! It's crocodiles."

"We literally flew back to the platform," recalled Hawkins.

Crocodiles. Sam Grashio sighed. "Nobody had even thought about *them* when we were struggling waist deep in the water and sword grass. With our luck so far, we should have stepped on a couple."

But their luck was about to change. The echo of gunfire was perhaps the most bizarre harbinger of good fortune imaginable. It was about 1800 hours when they heard the first shots. "By now we were so jumpy that the shooting shook us to the marrow of our bones," wrote Grashio.

The unexpected, unearthly clatter—rifle shots and the staccato tattoo of machine gun fire—was unquestionably that of a small battle. But where? And between whom? Jumping to their feet in unison, they stared silently at each other while trying to determine the direction of the gunfire, as well as the different types of weapons involved, skills that all soldiers who had spent time on or near a battlefield possessed. Shofner immediately recognized the distinctive crack of a Browning Automatic Rifle, or BAR. Another weapon sounded familiar to Dyess.

"That's a Nip burp gun. Ran into them on Bataan. Wonder what they're shooting at?"

"It's the Japs all right," added Spielman after a telltale thump. "Hear that knee mortar?"

With each exchange of shots came a corresponding exchange of whispers: How far away was this firefight? Did the Japanese have a fix on their position? McCoy attempted to alleviate the tense situation with his dry sense of humor, one, of course, flavored with logic.

"Those guys can't be firing at us. No one knows where we are, not even ourselves."

Suddenly, the sky was set aflame with an eerie red aura.

"They must have set a house or village on fire with that mortar," said Marshall.

Judging by the direction of the shots and explosions, which were now fading in both volume and intensity, they deduced that the battle was being fought near the supposed location of the railroad. "We could only hazard a guess on distance," explained Mellnik. "The reflective surface of the water complicated the problem." Shofner thought the fight—and thus the railroad—could not be more than three miles away, perhaps even as close as one mile. As the fiery, orange-red glow danced skyward, Hawkins reached for the compass. The needle pointed due north; they looked at each other knowingly.

"That way is out," said Dobervich. "Japs or no Japs."

• • •

No sooner had night fallen than the swamp symphony commenced. The fire flickered ever so dimly on the horizon, as their fears smoldered. Transfixed by the glow, no one slept, or spoke.

Sandwiched between Shofner and Grashio on the giant common bunk, Dyess was in a contemplative mood. There was something he needed to do, needed to say. He had never before assigned a task that he himself would not do, nor had he ever shied away from addressing his men, but he felt as though he was not the individual for this job. He nudged Shofner.

"Don't you think Sam ought to lead us in a little prayer?"

"I sure do think he ought to, Ed."

Dyess explained that he thought Grashio was probably the most religious of the group and therefore it would be appropriate that he led them in a prayer. Since there were no objections, Grashio dropped to his knees and began to recite the "Memorare," a prayer to the Blessed Virgin Mary that the Catholic nuns at Saint Aloysius school in Spokane had taught him. It had always been his favorite, and it seemed almost tailor-made for their current situation. He recited one sentence at a time and the other supplicants replied in kind:

> Remember, oh most gracious Virgin Mary, never was it known that anyone who fled to your protection or sought your intercession was left unaided. Inspired by this confidence I fly unto you oh Virgin of Virgins my mother. To you I come, before you I stand, sinful and sorrowful. Oh mother of the word Incarnate, despise not my petitions, but in your mercy and kindness, hear and answer me. Amen.

When Grashio finished, it was as if everything they had experienced, both physical agony and mental anguish, had disappeared. The heated confrontations, their aching limbs, the swollen, throbbing wasp stings, the fear and doubt—all vanished.

Yet it was not so much an absolution as it was a message. They had been slowly staggering toward inevitable collapse, dissolution, and death. And now, they had been shown, seemingly by some otherworldly phenomenon, a path—as well as the courage and strength to follow it. "I felt easier and more optimistic than I had since the start of the escape," recalled Dyess. Hawkins experienced a similar sensation. "That prayer drove anxiety and trepidation from my mind and left me with a feeling of peaceful calm and security."

To a man, the effect of Grashio's words was instantaneous, calming and curative. None of them would ever be able to explain just what had happened that night on the log. But Grashio knew.

"I thought a miracle had occurred," he would say. "I felt now that God would save us."

CHAPTER 14

Another Gamble

Thus hunger, thirst, fatigue, combine to drain
All feeling from our hearts. The endless glare,
The brutal heat, anesthetize the mind . . .

TUESDAY, APRIL 6–MONDAY, APRIL 12, 1943
Davao Province

Melvyn McCoy did not know if it had been an intervention of the divine or quinine variety, but he was nevertheless thankful to have awakened with none of the symptoms of the malady that had plagued him the previous day. The others, dressing and bustling with renewed vigor, shared McCoy's enthusiasm. Recharged by nearly eleven hours of sleep and a breakfast of oatmeal and tea, they sprang off the log at 0830.

The scene in the swamp was much the same—yet different. Their faces were red and puffy from mosquito bites, the mud still clutched at their feet, the water lapped their midsections, and the razor-sharp cogon mercilessly lacerated their bodies. Even so, "the sword grass looked less dreadful than the day before," noted Grashio. It was optimistic depth perception. The going was no easier, but the despondency that had made each step the previous day so laboriously difficult was absent.

On they pushed, slashing cogon with assured, mechanical efficiency, sloshing through the swamp water, wiping their brows, swigging from their canteens, oblivious to the swarming insects and stifling heat, the minutes running into hours, morning becoming afternoon.

Every few hundred yards, the column would halt and, after motioning for silence, Jumarong would cup a hand to one ear. The Americans looked at each other quizzically.

"He is listening for the cock crow," de la Cruz explained. "Wherever there are Filipino people you will hear the crow of the fighting cocks. The sound will travel for a long way."

The sounds of civilization eluded their ears, but another sign was visible: the swamp water seemed to be receding. When they halted for lunch at noon, it was hip-level. Each successive hour saw the water level drop; their spirits, correspondingly, soared. They also encountered sparser, smaller thickets of cogon, which enabled them to progress at a rate of roughly 500 yards an hour. They were soon joyfully splashing through ankle-high water. Finally, at 1400 hours, they exited the swamp and flopped onto the muddy jungle floor, leeches be damned. While they caught their breath, Jumarong loped into the brush. He returned fifteen minutes later with a grin on his face and some excited words: he had found a trail.

Forty-five minutes of effortless hiking brought them to an embankment perhaps five feet above the level path. The railroad, the goal that at times had seemed impossible to find, was within reach. Confident that the area was clear, McCoy gave the signal.

"Okay," he whispered. "Everybody up."

It was an oddly anticlimactic triumph. The railroad was little more than "two ribbons of rusty steel piercing the jungle and all but overwhelmed by it," recalled Shofner. Dazedly, they kicked around the rotting wood ties until someone let out an exclamation. There were footprints. Dozens of them. They were made by split-toed shoes with hobnail heels—Japanese footprints. Dyess had seen similar prints on Bataan. These shoes, he pointed out, not only provided Japanese soldiers with excellent footing on difficult terrain, they also made climbing trees a cinch for snipers. "The thing that jarred us," said Dyess, "was that the prints were fresh."

The startling evidence sent them into a copse of trees for a conference. There were lots of questions—Were the Japanese ahead of them or behind them? Did they patrol the railroad? If so, how often, and by foot, by locomotive, or both? Where were the guerrillas and civilians Acenas had spoken of? Spielman volunteered to scout ahead for intelligence, and with McCoy's blessing he, Jumarong, and de la Cruz left while the others prepared a camp in a clearing approximately 500 yards from the railroad. The scouting party returned at 1730 and Spielman reported on his findings—or lack thereof.

"No Japs, nobody," he said, shaking his head, "but we did find some deserted shacks about three kilometers north of here."

The tug-of-war between their hearts and minds—they were exhilarated to be out of the swamp, yet wary of what the next sunrise would bring—and the fact that the Marines' bunk had collapsed yet again, eliciting a barrage of expletives, made for another sleepless night. Hungry for answers, they skipped breakfast, struck camp, and set out in the predawn darkness along the railroad toward Lungaog.

"We'll be safe or dead in about four hours," reasoned McCoy. "The sooner we move, the better."

Slowly, fresh sunbeams poured into the emerald canyon, illuminating their narrow path north between the rusted rails. Because of the din of the waking jungle, they did not hear the sound of several feet sliding down the tapered trunks of the giant lauan trees towering several hundred feet above their heads and silently scampering into the undergrowth.

At the Marines' suggestion, they marched in a spread-out patrol formation of twos and threes staggered over several hundred yards, ready to melt into the jungle at the slightest hint of an ambush. With Japanese footprints appearing both in front of and behind them, heading north and south toward Anibogan and Dapecol, respectively, Hawkins did not want to take chances.

They had traveled only four kilometers when they discovered the most disconcerting evidence yet: more of the distinctive footprints, plus cigarette butts, spilled rice, and spent cartridges. The blood-spattered foliage and trampled brush suggested that they were standing on a battlefield, most likely the site of the battle they had heard on Monday evening.

"Looks like quite a fight," said Dobervich.

"Yep," agreed Shofner. "Wonder where the boys are who tangled with them?"

Hawkins noticed that the brush on both sides of the embankment seemed to be trampled in the direction of Dapecol, an indication of a retreat. But there were no sighs of relief just yet. "The Japs, we knew, would not give up easily in their efforts to kill or recapture us," said Hawkins.

"It was with great trepidation that we proceeded farther down the track."

Five hundred yards later, the escapees happened upon a small village. After deploying Dyess and Jumarong as lookouts, they entered what seemed to be a typical rural barrio—smoke issuing from cooking fires, water boiling, chickens, pigs, and dogs scratching around. But no people. They cautiously peeked into each of the half-dozen bamboo-and-thatch huts, but were left scratching their heads.

"Well, if this isn't the damnedest thing you ever saw," said Hawkins.

The bubbling cauldrons reminded them of their empty stomachs, so they decided to quan a breakfast of rice, papaya, cassava, and corn. They had just raised the food to their mouths when Dyess and Jumarong sprinted into the middle of the deserted village. The two lookouts were breathless and their faces deathly pale.

"Couple of armed men back there," reported Dyess, squeezing the words between deep breaths. "Filipinos. One of them drew a bead on me. Couldn't have missed."

Dyess said that he had called to the men—"Americanos!"—but after one raised his weapon they disappeared into the jungle. First the battlefield, then the abandoned village, and now this—each successive development was proving more unnerving than the last. The men could have been guerrillas, or guides for the Japanese. "In either case," wrote Shofner, "they would be inclined to shoot first then ask questions."

Stepping back between the rails, they could not shake the frightening sensation that they were being watched. "We could see nothing but dense jungle at each side, but hundreds of eyes seemed to be staring at us," said McCoy. "Were we walking into an ambush? We didn't know but we had to keep going."

They marched about two kilometers before crossing paths with a fifteen-year-old Filipino boy, their first encounter with another human since leaving Dapecol four days ago. Both parties were startled; the boy ran, but stopped after de la Cruz and Jumarong called out to him in Visayan. Staring at the Americans wide-eyed, he told them that his village, Lungaog, was nearby.

After three additional kilometers on the railroad and a thirty-minute hike along a muddy side trail, they entered the outskirts of Lungaog. Jumarong and de la Cruz approached some riflemen congregating in a hut in the middle of a clearing and explained that the group had escaped from the penal colony. The Filipinos initially seemed skeptical, but soon approached with handshakes and a warm greeting: "Brave American soldiers, sir. Brave soldiers, sir."

"At the moment, we looked like anything but brave soldiers," wrote McCoy. "We all had four day beards. Our uniforms were wet and dirty, our faces scratched by the sword grass of the jungle. . . . We weren't certain how brave we were, but we certainly were ten relieved Americans."

Runners were sent to notify local authorities, and food, including rice, cassava, and *baloots*, was brought out. A *baloot* is a duck or chicken egg taken after a ten-day setting. Boiled or baked, it is served cold and considered a delicacy in the Philippines. Though the sight of such a meal made their eyebrows arch, to refuse would have been in poor taste. So the escapees peeled the shells, revealing a partially formed bird, sans feathers, in a cloudy jelly, and hesitantly bit into their *baloots*; a ravenous McCoy was so hungry he gulped down two.

They then spied a well and instantly gravitated toward it. Lathering up with hoarded soap, they dumped buckets of clean water on each other to cleanse four days of collected filth. "The sensation was nearly as delightful as feeling solid ground underfoot had been the day before," remembered Grashio.

Their guard lowered, they were milling about the well in various states of undress, laughing, scrubbing, shaving, and celebrating when a sharp whistle ripped the air and a loud voice called out an unsettling command: "Hands up!"

Frozen and frightened stiff, they stood like statues at the well, dripping with water and suds as a strapping Filipino giant swaggered toward them. Brandishing two Colt .45 revolvers in his hands, with a campaign hat tilted on his head and two bullet-filled bandoliers across his barrel chest, he resembled a character they had seen in so many Hollywood movies.

The stern-faced Filipino—estimated by McCoy to be in his early thirties, at least six feet tall and 200-plus pounds—demanded to know who they were and what they were doing there. Wiping the lather from his face, McCoy motioned for de la Cruz and Jumarong to join him. The others, careful not to make any sudden movements, attempted to dress and present as dignified an appearance as possible. McCoy cleared his throat.

"We are your friends. Prisoners. We escaped from the camp. We're Americans."

"How did you come here?"

"Through the jungle," chimed in Shofner. "Through the swamp."

The Filipino was visibly perplexed.

"The Japanese send many spies. I don't like spies."

Though it was hardly advisable for one who was being interrogated at gunpoint, McCoy could not help but laugh. After all they had been through, the suggestion seemed preposterous.

"Spies?" wailed McCoy. "Look at us, we're Americans!"

The Filipino scanned the motley crew gathered around the well. Though months in the equatorial sun had darkened their complexions, their Western features made for a convincing argument. Still, the Filipino remained skeptical. Exasperated, McCoy yanked his dog tags from around his neck and held them out for inspection.

"Look at these. They say I am Melvyn H. McCoy, commander U.S. Navy. If that's not enough, ask our Filipino friends—they know who I am."

The Filipino scrutinized McCoy's dog tags and then rattled off several questions in Tagalog in the direction of de la Cruz. Evidently, the answers were satisfactory, for it was the first of many times they were to see a broad smile creep across the big man's round face.

"I'm Sergeant Casiano de Juan of the Mindanao guerrillas," he announced, thrusting one of the pistols into his belt and then moving forward as if to embrace all of the escapees at once. "We are happy to see Americans!"

"Big Boy," drawled Dyess while pumping de Juan's hand vigorously, "we're a helluva lot happier to see *you*!" (Thanks to Dyess, a nickname had been created in those first minutes of friendship. Casiano de Juan would henceforth be known to both the escapees and through guerrilla circles as Big Boy.)

"I have a surprise for you," said the grinning guerrilla, who then wheeled around, waved his pistol and let out a shrill whistle. "These are my guerrilleros."

At the signal, fifty-odd Filipinos erupted from the jungle and engulfed the escapees in a celebratory melee of whoops and cheers. The escapees had heard about the guerrilla movement that had arisen to resist the Japanese, but most of what they knew was hearsay. Now, they had actually encountered some of these guerrillas.

It was a most peculiar army. They were grimy and poorly clothed—some went barefoot—and carried weapons ranging from BARs, bolt-action rifles, and pistols to homemade shotguns, bolos, and Japanese swords, spears, bows, and quivers of arrows. Even so, their resolute appearance made a strong impression. Once in the depths of despair, Mellnik executed an about-face as the escapees moved out with the ragtag escort.

"Mac," he said, confiding to McCoy, "I think we'll make Cateel in a breeze."

"Look, Major," whispered Spielman, nudging Mellnik. "We're on display." Indeed they were. The entire barrio of Lungaog had turned out for their arrival. Adults crowded the building—a large nipa structure formerly filled with fighting cocks—and children crawled up into the rafters for a better view. While the Americans polished off their second, and in some cases third, helpings of cracked boiled corn, chicken, and stringbean soup, dozens of curious blinking eyes set amid the shadows watched with rapt curiosity. Many in the crowd had brought food, while others furnished their talents, such as the guerrillero who strummed "La Paloma" on his mandolin. "We were getting to see the justly famed Filipino hospitality," wrote McCoy. "These people were poor and our presence might mean retaliation from the Japs, but they were willing to share whatever they had."

"Now," said Big Boy, as they sat in a circular formation on the bamboo floor among the shadows created by the flickering light of a coconut-oil lantern, "how do you really come?"

"I told you," said Shofner, "through the swamp."

Dubious, de Juan shook his head from side to side.

"Nobody goes into the swamp. Nobody comes through."

Finally, accepting their protestations, he took their word.

"Brave Americans," laughed Big Boy. "Lucky too, eh?"

More lucky than they would ever know.

"We thought you were Japs at first," explained de Juan. "We were planning to kill you, but we found out you were Americans."

"We're certainly glad you found out in time," replied McCoy.

"What was all the shooting back on the railroad two days ago?" asked Hawkins. "Did you know about it?"

"Did I know about it? Ho, ho," chortled de Juan. "My men killed ten Japs there."

As de Juan explained, the bamboo telegraph—a primitive though highly effective network of scouts, swift runners, and drums—had alerted the guerrillas that a Japanese patrol had penetrated their territory. This, no doubt, was the search party sent out from Dapecol.

Ernesto Corcino, then a twenty-five-year-old guerrillero who would become an astute student of American history, compared his compatriots to the Minutemen in American Revolutionary War times. With the alarm, men from scattered farms and barrios dropped their tools, picked up their weapons, and gathered at dusk to lay an ambush near barrio Kinamayan—the deserted village where the escapees had eaten breakfast. Though heavily outgunned and outnumbered, sixteen to eighty-three by one account, they had the factor of surprise. Felling ten enemy soldiers with their first volley, they pulsed a shockwave of panic through the Japanese ranks.

"They fired their machine gun and the small cannon [mortar] but hit nothing," Big Boy told the Americans, adding that not one of his men had been injured. "They fought only a few minutes and then they tied their dead on poles like pigs and ran away."

For the escaped prisoners, this timely intervention by de Juan's men was freighted with fateful significance. Firstly, had it not been for the guiding light of the firefight, they might not have found their way out of the swamp. And even if the prisoners had found an exit, the Japanese, advancing unimpeded along the railroad, almost certainly would have eventually ensnared the Americans. Instead, the Japanese were forced to retreat south, back to Dapecol, providing the escapees a small buffer zone and enough time to enter deeper into guerrilla territory. Given the circumstances and recent revelation of information previously unknown to the escapees, their safe delivery into friendly hands seemed an improbable miracle. "One would think it a God-protected experience," Corcino would say.

According to Corcino, guerrilla sentries perched high in the lauan trees had spied the Americans at sunrise, shortly after they had begun traveling north on the railroad. These scouts also detected a detachment of Japanese approaching the escape party, though still several kilometers distant. Despite the distance, the keen eyes of the scouts could discern the differences between the groups, with Corcino noting that the more northerly one was composed of "ten tall white men" and that those trailing were "Japanese soldiers with their identifiable hats with hanging strips of olive green cloth." Because of the proximity of the groups, something seemed awry. The sentinels quickly descended from their lookout posts. While most of the outpost guards rushed to report the news of the intruders, two stayed behind to observe the movements of the nearer group.

At de Juan's camp, there was speculation that the Japanese were employing white-skinned German allies to masquerade as American POWs in an attempt to lure the guerrillas out and annihilate them with their superior firepower. "There are no Germans in Davao Penal Colony," countered a skeptical de Juan. But he could not afford to take chances. Three times he had made trips to Japanese-occupied Davao City and twice he had been questioned about the activities of the elusive guerrilla leader known as de Juan. During his third visit, the Japanese finally recognized him with the help of a spy. The wily guerrilla brokered a deal in which, on condition of his release, he promised to surrender his army. Once safely back in his own territory, he sent a needling message to the Japanese garrison commander: "Want us? Come and get us." Infuriated, the Japanese put a substantial price on de Juan's head of 100 pesos—roughly $500—as well as a sack of rice.

And so de Juan had little choice but to order another ambush. Tense with anticipation, the guerrillas had crouched at the edge of the clearing outside Lungaog as the intruders milled at the well. "Do not fire until I tell you to fire," de Juan warned them. For several anxious minutes, de Juan analyzed the situation. "Boys, these are not Germans," he told them in Ilonggo, a Visayan dialect, before stepping out into the clearing to confront the Americans up close.

When the Americans praised de Juan for setting the ambush at Kinamayan, the usually boastful leader just grinned and shrugged off the compliments.

"I do not know how to command troops," admitted de Juan. "I just use my tactics."

Sensing that the escapees needed their rest, Big Boy rose to take his leave and ordered the townspeople to do the same. He then reassured the escapees that though the Japanese were likely still licking their wounds from Kinamayan, he would post guards to stand watch.

"Do not be afraid," he said. "If the Japanese come again we will have warning."

Approaching Ed Dyess, one youthful guerrillero did not exhibit the same self-assurance as his commander and comrades. Visibly shaken, he told Dyess, apologetically, that he was one of the two scouts on the railroad that morning and that it was he, believing the escapees to be aligned with the Japanese, who had raised his shotgun and taken aim at Dyess. He then confessed that he had panicked and pulled the trigger, but fortunately for Dyess the cartridge did not fire. "God must have been with you, sir," Dyess was told.

"Little wonder," commented Grashio, "that Ed believed in predestination."

The distance between hell and paradise—the barrio Lungaog—the escapees discovered, had been only twelve miles. With no Japanese bugler to blast them from their bunks at dawn, they slept—ten hours on the first day. They went swimming, laundered their clothes, and caught up their diaries. And they ate. And ate. Sometimes, five meals a day. Whether he was taking them "papaya hunting"—in essence, fruit scavenger hunts in the jungle—or into his own home for sumptuous meals, Big Boy made sure that the Americans never went hungry or thirsty. At every opportunity, the Americans toasted their newfound freedom and friendships with *tuba*, a potent, rose-colored alcoholic beverage fermented from the sweet sap of the coconut palm. And they entertained a stream of visitors.

Thanks to the bamboo telegraph, visitors ventured from as far as ten miles to see the Americans who had escaped from the hated "Hapons." Most came bearing gifts of food, everything from eggs, fruit, vegetables, and boiled fish to live animals, which were tied to stakes and penned up outside the escapees' bamboo billet. "We soon had a private menagerie of our own," recalled Hawkins.

Shofner entertained the guests with photographs he had taken in Shanghai and on Corregidor and had smuggled through prison camp in the seams of his Marine football jacket. The locals spent hours looking at the pictures and listening to the Americans tell stories of the atrocities they had witnessed and survived, as well as the hair-raising tale of their escape. Some awestruck Filipinos asked the former POWs to serve as godfathers to their children.

"It was an odd sensation to be treated as if we were conquering heroes," said McCoy, "when in fact we were bedraggled fugitives from Japanese brutality." But that same brutality was the reason for the sympathetic hospitality they were now experiencing. It was what drove men like Casiano de Juan, a storekeeper from Capiz, Panay, to become guerrillas. Though they had not been corralled, starved, and tortured, they, too, had suffered abhorrent treatment at the hands of the Japanese. The visitors were rich and poor, educated and illiterate, old and young, but all told tales of poverty, oppression, and humiliation under the Japanese regime. All Filipinos, the Americans learned, were forced to bow to the Japanese. If not, they received a vicious beating. Shofner befriended a young boy who was missing his fore- and middle fingers, cut off by the Japanese so that he could not fire a rifle. If a woman resisted the advances of a Japanese soldier, they learned, she was severely beaten in public. "My daughters must not be defiled by the filthy Japanese," one Filipino, a cultured refugee from Davao, told Hawkins. "I will hide my family here in the interior until the Japs are driven out."

The escapees, however, had no such luxury. It would be only a matter of time until the Japanese picked up the fugitives' tracks. In fact, the sudden appearance of Sgt. Aquilino Baguilod on April 9 proved that their story had spread far and wide. It also served as evidence that the guerrilla movement was in fact a sprawling entity, not just localized. Baguilod introduced himself as an emissary sent on behalf of Capt. Claro Laureta of the 130th Regiment. The deference that Big Boy showed to Baguilod was immediately perceptible.

"[Laureta] is the leader of all people in this part of the country," explained Baguilod. "He heard that you were here and sent me to invite you to come and see him."

Though the request seemed more like an order than an invitation, the Americans communicated their intention to travel to the coast and procure a boat for a trip to Australia.

"The captain will be *The One* to assist you," countered Baguilod, telling them that it was a three- or four-day hike to Kapungagan.

"That's a long way," said McCoy.

"Yes, commander," agreed the messenger. "But it will be the direction you wish to go."

Since any direction away from Dapecol seemed a good direction in which to travel, and Laureta seemed to be an authority figure who could make things happen, they accepted the invitation. They would leave the next morning.

Big Boy furnished sixteen guerrilleros to serve as guides, armed escorts, and *cargadores*, that is, carriers of the Americans' accumulated gifts, which now included a sixty-pound pig that "rode protestingly" hanging upside-down on a bamboo pole, remembered McCoy.

The party proceeded first to barrio Luna, four kilometers north of Lungaog and the location of a sugarcane plantation owned by Onofre Beldua. Beldua's hospitality would rival that of Big Boy. Despite their endless eating, their food fixation seemingly grew even more powerful during this time. Consider Austin Shofner's diary entry for April 10:

> Hot coffee and bananas were served less than ½ hr. after our arrival. As I am writing this, I am listening to phonograph play the first American music I heard in a long time. For our noon meal we had corn with chicken—papaya and black eyed peas with basi (sugar wine). Pineapple desert. In the afternoon, we played bridge—read and listened to a 3 piece string band play native and popular music. In the afternoon we rambled around looking at the plantation and watching the sugar cook off. About 5:30 we had coffee, rice flour cake with molasses—real nice. For dinner we had rice with the pig we brought with us—the pig was cooked three ways—spare ribs, fried pork and another native way—very good. Tuba (much) was served with the meal and coffee and bananas after dinner. The moon was about ¼ new and the heaven was full of stars. We retired at 9:45 for a very restful sleep.

An easy five-kilometer hike the following morning brought them to Sampao—Lungaog's sister village, whose barrio lieutenant, or mayor, was the brother of Lungaog's chief civilian official—and another banquet. The inhabitants of each successive destination, it seemed, desired to outdo their predecessors in hospitality, a situation the escapees welcomed. Late in the afternoon, after they crossed a small river in an outrigger banca, their movable feast finally reached Kapungagan, headquarters of Captain Laureta. Surprisingly, they were welcomed not by Laureta, who was attending to affairs elsewhere in his district, but by the town's mayor, Eligio David, a Davao businessman who had fled to the interior with his wife and five children when the Japanese landed. David's hospitality would surpass that of all others.

The fun-loving Filipinos, they soon came to learn, would throw a fiesta, or party, on any pretext. In this particular case, as the twelve attractive Filipinas sent to their palatial quarters—the town's municipal building—informed them, the fiesta was being held in their honor. Moving toward the music, the escapees were escorted in a torchlight procession to a plaza crowded with people and tables heaped with food. Colored lanterns strung between trees, torches, and oil lamps arrayed throughout the jungle clearing lent a festive glow.

"Now this," said a smiling Ed Dyess, "is the way to fight a war."

Dyess was perhaps the only one capable of speaking. The others just stood, dumbfounded, waiting to wake up. "Less than a week earlier, we'd have called a man insane if he had predicted our presence at a dance," McCoy would write. It would take Grashio much longer, many years in fact, to find the appropriate words with which to describe the emotions they felt that night. "After twelve months of brutality, starvation, and degradation, an abrupt change to such hospitality left us midway between tears of gratitude and utter bewilderment."

They sat down to a dinner of chicken and roast pig, which they washed down with copious amounts of tuba while being entertained by a conga dance featuring small children and a hula dance by a pretty Filipina. Once lubricated, they mustered enough courage to join in the dancing. The Filipino men remained seated as a courtesy to the guests, and the Americans took off their bulky shoes before whirling their partners around the dirt dance floor. The crowd, however polite, could not help but snicker at the sight of Shofner's red socks. It was good-natured kidding, but Grashio was not game.

"As a dancer I was no Arthur Murray so I drank tuba and regaled an admiring audience of teenagers and children with my exploits as a P-40 pilot perpetually engaged in mortal combat with squadrons of villainous Japanese," he recalled. Grashio's performance was an infamous traveling act destined for other children in other barrios. Complete with hand motions and vivid descriptions, each story would invariably begin with Grashio seated among his audience: "There I was in my crippled P-40 at 20,000 feet . . ."

After a group of girls sang a set of native ballads, the hosts made a startling announcement: it was the guests' turn. "We had a hasty consultation," wrote McCoy, "realizing that this was a crisis. Our hosts might be offended if we failed to sing."

As per usual, it was Dyess who valiantly stepped forward. Despite the fact that his drawling rendition of "Beautiful, Beautiful Texas" was terribly off-key and the tiny band—which featured a trumpet, banjo, and guitar—struggled with the accompaniment, the applause was tremendous. Emboldened by Dyess, Paul Marshall stretched his vocal cords, too. Shofner then ascended the stage and proceeded to do his own version of the "Tennessee Stomp." The forceful performance almost brought down the house—literally.

At 2230, with the dance winding down, the crowd gathered and, at the request of Eligio David, sang "God Bless America." Once the moving tribute concluded, the crowd began to disperse. That's when McCoy stepped forward.

"We're not through yet," he announced in a choked-up display of emotional extemporization. After asking the crowd to make some minor lyrical changes, he signaled for the miniature orchestra to resume playing, saying, "Let's sing 'God Bless the Philippines.' "

At the conclusion of the song, remembered Grashio, it mattered little whether one was Filipino or American, "there were no dry eyes afterward."

SATURDAY, APRIL 17, 1943
Davao Penal Colony

Tears welled in the eyes of the POWs congregating outside the barbed wire boundaries of the special compound holding a group of prisoners. "Our friends who were working around the barracks came up with tears in their eyes and told us to take it like men, and that we were giving up our lives for other Americans, and that it was a wonderful way to die," remembered Bert Bank. Major Maeda and a phalanx of rifle-toting guards—the firing squad, no doubt—goose-stepped into the compound at 0845.

Japanese military jurisprudence dictated that *someone* had to pay. In the tension-filled days following the escape, the POWs at Dapecol had received regular news bulletins from the "manhunt front." They had been repeatedly assured that the search party had picked up on the escapees' trail, that the fugitives had been surrounded, that their recapture was imminent. Yet when Hozumi's patrol returned empty-handed (with the exception, of course, of their own dead), it became apparent that either the swamp had proven more competent than the search party or that the escapees had achieved the impossible.

But neither the POWs nor the Japanese had any way of knowing. Maeda was flustered. Prison camp commanders were given some autonomy, but since he had been unable to clean up his own mess and since mass escape was such a rare event, he had to report the matter to the Prisoner of War Bureau in Manila, under the command of Maj. Gen. Ichiro Morimoto, and await official instructions.

In the meantime, the Japanese, in keeping with their belief in mass punishment, had placed the entire camp on a diet of rice and salt and removed approximately 560 prisoners, more than one-fourth of the camp's total population, from the main POW enclosure into a special compound on April 11. In addition to the twenty prisoners who had slept next to the escapees, the Japanese had added the barracks' leaders, the American camp leadership, men who worked on the same details as the escapees, and others who had eaten, conversed, or associated with the escaped POWs—in short, anyone even remotely connected to the escape.

Tucked away in a banana grove almost 800 yards apart from the main compound on the other side of the railroad tracks, the special compound was a bestial relic from Dapecol's earliest days: five thatch-roofed barracks surrounded by three concentric barbed wire fences. The barracks, which radiated out from a central space, contained cages made of wood and wire mesh. These double-decked cages were seven feet long, three feet wide, and seven feet high, and predictably uncomfortable. "When we were all installed, crouching in our cages with heads poked out of the upper and lower 'apartments,' it . . . resembled nothing so much as the Bronx Zoo," wrote POW Alan McCracken.

Nothing, not even patchwork repairs of the mesh screens or homemade insecticides made of wood ash, water, and boiled tobacco stems could combat the colonies of bedbugs that infested the cages. The Japanese had placed severe restrictions on the entire camp. There was to be no smoking, no reading, no card playing. As Maeda had told all of the POWs in an address on April 15, they had "a moral obligation and must be penitent." But they were not going to be penitent in the camp chapel; church services were suspended. Less surprisingly, hard labor was deemed a suitable penance, but now, POWs headed out to the fields wore only G-strings. The Japanese believed that additional escapes could be discouraged if the prisoners were not permitted to wear pants, shoes, or other clothing crucial for jungle survival.

Another consequence was that Lieutenant Yuki's influence was all but eliminated since many of the Japanese believed that it was his liberal policies that had made the escape possible. Guards became correspondingly meaner, and beatings and incidents of physical violence committed against prisoners more commonplace. The interrogations continued unabated, too. "Why did they want to run away?" the Japanese repeatedly asked, with a frustratingly bizarre naïveté. "Because the prisoners are being starved," came the exasperated answer. Even so, rations were further slashed.

Guards patrolled inside the special compound to make sure that the Americans were not engaging in any restricted activities. When a guard was spotted, a code phrase alarm—"Heigh-ho Silver"—passed from cage to cage to curtail clandestine card games and conversations.

Though there had been little mention of shooting squads since Wada's impassioned speech on the night of the escape, most, if not all, of the men in the special compound considered themselves condemned. There was no way, they believed, that the Japanese would let something as monumental as a mass escape slide. And so they waited. The period was so mentally taxing, Bert Bank would later write that the ordeal lasted an entire month. It was, in actuality, slightly less than one week. "We really lived in agony," Bank said, "and prayed that they would come and shoot us right away instead of letting us suffer."

Not surprisingly, the debate about the escapees had hardly cooled. "To some they were heroes," said one POW. "To others names unprintable." Jack Donohoe, one of those awaiting his fate in the special compound, was both pessimistic and philosophical. "The way I felt was, you never knew, all of us might've been dead and they'd been the only ones to stay alive. At least somebody got to live."

Most notable, and perhaps peculiar, of the Japanese rules was that the imprisoned were not to exhibit any signs of emotion. "No hilarity" had been the decree. Bank had decided that he was going to do his best to violate that rule. After all, what else could the Japanese do to a condemned man? "Every individual has got their own idiosyncracies," he would say. "I never lost my sense of humor. While we were waiting for them to come and execute us, I told the guys, 'Hell, in the States, before they kill a guy, they give him a nice meal. Maybe they're going to bring us a steak tonight.' They didn't think it was funny. I thought it was funny as hell."

There was no steak that night, but no blindfolds or cigarettes were distributed in the morning, either. All of the special compound's occupants watched with apprehension as Maeda and Wada ascended a small box from which they could address the crowd.

The first order sentenced the entire group to confinement for a period of one month. Then a list of names was read: the American camp commander and his assistants; the barracks and bay leaders whose charges had escaped. Finally, the names of those who had slept next to the escapees were read. They were ordered to step forward twenty paces and salute. It was peculiar protocol, but, remembered Alan McCracken, "we who were about to only-Heaven-and-the-major-knew what, saluted." Maeda then took a folded piece of paper from his pocket and handed the document—in all probability the official order from Manila—to Wada.

"You will now hear your punishment," announced the interpreter.

To Bank, it seemed as though Wada was unfolding the paper in slow motion; the ordeal truly was never-ending. "Between the time he said this to the time he read the punishment, I think twenty years elapsed."

Twenty paces behind them, feet—some shod, most bare—kicked and shuffled nervously in the dirt. Otherwise, not a sound was heard. Every eye was focused on Wada's lips, every head turned, every ear strained to hear the verdict. Finally, Wada began to read.

"Men called here," he droned, "due to insufficient control and supervision of their men, neglecting their duties, causing the escape of war prisoners, which is the major crime, have been given the following punishments . . ."

Eyelids shuttered. Throats instinctively swallowed.

". . . And are directed to reflect their faults. They shall thereby spend the number of days indicated in meditation of the past incident and observing modest and model conduct at all times."

Individual sentences were read, but few heard them. All that those twenty men could hear were the words reverberating in their minds: *Directed to reflect their faults . . . meditation.*

Rendered immobile, trembling and trying to corral their disjointed emotions, Bank and the others opened their eyes to an unexpected, inexplicable reprieve and, for the time being, a new life.

SATURDAY, APRIL 17, 1943
Kapungagan, Davao Province

Despite their improved circumstances, the escapees were not totally free men. "We had escaped from Dapecol," admitted McCoy, "but never from the memory that [our friends] were still there." "All ten of us would have been consoled immensely had it been possible for us to know," Grashio would write, "that [Maeda] would not slaughter others for what we had done." They could not have known what had just taken place at Dapecol, nor could they refuse their hosts' hospitality. Feelings of guilt would hang over them like storm clouds, despite the fiestas and feasts.

The effects of the fiesta on the evening of April 12 had just about faded when two aides to the mysterious Captain Laureta, Lts. Jose Tuvilla and Teofilo Rivera, arrived to examine the escapees' credentials. "In cold, formal terms, they demanded to know who we were, where we came from and where we were going," said Mellnik. Both officers were spit-and-polish and menacingly serious—Tuvilla angular, Rivera muscular and bearded—as they went about their task with official efficiency.

"Which of you are Grashio and Shofner?" asked Rivera.

Evidently, Laureta had not discarded the notion that the Japanese were employing their Axis allies to dupe the guerrillas. That anyone could successfully traverse the swamp was apparently still too baffling to believe. "Grashio and Shofner were understandably indignant as they presented their papers showing they were officers in the United States Army and Marine Corps, despite their names," recalled McCoy. To suggest that they were anything but Americans, that their sores and cuts were not real, that their bodies did not ache and shake with pain and malaria, was an insult to the two men.

The escapees had little choice but to comply. Once satisfied that the escapees were who they represented themselves to be, Tuvilla and Rivera notified Laureta that it was safe to return to Kapungagan. Trailed by heavily armed bodyguards, Laureta finally emerged from the jungle at noon, as contrite as he was cautious, on April 17.

"My apologies, gentlemen, for being so suspicious," he said as they retired to his office. "But there is a price on my head and the Japanese have employed tricks before to get me."

Claro G. Laureta, compact, with tightly shorn black hair, was in his mid-thirties. Barely five feet tall, he wore a Japanese uniform shirt, carried a .45 automatic pistol and a sheathed bolo, and had the feverish look of a man who was weighed down by malaria attacks and the responsibilities of a sprawling command. As Laureta and the escapees shared their stories, mutual respect and admiration replaced the awkward hostility. Shofner described Laureta best: "A strange, paradoxical personality, he had a sentimentality which could set his eyes brimming with tears over a patriotic song, and a streak of granite toughness which could bring summary beheading for a guerrilla who transgressed his iron-clad rules."

While the Americans had been struggling to survive in prison camp, Laureta and his men had been struggling to survive in the jungle. The constabulary officer had arrived from western Mindanao in the midst of the panic that ensued after the civilian evacuation. Shortages of food, medicine, and clothing led to massive civil unrest, enabling bandits to seize power and Japanese spies and informants to proliferate. The erstwhile policeman labored instinctively and intensively to restore order. Once the intimidating, iron-willed dynamo had effectively turned the Davao area into his own district, he focused on the invader. His motivation was simple: to avenge the likely deaths of his wife and children.

"I do not know if they are dead or alive," he said tearfully, his black eyes flashing. "For months I have searched for them but I can find no trace. You can see why I hate these Japs and why I have devoted myself to killing as many of them as I can."

Though their presence was another burden on his shoulders, Laureta was sympathetic to the Americans' mission. He agreed with their stated desire to reach friendly forces and tell America the truth about what was happening to its men in the Philippines. Professing his loyalty to the United States, he readily volunteered whatever assistance he could provide. But first, he needed their advice.

Laureta unfolded a letter that had arrived by courier from Medina, a town on the coast of northeast Mindanao, several days earlier. Dated the 31st of March, it had been written by an American Army officer named Lt. Col. Ernest McClish, who claimed to command a sizable guerrilla operation in Agusan Province, north of Davao. McClish possessed 500 rifles, plenty of uniforms and supplies, and three diesel-powered boats. Most important, at least to the escapees, was McClish's brief mention that he was in radio contact with Allied forces in Australia. The letter was an invitation for Laureta to link up with McClish's outfit.

"I'd like to team up with a man like that," said Laureta, "but the Japs have hit me from so many directions that I'm afraid this letter is another trick."

Mellnik examined the letter. It was no trick, he told Laureta—he knew of McClish.

"In fact, I helped brief him on PA [Philippine Army] matters prior to his departure for Mindanao in November 1941. You can take that letter at face value."

"Well," added McCoy, "the letter seems genuine . . . Why don't you try contacting him?"

"Yes, that's what I had in mind," said Laureta thoughtfully. "Perhaps you gentlemen would be interested in this mission."

Laureta suggested that the Americans, traveling under an armed, fully provisioned escort, journey to Medina. There now were two options on the table in Laureta's office. The escapees could continue on to Cateel, a seven-day hike, and attempt to procure a vessel for a sea voyage to New Guinea and Australia. Or they could try to meet McClish in Medina, a challenging jungle journey of nearly 100 miles, with tough mountain trails and river navigation.

As McCoy saw it, despite the difference in distances and inherent risks, Laureta's plan was the better for two reasons: "our eagerness to repay Laureta for his kindness and the reference in McClish's letter about radio contact he had with Australia." McCoy was confident that if there was a radio, he could contact the Navy and arrange for a submarine to rescue them. Laureta concluded his pitch by promising that if they failed to reach Medina, or if McClish could do nothing for them, he would help them execute their original plan. It was put to a vote.

"What do you think, Shof?" asked Dobervich.

"Sounds like a natural."

Shofner turned to Dyess: "Ed?"

"Okay with me."

Around the room, heads nodded in the affirmative. Laureta cracked a rare smile—these were his kind of men. He made sure they understood that the trek would require them to travel through virgin jungle and over mountainous terrain. The fact that large sections of territory on the maps spread out before them—territory through which they would have to pass—had been ominously stamped "UNEXPLORED" was hardly comforting.

"You will be going where few white men have ventured before," said Laureta before clicking off the names of various native tribes rumored to inhabit the areas. "These people are headhunters. They kill for the sake of killing."

"Captain Laureta," piped up Grashio, "so do the Japs."

It was nearly impossible to fathom such an adventure, one perhaps more challenging than their last, and especially one in which the Japanese were an afterthought, but they were by now accustomed to long odds. A series of gambles, taken individually and collectively, had gotten them this far. Perhaps one more great gamble could get them home.

CHAPTER 15

Unexplored

There was no trail and I am wandering still
In search of something lost upon a hill . . .

WEDNESDAY, APRIL 21–WEDNESDAY, APRIL 28, 1943
Davao and Agusan Provinces

The flotilla glided through the morning mists hanging over the Libuganon River, the escapees watching wistfully as the Eligio David family, waving from the riverbank, receded into the distance.

In a procession reminiscent of a traveling circus, the expedition had commenced at 0800 after an emotional farewell during which the Davids were presented with a curious assortment of parting gifts: a pearl stud from Shanghai; quinine pills; some soap; a check for $40 drawn from a Quantico, Virginia, bank—all Mike Dobervich recalled having in the account. The Americans regretted that they could not give more, but there was no way they could ever repay the Filipinos.

They had left with warm memories—and supplies. In three days Laureta's men had assembled 300 pounds of rice and corn; six dozen eggs; nine blocks of sugar; twenty pounds of coffee; a bamboo tube of salt; pecks of tomatoes, beans, and dried peas. There were also 110 pounds of salted carabao jerky, plus twenty squawking chickens, housed in a portable coop.

McCoy had acquired a .45 caliber Colt revolver. Boelens left with a swollen jaw, thanks to the painful extraction of a wisdom tooth. And Dobervich was just plain lucky to leave. Racked with a fever and vomiting, he was quarantined in his own craft while the rest of the thirty-six-man detachment occupied the other five barotos, the twenty-foot dugout canoes that would be pulled, paddled, or poled up the shallow river on the first leg of their journey.

While roughly ten of Laureta's men accompanied the expedition as soldiers, the work of propelling the barotos was the responsibility of the Ata tribesmen who served as cargadores. Laureta, the escapees learned, had taken the Atas' elders hostage in order to pacify their territory. And though the Atas feared Laureta, the Americans stared uneasily at the pygmies' primitive yet deadly arsenal of spears and poison-tipped arrows.

Also along for at least part of the journey were Laureta, Lieutenants Tuvilla and Rivera, Sergeant Baguilod, and, much to the delight of the escapees, Big Boy. The sight of Big Boy cradling his BAR as they snaked along the shimmering river was reassuring. Another welcome addition was Sgt. Magdaleno Dueñas. Nearly thirty years old, yet barely five feet tall with a whistling, high-pitched voice, the hardworking Dueñas was responsible for their baggage. He wanted nothing more than to be an American soldier and citizen, so the next best thing for him was to serve alongside Americans.

At 1730, the party stopped for the night at a small outpost called Florida. "Here we were given an example of how Filipinos can throw things together. In no time at all they had built a serviceable table, served coffee, and then rice and meat," McCoy wrote in his log. The laborious process of setting up—erecting shelters, starting a fire, and preparing meals—then striking camp would be repeated daily and the Americans would never stop being amazed at the skill and efficiency of the Filipinos.

The serpentine river's strong current, 3 to 4 knots, made for slow progress. The barotos often ran aground in the rapids and all hands would have to splash out to push the canoes into deeper water. The first two days would prove such a struggle that they covered only about twenty kilometers. It was not surprising then that Shofner, Grashio, Hawkins, and Marshall decided to stretch their legs onshore late in the morning of the second day. In more ways than they imagined, the jungle was calling them. "Soon we rounded a bend and were out of sight of the barotos, savouring the feeling of being jungle explorers, treading the wild, uncharted heartland of Mindanao," recalled Shofner. Suddenly, a strange male voice beckoned to them from the brush: "I'm Mae West. Come up and see me sometime."

Startled, they stopped in their tracks. For several seconds, no one uttered a word.

"Hey, Shifty," said Grashio, breaking the silence, "am I going nuts?"

"I'm Mae West," repeated the voice, now sounding more like a command than an invitation. "Come up and see me sometime!"

At that moment, said Shofner, "a human apparition" appeared. It was a rail of an old man, toothless and bowlegged, wearing a shawl-like robe. Though fair-skinned, his appearance bore an uncanny resemblance to the Indian leader Mahatma Gandhi.

"Hot dog!" he exclaimed. "Americans! I'm glad to see you!"

He led the bewildered Americans to the bamboo hut that was his home. After somewhat translating the man's language—a bizarre smattering of Spanish, local dialects, and American slang, mostly movie dialogue—they deduced that he had once lived in the United States and was, in all likelihood, a fugitive from the law. Lonely and half-mad, he now lived with three old, raggedly clothed women whom Grashio referred to as his "antiquated harem."

After politely taking leave of their host, they pressed on, joined by Boelens, who had come ashore when the barotos were beached for lunch. They walked leisurely along the riverbank with their pant legs rolled up, crossing small streams and marveling at the pristine beauty of the jungle as birds and monkeys perched on hanging branches noisily heralded their passing. "We were about two bends ahead of the main party when we saw him," wrote Shofner.

Shofner was referring to an indigenous tribesman, not an Ata, but perhaps related, short in stature, bushy-haired, and with skin "as dark as mahogany." He wore only a loincloth and carried a ten-foot spear twice as tall as himself, as well as a bow and satchel of arrows. Ten others, similarly dressed and equipped, followed in single file. It looked to be a hunting party, but what these men were hunting became an immediate matter of speculation. "I thought of my bolo, but knew it would be useless if they attacked us with their long spears and bows and arrows," recalled Hawkins. "We did the only thing we could think of—just stood there trying to appear nonchalant until the party advanced and halted about 15 feet away from us."

The two sides stood face-to-face, motionless, each silently sizing up the other. Though the feral glint in the eyes of the hunters was unmistakable, "they seemed to be as spellbound as we were," said Hawkins, "for during those few moments they said nothing, but merely stared at us with a look of wonder. No doubt we were the first white men they had ever seen." Then, just as suddenly as the tribesmen had appeared, they melted back into the jungle.

Their lesson learned, the Americans would not stray from the barotos until disembarking at the home of Lieutenant Rivera, near the outpost of Gupitan, at dusk. There, light from an oil lantern revealed more of the incomparable hospitality of the Philippines, as well as the incredible speed by which the bamboo telegraph operated: their names had been carved onto the bamboo cups from which they drank. As they retired, massive thunderheads unleashed a fierce downpour.

The following morning, they learned that the heavy rains had raised the water level of the river, creating churning rapids. Not even the choppy waters nor the sporadic showers could dampen their enthusiasm. Not only were they leaving Dapecol behind, they were embarking on once-in-a-lifetime journey. They paddled along, pointing in wonderment at the sight of Ata tree houses lodged high above them. Stopping near one such residence for lunch, the Marines found a bow and some arrows and, with childlike glee, took turns firing the arrows into the brush.

Encounters with natives were few but noteworthy. McCoy did his best to limn the incredible journey in his log: "0730—met about 3 families of Atas floating downstream on bamboo rafts . . . the women's breasts are no larger than the men's. (P.S. Just passed another raft. I was wrong about the breasts.)"

Spellbound, they floated along, dazzled by the foliage lining the palm-fringed riverbank. The chatter and songs of parrots, kingfishers, and red-beaked toucans known as *kalaw* birds provided a fitting soundtrack. "I sure would like to take a movie of this trip," lamented McCoy.

Upon their arrival at Kapalong, an old constabulary camp fifty miles from Dapecol, the Atas were released from their indentured servitude and Laureta contacted the local chieftain to requisition more porters. It was the end of the line for Laureta, too. The next morning—Easter Sunday—after Grashio led a prayer service and before the group, which now numbered forty-six men, set out on foot for Agusan, Laureta placed Lieutenant Tuvilla in charge of the expedition. The Americans, effusive in their thanks, were sad to see Laureta return to his command.

"We'll be seeing you later," yelled Dyess, "when we come back with the Yanks in the tanks!"

"Bring the Marines, too," said Laureta. "And some Flying Fortresses!"

Regardless of the fact that the territory was marked "UNEXPLORED" on their maps, they had, metaphorically speaking, been here before. Less than a mile into their overland trek, their well-defined mountain path turned into a faint trail. And then it inexplicably vanished. The swamp fiasco was still fresh in Mellnik's mind, so he pulled Tuvilla aside to ask if the guide knew where he was going. "Yes," replied Tuvilla, reassuringly, "this is Main Street to him."

Warily, they shrugged their shoulders and continued onward—as well as upward and downward—through the Mindanao wilderness. They crawled up hills and slid down ravines, shimmied through rock formations, tiptoed across trickling streams, and waded rivers gorged with storm water. Clinging to thorny vines, branches, and saplings, they struggled to navigate the slippery terrain—45-degree slopes were the norm—cutting and puncturing their hands in the process.

As the meandering column ascended to higher altitudes, the trees loomed even taller, forming a canopy several hundred feet in height. These giant natural umbrellas failed to protect them from the incessant rain, which cascaded down rocks and hillsides in miniature waterfalls, threatening to knock them off their feet. The downpours and the crossing and fording of streams and rivers left the men soaked. At night, their shelters leaked, making sleeping and drying their clothes and gear impossible. On the bright side, there was little worry of encountering any Japanese.

The escapees had been impressed with the ability of their previous Ata porters to pole the heavily laden barotos through the strong currents of the Libuganon River, but they were absolutely amazed at the strength and agility of their replacements. Most of the new cargadores weighed no more than 110 pounds, yet, with the help of an ingenious harness of straps crossing their shoulders and forehead, each carried loads weighing between sixty and 100 pounds. And they did it barefoot, too. "How they managed to walk, climb or stumble all day long is beyond me," said McCoy. "And I would never have believed it if I had not seen it."

After supper, the Americans and Filipinos gathered around the fire for conversation and song. One of their fondest memories was that of Dueñas's rendition of "Home on the Range." But they were soon mesmerized by the sound of the Atas slapping out rhythms on long, narrow drums. A slow tempo steadily increased until it reached a furious, fluctuating cadence. "At that level," recalled Mellnik, "the wild and hypnotic rhythm touched the inner core of my being. I listened with fascination and dread as the weird messages sped into the night." At times, it must have seemed as though they were traveling not just through a wild jungle, but through time itself.

At Binucayan, the southernmost barrio in Agusan Province, they found a curiously empty collection of dilapidated huts. The village had been abandoned by its inhabitants for fear of the Japanese, a fact that struck McCoy as absurd. "No Jap would ever get near the place, it was so far into the hinterland." Twenty kilometers north was the peculiarly named town of Johnson, where they were honored not only with tuba, coconut milk, and a young pig, but also a smart presentation of arms from the motley-uniformed guerrilla garrison. Stiffening their aching backs, they returned the salute wearily.

It was the next village, Loreto, that made the most memorable impression on the weary travelers. Hanging from a pole atop the tin-roofed municipal building in the waning daylight was the first American flag they had seen on display in a year. "Seldom in my life have I been so shaken emotionally as I was at the sight," remembered Grashio. "For the first time since April 1942, I felt like an American again, rather than a prisoner of the Japanese perpetually on the run."

THURSDAY, APRIL 29–SATURDAY, MAY 8, 1943
Agusan and Misamis Oriental Provinces

Save for a surprise appearance by the Japanese, almost nothing warranted an interruption much less an abandonment of a meal, but the escapees were so excited on this morning that they could barely touch their bountiful breakfast of rice, chicken, fish, and carabao meat. The officer in charge at Loreto, Lieutenant Antonio, had confirmed that there was a radio transmitter and receiver operated by the guerrillas. It was located, as he understood, near the town of Amparo, just south of the Japanese-held coastal city of Butuan. That was not all. "And you may be interested to know that I have heard that American submarines are landing supplies," he added.

With the overland segment of their expedition concluded, they excitedly discharged the Atas and most of their escorts and waited long enough for a cobbler to affix a piece of rubber tire to the heel of one of Shofner's shoes before boarding five bancas, larger seagoing canoes, at 0930. The twenty-six-man group floated swiftly down the tributarial Umayam River for ten miles before merging at noon into the Agusan. Compared to the Libuganon, the Agusan was a broad, relatively straight and thickly populated waterway. McCoy, peering through the cogon and hyacinths fencing the riverbanks, noticed the river dwellers working near what seemed to be floating bamboo bungalows. These structures, moored onshore, were engineered to adjust to the rise and fall of the river. The men spent the night at one floating settlement called Teogum. A family had graciously vacated their home, but left behind a pet monkey, chicken, and yowling kittens, making for a restless night.

Red-eyed and in a foul mood, they returned to the river just before 0800. The sluggish current made progress difficult—at least for their bancas. It was early afternoon when a Filipino in one of the lead bancas began to gesticulate wildly. It was a giant snake, "as long as a telephone pole," recalled Shofner, knifing through the water perpendicular to their course at a rapid rate of speed. The oarsmen paddled frantically in reverse to slow their progress. Visibly concerned, Jumarong leaned over to Shofner and whispered "python," as if the oversize creature could hear him. "The big snake moved on relentlessly, unheeding—as if we weren't even there," said Shofner. "We watched it slither ashore on the far side and disappear into the underbrush."

Several hours of exhausting though otherwise uneventful paddling deposited them at the town of Talacogon, thirty miles south of Amparo. The icy reception they received from the town authorities worsened their mood. "They're probably afraid to befriend us," speculated Boelens. "The Japs are mighty close. These boys have to play both sides of the street if they want to keep their heads." This experience was taken as a portent, an indication of what kind of treatment they could expect, given their proximity to Japanese-controlled areas. But subsequent stops at the towns of Guadalupe, Esperanza, and Las Nieves suggested that Talacogon was an aberration. At Amparo, their fears were allayed.

It was one thing to be greeted by sympathetic civilians or an American flag, quite another to be welcomed by a genuine American. He was Lt. Walter Mester and he was the first Yank they had seen since leaving Dapecol. After filling him in on the story of their flight, they presented the letter from Lieutenant Colonel McClish and inquired about the guerrilla radio.

"It isn't here," said Mester. "Division HQ is at Medina . . . west of Butuan. That's where you'll find McClish, and the transmitter is supposed to be located not far from there."

"Can we arrange to get there?" asked McCoy.

"The Japs are real close. You'll have to go around them, then take a boat across the bay to Medina. You might want to send a couple of men ahead, and bring the others on later."

The decision to split up was a difficult one, much more so than choosing their representatives. There were eight sets of toes wriggling in the dirt. The only men with footwear durable enough to continue the journey were McCoy and Shofner.

Barrio Buenavista, bounded by palm trees, sugar-white sands, and the bright blue waters of Butuan Bay, was postcard-picturesque. In continuous motion since shoving off from Amparo at 0930, the men arrived at Buenavista at 1700. Here they found another guerrilla officer waiting for them—another American, no less. Capt. Tom Baxter told them that they had little time to rest.

"You will leave at high tide, around ten o'clock tonight," he announced. "I've arranged a banca for you."

"How long is the trip?" asked Shofner.

"Twelve to fifteen hours. It depends on how much Jap-dodging you have to do. They patrol the coast in a motor launch, and rumor has it they've got a two-masted banca with machine guns. You'll lay close to shore."

When it was time to board, Big Boy sidled up to Shofner and slid the strap of his treasured BAR off his shoulder. "Here," he told Shofner, "you might need this." Shofner was both humbly grateful and newly confident. "I felt armed," he would write. Joining McCoy and Shofner were Tuvilla, Baguilod, and a diminutive Dutchman named Kreickenbeek who before the war had sold dry goods along the rivers of Mindanao; his business in Medina was unknown.

McCoy's last pre-launch task was to send a runner with a message to the others to set out for Buenavista at once. Once settled, he pulled Shofner aside. "Whoever built her," he whispered, "must have been in a helluva hurry." Shofner was in agreement. "The banka [sic] was nobody's luxury liner. Sixteen feet long and built of rough planks caulked with shredded coconut husks, it was flimsy-looking transport at best."

There was little wind, so the oars rhythmically slapped the ink-black waters, gliding the banca along the coastline. Back in his element, lounging on the deck, McCoy sighed.

"It beats the bugs, old boy. Here we are, a tropic night, sky full of stars, no leeches, no snakes, no crocodiles."

McCoy's nostalgia, however, belied a palpable apprehension. "Both of us were edgy. We didn't know these people," recalled Shofner. "For a few pesos they might hand us over to the first Jap launch that came sputtering by." Shofner saw McCoy give his .45 a furtive check; he hugged his BAR.

The passengers dozed uneasily for most of the night, putting in to Cayugan at 0730. For twenty-five quinine tablets, they received camotes, bananas, eggs, two chickens, and a kid goat. It would be a slow, hot day of sculling. For Tuvilla, who became seasick, the voyage could not end soon enough. They had already exceeded Baxter's time frame, but Shofner did not hold it against him. The limits of Shofner's patience, however, would be tested when they landed at Linugos at sundown for more provisions. Clouds rolled in and a strong wind began to whip the sea. Their timid captain saw a fine opportunity to hole up in port and wait out what appeared to be an approaching storm.

"Very dangerous," he told Shofner. "Weather bad. Very dangerous in banca."

"We go anyway."

The captain was adamant, but could not match Shofner's trademark obstinance.

"Let's shove off, *now*."

"At last Medina is in sight," scribbled McCoy the next morning, May 5. "I was beginning to think it did not exist." The men were escorted by locals, children, and dogs in what became a procession down the palm-fringed, packed-coral streets of Medina, a prosperous coastal settlement of nipa and wood cottages located in the heart of a rich coconut-producing area in Misamis Oriental. They soon realized that their inquiries as to the location of the headquarters of McClish were unnecessary as the glare from the new corrugated tin roof atop a large building in the plaza was like a guiding star.

They soon caught a glimpse of the colonel striding toward them with a purposeful vigor, his pistol holster swinging from his belt. In his early thirties, he was sturdily built, with dark hair and olive skin. Two stolid Filipino riflemen followed closely behind.

"Welcome, welcome," said a smiling McClish while pumping their hands. "You must have had a difficult trip. Welcome . . . come in out of the sun."

"It all ran together in a rush of good-feeling; the firm handclasps, the ebullient nature, the smile," Shofner remembered.

"Pedro," said McClish, motioning the visitors inside and one of his bodyguards away, "something cool to drink for our friends."

Shofner's keen eyes noticed that McClish's holster flap was open. Sure enough, once they were out of the view of the onlookers, the curtain came down on his courteous act. He took a seat behind a table and narrowed his eyes into a steely, investigative glare.

"Who are you?" he snapped.

"I'm Shofner, Marines. This is Commander McCoy, Navy. We escaped from Davao Penal Colony. There are ten of us and guides, but the others are waiting in Buenav—"

McClish, unimpressed, interrupted and issued a stern challenge: "Prove it."

The routine—from a fellow American, to boot—was growing tiresome. "Sir?"

"How do I know who you are?" asked McClish.

McCoy and Shofner launched into a recap of their story, which they concluded by introducing McClish to Tuvilla and Baguilod.

"Yes," conceded McClish. "I sent a letter to Captain Laureta."

"That's why we're here," continued Shofner. "We understand you have a radio, and contact with submarines. We want to get to Australia, so we can report about the conditions in the camps. A lot of men are dying in there."

McClish's attitude softened when Shofner produced his collection of dog-eared photographs. Ultimately, the guerrilla officer rose to extend his hand. The missing bodyguard, Pedro, then emerged from behind a partition; the Americans heard the safety on his rifle click. This time, on the orders of McClish, Pedro went off to procure some tuba. McClish then turned to his stunned guests and smiled.

"Welcome to the 110th Division, gentlemen."

With refreshments in hand, the visitors hovered over several maps spread upon a table. McClish's dark eyes sparkled when Tuvilla detailed the size and disposition of Laureta's forces, for the forces at his command had now doubled.

"Captain Laureta instructs me to tell you, sir," said Tuvilla, "that he is anxious to cooperate in our common cause, to drive the enemy from our land and restore freedom to our people. God bless America."

Shofner cringed at the mawkish speech, but McClish's response moved him: "We who are privileged to stand beside our Filipino brothers are filled with admiration for their sacrifice and determination in the face of a vicious enemy."

The reply provided the escapees some insight into the personality of Edward Ernest McClish, a Native American of Choctaw heritage from Oklahoma who had come to his current assignment via official orders and his own initiative. McClish, formerly of the 57th Philippine Scouts, was sent from Manila in late 1941 to help mobilize the Philippine Army on Panay. After his unit was routed in a surprise attack near Malabang in Mindanao's southern Lanao Province in late April 1942, he escaped from a field hospital to Bukidnon, where he began to organize resistance forces. McCoy and Shofner listened attentively as he explained the magic behind the guerrilla army—one that seemed to have no central leader, no ascertainable organization, no supply chain, just individual, autonomous commands.

According to McClish, the island of Mindanao, with its 36,537 square miles of rugged terrain and thousands upon thousands of acres of virgin jungle, had been designated the Tenth Military District by General MacArthur's Southwest Pacific Area GHQ in Australia. With machine gun rapidity, McClish jabbed at the map and rattled off the names of enemy-held towns as well as the size and strength of their garrisons. The largest concentration of Japanese forces, including a whole division of infantry and several air units, he told them, was in the Davao City area. That revelation got McCoy's and Shofner's attention; they had escaped right out from under the noses of the largest Imperial Army presence between Luzon and New Guinea.

"How many men do you have?" inquired Shofner.

"Difficult question. The morning report is never quite the same two days running."

The muster rolls of the 110th Division fluctuated because the army was largely composed of local militias much like the outfit that had saved the escapees at Kinamayan. Personnel issues were only part of McClish's problems.

"We're short of everything," he added. "Organization and communications are difficult. Supply is critical. What we don't have we make, what we can't make we steal, and what we can't steal we do without."

Resourcefulness would be a guerrilla trademark. Bullets were made from brass curtain rods, highly volatile concoctions of ammonium nitrate and TNT, and gunpowder painstakingly extracted from firecrackers and Japanese naval mines. Foliage-concealed trenches dug in roads caused enemy trucks to careen and crash. The jungle was so littered with pits, sharpened bamboo spikes, trip wires, and other booby traps that Japanese troops refused to stray from the main roads, complaining that "even the grass bites." Foot pedals charged radio batteries, water power turned rice mills, and messages were delivered by horsemen and relays of fleet-footed couriers. Engines ran on fuel scavenged from shipwrecks and the tanks of mining operations. Tuba, too, was useful for more than just getting drunk; some vehicles had been ingeniously converted to run on alcohol distilled from the high-octane coconut booze. A former Manila millionaire and U.S. Navy Reserve officer supervised the printing of millions of "emergency" pesos on meatpacking paper. There was even a guerrilla newspaper, *The Freeman*, published by a Filipino who had majored in journalism at the University of Oregon.

The woeful shortage of trained officers and leaders was a bigger problem. The nascent movement, barely a half-year old in May 1943, was run by a handful of Americans, about forty officers and men like McClish who had refused to surrender, as well as others lucky enough to slip away from the POW enclosures at Dansalan and Malaybalay before being shipped to Dapecol. But there were other, unlikely leaders who stepped forward.

The guerrilla army was an outfit of irregulars, in terms of composition, background, and individual personalities. The dramatis personae of the guerrilla epic would eventually include representatives from every branch of the U.S. armed forces, the Signal Corps, quartermaster units, and the remnants of long-surrendered, dissolved outfits such as the 19th Bombardment Group and the 440th Ordnance. Some were Lt. Cmdr. John D. Bulkeley's PT-boaters left behind after MacArthur's flight. Others had previous service in the Philippine Constabulary. There were mestizos whose fathers, some of whom were African-American, had served during the Spanish-American War or the Philippine Insurrection. There were British, Swedish, Syrian, and Indian citizens, too. There was even a German who had been working as a mechanical engineer at the Mindanao Motherlode gold mine when war broke out. He had fought for his fatherland in World War I, but despised Hitler and threw in his lot with the guerrillas.

There was also a large number of American and Filipino civilians, from stranded businessmen to missionary priests, who were actively involved in the guerrilla movement. Many wealthy Filipinos provided financial and material backing. Others, extraordinary men like Vicente Zapanta, invested their entire lives in the cause. Reportedly a U.S. Navy veteran of World War I, Zapanta volunteered not only his services, but also the large, two-masted banca that he had used to make a nice profit in commercial trading. The ship would be christened the *Athena*, in honor of the goddess of war, and Zapanta promoted to admiral of the guerrilla navy.

Hatred of the Japanese transcended even bitter, centuries-old religious quarrels. The relationship between the Moros, the Muslim inhabitants of western Mindanao, and Christian Filipinos had been at best tenuous, at worst bloody. Because the Japanese were equal-opportunity oppressors, Moro *datus*, or chiefs, decided to join forces with the Christian guerrillas. It was an uneasy truce, one that would end with the war. Tribes such as the Manobos and Negrito pygmies were also brought into the guerrilla fold. Whether one was white, black, yellow, or brown, Christian or Muslim, male or female, young or old, rich or poor, illiterate or educated, all were united in their efforts for a common cause: the defeat of the Japanese empire.

The guerrillas had been able to put aside most of their differences. The bigger conflict was between Mindanao and Australia.

"As far as MacArthur's headquarters are concerned, our prime mission is intelligence—report on Japanese shipping, air traffic, troop movements," said McClish.

To that end, once contact with Australia had been established, GHQ had begun to supply the guerrillas via submarine. The first landing, McCoy and Shofner learned, had taken place just two months earlier. Some weapons and ammunition had been delivered, but the supplies consisted mostly of cash, medicine, and the radio equipment, codebooks, and batteries needed to set up coast watcher stations. Also included were cigarettes, matchbooks, and other small items imprinted with the words "I Shall Return," which were designed to further engender the cult of Mac-Arthur in the Philippines. From chocolate bars to carbines, these items, though meager in sum, were a tantalizing taste of what came to be called "The Aid," symbolic, appetite-whetting samples of the fulfillment of Mac-Arthur's promise of liberation. But in order to prevent the guerrillas from initiating any major engagements and unwinnable battles, which might jeopardize the overall mission, GHQ would deliberately not supply enough firepower.

While the Filipinos seemed willing to work and wait patiently for "The Aid," as well as MacArthur's return, they were not content simply to spy on the Japanese. They cared little about global strategy and even less for the mandates of officers in Australia or Washington. They supplied and sheltered the guerrillas, and in return wanted tangible results—dead Japanese. This demand forced the men on the ground in the Philippines, men like McClish, to burn a small candle on both ends.

"We're an army of bamboo, rattan and courage, gentlemen," summarized McClish.

Lastly, McClish admitted, somewhat hesitantly, these were not solely his problems. As just one of what would eventually be eight subcommanders in charge of separate territorial jurisdictions on the island, he was in command of only the 110th Division, which was composed of the 110th, 113th, and 114th Regiments, units spread across the provinces of Misamis Oriental, Agusan, and Surigao. Overall command of the Tenth Military District, he told them, was held by a brigadier general named Wendell W. Fertig, whose headquarters was in Misamis City in Misamis Occidental, 150 air miles from Medina in northwestern Mindanao.

"I have a radio transmitter in Gingoog, about fifteen miles from here," said McClish. "It is in contact with Fertig's headquarters, which relays our messages to Australia."

McCoy and Shofner, still dazed by McClish's briefing, excitedly asked if a trip to Gingoog could be arranged.

"I'll take you there myself," offered McClish. "It's a horseback jour-

The island of Corregidor in Manila Bay was home to nearly 15,000 American and Filipino troops before its surrender to Japanese forces on May 6, 1942.

This cartoon appeared in the *Chicago Tribune* in late January 1944, upon the long-awaited release of the Dyess Story.

First Lt. Austin "Shifty" Shofner on
Corregidor in early 1942.

Then-Major William Edwin Dyess just
months before his tragic death on
December 23, 1943.

Thirty-six-year-old Lt. Commander
Melvyn H. McCoy was the oldest
as well as the highest-ranking member
of the escape party.

Nearly 1,000 American prisoners of war were crammed aboard the
Erie Maru, a decrepit, coal-burning 7,000-ton merchant vessel, for the
voyage from Manila to Mindanao.

The main gate at the Davao Penal Colony, through which nearly 2,000 American
prisoners of war entered the camp in the fall of 1942, would be the escapees'
first barrier to freedom.

The American POWs in Dapecol were housed according to rank in these long, poorly maintained, barnlike barracks.

Claro Laureta, the diminutive, yet dynamic commander of the 107th Infantry Division, as well as all guerrilla forces in the Davao area, provided aid and assistance to the escapees following their breakout from Dapecol.

The escapees' Filipino allies: (from left to right) Juan Acenas, assistant superintendent of the Davao Penal Colony; Mrs. Candido Abrina; Candido "Pop" Abrina, raconteur and Dapecol agricultural supervisor, 1946.

Lt. Commander Charles "Chick" Parsons (left), the man described by General Douglas MacArthur as "the bravest man I know," and Colonel Wendell Fertig, leader of the Mindanao guerrillas.

The USS *Trout,* the submarine that extracted the first group of escaped POWs from Mindanao on July 9, 1943, had a unique history of special missions.

From left to right, Major Ed Dyess, Lt. Cmdr. Melvyn McCoy, General Douglas MacArthur, and Major Stephen Mellnik conversing in MacArthur's office in the A.M.P. Building in Brisbane, Australia, on July 30, 1943.

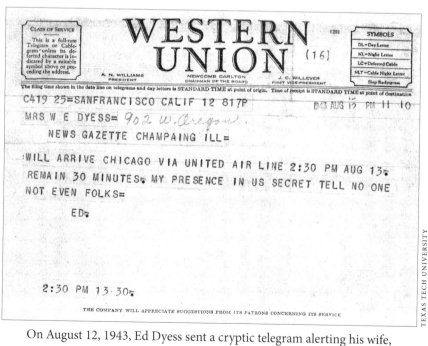

On August 12, 1943, Ed Dyess sent a cryptic telegram alerting his wife, Marajen, that he would be returning home to the United States.

Five members of the escape party are reunited at the Marine Corps Barracks in Quantico, Virginia, in the summer of 1944: (from left to right) Major Michiel Dobervich, Lt. Col. Austin Shofner, Commander Melvyn McCoy, Major Jack Hawkins, and Major Samuel Grashio.

After the war, Robert Spielman returned to his home state of Texas with a lieutenant colonel's oak leaves on his shoulders, and a wife and family, too.

Paul Marshall, an erstwhile enlisted man, returned to the United States at war's end a decorated guerrilla commander and Army lieutenant colonel.

Lt. Leo Boelens, the master mechanic and the only escapee not to return to the United States, was killed on Mindanao in early 1944.

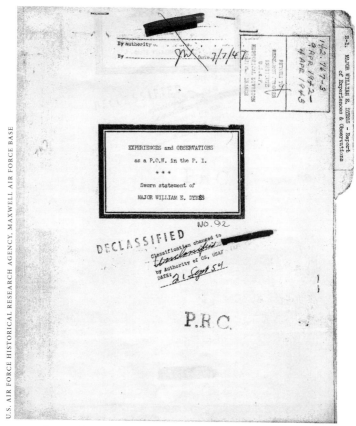

EXPERIENCES and OBSERVATIONS

as a P.O.W. in the P. I.

* * *

Sworn statement of

MAJOR WILLIAM E. DYESS

DECLASSIFIED

P.R.C.

Ed Dyess's deposition would form the foundation of what the War Department would later call "the greatest story of the war in the Pacific."

ney of course; the country's too rough for anything else. . . . We'll go tomorrow. But first, the governor would like to have you as his guests for dinner."

That evening, ex–Provincial Governor Don Gregorio Peleaz, a wealthy white-haired gentleman of the landed aristocracy whose speech was affected with a Castilian lilt, entertained the two former prisoners of war like visiting dignitaries in his Spanish villa. An eleven-piece orchestra played while they enjoyed a multicourse dinner with shiny silverware and white linen napkins. While puffing on their after-dinner cigars, McCoy and Shofner knew that the others would not believe the dream world they had discovered.

Laden with a requisition for food, a pair of rubber shoes, and thirty bars of soap, as well as $100 with which to buy salt for his men and a box of face powder for Sergeant Baguilod's girl (the cash was a gift on behalf of all the escapees), and, last but certainly not least, a message for Captain Laureta prepared by McClish, Tuvilla left at midnight aboard the *Athena* for Buenavista. On the orders of McClish, the guerrilla flagship would ferry the rest of the Dapecol fugitives to Medina on its return trip. It looked to be a joyful reunion—if all went well in Gingoog.

Just past noon on Thursday, May 6, McClish, McCoy, and Shofner were saddled atop three native ponies clipping down a colorful jungle corridor. His spirits brimming, Shofner thought it appropriate for another lecture on the proud history of the Marine Corps.

"Have you ever heard of the Horse Marines?" Shofner yelled as they bounced along. "The cavalry unit that protected American citizens in China from 1912 to 1938? Don't you know that the Marines have a great tradition in all forms of sport, as well as all forms of warfare?"

Greeting them at the expansive Anakan Lumber Company, some five miles from Gingoog, was the mill's manager, a fifty-something American named Cecil Walter, who was trapped behind enemy lines. Walter showed them to the powerful transmitter, which had been used before the war for business purposes, mainly communication with Manila.

For the first time since the fall of Corregidor, exactly one year to the day earlier, McCoy assumed a familiar position and sat down at the transmitter to dispatch two messages. "It was an exciting moment for us," Shofner would write. If McCoy realized the significance of the day, he did not acknowledge it in his log. Nor did any hint of emotion appear in his copy. He followed procedure by identifying himself and reporting in to his superiors before communicating the facts.

> FOR COMMANDER NAVAL FORCES SOUTHWEST PACIFIC
> INFO COMMANDER MARINE FORCES
> FROM LIEUTENANT COMMANDER MELVYN H. MCCOY
>
> ARRIVED AFTER ESCAPE FROM AMERICAN PRISONER OF WAR CAMP DAVAO WITH THREE MARINE OFFICERS CAPTAIN SHOFNER, THREE AIR CORPS, CAPTAIN DYESS, ONE CAC [COAST ARTILLERY COMMAND], MAJOR MELLNIK AND TWO SERGEANTS X ALL CAPTURED BATAAN AND CORREGIDOR HAVE EXTENSIVE INFO REGARDING CORREGIDOR X BRUTALITIES AND ATROCITIES WITH EXTREMELY HEAVY DEATH TOLL TO WAR PRISONERS DUE SAME X HAVE SOME INFO RE DAVAO PROVINCE X IF PRACTICABLE REQUEST ENTIRE PARTY PLUS TWO FILIPINOS WHO AIDED ESCAPE DEPART HERE VIA NEXT TRANSPORTATION AVAILABLE X

The second message, previously prepared by Mellnik, was sent to the attention of Lt. Gen. Richard Sutherland, MacArthur's chief of staff. Given Mellnik's relationships with members of MacArthur's inner circle, this message was more personal, as well as alarmingly detailed, in order to elicit a rapid response.

> FOR LIEUTENANT GENERAL RICHARD K. SUTHERLAND,
> GENERAL HEADQUARTERS
> U.S. ARMY FORCES IN AUSTRALIA
> FROM MAJOR STEPHEN M. MELLNIK
>
> HAVE ESCAPED WITH SEVEN OFFICERS AND TWO ENLISTED MEN FROM JAPANESE WAR PRISONERS CAMP IN DAVAO PENAL COLONY X LIEUTENANT COMMANDER MCCOY US NAVY HAS REQUESTED SENIOR NAVAL OFFICER IN AUSTRALIA FOR SUBMARINE TRANSPORTATION TO AUSTRALIA X WILL YOUR OFFICE ASSURE A FAVORABLE ANSWER X JAPS VIOLATING ALL RULES OF WARFARE AND DECENCY X FIFTY PERCENT USAFFE

FORCES SURRENDERED IN BATAAN NOW DEAD FROM MALNU-
TRITION AND DISEASES X REMAINDER IN VARIOUS STAGES OF
BERI BERI, DYSENTERY, MALARIA AND BLINDNESS DUE TO VI-
TAMIN DEFICIENCY X WAINWRIGHT, MOORE, BEEBE, DRAKE
GOOD HEALTH AT SURRENDER X REGARDS COLONEL DILLER,
GENERALS MARQUAT AND WILLOUGHBY X HOPE TO SEE YOU
SOON X

Their mission completed, McClish, McCoy, and Shofner rumbled back to Medina along a rutted roadway in a battered, alcohol-fueled Chevrolet, estimated to be of 1931 vintage, that McClish had procured. Though in constant pain from blisters caused by his saddle, Shofner could not help but ponder the whereabouts of the other escapees in the closing sentence of his diary entry on the evening of May 7: "I wonder whats wrong with the rest of the gang—they should have been here by now—sickness—Japs or they didn't get the word[?]."

There was still no sign of their comrades the next day, but McCoy and Shofner did meet McClish's chief of staff, Maj. Clyde C. Childress. Childress, a twenty-five-year-old officer from Fort Worth, Texas, had fought in the ill-fated action at Malabang and had headed into the hills rather than surrender.

A fearless warrior and a straight shooter, Childress would be a trusted friend to the escapees. He tempered the enthusiasm of the two messengers, who believed they had just accomplished an essential part of their mission at Anakan. McCoy would write in his diary of a warning from Childress that, for reasons unknown, "communications with GHQ were slow and none too satisfactory."

CHAPTER 16

Little Time to Rest

I find my way with weary stumbling feet
Between the broken fragments of defeat
"We have our honor; we were meant to fail"
I hear the words but still there is the trail.

SUNDAY, MAY 9–MONDAY, MAY 10, 1943
Medina, Misamis Oriental Province

It was 0520 when Mellnik reached under the mosquito net to shake McCoy awake. To McCoy, just returned from a guerrilla dance, it seemed like a bad dream. Mellnik must have thought he was dreaming, too. He stood there, absorbing the lace curtains, the frame-shuttered windows and the fancy, four-poster bed from which McCoy was now stirring, his mouth agape.

"Stop gawking," said McCoy. "Let's clean you up and put you in some decent clothes."

Haggard from two days of dodging shoals and shore-based small-arms fire, the escapees had not seen anything yet. Outfitted in new khaki and shoes—donations from Chinese merchants and McClish's stores—the entire escape party celebrated the seventy-fourth birthday of Governor Peleaz with a lavish lunch. They were then whisked by sailboat to a fiesta celebrating the Queen of May in the village of Daan-Lungsod, about fifteen miles southeast of Medina. The fiesta, as much as Marshall could remember of it, was a wild affair. "Jeez, everybody got snookered to the gills."

After a succession of speeches from assembled dignitaries, the escaped POWs were summoned to the stage for the coronation of the May Queen and a standing ovation. But their celebrity was taking its toll. "We went to such events both because we were guests and because by so doing we helped maintain esprit de corps in the guerrilla army," said McCoy. "But we never forgot for an instant that our friends were still rotting in Jap prison camps."

There was something else bothering McCoy: he had had no confirmation of his messages from General Fertig's headquarters. Perhaps there was more to Clyde Childress's warning about communicating with Australia than they knew. A group conference determined that a face-to-face meeting with Fertig was in order. McCoy and Mellnik, as ranking officers, were selected for the task. The others offered their services, however temporary, to the guerrilla army.

On the afternoon of May 10, after lunch at Vicente Zapanta's home in Daan-Lungsod, McClish promoted each of the remaining escapees one grade. Thus, by the orders typed by McClish's adjutant on ruled school tablet paper, they officially became officers—brevet, or "bamboo grade"— in the Army of the United States, USFIP. Though de la Cruz and Jumarong exchanged their prison stripes for enlisted chevrons, perhaps the biggest leap was made by Marshall and Spielman, newly minted second lieutenants who were assigned to the 114th Regiment. The arrangement was confusing, but each escapee felt as though he owed a debt to the guerrillas. "I don't know how we can be officers in the Marine Corps and the Army at the same time," remarked Dobervich, "but if it's all right with McClish, I guess it's all right with me."

As their comrades rummaged for insignia and weapons, McCoy, Mellnik, and Childress boarded the *Athena*. They would be taking an indirect route to Misamis Occidental, stopping first at the town of Talakag in the northwest corner of Bukidnon Province to investigate a rumor.

"My intention," McCoy wrote in his log, "was to see a Lt. Commander Parsons, USNR, who had been left here by submarine in March, on a special intelligence mission."

WEDNESDAY, MAY 12–THURSDAY, JUNE 10, 1943

Misamis Oriental, Bukidnon, Lanao, and Misamis Occidental Provinces

McCoy knew that the popular flagship of the guerrilla navy was not a commissioned U.S. Navy vessel, but he had no objections with its designation as the USS *Athena*. Not that he would have dared say anything.

"The swarthy, husky members of the *Athena* crew needed only daggers in their teeth to make them look like pirates," he commented.

The *Athena*, in McCoy's words, was "the strangest flagship that ever flew the Stars and Stripes." Stretching forty feet from bow to stern with outriggers and two tall sail masts, Zapanta's diesel- and wind-powered ship was equal parts yacht, gunboat, and Chinese junk. There was no delineation between steerage and first class: the *Athena*'s food supply of chickens, pigs, and even a cow mingled on the deck with the human passengers and crew, which Zapanta had divided into sailors and Marines in imitation of the U.S. Navy. Despite Zapanta's hard brand of discipline, noted McCoy, his crew was fiercely loyal and "would have attacked a Jap battleship if he had given the order." Fortunately for the *Athena* and her passengers, there were no hostile encounters. The ship's most formidable piece of armament was a homemade three-inch cannon mounted on the bow. It was fired by hammering on a nail, which set off a dynamite cap. Mellnik, the artillery expert, asked a gunner about its range. "Seer," came the proud reply, "it fired so far we did not see."

Zapanta guided the *Athena* from Medina by hugging the coast, but to reach El Salvador, the town closest to their ultimate destination, he would have to proceed across the breadth of Macajalar Bay, an area filled with Japanese traffic. The *Athena* departed an intermediate stop at Balingasag in the afternoon in order to reach El Salvador at dawn, but the wind blew up during the night, creating rough seas. Daylight revealed three large armed enemy transports, well within range of observers. As the Americans ducked beneath the gunwales and covered up with burlap bags, Zapanta followed discreetly behind the convoy until the ships turned to Cagayan, then aimed the *Athena* toward El Salvador. Recalled McCoy, "Had we left Balingasag an hour later we would probably have ended up in the middle of these three Japanese ships."

From El Salvador, the Americans and their local guides set out on foot and horseback for Talakag, thirty miles due south. For two days they followed a ridgeline trail, past breathtaking waterfalls into the high plateau country of Bukidnon, territory that (if one could ignore the omnipresent coconut palm trees) closely resembled Great Plains farmland. The infinite cornfields and grassy hills provided a stunning contrast with the jungles of weeks past. For McCoy, a Midwesterner, never had home seemed so close, yet so impossibly distant.

They ferried the Cagayan River and then boarded a bus that deposited them in Talakag, headquarters of the 106th Division, commanded by Lt. Col. Robert V. Bowler, at about 1300. Bowler, a thirty-five-year-old former college economics professor, was hungry for information about his brother, Col. Louis Bowler, who had been on Corregidor. Mellnik reported that the elder Bowler had been in good health when last seen in Cabanatuan. Bowler then reciprocated with information of his own: he confirmed that a Navy officer named Parsons was indeed in this locality. And then as if to shroud the presence of Chick Parsons in the Philippines storm clouds arrived and rain fell.

The message reached Chick Parsons at the ranch where he was staying with a Jesuit missionary priest named Father Edward Haggerty. The sopping-wet courier unscrewed the cap on the bamboo tube that he had clenched in his teeth as he swam the raging Ipanan River. Parsons swiftly scanned the note, then readied to head out into the storm.

"You'll want to come, Padre," he said. "These men have just escaped from the Davao Prison Camp."

Despite their incredible story, the escapees did not make a good first impression on Haggerty. He seemed put off by the escapees' insistence that they be immediately evacuated to Australia. "We needed good men here to help us, and we didn't consider escaped prisoners any more heroic than the rest of us who had never surrendered," wrote Haggerty, an active guerrilla in spite of his priestly vows.

But Parsons understood the titanic effort it had taken to escape from the Japanese, and the escapees' determination to help their still captive comrades. He empathized with them in a way that only one had who shared nearly the same experiences could. Parsons, after all, was a member of their exclusive fraternity, although he could not tell them that. "Though outwardly frank," recalled Mellnik, Parsons "was most mysterious about his origin and mission."

Neither McCoy nor Mellnik knew that Parsons, while playing the role of Panamanian consul, had witnessed their humiliating march down Dewey Boulevard. It's unlikely that they would have believed the amazing story of how Parsons had managed not only to sneak his family out of the Philippines in a repatriation of diplomats, but, with the help of his son Peter, to smuggle a briefcase containing intelligence documents. Or how, just before boarding a Douglas DC-3 in Formosa, he had so thoroughly charmed the police commandant that the official requested that he "remember to tell the people at home"—referring to Panama—"the truth about Japanese hospitality."

"Believe me," promised Parsons, thinking of American authorities, "I'll certainly do that, *amigo*."

Nor would the Americans have believed that he had managed to keep his true identity secret during voyages on neutral ships from Shanghai to Singapore to South Africa and, ultimately, to New York, where his escape had ended on August 29, 1942. After all, the FBI did not believe Parsons.

"I'll radio your story to Australia," Parsons reassured McCoy and Mellnik. "MacArthur will be glad to hear someone finally broke out of a Jap PW camp."

Parsons's war, in all actuality, had only just begun when he arrived in New York Harbor. Shortly after he began work on a joint Army-Navy intelligence-gathering plan, a telegram arrived at the Navy Department: "SEND PARSONS IMMEDIATELY." It was signed, "MACARTHUR." Freshly promoted, Parsons trekked back across the Pacific to become the one-man office of Spyron, a derivative of the words "spy squadron," a unit that had been created under the aegis of the Philippine Regional Section of MacArthur's Southwest Pacific Area GHQ in Brisbane. There, Parsons convinced the Navy that using submarines to ferry supplies and agents to the Philippines would ultimately pay dividends with the establishment of coast watcher stations. He was joined by an Army officer named Charles Smith, who had effected his own astounding escape from Mindanao to Australia on a small yacht. It was Smith who suggested that Mindanao be Spyron's initial objective and that he accompany Parsons on the first of several trips to the occupied Philippines.

Some in GHQ thought that Spyron's plans were a waste of time and resources and that Parsons was insane for agreeing to return. He had slipped through the grasp of the Japanese once; they would not let it happen again. But Parsons was not about to sit out his family's personal war with Japan. His businessman brother-in-law, Thomas Jurika, had stayed behind to fight the Japanese in Cebu and Mindanao. Jurika's older brother Steve, the former naval attaché in Tokyo, had briefed the Army B-25 pilots on the USS *Hornet* prior to the Doolittle Raid. Parsons's mother-in-law, Blanche Jurika, had remained in Manila and was working clandestinely with the resistance. Parsons was sure of himself and his mission, which was to set up a communications net, learn the extent of the guerrilla movement, and determine the competence of its leaders.

He had been in the midst of that mission when the escapees arrived. He had planned on leaving that morning for Malaybalay to negotiate with a renegade Moro leader, so it was sheer luck that he was still in Talakag. Parsons asked the Americans to wait. He promised that upon his return, he would take them to Misamis City and the mysterious Fertig. They agreed.

Later that evening, as Parsons and Haggerty swam their horses across the Ipanan River, they discussed what they had heard and learned. Once he had been able to absorb the whole sordid tale of the escapees' imprisonment, Haggerty's sympathies were squarely on their side. He told Parsons that he hoped McCoy and Mellnik "would get south and inflame America." Parsons was optimistic about their chances to do so, but also guarded.

"They will do some good," he said, knowing what—or, more precisely, who—awaited them back in the States. "If they're ever allowed to talk. . . . I tell you, because I argued with some of them, as Mellnick [sic] and McCoy will do. They are an unsentimental bunch."

In Medina, it was hard to tell which traveled faster: the rumors of pending Japanese attacks or the crowds of panicky, evacuating civilians. Leo Boelens knew a retreat when he saw one. "Nips push a little on Tagoloan," he wrote in his diary on May 21. "Maybe this is it all over again."

Not long after McCoy and Mellnik's departure, the word from agents in the enemy stronghold of Cagayan was that the Japanese were preparing for an expedition against Medina. "We get rumors like this all the time," said an unruffled McClish. "If the Japs actually make a move, we'll hear about it before they get here."

Despite McClish's confidence, the civilians had evacuated most of the coastal towns and barrios by late May. To American ears, the Filipino pronunciation of the word "evacuate" sounded more like "bokweet." They soon further Americanized it to "buckwheat," which would become guerrilla slang meaning to place as much distance between oneself and the Japanese as possible.

One could not fault the escapees had they wanted to buckwheat, too.

Paul Marshall strolled into McClish's office one day holding a mimeographed leaflet that had been brought in by a Surigao-based spy. Printed in red ink, the flyer proffered a business proposal—of a sort:

> The commanding officer, Japanese Imperial Forces at Butuan, hereby offers a reward of 1,000 pesos to any loyal Filipino who will deliver . . . the severed head of the American known as Paul Marshall. All Filipinos are warned that any person who aids, comforts or harbors an American will be put to death.

The notice, signed by a Japanese captain, meant that not only had the Japanese not given up on their pursuit of the escapees, but that the bamboo telegraph was a two-way communication device; informers had evidently reported the presence of the Americans in northern Mindanao.

Unfazed, Marshall drew up a leaflet of his own, decorated with a skull and crossbones, offering 1,000 pesos for the head of the Japanese captain. Following Marshall's instructions, the intrepid Filipino tacked the flyer to the door of the captain's house in Butuan one dark night.

Despite Marshall's brazen riposte, it did not take long for additional circulars promising rewards for the heads of the other members of the escape party to start appearing. It was unsettling that the Japanese always seemed to know where they were. "Apparently, they don't want us in one piece," remarked Dobervich wryly.

The Japanese were clearly closing in. The escapees hoped, for all of their sakes, that McCoy and Mellnik were also closing in on their goal. "I'm running at bowels," bemoaned an ill Boelens, and soon, "probably at feet."

Dawn had just broken over a seemingly still slumbering Misamis City as McCoy, Mellnik, and Parsons made their way along weed-covered roads lined with run-down residences being reclaimed by the jungle. It was Sunday, May 30, and there was not a living soul present, much less the typical welcome party. Misamis City was more ghost town than guerrilla capital. "Why did people abandon a town?" Mellnik recalled. "Were they afraid of disease? Enemy attack? There was something scary about the ghostly structures; we trotted in silence."

During the sixty-mile, one-week, land-sea voyage from Talakag, they had been competently conducted from one safe area to another, "like batons in a relay race," said Mellnik. Their experiences in the charge of Bowler's men had been nothing short of outstanding, and consistent with the treatment they had received from the guerrillas since their first encounter with Big Boy's men outside Dapecol. That was what made Fertig's behavior so bizarre. While waiting for Parsons, McCoy had radioed Fertig to inquire about the messages sent from Anakan. Despite the fact that communication with Misamis City was easy, there had been no answer.

As Parsons headed to Jimenez—a town fifteen miles farther up the coast, halfway between Misamis City and Oroquieta—where he would be staying as the guest of the politically powerful Ozamis family, McCoy and Mellnik were led to a large house surrounded by a massive stone wall and then directed by a sentry through an iron gate into an anteroom outside Fertig's office. The perceptible "pomp and formality," said Mellnik, made an impression on McCoy.

"Your Army big-shots do well by themselves," he quipped to Mellnik.

When they were finally ushered inside, Mellnik recognized the face of General Fertig as that of a hastily commissioned civilian whom he had seen fleetingly during the last days on Corregidor. Native soap had tinged his sandy gray hair an auburn red, but it was Wendell W. Fertig, a tall and lithe figure in his early forties with a Vandyke beard. Mellnik sensed that Fertig seemed "aloof and preoccupied." He wore a major's oak leaves when Mellnik had last seen him on the Rock; he now wore stars on his collar. Something seemed awry. An icy glare from Fertig's blue eyes guided his guests to their seats.

"Chick told me you were here," said Fertig with cold formality. "What are your plans?"

"We're anxious to reach Australia," answered McCoy. "We understand you have communication with GHQ. A radio message might save us a risky, two-month ocean voyage by banca. We'd like to tell General Mac-Arthur that ten ex-PWs from Bataan and Corregidor want to rejoin U.S. forces."

"If you change your minds," replied Fertig, "you're welcome to join my command."

"Out of the question. We've had a rough time. Most of us need medication before returning to duty. Lord knows what diseases we're carrying. When can I send a message?"

"Since my equipment is not the best, communication with GHQ is uncertain," said Fertig evasively. "In fact, we barely arranged the rendezvous that brought Parsons to Mindanao."

"Then I suppose that sub will come back for Parsons?" mused McCoy. "When will that be?"

"I'm not at liberty to say."

"Ten of us would like to be around when it surfaces," added Mellnik.

"You don't thumb a ride on a submarine just like that," snapped Fertig. "GHQ determines who boards the sub."

By now, their patience was all but exhausted. They had not escaped and journeyed hundreds of miles only to quarrel with someone who, it was plainly obvious to them, was playing war. Without further reservation, they frankly informed Fertig that as professional soldiers and graduates of West Point and Annapolis, they did not consider themselves outranked by seemingly self-promoted ex-civilians, nor did they plan to join any irregular forces commanded by such men. Furthermore, they pointed out his ignorance of military procedure. McCoy had never suffered fools easily, and he could no longer control his temper.

"I'm more familiar with Navy customs than you are," he barked. "A sub skipper will rescue any American stranded behind enemy lines. But that's beside the point. As a commander in the U.S. Navy, I'm entitled to use U.S. facilities to communicate with my superiors."

Neither officer knew that on May 14 and 19, most likely after the promised prodding from Parsons, operators at Fertig's station had tapped out two brief messages to GHQ—but not the messages McCoy had sent from Anakan. The second, though error-filled, was more detailed:

TO GEN MACARTHUR
FROM WYZB

ELEVEN PRISONERS REPORTED ESCAPED ON NINE APRIL. TEN ARRIVED IN ORIENTAL MISAMIS AND TWO ENROUTE HERE NOW . . . RADIO STATES THAT MISTREATMENT STORIES ARE TRUE. THEY ARE FROM CORREGIDOR AND BATAAN. WILL FORWARD DETAILS.

But Fertig, for reasons known only to him, decided against sharing that information with the two livid officers. Instead, he chose to maintain his curiously hostile stance, saying, with an air of dismissal, "I'll notify GHQ that you are here and request instructions."

Back in their billet, McCoy and Mellnik shook their heads. "We critiqued Fertig's strange behavior for hours," said Mellnik. Perhaps Fertig was fearful that they would debunk his phony rank in Australia. Or maybe Fertig, who was in desperate need of officers, harbored hopes that he could forcibly conscript all of the escapees. They were unaware that Fertig harbored a resentment against any American that had surrendered. He had not done so himself and had contempt for anyone who had, regardless of the circumstances. Fertig also believed that anyone who had spent time in a POW camp was damaged goods. He offered a comparable diagnosis for his visitors in his diary that evening: "They are a bit stir crazy."

In Fertig's defense, the burden on his shoulders was unimaginably heavy. He suffered from persistent headaches and generally poor health, largely due to the Japanese. The rumors of imminent attacks were growing more believable by the day, hence the emptiness of Misamis City. Fertig did not have the training, ability, or resources to juggle multiple crises. An accomplished mining engineer from Colorado who had been commissioned in the Army Corps of Engineers at the start of the war, he had no military or leadership experience. Fertig was used to working with machinery, not men, and that calculated detachment, an inability to relate to others, was a major detriment to his command. Nevertheless, Fertig deserved substantial credit for successfully uniting various factions under one organizational structure during a period of rampant lawlessness and upheaval.

Fertig would argue that it had been possible for him to do so only because he had assumed the rank of general. He believed that none of the bandits, the renegade guerrilla leaders, or the rank-and-file Filipinos who made up the bulk of his forces—even civilians, for that matter—would respect a lieutenant colonel, his rank at the time of the surrender. He had to make them believe that he was "The One" who could deliver "The Aid." The stars on his collar, fashioned by a Moro silversmith, had thus far accomplished that goal.

But now, Fertig's bizarre behavior was due to his own engorged ego. Clyde Childress believed that the escaped POWs clashed with Fertig because "they were not subservient enough to him." Mired in his own megalomania and with his command crumbling around him, Fertig could not see that the escaped prisoners had not arrived to usurp his throne. They simply wanted to get to Australia. Yet as long as Fertig had a say in it, they were not going anywhere.

The next day, McCoy and Mellnik were given a list of regulations under which they were to live as Fertig's guests, the most notable of which stipulated that they were free to travel only "within the coastal areas, provided such travel was made by horse-drawn vehicle." Fertig would claim that this stipulation stemmed from the shortage of gasoline, but it was most likely an attempt at keeping them under his thumb.

It certainly seemed as though McCoy and Mellnik would have plenty of time to try to figure out Wendell W. Fertig, as well as find a way out of their current predicament. They were, in effect, captives once more.

THURSDAY, JUNE 10–FRIDAY, JULY 2
Misamis Occidental, Misamis Oriental, and Zamboanga Provinces

The bolt of lightning struck perilously close to the *Narra*, mere seconds after the launch had docked in Jimenez. The real shock, however, awaited the two passengers who were now making their way to the Casa Ozamis.

Inside the spacious, adobe-walled residence, McCoy and Mellnik, on a rare furlough from Misamis City, were discussing strategy. Ten days had passed and they still had not received any word from GHQ or Fertig. And a courier would soon be leaving for Medina.

"I'd like to tell our people about a possible change in plan," McCoy told Mellnik, "but until GHQ answers, I can tell them nothing."

They had no idea whether Fertig had sent their message. His promise to do so during their first, inauspicious meeting sounded less than convincing and their most recent conference, a few days ago, had not gone well, either. McCoy had recently begun to reconsider their original plan, a trip to Australia via sailboat. Though recent news of fierce fighting in the Port Moresby area of New Guinea meant that a voyage south would be considerably difficult, the odds of boarding a submarine hardly seemed better, given their relationship with Fertig. One final visit with Fertig, they decided, was in order.

"I hope we don't have to use this persuader," said McCoy, patting the .45 caliber revolver in his pocket, "but we must get word to GHQ."

At that moment, the door swung open, revealing Ed Dyess and Leo Boelens, just arrived from Medina. The escapees had been waiting for weeks for word from McCoy and Mellnik, so when Dyess had learned that Childress would be sailing to Misamis City to procure ammunition, he volunteered for the journey to see for himself what was causing the delay.

"So this is how you two look after our interests," said Dyess as he gazed around the palatial Ozamis residence, with its electric lights, running water, and rotating fans.

When he learned the reason for the protracted wait, he was outraged.

"Hells bells! Let's light a fire under this guy. We've been through too goddamned much to be stymied now by jealousy or protocol."

Returning to Misamis City, all four ex-prisoners strode into Fertig's office the next day. As Dyess "stared belligerently," recalled Mellnik, McCoy took his .45 out of his pocket and placed it on his lap.

"GHQ seems slow about answering your message," opened McCoy. "Maybe you should remind them. Don't you agree?"

"Yes," said Fertig, who could not help but notice the pistol, as well as the message it conveyed. "But don't place all the blame on GHQ—our transmitter has been out of order."

While maintenance records from the Tenth Military District remain lost to history, surviving communication records serve as evidence that Fertig's reply was a lie. Fertig's headquarters had been in contact with GHQ regarding the evacuation matter in messages dated June 9–10, and just one day earlier, Fertig noted in his diary that "MacArthur advises that [the POWs] will be taken out on first opportunity." In view of his desire to rid himself of them, his decision to not share this information is telling about Fertig's emotional and mental state. Of course, Fertig did have a lot on his mind.

On June 7, Camiguin Island, ten miles from the northern coast of Misamis Oriental, was reported secured by the Japanese. Less than twenty-four hours earlier, Lieutenant Colonel Bowler had radioed that a detachment of 200 enemy troops had taken Talakag. It seemed only a matter of time before the Japanese advanced on Medina, and ultimately, Misamis City. Although the empty streets of Misamis City should have been an early clue regarding the serious of the situation, Fertig did a masterful job keeping this news from the escapees. According to Fertig's radio operator, Lt. Robert Ball, McCoy and Mellnik had been blissfully unaware of the danger until Ball warned them that a massive enemy invasion was afoot. All the same, McCoy was confident that he and the escapees would be out of harm's way when the Japanese showed up.

"I think we'll get an answer this time," he told the others as they departed Fertig's office, "and in less than ten days."

The shrewd cardsharp's confidence stemmed, in all likelihood, from the ace tucked up his sleeve: Chick Parsons. Though Parsons apparently enjoyed a genial relationship with Fertig, his sympathies lay squarely on the side of the escaped POWs. In all probability, an agreement in which Parsons would intercede on their behalf with MacArthur had been worked out. Parsons did, after all, possess a special cipher—called "Q-10"—which enabled him to communicate privately with GHQ in coded messages that could not be read by Fertig. And Parsons did promise McCoy and Mellnik that he would send a message regarding the prisoners' escape and plight to Australia during their first meeting in Talakag nearly a month earlier. The officers shared a hint of these continued, covert maneuverings during a visit with Boelens, who remained in Misamis City to recuperate from malaria attacks after Dyess returned to Medina on June 12. "Commd'r McCoy and Mellnick [sic] over," wrote Boelens on June 15. "Thinks [Parsons] double-cross, has worked."

It did. Although Parsons was a prime mover, the escapees unknowingly had, once again when they needed it most, received some additional, providential assistance. The strange messages emanating from the Mindanao jungles regarding escaped POWs were initially viewed with some skepticism by GHQ. No one, after all, had escaped from the Japanese, much less a large group of POWs. Some in the Allied Intelligence Bureau, in fact, believed the messages a clever Japanese ruse. Gen. Courtney Whitney, the head of AIB, referred the matter to his deputy controller, Lt. Col. Allison Ind, for further investigation. Though the messages were bereft of details (only a few of the escapees were mentioned by name), Ind's eyes widened when he saw one of the names: Dyess. Ind had been Gen. Hal George's intelligence officer when Dyess was in command of the Bamboo Fleet on Bataan. It was a matter of fate, pure and simple, that Ind was the one at AIB tasked with verifying the startling, static-filled messages. "If the man claiming that name was genuine, he would know the answers to some questions I could send," reasoned Ind. Whitney ordered Ind to proceed and Dyess, in turn, responded correctly, setting in motion a course of events that would lead to Parsons's crucial involvement.

The long-awaited reply from Australia, however, was bittersweet: Fertig informed McCoy and Mellnik that they—and only they—had been cleared for evacuation. They had planned their breakout, escaped, survived the swamp, and journeyed throughout Mindanao as a team. Each had taken an equal share in the risk, but now the reward was to be for only two. McCoy and Mellnik were furious, but GHQ refused to budge.

GHQ, however, made an exception for Dyess, who, in a long interview before his departure, had impressed Fertig with the idea that "The Aid" could be delivered by air. In McCoy's and Mellnik's absence, he and Boelens had scouted sites for potential airfields that could be used by the Allies during the retaking of the Philippines. Fertig wanted Dyess to explain his theories in person at GHQ and on June 15 radioed MacArthur to recommend that he be added to the evacuation list. However transparent Fertig's motives, Whitney agreed and Dyess was ordered to evacuate with the others in early July, according to a message received from GHQ on June 21. Dyess, already back in Medina, presumably knew nothing of these developments. If his behavior on Bataan was any indication, he probably would not react favorably to the order. But Dyess would have little choice. He had already ignored one evacuation order on Bataan; two instances of insubordination would not have been looked upon kindly by his superiors.

For McCoy, who considered himself the group's shepherd, this was proving a difficult, unexpected quandary. He knew that someone had to get out and tell their story. He also knew that he could arrange to bring the others out only if he was successful in getting to Australia himself. Nonetheless, he found the idea of leaving the others behind morally repulsive. With little other recourse, he composed a letter to the other members of the escape party in which he explained the situation and requested their immediate input. In view of the rumors of looming Japanese attacks, he hoped that they would still be in Medina—or alive, for that matter—if and when his letter arrived.

Shofner knocked on the door of the room that Jack Hawkins shared with Mike Dobervich. A groggy Hawkins could tell by the look on his friend's face—the telltale way he pursed his lips—that Shofner was angry.

"What's the matter?" asked Hawkins.

"I've got a letter from McCoy. Just came in by launch . . . Fertig didn't send our messages," growled Shofner, "and wait 'til you hear the rest!"

By the time they finished McCoy's missive, Hawkins and Dobervich shared Shofner's indignation. The fact that Fertig could not even have forwarded their names to American authorities so that their families would know that they were alive was "downright distressing."

"If you say so, we'll give up our transportation, rejoin you, and we'll carry out our original plan," McCoy signed off his letter. "If you prefer to have us go now by submarine, we'll do our utmost to see that all of you get back later."

"Maybe we should go over and try to force the issue with Fertig," suggested Shofner.

"I believe McCoy would have suggested that if he thought it would do any good," said Dobervich.

"You're probably right. Maybe it would be just as well to sit tight here . . . and wait for McCoy to handle things. Once he gets with the Navy in Australia, I'm sure he can make arrangements for us. You know Mac. He won't forget us, and he won't give up."

The news was typical "stragedy," a Bataan buzzword that combined strategy with tragedy, in the judgment of the escapees. They almost expected such developments. "Shifty," lamented Sam Grashio upon hearing the news, "it looks like we have the enemy right where they want us."

This "stragedy" meant that they would have to keep moving, albeit in different directions, toward decidedly separate fates. Grashio, the Marines, Marshall, and Spielman would retreat east to Daan-Lungsod and the new 110th Division headquarters. Dyess would reluctantly journey westward to Jimenez, the rallying point for the sub extraction party agreed upon by GHQ and the expedition's leader, Parsons. On the 15th of June, Dyess, McClish, and Ensign Iliff Richardson, an emissary from Leyte guerrilla commander Col. Ruperto Kangleon, accompanied by twenty-odd troops, put out on the diesel-powered launch *Rosalia*. Both McClish and Kangleon, facing imminent attack, were seeking Fertig's help.

But Fertig was in trouble, too. The recent flurry of radio traffic regarding the secret submarine rendezvous had attracted the attention of Japanese radio operators aboard naval RDFs—radio detection finders— that had formed a floating picket around Mindanao. Signals, recalled Allison Ind, beamed from ship to ship, from one vessel bobbing quietly in the Mindanao Sea, just off the island of Bohol, to another anchored near Leyte, in the Surigao Sea. Within no time, these electronic eavesdroppers would triangulate the locations of the guerrilla radio stations. "Japanese Naval Air Operations would be glad to hear of this 'fix,' " Ind wrote.

Early on the morning of June 26, Misamis City was bombed, precursory action to a multipronged invasion involving landings in the north along the coast of Misamis Occidental and in Pagadian Bay, fifty miles to the south in Zamboanga Province. The Japanese, once content to rule Mindanao's coastal cities while strip-mining the island of its resources, now seemed intent on conquering Fertig's fiefdom.

A combination of luck and foresight had kept Fertig one step ahead of the Japanese—he had escaped to Corregidor just before Bataan fell and had left for Mindanao on one of the final flights from the Rock on April 29, 1942—so where he and his mobile headquarters went, so did the others. It was a mad blur of perspiration, packing, and profanity. Documents were incinerated, aerials were taken down, wires coiled, and radio sets strapped to the backs of guerrillas for hasty flight. Leo Boelens, recovering from malaria, would slip out of Misamis City on a sloop just forty minutes before the arrival of the Japanese landing craft. Going to bed fully clothed and ready for another quick flight, Boelens would write in his diary, "Wonder about Ed."

McCoy and Mellnik, biting their nails as exploding bombs could be heard from the direction of the nearby town of Aurora, also wondered if Dyess would arrive in time. Both Charley Smith and Chick Parsons had already reported in to Fertig's latest headquarters approximately six miles west of Bonifacio, the latter on July 1 after narrowly escaping through the backyard of the Casa Ozamis as Japanese soldiers splintered the front door with an ax.

Dyess would follow in Parsons's footsteps. According to Richardson, the *Rosalia* was making about six knots, "going along with a good, smooth gush" off Jimenez at 0400 on June 26 when a searchlight from a Japanese landing barge splashed a bright, bluish green light across the vessel. "It was an awful feeling," Dyess would say, "like men must feel in a police show-up. There was no place on that damn boat where we could get out of the glare." Richardson ran the *Rosalia* onto the beach and the passengers sloshed through the knee-deep water and melted inland. They were working their way through some rice paddies at dawn when a woman, much like a Filipino Paul Revere, came running down the road to alert them. "Hapons!" she cried. "Hapons coming!" They crouched silently in the underbrush as an enemy column passed by. The soldiers were so close that you could hear the sound of their equipment clinking as they marched. "They padded past us like figures in a dream," recalled Richardson.

It was therefore necessary to take an elongated detour around Jimenez and, after a forced march of several days through the jungle, a weary Dyess finally staggered into Fertig's mobile command post at 1700 on Friday, July 2.

There would be little time, though, for him to rest. A date with a submarine awaited.

CHAPTER 17

A Story That Should Be Told

Westward we came across the smiling waves,
West to the outpost of our country's might . . .
Eastward we go and home, so few—so few—
Wrapped in their beds of clay our comrades sleep . . .

SATURDAY, JULY 3–FRIDAY, JULY 9, 1943
Zamboanga Province, Mindanao

T he raindrops pattered, then ran in rivulets off the eaves of the thatch roof, much in the same way that Ed Dyess's scattered thoughts connected and poured through his pencil. There was so much to say, so much to write on this steamy Mindanao morning, yet so little time.

Dear Sammy—

I just arrived here and "got the dope." By the time you receive this things will be "all off" or I'll be long gone. Sam, you know I wouldn't go if I didn't think it was best for us all; Leo and I have talked the situation over. With me there I am sure we can be together again soon; however, if I stay none of us will have a prayer.

It had taken Dyess time, plus the help of Boelens, to understand that he had to go. Someone had to tell the story of the escape and speak for

263

the thousands who had perished, as well as the thousands still suffering in captivity. His was to be that voice. Dyess, though, was the last one to realize it. As those drawn into Dyess's orbit would attest, his magnetic aura had become increasingly powerful since the escape. The proof? Even the not easily impressed Father Edward Haggerty had been captivated by Dyess. Wrote Haggerty: "And all who heard him thought as one: 'Here is a man to put the plight of our prisoners before the public.' " Still, Dyess felt the need to explain his actions to those, like Grashio, who knew him best.

> It is not a run out boy, *because you and Leo are closer to me than brothers. It gives me a helluva empty feeling to say farewell, but believe me it won't be for long; I wish it could have been otherwise, but mother fate stepped in. I'll see that your wife, folks & uncle are notified, but it won't be long before you can tell them yourself. I don't feel right without having you along Sam, & I'll never be satisfied until we are flying together "knocking sparks out of [the] flaming assholes." May the "pickins" always be good.*
>
> > *Your Bud & Pal,*
> > *Ed*

Entering Fertig's mobile headquarters, Dyess and Boelens found the others—Fertig, Smith, McCoy, and Mellnik—sweating the details of the submarine rendezvous. An extraction from Jimenez or Misamis would have been ideal, but the Japanese presence scotched that. They had then planned to travel south by truck to Pagadian City, a distance of no more than fifteen miles, for a rendezvous near Pagadian Bay, but reports of increased Japanese activity in the south now rendered that alternative useless, too. Neither the humidity nor the stress of the situation seemed to affect Chick Parsons. Shortly after his arrival at Fertig's temporary headquarters, a radio message was received at AIB in Brisbane. The Q-10 code, once deciphered, revealed that Parsons, as per his persona and reputation, was prepared for such eventualities.

ARRIVE HQ TODAY FROM NORTH. WARN SUB COMMANDER
SITES ONE AND TWO FOR MEETING NORTH COAST IN HANDS
ENEMY SITE THREE NOT FEASIBLE. RECOMMEND MEETING

ONE HOUR BEFORE SUNSET NINTH VICINITY NORTHEAST
COAST OLUTANGA ISLAND FROM SAME LAUNCH THAT MET
SUB. IF POSSIBLE THIS MEETING SHOULD BE ARRANGED SPE-
CIFICALLY TO AVOID ENDANGERING SECURITY. AREA SECURE
AT PRESENT NO AIR OR SEA PATROLS. PORTABLE TRANSMIT-
TER MALANGAS WILL WARN IF SUDDEN CHANGES. MORE
TOMORROW.

Parsons's plan required an intense hike to Margosatubig, a five-day
trip spanning some sixty-five miles, on the Igat Bay inlet. After mapping
out a route that would take advantage of his knowledge of the labyrin-
thine network of trails, Parsons added a cushion of an extra day since
they would be traveling over some difficult terrain, much of which was
mountainous and marked with the familiar "UNEXPLORED" on maps.
And that looked to be the easy part.

Upon reaching Margosatubig, they would sail to the rendezvous point,
approximately five miles into the heart of Dumanquilas Bay, a small body
of water more than forty miles east of Pagadian City and just northeast of
Oluntanga island. When Fertig's finger indicated the point about where
the pickup would occur, Mellnik was stunned.

"Out there?"

"That's how it is," said Fertig. "But you'll have the advantage of knowing when and where the sub is coming, which the Japs won't. To reduce
the time you'll be on the water, I'm sending you out in the *General Fertig*."
That ship was a fast, sixty-foot, steam-powered launch that had formerly
been the property of a lumber company.

Although Fertig got in the last word in his rivalry with McCoy and
Mellnik, Parsons had the final say in regards to the expedition. Because
he preferred to travel light—he favored a uniform of shorts, tennis shoes,
and a Navy officer's cap and rarely, if ever, carried a weapon—the others would, too. The group—five Americans, an armed escort composed
of Lt. Roberto de Jesus and five soldiers from F Company, 2nd Battalion, 115th Regiment, a unit based in southern Zamboanga, plus guides
and porters furnished by Fertig—would carry no food, little baggage, and
only a Thompson submachine gun and some pistols. Parsons knew he
could count on Filipino generosity to feed them and that it would be wise
to avoid entanglements with the Japanese. It would be his knowledge of

the land and its people, as well as his ingenuity, that would give the group a fighting chance.

The expedition commenced at 1000; they would not have to wait long to see Parsons in action. They had hiked for only a few hours when they happened upon a river with a burned-out bridge. An excellent swimmer, Parsons disrobed and plunged into the water to begin assembling the remnants of the smoldering timbers into a pontoon bridge. As the others followed Parsons into the water, the Filipinos were both impressed and frightened by their leader's bravado. One approached McCoy. "Sir," he cautioned, "there are many crocodiles in this river." McCoy immediately ordered the guerrilla carrying the tommy gun to stand guard over the operation. Only when the group had successfully crossed did McCoy decide to tell Parsons about the crocodiles. "His skin is naturally dark," wrote McCoy, "but he turned pale."

Spurred by thoughts of a good meal and solid sleep, they reached a barrio at sunset only to discover a squad of Japanese troops bathing in the schoolyard. Dyess yelled an alarm and they immediately buckwheated as the startled Japanese fumbled for their clothes and weapons.

The Americans and Filipinos clambered up a muddy trail leading to the mountains and, flush with adrenaline, did not stop for a moment's rest. Unable to shine a flashlight or torch, they groped along in the darkness, miserably hungry, for four or five hours until the terrain leveled off. Out of breath, they filtered into a clearing where they found a small cornfield, "always an indication that a house was near," Parsons would say. Wandering along the rows, they snapped ears from the stalks and gnawed the raw corn from the cobs.

They spotted a bamboo structure at the edge of the clearing. Inside, in a space no more than fifteen feet square, were crammed some thirty men, women, and children, plus an assortment of dogs, cats, and other animals—the entire population of the town from which they had just fled. As they learned from the friendly Filipinos, who shared some cooked chicken, a patrol of fifty Japanese soldiers had entered the town and the townspeople also had just barely escaped.

While the others shoehorned into the hut for the evening, Parsons and Smith attempted to sleep in the chicken coop after first shooing out the occupants. Evidently, the evicted fowl resented the foul treatment and returned during the night to take their revenge; when Parsons and Smith awoke at 0400, they found several chickens and roosters perched on top of them, as well as an entire night's worth of droppings. It was a harbinger of events to come.

One of the residents of the town, claiming to know a shortcut to the next barrio, offered his services as a guide. True to form, the group promptly got lost. It would take several hours of stumbling around and down the mountain before Charley Smith, holding the group's compass, assumed control of navigation and returned them to the trail. The column proceeded along the path, whistling cheerfully, until Parsons and Smith called an abrupt halt. The others caught up and congregated over a parcel of soft mud freshly dotted with footprints, shallow imprints made by split-toed shoes—*that* kind of footprints.

The Japanese, it seemed, had divided their patrol, with half going around the mountain and the other half coming over it in an effort to flush out their prey. In fact, the latter group "had actually passed us as we were scrambling around taking our shortcut," claimed Parsons. The escapees' luck in getting lost had likely saved them from being trapped between two enemy patrols and some unwanted fireworks on this Fourth of July. But they were hardly in the clear.

They were now in effect tailing the Japanese who were chasing them.

"There was only one trail and nothing to do but march on, taking what precautions against ambush we could," said Parsons. Two guerrillas removed their uniforms, so as to look like locals, and scampered off to scout ahead. It was an agonizingly irrational situation: despite having found the path, they could not speed their advance for fear of overtaking their "pursuers."

Marching on edge, they found it difficult to maintain the snail's pace for more than several hours. By 1500, they began to spot cigarette butts on the trail at their feet—some still burning. Not long after, at the top of a rise, they were startled by an old Moro woman. Through her gestures, they understood that the Japanese had questioned her about the presence of Americans on the trail. She decided to wait and issue a warning. "There was no rhyme or reason for her warning us," stated Parsons, "except friendship for everyone but the Japanese."

Peering down at the Japanese resting in a grove, they weighed their options. Watching the enemy soldiers lounging, eating, and drinking coconut milk—they themselves had not eaten since early morning—was more than they could bear. Smith wanted to attack the patrol, but cooler heads prevailed; even if each of their bullets found its mark, they still would not have enough ammunition to dispose of even half the patrol. All they could do was chew on palm leaves to calm their nerves and stomachs—and cross their fingers. At the edge of the grove, the trail forked in two directions. If the Japanese took the left trail, they were safe since their route lay straight ahead. But if the Japanese continued on their current path, they would have to continue playing their game of reverse cat-and-mouse.

Luck, as it had been so many times in the past, was with them once again. The Japanese moved out and chose the left fork. Once the patrol was safely out of sight, they picked their way down to the path and continued on for several hours, stopping only at an abandoned homestead at dusk to prepare an impromptu meal from a chicken that Dyess had chased down. They were forced to continue on well into the night to make up for lost time. Parsons knew that if they did not make the rendezvous, it was doubtful that they could arrange another, due to the increased enemy activity in the Mindanao area.

Nature, not the Japanese, would be their primary adversary on the third day of their trek. They traversed arduous mountain trails thick with mud that often reached to their knees. Streams consistently barred their path, forcing them to build rafts or else clumsily wade across. While Parsons traveled barefoot most of the time, the others were always stopping to empty their shoes of gravel. Parsons seemed to move with ease along the jungle trails, almost as if he had been there before. Perhaps he had. The ambitious Tennessean had left home for the Philippines in the 1920s and, within a few short years, had been everywhere from Luzon to Zamboanga while working for the American administrative government and honing his commercial talents.

The succession of water barriers and sudden downpours left them continuously waterlogged at the same time that their endless perspiration left them dehydrated. McCoy had the only canteen in the group and it was almost always empty; the laborious process of purifying water with halazone tablets took too long to meet the demands of their thirst so they invariably dropped to their knees to gulp water from streams.

Their tremendous expenditure of energy left them ravenously hungry, too, but they found it difficult to make any concessions, even when they happened upon a barn containing a large amount of livestock. A handful of goats "made such a human bleating" recalled Parsons, that they could not bring themselves to kill the animals. Happily, the situation was re-solved when the scouts located a group of locals who offered to kill a pig for them. The detail returned with a feast of barbecued pork and a dish of ground steamed corn that tasted like hominy grits. "The finest meal of our lives," Parsons recalled. "It just was like sitting at the Waldorf-Astoria in New York City with thirty waiters bringing on course after course."

The following morning, both their ranks and their spirits swelled with the arrival of a handful of guerrillas who had recently buckwheated from Aurora—they were now capable of defending themselves should they en-counter any more enemy patrols. "At this point, we felt that the situation was well in hand and were in fact hopeful of making our rendezvous on schedule," Parsons would write, "when we ran across the worst river we had yet encountered."

It was the Dinas, located midway between the barrio of Balongating and their next destination, Libunganan. While the rest of the group began raft construction, Parsons and Dyess went off in search of a guerrilla en-campment rumored to be nearby. Parsons hoped to find a radio that they could use to warn the submarine of a possible delay. They inflated their trousers and then tied them around their necks before kicking their way across the river. Their advance work, however, was for naught; they would hike in a circle for nearly two hours, returning to their starting point just as the others, exhausted and scared stiff, landed ashore. The rafters had lashed a vine to a tree on the opposite bank, but the towline had snapped, sending the raft careening downstream with the powerful 8-knot current. Only a bit of topographical luck, the fortuitous appearance of a sharp bend, had enabled them to beach the runaway raft.

Parsons had noticed that the former escapees were showing signs of strain, so it was with some apprehension that he allowed McCoy to march ahead with a guide. Parsons and the others failed to reach the guerrilla camp at nightfall and worse, lost contact with McCoy altogether. The next morning, they were relieved to find that McCoy had preceded them to Libunganan. "He gave a very hazy explanation of his actions . . . and we realized that he was badly in need of medical care—further necessity for making our rendezvous on time," Parsons wrote.

Captain Medina, commanding officer of the 115th Regiment, wel-comed the travelers with open arms, as well as some interesting enter-tainment. The Americans had arrived in time to witness the trial of a captured spy. The accused's testimony was collected in due form and affidavit and the man ultimately confessed to supplying the Japanese with information. Guerrilla justice was swift, meted out with a Moro *barong*, or long sword, which Dyess asked for and received as a souvenir from the sergeant who performed the execution.

They rose early on the sixth day and took a southwesterly course. Parsons estimated that they traveled nine kilometers from Libunganan to the barrio of Sayog, which was located approximately ten kilometers from the municipality of Lapuyan. Beyond that, somewhere, was their ultimate destination, Margosatubig. It was nearly a guess. Shoulder-high cogongrass swallowed up the trail, making speculation a necessary part of navigation. They also had to deal with another wayward guide they sensed was leading them astray. Consultations with their compass and the guide revealed that the latter wanted to eat lunch at the home of a girlfriend who lived out of the way.

For most of the afternoon, they wandered from hill to hill and fought through fatigue and hunger to breathlessly summit miniature mountains, each time expecting to see the blue waters of Igat Bay, but instead they peered out over more green jungle. "We kept plugging along at any trail we could see, wondering if we had suffered all these hardships and come this long way only to fail when our mission was so nearly complete," remembered Parsons.

And then, after another strength-sapping ascent at 1600 hours, Igat Bay suddenly appeared. By 1900 they were in Lapuyan, where Capt. Joe McCarthy, an American mestizo guerrilla, was waiting with a launch that would transport them through a driving rainstorm to Margosatubig.

Parsons was pleased to learn that McCarthy had had the foresight to radio a warning to Australia that the extraction party might be delayed. Parsons sent an updated message confirming his arrival in Margosatubig, but since the communications station was a one-way operation, there was no way for him to know if that message, or McCarthy's message, for that matter, had been received. They could only follow through with the mission and pray that the rendezvous would go off without a hitch.

They departed Margosatubig at dawn on the 9th of July, puttering first through the narrow channel separating Zamboanga from tiny Igat island and then striking out across the middle of Dumanquilas Bay for the village of Naga Naga. It was there that they found the *General Fertig*. The launch was armed with a machine gun salvaged from an aircraft wreck, but it was hardly a match for the Japanese destroyers that had been reported to be operating in the bay. They immediately set to work camouflaging the craft. By the time they finished, banana leaves and palm fronds hung from guy wires and no fewer than a dozen potted palms, plus piles of fresh fruit, were arranged on the deck. Mellnik noted, with some amusement, the lone coconut palm tree that flew from the mast: "Only a slight ripple at the bow and the wake at the stern belied our appearance as an island."

It was not until 1600, after stealthily slipping from cove to cove, that the *General Fertig* released into Dumanquilas Bay. Upon arriving at the rendezvous coordinates, Parsons ran an upside-down American flag up the mast, the agreed-upon recognition signal. But for the waiting, their work was done. (In U.S. Navy tradition, an inverted ensign is recognized as a distress signal.)

Without the rumble and hum of the boat's diesel engines, they bobbed in unsettling silence for what seemed like hours. The glassy sea lapped audibly on the ship's wooden hull. Their hearts pounded inside their chests. "Dyess and Mellnik were pale and tense," recalled McCoy. "I played solitaire to keep from going crazy."

Ever so slowly, the minutes ticked by. One hour turned into two. The escapees could not help but let dark thoughts enter their minds: that a Japanese ship or seaplane would discover them; that they had missed the rendezvous; that the Navy had called off the operation. Perhaps they were doomed to a life as fugitives perpetually on the run.

"Think they'll find us?" Mellnik asked Charley Smith.

"Sure," said an outwardly calm, confident Smith. "I'll bet they're watching us through a periscope right now."

Smith was described by Parsons, affectionately, as a "cold-blooded, unemotional sourpuss. I have never seen him smile, much less laugh. Just at sunset he grabbed me around the neck and let out what would almost be a scream." Hearing a gurgling rumble off the bow, they turned to see a "great big black bulk rising out of the water," recalled McCoy.

"There it is!" shouted Smith.

The submarine launched from the water at a 45-degree angle before toppling onto the waves in a giant cloud of spray. It was merely a routine surfacing, but to each of the five Americans it was an overwhelming sight that none would ever forget. The event was especially poignant for the former POWs. According to Parsons, one burst into tears. Another simply sat, frozen, unable to tear his gaze from the sub. The third arched his arms around Smith and Parsons in communal "silent witness of what seemed to us to be a miracle."

A shrill burst from an air whistle initiated a dizzying surge of activity. Steel hatches clanked open and American sailors poured forth to man the deck gun, to lash the *General Fertig* to the sub's hull, and to help load the fruit and the human cargo.

"All aboard and make it lively!" came the command from a crisp, God-like voice from high up in the conning tower. Heeding the voice, Parsons and the others paused long enough to empty their pockets of quinine, ammunition, and other items they knew the guerrillas needed.

Stepping aboard the sub, McCoy's legs buckled. "The thing I remember most clearly about going on that ship is the sensation of standing on armor plate—good, hard American armor plate," he would write. "We were saying goodbye to bamboo and rattan."

Dazedly, they descended from the conning tower into what Mellnik called the "vaguely unreal and frightening" interior of the sub, inhaling the sharp smells of fuel oil and sweat as they passed through dim, narrow corridors lined with gauges, valves, pipes, and switches and filled with the sounds of commands, whistles, and clacking heels. And then they were ushered into a quiet, "cozy" wardroom where a deck of cards and a sugar bowl rested on a green felt table and pots of coffee bubbled on a hot plate. Mellnik dropped his head onto his hands. "I closed my eyes," he said, "to let the thought sink in."

This floating 307-foot, 1,475-ton steel oasis was the USS *Trout*, a submarine whose decorated crew had acquired a reputation not only for bravery—the battle-scarred boat was credited with damaging a Japanese aircraft carrier, challenging an Imperial Navy battleship, and sinking a sub—but also for relentlessly harassing enemy shipping: the *Trout* had sunk or damaged more than 100,000 tons everywhere from the Solomon Islands to the Singapore trade route. Unique, however, was the *Trout*'s special history of secret missions, including one that occurred during its second war patrol in February 1942. The *Trout* delivered 3,500 rounds of antiaircraft ammunition to Corregidor, but the mission was more important for what the *Trout* returned to Pearl with as ballast: twenty tons of gold bullion, silver pesos, and securities of the Philippine Commonwealth's currency reserve worth more than $10 million.

In the midst of the controlled chaos, the passengers were welcomed aboard by the *Trout*'s skipper, Lt. Cmdr. Al Clark. They told Clark that they had heard that three Japanese transports were moored in a harbor ten miles west of their position and that an enemy warship might also be in the neighborhood. Clark assured them that the boat would get under way at once, and no sooner had he done so than a clamor of bells and whistles resounded throughout the ship, signaling their imminent descent into the depths of Dumanquilas Bay.

The close presence of enemy vessels was not the only reason for the alacrity with which the crew moved. The *Trout* had once again taken on some extremely valuable cargo. And someone in Australia was waiting for the delivery.

SATURDAY, JULY 24–FRIDAY, JULY 30, 1943

Perth, Western Australia, and Brisbane, Queensland,
Commonwealth of Australia

Squinting through the bright sunlight, a light-headed and confused Steve Mellnik struggled to bring the figure lying in the adjacent bed into focus.

"Where are we?" he asked, groggily.

"In an Australian army hospital in Perth," replied Charley Smith.

Thanks to a malaria attack, Mellnik had been out for four days. He had only hazy memories of being strapped to a stretcher and carried up out of the conning tower of the *Trout* after the sub had entered Fremantle Harbor on July 20.

"Where are McCoy and the others?"

"Took off for GHQ in Brisbane two days ago. Said they wanted to see bright lights! You and I are lucky; we're sick enough to loaf legitimately for two weeks."

Mellnik would have no such luck. The following day, a confidential telegram arrived.

DO NOT, REPEAT NOT, DISCUSS EXPERIENCES WITH ANYONE.
IMPERATIVE YOU ARRIVE BRISBANE AS SOON AS POSSIBLE.
HAVE NOTIFIED YOUR FAMILY OF SAFE ARRIVAL.

MACARTHUR

Mellnik soon wobbled off a bumpy, 2,500-mile flight to find McCoy and Parsons waiting for him. They provided more of a briefing than a welcome.

"So far as the public is concerned," said Parsons, "you're a nonperson. Stay inconspicuous. We'll get you some uniforms today—those rags look like hell. Tomorrow you'll be seeing lots of brass, so get a good night's rest."

The rapidly unfolding series of events was overwhelming. But regardless of the cryptic warnings from MacArthur and Parsons, as far as GHQ was concerned, the *Trout's* special passengers were anything but nonpersons. They would spend the next few days behind guarded doors at AIB headquarters in an exhaustive succession of debriefings, interviews, and conferences. The interrogations, recalled Allison Ind, "were pushed as rapidly as the strength of the pale, drawn-featured escapees would permit." On July 26, Dyess and Parsons attended a morning conference with four staff officers regarding the construction of secret airfields on Mindanao. At the same time, Mellnik was being quizzed on "everything from the effects of artillery fire on Corregidor to the availability of rice on Mindanao."

GHQ's appetite for information was insatiable, but Dyess, McCoy, and Mellnik were having a difficult time getting their interrogators to listen to what they felt was the most important intelligence they had brought out of the occupied Philippines: the revelation of what the Japanese had done and were continuing to do to American prisoners of war. They had not escaped to talk about tons of rice or rounds of ammunition, but those seemed to be the only statistics that interested MacArthur's men. The thousands of corpses occupying mass graves at Camp O'Donnell and the 500 grams of rice—starvation rations—that the men in Dapecol were subsisting on seemed to be of no interest. The frantic pace of questioning slowed only when it finally came time to discuss the atrocities they had witnessed and their experiences as prisoners of war, because, explained Allison Ind, "the stories were so horrifying that the stenographers could take it for only twenty minutes at a time."

Predictably, McCoy's patience began to wear thin. Like Dyess and Mellnik he was haunted, not only by the men left behind at Dapecol, but by the knowledge that the other members of the escape party were still on Mindanao, presumably running for their lives. He had given his word and was determined to get them out. He strenuously argued that any submarine operating in the vicinity be sent immediately to pick up his comrades. It was, he believed, the least their country could do for them. "These men escaped from the prison camp, not to join the guerrillas, and not just to effect their own personal freedom," he told his Navy superiors, referring to the paramount goal behind their escape.

General Whitney was sympathetic, yet offered a warning. "Though the Old Man told me to bring your friends out," he told Mellnik, "don't expect overnight service." Despite the bewildering logistical buildup of Allied forces in Australia and the fact that the United States was locked in a defensive stalemate in the Pacific, interservice rivalries were still prevalent. MacArthur's GHQ was an Army show. The submarines were controlled by the Navy. GHQ's Philippine Regional Section was allowed only five tons of cargo, or five men, on subs transiting Philippine waters. "Now that we've demonstrated a capability to conduct safe rendezvous, we hope the Navy will give us sub space more frequently," added Whitney. It was not the answer that Dyess, McCoy, and Mellnik wanted to hear, but they would have to be content with that assurance for the time being.

Their feelings of powerlessness and guilt were magnified when they walked into General MacArthur's office in the Australasian Mutual Provident Society, or AMP Building, on Edward Street at 6:05 P.M. on the evening of July 30. There, they found the famed four-star general, as well as a phalanx of senior staff officers, standing rigidly at attention. As an adjutant read their citations, MacArthur pinned a Distinguished Service Cross, the second-highest military decoration in the United States Armed Forces, on each of their chests.

The adjutant's words—"For extraordinary heroism during operations against an armed enemy . . ."—troubled Mellnik. "As Gen. MacArthur pinned DSCs on McCoy and Dyess, I thought of the heroic thousands who died anonymously on distant battlefields and PW camps. . . . Feeling contrite and unworthy, I silently prayed my fallen comrades to forgive me."

The office emptied after the ceremony, leaving only MacArthur and the escapees seated around the general's desk. Typically, a "conversation" involving MacArthur and a guest consisted of the general doing most of the conversing and the guest doing most of the listening. That was not the case on this evening. MacArthur inquired about the fates of mutual friends and then listened intently as Dyess told his firsthand account of the Death March and as McCoy and Mellnik added the horrific tales of their respective prison camp ordeals. MacArthur was revolted by what he heard. A lone photograph taken during the occasion shows a different MacArthur, without the characteristic theatric regality. Instead he appears tight-lipped, uncomfortable, even grim. Despite MacArthur's well-chronicled narcissism, he was, in all likelihood, haunted by the thoughts of the price that his men had paid—and that those in captivity continued to pay—for his failure in the Philippines. MacArthur may have left the Philippines, but the Philippines and memories of his men had never left him.

When the former POWs finished their informal debriefing, the typically eloquent general's reply was unusually brief, yet threateningly powerful.

"The Japanese will pay for that humiliation and suffering," MacArthur promised them in a grave voice.

After all of the meetings and conferences with seemingly uninterested subordinates, it was reassuring for the escapees to know that MacArthur, at least, was on their side.

"It's a story that should be told to the American people," said MacArthur, singling out Dyess as the person to tell that story, much as Father Haggerty and others on Mindanao had. "But I am afraid, Captain, that the people back home will find it hard to believe you."

MacArthur did not specify to whom he was referring in regards to "the people back home." The American public? The top military brass who were running the war from Washington? Or was he referring to the U.S. government?

But that mattered little to Ed Dyess. After all, whether it was a stage performance at John Tarleton College in Stephenville, Texas, a briefing at Bataan Field, or a fiesta in the middle of the Mindanao jungle, he had yet to encounter an audience he could not win over.

CHAPTER 18

Duty

You say I'm jesting, talking like a fool?
Perhaps you're right, here in your crowded hive
Safe in your comfort. The misguided tool
Who earned that comfort now returns alive . . .

SUNDAY, SEPTEMBER 5, 1943
White Sulphur Springs, West Virginia, United States

On this morning Ed Dyess awoke in a bed in the high-security wing of a military hospital secluded in the Allegheny Mountains of West Virginia. Following his homecoming journey to the United States from Australia, Dyess had suffered a physical collapse that was as dizzying as any malaria bout. A cargo plane had transported Dyess, McCoy, and Mellnik across nine time zones in a mere thirty-six hours. Back home they discovered a nation firmly on a war footing, military personnel wearing new styles of helmets and uniforms and so much else. Dyess must have been especially bewildered at the sight of unfamiliar new aircraft adorned with new logos and new names, "fighters." To top it off, a chaotic routine of conferences and debriefings left the men little time to catch their breath, much less adjust to the bizarre new surroundings.

Dyess had not been admitted to Ashford General—formerly the luxurious Greenbrier Resort—entirely for physical recuperation. Anyone with enough security clearance to read his fourteen-page Pentagon deposition would have realized the significance of his words. There were those in the upper strata of the U.S. government who were deeply concerned

277

by his revelations, so Dyess was sent to Ashford until the government could figure out what to do with him. In the meantime, a gag order was enforced. If Dyess spoke of his experiences to anyone but authorized personnel, he risked his commission and possible criminal proceedings. His only outlet was his deposition, which revealed his deep feelings about the consequences he and his comrades suffered from following orders: "Had the Americans and Filipinos of Bataan known the fate in store for them . . . never would they have surrendered to our dishonorable foe."

Despite his officer's oath, he knew that he also had a duty to those left behind, and he ended his deposition with an expression of his strong personal convictions. Though he had no intention of being insubordinate, these words had probably been enough to land him at Ashford: "In my opinion, it is not only advisable, but absolutely necessary that all civilized people of the world know the conditions of the Japanese prison camps and the atrocities against American prisoners of war. . . . It was my idea when I escaped from the prison camp that if I could bring conditions before the American people we could force the Japanese into . . . giving us better treatment."

Ashford was the perfect place to quarantine Dyess and his story. Located 250 miles from Washington in southeastern West Virginia, the resort had first served as a detention center for enemy diplomats. Before war's end, more than 24,000 Army patients would be treated there. But for Dyess, Ashford was no sanctuary. Although one needed a special pass to gain access to him, he had nevertheless been besieged for two weeks by what one newspaper would call a parade of "literary sharks, Hollywood stooges, and syndicate agents."

He had the Associated Press and well-meaning friends to thank for that. The Dyess legend might have begun with his raid on Subic Bay, but in the States stories about him had been appearing since he had passed into captivity. The earliest appeared in the *New York Times* on July 26, 1942. In that article, correspondent Byron Darnton told of being summoned to an Australian field hospital. "I didn't want you to come to see me so I could talk about myself," Lt. Ben Brown told Darnton, "I want to tell you about Captain Ed Dyess. I don't think his story has been told back in the United States and it ought to be." Brown briefed Darnton on Dyess's exploits, and Darnton relayed the story to the *Times* Manhattan headquarters. Ensuing stories effectively built up Dyess's legend. Some of his visitors had informed him that arrangements had already been made for the publication of his story, regardless of his cooperation. He summoned his wife's attorney, August Meyer, to deal with his unwanted visitors. All Dyess wanted was to tell his story and return to the Pacific in the cockpit of a fighter plane as soon as possible. Then Marajen Dyess remembered that the *Chicago Tribune*, one of the nation's largest, as well as most powerful, daily newspapers, had been the first to request an interview with her husband.

Meyer contacted Walter Trohan, the *Tribune*'s Washington bureau chief, and Trohan transmitted the facts of the situation to assistant managing editor Don Maxwell in Chicago. Wasting little time, Maxwell selected Charles Leavelle, an experienced, middle-aged reporter, to accompany him on a trip to West Virginia. Maxwell arrived at Dyess's bedside and told him that the *Tribune* would beat any offer. But, as Dyess explained, money was not the most important consideration.

"The thing I must do—the thing I'm going to do—is to tell the American people what the Japs have done and are doing to their sons and husbands and brothers out in the Philippines. I want the American people to understand Japanese psychology and the way they make war. I am going to tell my story through the medium that will get it to the most people most effectively."

"We gave him the facts," Leavelle would write. "The best of the magazines could tell his story to two or three million people a week. The *Chicago Tribune* and associated newspapers could tell it to 12 to 14 million people a day." Maxwell also told Dyess that he would not have to pay for Leavelle's services. This saccharine concession was not lost on Dyess, who had, in fact, offered what amounted to a disclaimer in his deposition. "I had tried to put into words some of the things that I have experienced and observed during these past months, but I fail to find words adequate to an accurate portrayal. If any American could sit down and conjure before his mind the most diabolical of nightmares, he might perhaps come close to it, but none who have not gone [through] it could possibly have any idea of the tortures and the horror that these men are going through."

The *Tribune* offered $21,000, only $1,000 more than the highest standing offer from *Collier's*, but Maxwell and Leavelle had impressed Dyess.

"It's a deal," said Dyess, raising himself off his pillow to extend his right hand. "In the last few days all I've heard is talk about percentages on this, cut-ins on that, and slices of something else. Nobody would talk about how they were going to present this story . . . or about the number of people that would read it. That's all I'm interested in. I don't care about money and apparently you don't either. I want the story told and that is what you seem to want above everything else. We'll start work as soon as you can fix it up in Washington."

THURSDAY, SEPTEMBER 9–TUESDAY, SEPTEMBER 28, 1943
Washington, District of Columbia

THE WHITE HOUSE
WASHINGTON

September 9, 1943

SECRET
MEMORANDUM FOR:

The Secretary of War.
The Secretary of the Navy.

Subject: Japanese Atrocities—Reports of by Escaped Prisoners.

1. I agree with your opinion that any publication of Japanese atrocities at this time might complicate the present and future missions of the GRIPSHOLM and increase the mistreatment of prisoners now in Japanese hands. I request, therefore, that you take effective measures to prevent the publication or circulation of any stories emanating from escaped prisoners until I have authorized a release.

2. It might be well for the Joint Chiefs of Staff to make recommendation as to the moment when I should inform the country of the mistreatment of our nationals.

s/FRANKLIN D. ROOSEVELT

Copy to: Admiral Leahy

Mindanao's bamboo telegraph had nothing on wartime Washington. So fast did news travel—even of top secret White House memoranda—that the ink had hardly dried on FDR's signature when an alarmed Don Maxwell learned of the executive moratorium on atrocity stories. Maxwell called Walter Trohan. Trohan, in turn, dialed up Brig. Gen. Alexander Surles, chief of the War Department's Bureau of Public Relations. Trohan reached Surles at 5 P.M., September 9.

"I wanted to put a couple of things up to you because I know you will be fair and honest and want to do the right thing," opened Trohan. "Between you and me, we want the prestige of releasing it. . . . That's laying it completely and coldly on the table."

Trohan then suggested that until publication permission was granted, only three copies of the story—in addition to Dyess's, one each for the Army and *Chicago Tribune*—would be printed.

"Nothing is going to happen on this thing for at least six weeks," Surles assured him.

"Yes, but we'd like to spend about that much time writing it, if it could be arranged."

"I'll see what they say on it and let you know."

After Trohan and Surles hung up, the discussion about what would eventually be called "the Dyess story," as well as the larger subject of censorship, began in earnest.

On the home front during the dark days of early 1942, before the advent of ration stamps and gasoline stickers, America's first chronic shortage was war news. Censorship restrictions were responsible for the information famine, and though these restrictions originated from the highest levels of the military and the civilian government, two government agencies were largely responsible for waging the news war: the Office of Censorship and the Office of War Information, more commonly referred to by its initials, OWI. These agencies were separate entities and their missions entirely different.

Censorship, headed by Byron Price, the former executive editor of the Associated Press, was tasked with reading, evaluating, and editing news content before it appeared in the nation's print publications and radio broadcasts. Whereas Censorship was largely a filter between writers and commentators on one side and the country's printing presses and microphones on the other, OWI was charged, in the words of President Roosevelt, who signed the agency into existence with Executive Order 9182, "with the duty of formulating and carrying out information programs designed to facilitate the development of an informed and intelligent understanding, at home and abroad, of the status and progress of the war effort and of the war policies, aims and activities of the Government." OWI, in so many words, was the public relations arm of the wartime U.S. government.

The mission of OWI chief Elmer Davis, a popular CBS commenta-tor, was extraordinarily difficult. As *Time* magazine explained, Davis and those at OWI had, in effect, taken an oath "to tell the truth, but not the whole truth about the U.S. to its friends and enemies, and to neutrals abroad." Davis, a fifty-something Hoosier with horn-rimmed glasses, was the quintessential American journalist—Edward R. Murrow called him "fair and tough-minded." He would have to fight not only enemy propaganda abroad, but public misconceptions (the residual effects of American propaganda during the First World War), Washington policy-makers, and military brass at home, all while trying to keep a lid on inter-nal squabbles. Though the tide of war seemed to be turning in America's favor in the fall of 1943, Davis, and Price to a certain extent, were steadily losing ground in their efforts to educate the American people.

So stringent were the censorship regulations that it was not until the September 20, 1943, issue of *Life*—a full twenty-one months since Pearl Harbor—that the public saw the first images of dead U.S. servicemen in the war. Previously, thousands of images captured by combat photogra-phers had been locked in a War Department vault known as the "Cham-ber of Horrors." Written accounts of battles were also edited to eliminate gory details. In order to foster optimism, authorities believed that it was best to withhold the truth concerning the state of the Allied war effort, not just the casualty statistics and strategic failures, but also the visual proof of the dead and maimed bodies that was real war. The Office of Censorship had asked American journalists and media outlets to "lay off" reporting atrocity stores as early as February 1942.

The government, mindful of the effect on the public of the most re-cent war news from the Philippines, had no wish to reopen old emotional wounds at this time. The news of Bataan's surrender had been devastating when finally delivered in full, deflating detail in the spring of 1942. A fu-nereal gloom had shrouded the country as newspapers, radio, and news-reels revealed that approximately 36,000 U.S. troops were believed to have surrendered to the Japanese, qualifying the defeat as the largest and most ignominious in U.S. military history. The reverberations caused by the capitulation had rippled through the nation. It was not long after the fall of the Philippines that Americans began to question the "Europe First" strategy. A Brooklyn man sent $100 to Secretary of War Henry Stimson with the stipulation that the money be used to purchase "bullets or bayo-nets to avenge Bataan." Perhaps the most noteworthy national response was the formation of grassroots organizations designed to lobby for action in the Pacific and for POW support. Among many others, there was the MacArthur Club of Fort Worth, Texas, the American Bataan Club of Maywood, Illinois, the Sponsors of Philippine Heroes in Hollywood, California, the Philippine Society of Kansas in Wichita, and the Philippine Hero Club of St. Joseph, Missouri. Foremost, however, was the Bataan Relief Organization, created by Dr. V. H. Spensley, an Albuquerque dentist whose son was a Japanese POW. Within months of the Philippines disaster, the BRO would claim more than one million members in affiliate chapters nationwide.

Despite the efforts of these organizations, the martyrs of Bataan and Corregidor faded from the national consciousness in 1943. As the war in Europe took priority in terms of strategic planning, personnel, supplies, and media coverage, it seemed to many Americans, among them Mrs. August Mensching, a member of the American Bataan Clan from Des Plaines, Illinois, that "too many people have forgotten that there was a Bataan."

Perhaps some occupying the loftiest levels of the government would have preferred that. In a telephone conversation with one of General Marshall's aides on September 14, General Surles stated his belief that the mounting confusion concerning Roosevelt's memorandum and the buzz in official Washington behind the Dyess story were "all tied up with a great many factors, including the visit of the GRIPSHOLM and other things."

The *Gripsholm* was a merchant ship of neutral Swedish registry that was carrying medical supplies and food for Allied POWs in the Pacific. The U.S. government was worried that publicizing Japanese atrocities might jeopardize the delivery of those supplies. The government was also concerned about the possible reaction of the volatile Japanese to any atrocity claims of Allied POWs. But there were other reasons behind the executive suppression of Dyess's and any other atrocity stories.

While civilians, some segments of the press, and certain high-ranking brass clamored for action against the Japanese, the Pacific war remained the stepchild of the global conflict. Stories about the war with Germany dominated front pages, while the Pacific war was relegated to the inside pages.

Worse, the Pacific theater was working on a shoestring budget. In December 1943, the U.S. Army had slightly more than 900,000 men deployed in the Pacific and China-Burma-India theaters, as opposed to nearly 1.5 million men in the European, Mediterranean, and North African theaters. And only a fraction of supplies was allotted to the Pacific. Fleet Admiral Ernest J. King, an outspoken critic of the Europe First strategy since the Arcadia Conference of late 1941 and early 1942, estimated that in late 1943, despite the fact that most of the noteworthy battles of the war thus far had taken place in the Pacific, only 15 percent of the prodigious amount of supplies rolling off American assembly lines was reaching the Pacific. King believed that American industry was capable of producing enough war matériel for simultaneous offensives against Germany and Japan; he also thought Britain was shirking her responsibilities as an ally in the Pacific struggle.

No amount of redistribution of aid could pacify Douglas MacArthur. MacArthur believed himself to be fighting a two-front war, one against the Japanese and another against Washington. MacArthur predictably and immediately seized on the revelation of Japanese atrocities as the reason why he must make good on his promise to return to the Philippines with all deliberate haste. In a private letter prepared for FDR not long after his conference with Dyess, McCoy, and Mellnik in July 1943, MacArthur passionately stressed that:

> our quiescent policy with respect to the Philippines . . . is in no small degree responsible for the unfolding of a drama the stark tragedy of which has no counterpart in American history. Our prisoners of war are being subjected to slow and deliberate extermination through disease, starvation and summary execution. So, have many thousands already perished and few, if any, will ever survive unless we arouse ourselves into a more dynamic Philippine aid policy . . . Never before in the service of my country have I found it necessary to defend her honor and dignity . . . before all humanity, by the advocacy of military and moral considerations more elementary than those that should now form the framework of our Philippine policy if we are to redeem ourselves before God, before the shattered remnant of our Army that lies shackled in the stench of Japanese imprisonment and before our wards, the Filipino people.

MacArthur thought that the Dapecol escapees had not been muzzled merely to ensure safe delivery of the *Gripsholm*'s cargo. "Perhaps the administration, which was committed to a Europe first effort, feared American public opinion would demand a greater reaction against Japan," MacArthur would speculate in his memoirs, "but whatever the cause, here was the sinister beginning of the 'managed news' concept by those in power."

MacArthur's supposition that the government was deliberately suppressing the atrocity stories should not be dismissed out of hand. War correspondent Raymond Clapper, a veteran of several Pacific battles who was also a supporter of FDR, confirmed MacArthur's claim, complaining that Roosevelt "was taking the whole technique of a controlled press far beyond anything we have experienced in this country."

No matter what their government was—or was not—telling them, Americans had long been aware of the brutal nature of their Pacific enemy, due to atrocity stories emanating from China (Nanking, among other places). It was not until 1943, however, when several stories detailing atrocities committed against U.S. prisoners were released, that the public's blood began to boil. In late April, Americans learned of the October 1942 execution of three American fliers who had been captured in occupied China following the Doolittle Raid. Roosevelt condemned the Japanese as "barbarous" and "depraved," and the public's reaction, noted historian John Dower, "was comparable to the rage that greeted the news of Pearl Harbor." Observing the emotional response, the British embassy in Washington reported to London that the uproar was such that it "sharply increased the stimulus of national anger and humiliation which makes of the Pacific front permanently a more burning issue than [the] European front is ever likely to be."

Why was Dyess encountering so much resistance? Perhaps because his story was unlike anything America had known before, a story that described not a handful of heinous acts committed against a few downed airmen, but the systemized torture and extermination of thousands of abandoned American troops. The story possessed so much emotional and political dynamite that it was no wonder Colonel Robert McCormick, owner of the *Chicago Tribune* and other papers, was heavily invested. The maverick publishing baron had long been an enemy of FDR and the Democratic Party. The Dyess story was only the latest in a series of tangles that the *Tribune* had had with censorship and the White House. Months earlier, the paper had been accused of compromising national security by publishing a story about the Navy's successful breaking of Japanese codes, which helped lead to the Midway victory. A grand jury was convened, but the case was dropped because the Japanese never changed their codes as a result of the *Tribune*'s story, thus exonerating the paper. Dyess's story of widespread atrocities and the sensational story of the only mass escape of American POWs seemed tailor-made for McCormick and the *Tribune*.

The fact that it was the *Chicago Tribune* sitting atop this ticking media time bomb was beginning to light up switchboards throughout Washington. Upon his return from a meeting with *Tribune* editors in Chicago, Capt. Leland P. Lovett, head of the Navy's Office of Public Relations, alerted Surles that it seemed as though the paper was preparing to take an aggressive stance. McCormick's likely impatience presaged a censorship showdown. "The thing I'm a little doubtful about," Military Intelligence Service chief Gen. George V. Strong told Surles in a phone conversation on September 13, "is to whether the *Chicago Tribune* wants to play the game." In anticipation of an attempt by the *Tribune* to circumvent established channels, Strong and Surles were prepared to invoke the Espionage Act, if necessary, to ensure the paper's cooperation. (Passed shortly after America's entry into World War I in 1917, the Espionage Act prohibited the transmission of national defense and security information, interference with military operations, and other treasonous and/or subversive activities. It was amended in 1940.)

Meanwhile, Dyess was not the only one being muzzled. Both McCoy and Mellnik had undergone extensive debriefings and submitted reports, only to encounter the same mysterious roadblocks. As in Dyess's case, their silence had reportedly also been secured under the threat of the loss of their commissions and careers. McCoy's situation had not been made any easier by Wendell Fertig, who had sent a letter to an old friend, Gen. Hugh J. Casey, in a bundle of papers taken out on the *Trout* in July. Fertig's warning to Casey, likely circulated among the elite levels of command, undoubtedly raised red flags for McCoy's superiors:

> In general personalities have not been as serious as anticipated. However, the escape of ten prisoners from Davao has complicated the situation somewhat, since the escape was led by Lieut. Comdr. Melvyn H. McCoy, who, to put it as pleasantly as possible, is a bit "stir-crazy." He must be watched upon his arrival in Australia, because he may do some injudicious talking.

McCoy had had enough. First he had to fight the Japanese. Then Wendell Fertig—twice. And now his own Navy, as well as the bureaucratic machinations of the U.S. government? The memories of those comrades he had left behind, both the escapees still on Mindanao and the POWs still behind barbed wire, would not allow him to remain quiescent.

"In view of what's happening to the prisoners out there—they've died by the thousands, they're continuing to die and they're probably all going to die if something isn't done about it—I cannot accept the order to remain silent," he told his superiors. "One reason we escaped was to let the world know what is happening to the prisoners. I will reveal this and . . . will sacrifice my career if necessary. This must be told and I will tell it."

With that brazen pronouncement, McCoy waited to see if the Navy would call his bluff. In the meantime, he entered into negotiations with several publications for the rights to his version of the escape story.

Mellnik, too, was obsessed by thoughts of those left behind, but he remained more reserved than McCoy. He followed orders to the letter, telling his astonished family very little, if anything, about how he had found his way home. At the same time, Mellnik seemed equally confused by the general lack of knowledge about or passion for the Pacific war, not to mention his ordeal. "It seemed hard for him to realize we in America didn't know of the Japanese cruelty to our men," his wife would tell a newspaper reporter.

Believing that he could do more for his comrades in the Pacific than in the Pentagon, Mellnik arranged for a transfer to MacArthur's GHQ in Brisbane. But before his departure, he traveled to Saranac Lake, New York, to fulfill a promise. It was there, the Western Hemisphere's foremost location for the treatment of pulmonary tuberculosis, that Mellnik found a frail, sickly Manuel Quezon racked with coughing spasms and entering the last months of his life. Mellnik told Quezon of the invaluable assistance that Ben de la Cruz and Victor Jumarong had provided the escapees and asked that the Philippine president-in-exile grant pardons to both men.

"If you'll give their names to my secretary," said Quezon, "she'll prepare the papers, and I'll sign them, before you leave."

By mid-September, the powers-that-be decided to buy time, presumably for the *Gripsholm*, perhaps to explore other methods for resolving the pending showdown involving the *Chicago Tribune*, Dyess, McCoy, and the government, and maybe for "other things," as Surles had stated.

Charles Leavelle was granted permission to take down Dyess's story—but nothing more. An awed Leavelle spent several days at Ashford before Dyess was discharged. "At first it was difficult to believe he held the Legion of Merit, the DSC with Oak Leaf Cluster, the Silver Star, and the two cluster group citation," he would write. "He was a thin, blond youngster, slow of speech. But after a couple of minutes in his presence you recognized the qualities of leadership that made him great."

Usually, Dyess reclined in his bed and dictated his story to Leavelle. Humble, Dyess seemed to consciously avoid any inclusion of himself in the story. On occasion, the pilot would hover over Leavelle's shoulder, reading as the latter typed. "Tst, tst," Dyess would say, shaking his head. "You must have a strong 'I' key on this typewriter. It's a wonder to me it didn't break somewhere along here."

Dyess eventually relented to being the centerpiece of the story, conditionally. "If you triple my troubles and multiply the result by several thousand, you'll get a rough idea of what went on," Dyess remarked, putting his experiences into perspective. "And when you do that, you must bear in mind that I got out alive. Thousands of the boys didn't—and won't."

In early fall, Leavelle and Maxwell traveled to Washington for a conference with General Surles, having brought five completed chapters for the latter's review. Surles, however, declined, stating that a blanket ban had been placed on all atrocity stories from the highest authorities and, recalled Leavelle, that "there would be no point in his reading the story."

Despite all of the obstacles they had overcome, Dyess, McCoy, and Mellnik had arrived home only to face another lengthy battle. This time, wrote Leavelle, they would be fighting their own government, "official reluctance, indecision, resistance and actual hostility in high places."

THURSDAY, SEPTEMBER 30, 1943
At sea aboard the USS Bowfin

At last, Sam Grashio's hands had stopped trembling. Calmly, as the submarine *Bowfin* ran safely and silently in the depths of the Mindanao Sea, Grashio pulled out the envelope on which was written, in the handwriting of Leo Boelens, the following instructions: "Sam—Not to be opened until after shove'n." Earlier in the evening, Grashio's hands had quivered so much that he could not pick up a cup of coffee in the officers' wardroom. But now, as he had steadied to the realization that the submarine truly existed, that he was indeed going home, he opened the parcel to find two parting gifts: a letter and a poem.

Taking a leave from his duties as guerrilla quartermaster, Grashio had spent several weeks with Boelens on the site of Farm Project No. 1 about four kilometers south of Lala, Lanao. Boelens, though, had not returned to his roots; Farm Project No. 1 was the code name for a secret, 1.4-million-square-foot airfield that Wendell Fertig had ordered Boelens to carve out of the Mindanao wilderness. The name was a disguise—should the Japanese capture Fertig's papers or a spy overhear a conversation, there would be little to indicate the true nature of the project. Boelens supervised a small team of three officers and five enlisted men as well as a number of civilian laborers. In typical Boelens fashion, it had become an all-consuming task.

Years later, Grashio would wistfully recall the period of his visit, the memories of feasting on monkey meat with local Moros and him and Boelens reading stories from old *Reader's Digest* magazines to each other near a beautiful waterfall. Grashio's visit was cut short when a runner from Fertig's headquarters arrived with the news that he had been cleared for evacuation. "I was simultaneously gladdened and saddened," Grashio would write.

Grashio had offered to stay behind, but Boelens would hear none of it. Just as he had with Dyess, Boelens seemed to possess a greater sense of Grashio's destiny than Grashio himself. On his departure two days earlier, Grashio had awakened at 2 A.M. to find Boelens awake, writing by the meager light of a coconut oil lamp.

Sam—

We've come a long way together, 10,000 miles or more
To find the going tough but we've much to be thankful for.
Our friendship was cast into brotherhood amidst the blood and jumble, and bound by mortar made of hardships that time can never crumble. Our paths diverged from time to time common of circumstance, but always joined at happy stands of joyous consequence.
We have reached another junction; the sign says you must go,

until the paths converge at a happy stand where the pickens are
good we know.

Leo

In the letter, the message was more of the same. Their duty as officers, wrote Boelens, was of paramount importance. Personal loyalties and relationships must be set aside for the good of the nation. "His duty was to stay and complete the airstrip," Grashio said. "Mine was to go." But for what reason, Grashio could not immediately understand.

CHAPTER 19

Greater Love
Hath No Man

I kneel to thee and hail thee as my Lord.
From such a God as thee I ask not life . . .
I ask but strength to ride the wave of fate . . .

FRIDAY, OCTOBER 8–THURSDAY, NOVEMBER 4, 1943
Washington, District of Columbia

The arrival of autumn brought cooler temperatures, but America's emotional furnace needed little stoking. In early October, the government released the translation of a diary found on a dead Japanese soldier in New Guinea that poetically described the beheading of an Allied airman. Addressing an inflamed nation, the *New York Times* editorialized that the diary exposed "the real nature of our Asiatic enemy," one of "primitive blood lust and brutal butchery."

Writing a secret memorandum for Secretary of War Henry Stimson on October 8, General George Marshall sensed the change in the barometer of public opinion. The pressure in Washington was increasing with the release of each atrocity story. Believing that it was only a matter of when, not if, the public heard the Dyess story, Marshall forecast a tempest. He wanted Stimson to be prepared for the worst, but also to prepare to harness and manage the public fury.

The problem is exceedingly complex and of course requires the most careful handling both in relation to our actions at the present time and as to future developments. The storm of bitterness which will arise, once the public is aware of the brutalities and savagery displayed by the Japanese towards our prisoners, should be directed along carefully thought out lines rather than left to dissipate itself in a lurid press and unpredictable reactions. . . . I don't want to burden you unnecessarily in this matter, but you have had it somewhat in hand and it pertains to the highest governmental policy.

That policy greeted Sam Grashio when he reached Hamilton Field in mid-October. "Here, as in Australia, I was reminded repeatedly that my past was a military secret, that I was not to discuss life in prison camps with anyone," Grashio remembered. "At the moment I thought this merely silly. Within a few days, the gag was to be exceedingly irksome."

Grashio proceeded to Washington, stopping briefly in Chicago at the request of Don Maxwell to sign a waiver that would ensure the *Tribune*'s monopoly on the Dyess story. For his signature, Grashio was "rewarded with the princely sum of $100." In Washington, Grashio found the exchange even less lucrative. The functionaries at the Pentagon and State Department were "patronizing" and unsympathetic: "To me, they seemed unreasonable, even inhuman; preoccupied with Europe when American soldiers were starving, rotting and dying in squalid prison camps; far too concerned about the reactions of the Japanese and too little about the fate of Americans abroad and the anxieties of their loved ones at home." Grashio could not comprehend the foot-dragging in an otherwise bustling capital. "In my opinion," he said in his official statement, "at this time there is approximately 25% of the original Americans taken in the Philippines still alive and in another six months to a year, if something is not done to improve their diet and medical care, very few will be living to tell their experiences."

Shortly after his Washington trip, Grashio experienced his own breakdown. As with Dyess, his was a long time coming. In prison camp, the prisoners' energies had been devoted to survival. After escaping, they needed to stay one step ahead of the Japanese; there was no time to look back. Thrust back into home life, Grashio grew chronically nervous and restless. His moods became "dark and petulant." When he wasn't suffering from insomnia, he endured nightmares, frightening visions of the prison camps and the Japanese.

Grashio was soon admitted into Spokane's Fort Wright hospital for six weeks of "rest, recuperation and repairs." While doctors fought his malaria and a dentist reconstructed a mouthful of teeth that had been decimated by malnutrition, he searched for the source of his debilitating depression. It did not take long: it was *them*—Bert Bank, Motts Tonelli, and the others still in Dapecol. "Now I found myself muzzled," he would say, "seemingly unable to do anything for those left behind, and at the same time ignorant of what had happened to them."

His inability to respond to the "avalanche of questions, calls and letters," the information requests from relatives of POWs, plunged him deeper into despair. "It was maddeningly frustrating to be unable to divulge what I knew, especially when some of the beseechers were aware that I was holding back on them and when I was convinced that there was no sufficient reason to hold back." All that the escapees had been through seemed for naught. It was the cruelest of ironies. "The whole purpose of our escape," he said, "seemed thwarted, mocked every day."

As bad as it was, Grashio admitted that "Dyess came much closer than I to being destroyed by the consequent frustration." Dyess had absorbed one bitter disappointment after another. Not only had he been forced to ignore the families of his men and essentially been removed from public circulation for several weeks at Ashford, his request to return to combat duty in the Pacific had also been denied. Months later, Marajen Dyess attempted to explain what her husband was going through. "I saw it in his eyes—that suffering—when I first greeted him," she said. "I was the only one he could tell. He had to tell someone. He was breaking inside. Hundreds of people with relatives who are Jap prisoners called or wrote him daily and he couldn't tell a single one about the dreadful happenings in the Philippines. It hurt him so."

Dyess, however, was temporarily placated with another promotion, as well as General Arnold's promise of a fighter command in Europe. And Grashio's orders were changed so that he could join Dyess as a squadron commander. Even more important, Dyess had been granted one more special permission: he was going home to Texas.

FRIDAY, NOVEMBER 5, 1943
Albany, Texas

Ed Dyess no sooner rose from his seat than the overflow crowd at the Albany High School stadium jumped to its feet and erupted in thunderous applause. He had not even opened his mouth.

"Hello folks," he said, leaning toward the microphone sheepishly. Then, waving the audience down, he pleaded, "Everybody sit down."

Dyess had sat through the invocation and introductions waiting nervously for his turn at the rostrum. The stadium floodlights shone down upon the highly decorated, twenty-seven-year-old new lieutenant colonel on this Friday night with greater intensity than at any time during his playing days. But butterflies were not the problem.

"I feel like I have a ten-gallon hat caught in my throat," he opened. "You know, I really am embarrassed up here. . . . I don't know of any other time when I have felt like this—except I remember one morning I was standing in a cow pasture with a parachute on while the Japs were bombing Pearl Harbor. I feel now like I felt then, except I don't have a parachute now. . . . If you have ever gotten up to make a speech and can't say anything—you know the jam I'm in now."

Dyess had been permitted to stop in Texas before reporting to his new assignment with the 4th Air Force in California. It would be the briefest of homecomings—six days—and an uncomfortable one at that, given the entourage of officers and bodyguards that accompanied him to Albany. Whether he was in the parlor room having a conversation with an old friend or outside tossing around a football with some Cub Scouts, the escorts were omnipresent. In the latter years of her life, his mother, Hallie, would remain convinced that the telephones in the Dyess home had been bugged at this time. Throughout Dyess's brief stay, hundreds of calls, letters, and telegrams—many were from well-wishers, but most were from worried parents, wives, and loved ones of people declared missing on Bataan—streamed into his parents' residence. He had no choice but to answer each the same: "I can't say a thing." He could not even tell his parents about what he had seen and experienced, or how he had escaped. Invitations to speak in nearby Cisco and Abilene had to be turned down. Dyess was probably fortunate in that regard.

The giant crowd jammed in and around the stadium on this night—by most accounts, the entire population of Albany, approximately 2,000— was starving for information about the adventures of their native son. Dyess tried his best to nourish them with his charm and sense of humor. One friend, he told the audience, had suggested that Dyess just count to 100 to fulfill his speaking obligation.

"But I see Miss Jackson, my old math teacher, out there," cracked Dyess, "and she knows I can't count that high."

Dyess then turned to a subject that he could talk about indefinitely: food.

"One thing I know for sure—it is wonderful to be here. I didn't know that when I sent a telegram asking that a steak be saved for me that I would get all of the food I am getting now."

The gag order had forced the pool of reporters covering the homecoming to file stories on what Dyess was putting into his mouth, rather than what was not coming out. Judge and Mrs. Dyess had dutifully saved up their ration points in order to provide their son with a steak for nearly every meal, leading to headlines such as the one appearing in this day's edition of the *Dallas Morning News:* "One-Man Scourge of Japanese Turns Talents on Texas Steak."

"I am going to have to get out of town before I give my dad a race," Dyess, said, laughing and patting his midriff as the crowd roared. "In my lifetime, I have tried practically everything there is to eat. In fact, in Shackelford County, I tried to eat a barbecued sparrow and a hawk. I have eaten a little monkey, horse, mule and carabao. Our cooking recipe for carabao was simple. Put two rocks in with the carabao. When the rocks melted, you knew the carabao was tender."

On Bataan, Dyess added in all seriousness, U.S. troops ate everything but rats.

"Yellow rats! If you don't know what a yellow rat looks like—well, it is larger and rattier and yellower than any rat you have ever seen. We had a lot of trouble with these rats and killed a good many of them."

The implication was clear. It would be Dyess's only reference to his combat experiences.

"I'll tell you where I've been," continued Dyess, returning to humor in an effort to address some of the rumors that had prefaced his presence in Albany. "This is my story and I will stay with it. My boat sailed from San Francisco two years ago—and I jumped the ship. Since then I've heard that I've been in Shangri-La—you've all heard of Shangri-La. But I haven't been in Shangri-La. I've been incognito in a zoot suit."

Dyess, whose eyes were beginning to turn glassy, did not need to glance down at his diamond-studded wristwatch, a gift from his parents for two missed Christmases and three birthdays, to know that it was time to wrap up his speech.

"But seriously, it is probably a pretty good thing that I can't talk too much on a few subjects. This is the greatest tribute I will ever get—past, present or future . . . I don't think that this should be a tribute to me. I am back. I am here. Let's make this a tribute to those boys who are not back but who are still over there." Dyess paused momentarily as his amplified voice reverberated into the crowd. "This is the greatest honor I shall ever receive. When the folks at home are glad to see you home—you can't beat that."

Dyess could barely choke out the last words when hundreds from the crowd—men, women, and children, friends and strangers alike—surged from their seats and pressed the speaker's stand to pump his hand, ask for autographs, embrace him, or, in the case of some, merely touch him.

"I want you all to know that I love every one of you."

MONDAY, NOVEMBER 15, 1943
Nasipit, Agusan Province, Mindanao

It was almost 1600 hours and Austin Shofner was, as usual, in a betting mood. An hour earlier, Shofner, Mike Dobervich, Jack Hawkins, Wendell Fertig, and Ernest McClish had boarded the launch *Agusan* and puttered out from Nasipit to meet the submarine that had been dispatched to evacuate the three Marines, as well as a number of civilians and children, from Mindanao. The sub was slightly overdue and Shofner sensed that the group needed a boost.

"Who wants to make a little bet?" he challenged. "I'll say she surfaces at four-thirty. How about you, Beaver? Think you can outguess me?"

"Okay, Shof," said Dobervich, ever indulgent. What do you want to bet this time—the usual?"

"Yep. One steak dinner, payable in Frisco."

"All right, you're on. I say five o'clock. You say four-thirty. Whoever's closest wins."

"Beaver, you already owe me twelve steak dinners, you know."

"Don't worry, Shof. When we hit Frisco I'll buy you those twelve steaks—all at one time. And I hope you choke on 'em."

The lighthearted banter did little to alleviate Hawkins's gnawing fears.

"I could scarcely believe that the submarine would actually appear," he would say, "that this, at last, was to be the day of deliverance."

Reaching this point had not been easy. The remaining escapees had spent the last four months buckwheating from headquarters to headquarters, town to town, hideout to hideout. Hawkins was lucky to be alive, let alone here for this moment. In June, soon after being sent to Tubay in the Lake Mainet area of Surigao to prepare a new camp, Hawkins had been stricken with blackwater fever, a virulent complication of malaria. The devastating attack immobilized him at a most inopportune time: almost simultaneously, the Japanese launched an assault on Tubay. Amid falling bombs, Filipinos carried a semiconscious Hawkins to the remote home of a man named George Tirador. For nearly a month, Tirador and his family nursed Hawkins back to health with around-the-clock care and some of the quinine that Ed Dyess had pilfered from the Dapecol dispensary prior to the escape.

The Marines' departure would leave just three of the original American escapees on Mindanao. Leo Boelens, still laboring on his airfield in Lanao, steadfastly refused evacuation. Spielman had made a habit of visiting the homestead of Frank McCarthy, a Spanish-American War veteran who had stayed in the Philippines to build a fortune in lumber and mining in Surigao, purportedly because of McCarthy's stockpile of cured meats. "[McCarthy] had hams, bacon and a pretty little girl," Paul Marshall revealed. Her name was Lucy, and Spielman was smitten. Marshall would be the best man at their wedding that fall. It was not a large affair, for fear of unwanted guests. "We were afraid if [the Japanese] knew about it, they would come," remembered Lucy Spielman.

Marshall, now a captain, was CO of the 114th Infantry Regiment. Spielman, in turn, became his executive officer. The two youngest members of the escape party understood the unique opportunity they had with the guerrillas. If they returned to the regular army, they would return as enlisted men. There was unfinished business, too. "Bob and I had a little grudge, shall we say it, with the Japs," explained Marshall. "It was payback time."

Much to the relief of the Marines, the sub finally surfaced—"like some great sea monster from the depths," remembered Hawkins—around 1700. More than 370 feet long and with a displacement of 2,730 tons, the USS *Narwhal* was the largest sub in the U.S. fleet, along with her sister ship, the *Nautilus*. But to many of the Americans and Filipinos waiting at Nasipit, the *Narwhal*'s sheer size and two 6-inch deck guns made her look like a battleship. None present that day would ever forget the sight of the massive vessel docking at the rickety pier. Nor would the crew of the *Narwhal* ever forget the welcome they received.

Sailors pouring out of the ship's hatches could not believe their eyes—

nor their ears. A guerrilla band began belting out "Stars and Stripes Forever," and dozens of stevedores appeared almost magically to begin unloading the *Narwhal*'s cargo of much needed supplies. "The place was lit up by native torches eight feet tall, flickering and sputtering and sending up thick, oily smoke," one of the *Narwhal*'s chief petty officers later told *The Saturday Evening Post*. Other sailors saw barbecued pigs and kegs of beer laid out as if in presentation for a banquet. Soon there were hundreds of inquisitive locals swarming the pier. The band alternated sailors' requests with some favorite tunes such as "The Eyes of Texas," which Ed Dyess had taught them, as well as "Anchors Aweigh" and "Yankee Doodle."

So much for secrecy. Shofner, standing on the deck next to Cmdr. Frank Latta, skipper of the *Narwhal*, while savoring a cup of American coffee and a cigarette, noticed that Latta's face, previously beaming in wonderment, quickly drooped. It must have dawned on the bewildered skipper that this surreal scene was taking place deep in enemy territory. The Japanese garrison at Butuan was, after all, only fifteen miles away.

"You say we have good security?" asked Latta.

"Every road, every trail is covered by sentries," Shofner reassured him. "If a Jap goes to get a drink of water in Butuan, the bamboo telegraph will tell us about it."

When the unloading was finished, Filipinos brought forth baskets of fruit, as well as long bamboo tubes, which Latta, once he understood the contents—tuba—apologetically refused. Touched by the Filipinos' generosity, the crew reciprocated by emptying their lockers of candy, cigarettes, and clothes, which they distributed to the crowd. The Marines did likewise. Shofner unslung his BAR from his shoulder and handed it to McClish.

"Big Boy will need this back," he said.

Dobervich characteristically slid off his battered shoes and tossed them to a shoeless Filipino on the dock. Hawkins handed his pistol to McClish. "I choked up and had difficulty saying goodbye to him and to my other friends on the dock. I had come to love these warm and brave people and this wild and primitive land," he would say. "I had a feeling that the high point of my life was at hand and would soon slip into the past. Nothing in my future, I thought, could ever equal these experiences in these two years."

One could certainly sense the sentimentality in the sultry, smoke-choked air. With the human cargo embarked, a total of thirty-one evacuees, including several women and children, among them a baby, the sub shoved off to farewell waves and the strains of "God Bless America."

The *Narwhal*'s eight-day voyage to Australia became the stuff of legend. In a matter of days, the wardroom became a dispensary for chewing gum and gumdrops. Grizzled torpedomen hauled children over hatch coamings by their diapers. Crewmen taught children how to make sailor's knots so that the kids would quit "monkeying with the valves, levers and electrical switches." According to *The Saturday Evening Post*, "frilly and pastel-hued underthings" appeared "upon improvised laundry ropes in those portions of the Old Girl's innards that were warmer and dryer than the others." There were lines for the head and many surprises, such as the time Latta turned on the shower jets, only to be ambushed by a pair of pink pants and a brassiere.

The high jinks, however, hardly bothered the Marines. Just about the only problem they recounted was an inability to sleep, but that had nothing to do with their fellow passengers. As Shofner remembered, not even Latta's soft bunk helped. Nearly two years of sleeping in foxholes or on concrete floors, wooden slats, and bamboo cots had adversely conditioned him. So one day he climbed down onto the hard steel deck plating and, much to the surprise of the sailors stepping over his body, fell asleep immediately.

THURSDAY, DECEMBER 16, 1943
San Francisco, California

The Pan Am Clipper skimmed San Francisco Bay, its propellers whirring to a stop at 0900. Exhausted after eight days of island hopping across the Pacific—their flight itinerary covered a total distance of more than 7,000 miles and included stops at New Caledonia, Espiritu Santu, the Ellice and Phoenix Islands, and Pearl Harbor—the three Marines were also cold and hungry. With another plane waiting to whisk them to Washington, they would have to hurry if Shofner was to collect on his bets.

Strolling down the dock and shivering in their thin field jackets, they found a cozy restaurant decorated for the season with tinsel and holiday bunting. Wearing decorations of their own, Distinguished Service Crosses awarded to them by MacArthur during an unforgettable ceremony in Brisbane, they took a booth near a small Christmas tree.

"If General MacArthur had gone into the movies, you would never have heard of John Barrymore," Shofner said. "I went in hating his guts—we used to call him 'Dugout Doug' and a few other nice choice words—[but] he told me what a great job I had done and gave [me] the Distinguished Service Cross. I thought he was God and I was his right-hand angel when I left."

But nothing could compare to the elation that accompanied being back in the States. They were so caught up in the holiday atmosphere and in the joy of being home that they could barely finish their meals.

"I still can't believe it," Hawkins muttered aloud, "it's like a dream."

The tune playing on the restaurant's nickelodeon, Hawkins would recall, had a familiar ring to it. Had it really been one year since he, restless in Barracks Five in Dapecol on a cold, rainy, miserable Christmas Eve, had awakened Dobervich with a strange premonition?

The name of the song was "I'll Be Home for Christmas."

WEDNESDAY, DECEMBER 22, 1943
Burbank, California

No one could accuse Ed Dyess of not taking time to stop and smell the flowers. Not today, at least. It was late morning and though somewhat in a hurry, Dyess was all smiles walking down Crescent Heights Boulevard, his arms filled with the fresh-cut flowers he had personally selected for the dinner party he and his wife were hosting in their Hollywood apartment that evening. Marajen Dyess counted a number of Hollywood elite, including several movie stars, as close friends, so the event promised to be star-studded.

Nothing could ruin Dyess's mood, not even the preposterous stall tactics being employed in Washington. Exactly three weeks earlier, the *Gripsholm*, her cargo delivered, had docked safely in New York. The *Chicago Tribune* immediately petitioned for permission to release the Dyess story, but "the War Department said that the American people were not yet ready for such an appalling story of Japanese atrocities," recalled Charles Leavelle. The situation, it seemed, had morphed from a matter of supposed practical pretexts to one of transparent, official obstinacy. Just when did the government think that America would be ready?

Dyess went to Washington to consult with General Hap Arnold, but Arnold could offer Dyess little in the way of answers or assistance. The

War Department had classified the matter as one of national security, Arnold told Dyess; he had no power to intervene. The War Department had reiterated that any revelation of Japanese atrocities would possibly result in reprisals against American POWs. Dyess was incredulous. Those men still behind Japanese barbed wire, he argued, would want the people back home to know what was happening. It was a chance that needed to be taken.

The *Tribune* then began to wheel out its First Amendment field artillery. The paper first enlisted the help of Roy Roberts, editor of the *Kansas City Star*, president of the American Newspaper Editors Association, and chairman of the Newspaper Advisory Committee of the Domestic Division of OWI, to lobby Elmer Davis on the paper's behalf. Next, the *Tribune's* research staff assembled a massive file containing hundreds of atrocity and escape stories—organized by theater, enemy, publication, and date of publication—that had been printed with military censorship approval and submitted this package of precedents to OWI.

Dyess could only wait. In the meantime, he had plenty to do, including finding his crucifix and Saint Christopher medal, the treasured talismans that had accompanied him on his journey through combat and captivity to freedom. He had been wearing them during his stay at Ashford and had allowed the *Tribune* to photograph the objects, remembered Leavelle. But on December 20, the items mysteriously disappeared. A full-scale search was initiated, but nothing turned up. "On the night of December 21st [Dyess] still was hopeful of finding his talisman," wrote Leavelle. "He spoke of it to Mrs. Dyess as they addressed Christmas cards."

One of those cards was addressed to Sam Grashio. Dyess had been planning to visit Spokane, but poor weather had grounded him. No matter. He would get there after the holidays.

> *Dear Sam—*
>
> *I was to leave here this morning, but O-O kept me on the ground so now I'll have to put it off until after Xmas as the weather is supposed to be bad all day tomorrow. Listen "knucklehead" if it isn't too much of a secret just where in the hell do I find you after I get there, or have you moved into the jail to feel at home.*

There were some additional matters that Dyess needed to attend to before the holidays. Depositing the flowers at his apartment, he then headed to Grand Central Air Terminal in Glendale to sneak in some flight time on the P-38 Lightning, the Army Air Force's new ultrafast twin-engined fighter. Armed with four .50 caliber machine guns and one 20-millimeter cannon, the P-38 was capable of reaching speeds in excess of 400 miles per hour. It was the kind of warplane that aggressive, talented pilots salivated over—Dyess's kind of plane. He needed to log some hours in order to assume command of the outfit that he was preparing to take into combat in Europe, the 479th Fighter Group, a component of the Eighth Air Force.

Just before Dyess's arrival at the field, Lt. Robin Olds, a twenty-one-year-old West Pointer, was given his orders. "The operations officer said, 'I want you to check out this colonel in a P-38,' " Olds would say. "Nobody told me who he was or anything else about him."

As Dyess settled into the cockpit of P-38H-5-LO, Olds crouched on the wing and explained the controls. Dyess was not curt or overbearing, but, recalled Olds, "I realized that he wanted to hurry up." Though Dyess had logged only ten total hours of flight time in the P-38 and Olds had extensive training on the model, Olds deferred to Dyess's rank and distilled his preflight check into a handful of necessary items. Olds told Dyess that warplanes in the United States were provided with lower-grade gasoline in order to conserve high-octane, high-performance fuel for combat aircraft. As a result, the engines of stateside birds frequently became congested and tended to detonate, or backfire. Sometimes, they even locked up mid-flight. These problems were particularly prevalent with the P-38.

"As you line up," Olds told Dyess, "if you hear bang, bang, bang, shut 'em [the engines] down and stop. Hit the brakes. Go off the end of the runway if you have to."

Dyess signaled that he understood, but Olds would later say that it seemed as though Dyess was dismissive of the briefing. Of course, Dyess had logged thousands more hours of cumulative flight time in his career than Olds, a recent flight school graduate. And, as a pilot who had actually tangled with the Japanese in aerial combat, Dyess was unlikely to be frightened by something as seemingly harmless as bad gasoline.

After Olds hopped down from the wing, Dyess gunned the plane's engines. At approximately 1206, he called the tower for taxi instructions. Dyess was notified that he was cleared to runway 30, but when he rolled onto the flight line, he found himself waiting for several minutes as a B-25 prepared to take off. This likely tried Dyess's patience; it was now past noon and he had plenty of other errands to attend to. At 1209, Dyess radioed the tower again—permission to take off was finally granted.

Tech Sergeant Roy E. Davidson, flight chief of the 337th Fighter Squadron, watched as Dyess zipped down the runway, gaining velocity for takeoff. He had noticed that Dyess did not check the mags—the plane's wheels, or landing gear—a normal preflight precaution.

What happened next, as Olds remembered it, took place in a matter of a few seconds, but it seemed to occur in slow motion. As the P-38 streaked along, the left engine began cutting out. Olds heard the telltale popping sounds from the operations shack and remembered that several officers and men had rushed out to investigate the source. The plane, instead of braking, feathered ever so slowly into the air, reaching an altitude of approximately twenty feet, according to one eyewitness, Capt. Gerald R. Rounds of the 329th Fighter Group. The left engine, recalled Rounds, began "backfiring violently," causing the plane to bank to the left. While Olds estimated that Dyess was able to loft the P-38 up to about 200 feet, he and several other eyewitnesses noticed that the plane's landing gear was still fully deployed, creating an excessive drag, which prevented the plane from gaining more altitude. "[There was] no way to control it in those circumstances," said Olds.

Dyess must have arrived at the same frightening realization. He called the tower to request that the field be cleared for an emergency landing. The tower acknowledged Dyess's message and advised him to pull up his wheels, as the plane was rapidly losing altitude. At this point, approximately thirty seconds had elapsed and Dyess's plane disappeared out of sight of the tower, "below tree top level, with wheels still down." Neither Olds nor anyone else at the field could see what happened next.

The airfield was adjacent to Burbank and tightly bounded by a crowded residential area that began almost at the end of runway 30, so there were plenty of civilian eyewitnesses. Mrs. Oscar Schuetz was in the kitchen of her home, which was located directly behind Saint Finbar's Catholic Church on the corner of Sparks and South Myers streets, at 12:10 P.M. when she saw an airplane roaring out of the sky that "appeared to be on fire while still in the air." Seconds later, service station owner Howard C. Gowman was at his place of business on 1250 West Olive Avenue when he saw Dyess's smoke-belching plane cough overhead at no more than

100 feet. According to Gowman, the plane was somehow operating "with one motor out" and despite the fact that "the other motor did not seem to work right." It was plummeting fast.

Gowman saw the plane swing in line with Olive Avenue, a four-lane highway, about two blocks west of his station; evidently, the pilot was going to attempt a landing on what looked to be an empty city street. Dyess had no other option. He could not guide the crippled plane back to the airfield, nor could he bail out and let his plane career into a heavily populated area. Even if his conscience would have let him, his parachute would likely not have had time to deploy. The attempt to land would be his best chance of saving his own life and those of the civilians living in the neighborhood. Dyess was just about to attempt the daring maneuver when fate—as it had so many other times in his young life—intervened one last time.

The smoking, fire-licked P-38 was only a few feet from skidding to a miraculous emergency landing when a car unexpectedly appeared out of a side street and proceeded east on Olive Avenue, directly in the line of Dyess's landing path. Dyess jerked the stick and the ship responded by lofting into the air just high enough for the car to pass underneath. In the ensuing split second, while Dyess had floated up to perhaps forty or fifty feet, he noticed that there was a small vacant lot at the southeast corner of Myers and Olive. Instinctively, he banked his plane for it. But there was not enough altitude or time for any more evasive action.

Roland Ellis of North Hollywood was sitting in his car, which was parked about one and a half blocks northeast of the intersection of Myers and Olive, when he saw the left wing and left wheel of the P-38 strike the steeple of Saint Finbar's, just east of the vacant lot. In an earth-shattering crash, the plane struck, left wing first, metal upon asphalt, and cartwheeled into the vacant lot. Ellis testified that he was the first adult on the scene, some children having arrived before him. The plane, Ellis would claim in his deposition, had fragmented upon impact, with por-tions coming to rest in both the vacant lot and in front of a residence.

By the time an ambulance, crash truck, and military escort arrived, a large crowd of onlookers was already on the scene, pressing forward to gawk at the fiery wreckage. The officer in charge, an Army major, notic-ing the fuel leaking from the plane's mangled fuselage, ordered everyone to put out their cigarettes. When the request went unheeded, he ordered the cordon of soldiers to load their rifles. Hurriedly, people stamped out their smokes, speculating in nervous chatter the circumstances behind the crash and the identity of the pilot. By the looks of the crash site, Ed Dyess had died instantly.

Official inquiries into Dyess's death began shortly after the wreckage was cleared. Whether Dyess had been prevented from raising the landing gear of his plane by some mechanical malfunction or "temporary mental deficiency," the underlying cause of the accident as stated in the official report, will never be known. There were many ridiculous and far-fetched explanations for the accident proposed, but the "underlying nature" of the accident was perhaps appropriately listed as "91 octane gasoline." Dyess's crucifix and Saint Christopher medal were never found.

"Almost every pilot we knew carried a talisman of some sort," Marajen Dyess would later say. "They guarded these objects more closely than any other possession. Edwin's accident, following closely on the loss of his crucifix, may have been coincidence. It may have been something more."

WEDNESDAY, DECEMBER 22–MONDAY, DECEMBER 27, 1943
Albany, Texas

Sam Grashio recognized the troubled voice on the phone as that of the *Chicago Tribune*'s Don Maxwell. Ed Dyess, Maxwell told Grashio, had been killed in a plane crash. Stunned, Grashio immediately placed a long-distance call of his own, to Albany, Texas. Someone—it was Judge Dyess—answered, remembered Grashio, but evidently he was even more shocked than Grashio because he had been rendered speechless, unable to utter a single word beyond hello. The news was true.

It made no sense. Dyess had dodged bombs and bullets. He had survived starvation, brutality, disease, and humiliation. He had traversed swamps, jungles, and oceans, only to have his life snuffed out in a routine practice flight? To Grashio, who loved Dyess like a brother, the flier's death was an amazing anticlimax to an extraordinary existence. "Every circumstance of his death seemed to mock reason and justice, even more proportion," Grashio would write.

Yet there was in fact symmetry to this horrific tragedy. Dyess had died as he had lived—heroically and unselfishly. The Ed Dyess who flew a crippled P-38 to his death in order to avoid hitting an unknown motorist was the Ed Dyess who was concerned with evacuating everyone but himself from Bataan; it was the same Dyess who had selflessly exposed himself on the Death March to lead others; the Dyess who had given up a can of sardines to a sick enlisted man in Camp O'Donnell; the Dyess who had volunteered to take the escape party's gear out of Dapecol on his bull cart; the Dyess who had sung off-key at a jungle fiesta so as not to offend their hosts. At the moment, however, it was little consolation to a grief-stricken Grashio. "Ed would never know if the story he wanted so badly to tell would ever be released," Grashio lamented.

In the succeeding days, Dyess's hometown mourned his loss. While the family waited for his body to arrive by train from California—it was the desire of his parents that he was buried in Albany, rather than Arlington National Cemetery—the huge American flag flying on the lawn of the town's limestone courthouse was lowered to half-mast.

In the immediate aftermath of Dyess's death and for several weeks afterward, a deluge of letters, cards, telegrams, and telephone calls, outpourings of support and sympathy, flooded the Dyess residence. There were missives from politicians and the general public. The lieutenant governor of Texas, John Lee Smith, sent his condolences, as did college friends, flight school chums, and other acquaintances with return addresses spanning all corners of the country. Some were from strangers, people who had heard or read of the tragic crash and, despite the secrecy surrounding Dyess, somehow felt that he was significant, as was his yet untold story.

News of the tragedy even circled the globe. One of the most poignant letters was written by Lt. Cmdr. Al Clark, skipper of the *Trout*. "I want to say that Ed was the grandest, toughest, good natured hombre that I have ever had the pleasure of knowing or ever hope to know," wrote Clark. "If any of my three boys grow up to be the man that Ed was I would feel that I had done one hell of a fine job."

Several hundred men, women, and children who shared those sentiments waited in line on the cold, rainy, wind-whipped day of December 27 to fill Matthews Presbyterian Church for Dyess's memorial service. There were so many that the overflow crowd was directed to a nearby building where a public address system had been rigged.

One of the many military dignitaries present was Brig. Gen. Russell Randall, commanding officer of the 4th Fighter Command. Randall, who had flown to Abilene under zero-zero conditions to attend the service, informed the crowd that he was personally recommending Dyess for the nation's highest military honor, the Congressional Medal of Honor.

Those present inside the church and at the graveside ceremonies that somber day witnessed many moving gestures and tributes to Albany's favorite son—an appropriate solo, "Ah! Sweet Mystery of Life," was sung by a woman named Helen Gordon during the funeral service—but none was as touching or appropriate as the eulogy delivered by Rev. J. A. Owen.

According to Owen, amid all the sacks of mail and stacks of telegrams received by the Dyess family, one piece of correspondence in particular had stood out. It was a telegram addressed to Dyess's parents. Only thirty-four heartfelt words, it was a fitting epitaph, one that perhaps not even the still suppressed *Chicago Tribune* story, comprising tens of thousands of words, could surpass. It was the real story of William Edwin Dyess, and, perhaps most significantly, helped solve at least one of the many mysteries swirling around the hero pilot at the time of his death. Owen read it in its entirety:

PLEASE ACCEPT EXPRESSED PROFOUND SYMPATHY OF THE MAN SPARED FROM DISASTER BY THE FINAL BRAVE DEED OF YOUR SON. GREATER LOVE HATH NO MAN THAN TO GIVE HIS LIFE TO SAVE ANOTHER.

CHAPTER 20

Legacies

We want no unearned plaudits, nor acclaim . . .
Let others praise "our hopeless gallant fight":
We know to whom the praises should belong.

WEDNESDAY, DECEMBER 29, 1943–SATURDAY, JANUARY 8, 1944
Washington, District of Columbia

Ed Dyess had been laid to rest, but his story would not be buried without a fight. That much, his father had promised. "My son kept his promise to his superiors not to reveal anything," an angry, grieving Judge Dyess told reporters. "He . . . told me that his story would help stir folks up to fight harder to win the war in the Pacific. It was his opinion that every man who was captured with him on Bataan and who is still living would want the people at home to know how America's fighting men were treated by Japan. He said he was afraid the people at home did not understand the psychology of the Japs.

"I suffered in silence during the period Ed was receiving strange treatment at the war department office in the Pentagon building in Washington, D.C. I never have been there but if I weren't afraid of what I might do, I would like to meet some [of these] pencil-pushing officers who probably would faint if they smelled gunpowder."

Despite Dyess's vow of silence, news of Japanese atrocities was already being disseminated by repatriated missionary priests and correspondents, as well as Col. Carlos Romulo, the man who owed his life to Leo

Boelens's mechanical skill. Romulo was in the United States campaigning for MacArthur's cause and his stories served as ammunition.

These stories inevitably filtered to the Bataan Relief Organization and similar Pacific and POW lobby organizations, the members of which were nauseated by the government's handling of the situation in the Philippines. American Bataan Club president Albert C. MacArthur (no relation to General MacArthur) issued a scathing accusation after Dyess's death. "Our thought is that Washington officials and brass hats made one big mistake at Bataan—we don't know what—whether or not it was a failure to furnish ample equipment to the boys there, but they want to forget the whole thing, and want the nation to forget Bataan," said MacArthur. "And we won't do it."

The *Chicago Tribune* had a sizable stake in the saga and was determined to see the Dyess story delivered to American doorsteps. So skillfully, however, had the story been concealed that the Office of Censorship was not even aware of its existence until mid-November, when a PR officer from General Surles's staff called Jack Lockhart, a Scripps-Howard newspaperman working under the *Trib*'s Byron Price, and, in Lockhart's own words, "cleared up the mystery of why the *Tribune* is so interested in Lieutenant Colonel William Dyess of Albany, Texas and a couple of other things."

Christmas Eve 1943 would prove a pivotal time in the war to release the story. That morning the *Chicago Tribune*'s Walter Trohan paid a visit to Lockhart. Not only did Trohan clue Lockhart in on the full story of the *Tribune*'s relationship with Dyess, he illustrated the paper's resolve. "If necessary," Trohan informed Lockhart, "we will get somebody in Congress to read this series into the *Congressional Record*, thus providing appropriate authority."

To OWI chief Elmer Davis, who was preparing to write a letter on December 24, the atrocities story was more than sensational—he saw it as crucial not only to his job of keeping the American public informed about the war and protecting the fundamental constitutional right of a free press, but to the war effort itself. Davis attempted to communicate those views to Fleet Admiral William Leahy, the chairman of the Joint Chiefs of Staff and a trusted friend and adviser to FDR. The president, wrote Davis, had requested in his secret September memorandum that the Joint Chiefs make a recommendation when the White House should inform the nation of the mistreatment of her fighting men. "I should like to recommend to the Joint Chiefs of Staff that the time has now come to recommend to the President that he authorize publication of such information."

In six concise paragraphs, Davis laid out his argument. He stressed that the prevailing public opinion was that the war with Germany was nearing its end and warned against complacency on the home front. Without a compelling reason to carry the war with Japan to unconditional surrender, America's efforts in the Pacific "could easily degenerate after a few victories . . . into a feeling that we had vindicated our honor and could afford to negotiate a peace short of complete victory." Although most Americans felt that the antiwar groups—Professor George Hartmann's Peace Now movement, for example—agitating for negotiated settlements were largely semi-traitorous fringe elements, Davis did not want these ideas gaining any traction.

"The nature of the Japanese enemy is much less widely understood than the nature of the German enemy," Davis added, echoing the sentiments of Judge Dyess. "When the feeling is at all widespread that the enemy is 'incomprehensible,' it is more difficult to demand of the nation the exacting sacrifices necessary to win the kind of victory that can be expressed in comprehensible terms." Davis also disagreed with the prevailing opinion that any revelation "would stimulate fresh atrocities." On the contrary, now that Japan was on the defensive, the Japanese would have a pressing interest in producing evidence of "civilized conduct" in order to negotiate more advantageous peace terms.

A carbon copy of the letter to Leahy was sent to Owen Lattimore, a noted Far East specialist, former adviser to Generalissimo Chiang Kai-shek, and current head of OWI's Pacific overseas office. Lattimore had been consulted on the matter by Edwin Palmer "Ep" Hoyt, publisher of the *Portland Oregonian* and a self-anointed "people's advocate" serving as chief of OWI's domestic branch. It was Lattimore, an old Asia hand and Oriental psychology expert, who had previously convinced Davis of the need to release the story of Japanese atrocities. As *Newsweek* would write, Lattimore "argued that exposure and warnings would impress the Japs, while continued suppression of the atrocity stories might give them a feeling of impunity."

Gen. George Strong of the secret military Intelligence Service did not appreciate Davis's attempt to circumnavigate the channels of command and sent a terse note telling Davis, in so many words, to mind his own business. Undeterred, Davis launched a written counterstrike on December 27 in which he called the atrocity story ban one-sided, pointing out a noticeable bias against stories taking place in the Pacific theater. As the *Chicago Tribune*'s crack research had indicated, for every story on the execution of the Doolittle fliers published, there had been many more stories regarding European theater–based atrocities cleared. "Your MID 912 confuses me a little," wrote Davis, provokingly. "Does this refer to all enemy atrocities?" Nevertheless, Davis stated that he would continue to obey the presidential order, even though he believed "that the policy has outlived its usefulness."

Strong must have thought he was listening to an echo of his own thoughts when he answered a call from General Surles just before noon on December 29.

"I just wanted to tell you that this damn Dyess story is going to be tough to hold," warned Surles.

Surles told Strong of Trohan's threat to have the Dyess story read into the *Congressional Record*, most likely by sympathetic members of the Texas delegation to the House of Representatives, and added that the *Tribune* could now count as allies in its cause Roy Roberts, Ep Hoyt, and soon possibly Byron Price. Surles went on to inform Strong that the *Tribune* had submitted the story to the Office of Censorship in order to have Price scrutinize it for anything that, in his professional opinion, might endanger national security. Price, Surles explained, was likely to clear the story, a development that could make their jobs difficult.

"Now in view of the fact that we've got this directive that came from the White House on that atrocity business, of course we've been protesting every time it comes up and Price had taken the attitude, I think, that he wasn't consulted directly by the president, therefore he will make his own decision on the thing. We sent him a copy of our directive but he claims that he didn't get communicated with directly so he'll do as he sees fit on it. Now in view of that, do you want me to talk to the White House on that—or do you want me to talk to Price?"

Strong suggested an appeal to the highest authority—FDR—from Stimson to hold off what seemed to be an impending allied charge by the *Chicago Tribune*, OWI, and Censorship.

"What I'd do if I were you," said Strong, "I'd draft a memo for the S/W's [Secretary of War's] signature and let him send it over to the President. I think that's the only thing we can do."

In the meantime, Strong suggested that Surles ask Price to stand pat until the memo reached the Oval Office. Later that day, the aggravated fifty-eight-year-old brigadier placed a call to Price to gauge his thoughts. Price, Surles must have been relieved to learn, seemed as though he was still trying to wrap his hands around the situation.

"What I know about [the Dyess story] is rather sketchy," said Price. "I haven't seen any of the manuscript but I do understand that the *Tribune* has signed up a contract which they say they won't publish this unless it clears Censorship."

"Well, as long as Dyess was alive he had to clear thru military censorship—that was the directive Dyess had—but he's dead now you see and that's why they're pushing ahead on the thing," Surles responded.

Price reassured Surles that his office was far from making a decision, and even suggested that he would "stall it for a week or two until you find out around town here what's going on?"

Much like Davis, the career journalist had probably realized the importance of the atrocities story: what its release could conceivably mean to the American public, his profession, his job, and the war itself. And perhaps he had also realized that perhaps with time he could convince Surles to look at things from his point of view. He seemed to sense that the constant grating of all these government entities against one another, with the *Chicago Tribune* applying relentless pressure, was creating too much friction—friction that was keeping all of the interested parties from reaching a solution. Price probably also sensed Surles's growing frustration with the situation and the opportunity that teamwork might present. Price then brought up the Davis letter, probably to see where Surles stood on the matter personally.

"Everything I hear about [the letter] supports the view I've had all the time that you can't suppress atrocities," Price told Surles. "The Japs will do as they damn please regardless of what we publish in this country."

Price then summarized for Surles a conversation he had had with Ray Cronin, the AP's recently repatriated Manila bureau chief. Cronin nullified the government's claim that the *Gripsholm*'s mission was of paramount importance for the POWs. According to Cronin, Red Cross supplies rarely reached the POWs. Most of the food, medicine, and cigarettes were kept by the Japanese or else later appeared on the black market. Surles sounded somewhat sympathetic.

"I hope you can give your support to loosening up this atrocity business because I don't think it's getting us anywhere," Price concluded.

Nineteen forty-four was slightly less than a week old when it became apparent that the initiative of Davis and Price was beginning to pay dividends. Davis's letter to Leahy had been circulated throughout Washington—in the upper strata of government, at least—and he soon found that he had quite a number of supporters, including Secretary of State Cordell Hull. "The policy in regard to the publication of atrocity stories is in my opinion one of great importance in connection with the war effort," Hull wrote Davis. "It is further my opinion that these stories should be used to further the ultimate national interest."

The question remained whether the White House and War Department were aware of the forces arraying in favor of the story's release. At half past noon on the 8th of January, Price called Surles with a proposition.

"Two things," Price began. "One, Walter Trohan was in here this morning needling me up. He's been calling every day about this Dyess. I said, 'I'm going to New York Tuesday and will probably be gone about a week. If you want an answer one way or another by Monday, I'll give it to you and you'll have to take your chances on what it is. But if you'll lay off for a couple of weeks and keep your shirt on, I think there may be some hope that this thing can be settled amicably all around.' So he said that he liked that proposition of laying off and unless I heard from him to the contrary that they would accept a two-week's moratorium."

"Fine," agreed Surles. "That'll help a lot."

"In the meantime, I hope that we can get some action one way or another on this."

Surles then told Price that his recommendation—Price had composed a complement to Davis's letter—had been submitted to the Joint Chiefs. It certainly seemed, at least to judge from the view provided by Price's office in the Federal Trade Commission building on Seventh and Pennsylvania avenues, that his strategy was succeeding.

"Anything you can do to expedite it will help," said Price. "I think we ought to get [the Dyess atrocities story] out."

"Well, I certainly liked what you submitted," Surles replied

"I'm afraid General Strong won't but I don't know what we can do about that."

"I think what we've got to do is—we can't move in with a slam and a banging of doors, etc. I think we've got to move in quietly and with [the Joint Chiefs'] full concurrence."

"I'll keep you posted about this Dyess business," promised Price. "As I told you, we won't take any action without consulting you further about it."

"Yes," closed Surles, "because it is a pretty hot thing."

For a number of reasons, as all of the involved parties seemed to agree— the *Chicago Tribune*, the Army, the Navy, the Office of Censorship, OWI, the State and War Departments, and the White House, plus others soon to be revealed—much better timing was of the utmost importance.

TUESDAY, JANUARY 18–SATURDAY, JANUARY 22, 1944
Washington, District of Columbia

The two-week moratorium was not destined to last that long. The Joint Chiefs convened on January 18 to decide whether to issue a recommendation to the president regarding the release of the atrocities stories. Official Washington waited anxiously for the decision.

With Price in New York, Jack Lockhart began making calls in an effort to glean some information. At 11 A.M., he reached George Healy, Hoyt's successor as OWI domestic chief; Healy had heard nothing. Forty minutes later, Lockhart spoke with Stephen Early, FDR's press secretary, who informed him that the matter would soon be brought to the president's attention. Apparently it was, because at 3:50 that afternoon, Early telephoned Lockhart to say that he had some information on "the Dyess and related stories which he could tell me confidentially."

Early told Lockhart that the White House no longer held out hope for future relief missions. He then went on to say that Great Britain had more POWs in Japanese hands than the United States and, in view of that, Roosevelt now felt it necessary to consult the British. The following morning, Early reported that the British had signed off, asking only that they be kept apprised of the situation and release schedule so that they could prepare a parallel release of their own. "As a result," Lockhart would write in an office memorandum, "the President is now willing to have atrocities [story] released in an orderly fashion."

A date was set: Monday, January 24. "That's the way she lies," a surprised Early told Col. Stanley Grogan, an Army PR officer under Surles, during a phone conversation that afternoon. "I thought [Roosevelt] would kick a little bit about that but nevertheless she's going."

A subsequent conversation between Grogan and Maj. Gen. Clayton Bissell, George Marshall's G-2, the following morning reveals that Secretary of War Stimson was caught off guard by the president's apparent about-face.

"The Secretary was pretty disturbed last night," revealed Grogan.

"Well, the Secretary didn't have the facts presented properly to him," said Bissell. "If I had known the Joint Chiefs of Staff had taken as firm a stand as they did I would have told him that the action was based on their recommendation."

That firm stand should no doubt be credited to Davis and Price. They had swayed Leahy and the Joint Chiefs to the point that the latter realized that the release of the atrocities stories could conceivably be a boon to American arms. The change in policy was also a seminal victory for Davis, Price, and their staffs, not to mention the *Chicago Tribune* and the Fourth Estate. Yet there was hardly a hint of a congratulatory tone in the announcement Davis distributed to his staff. Time would not allow for a celebration.

Via Early, Davis had been directed by the president to coordinate with the British on the release of the atrocity announcements by both nations. The Army and Navy, meanwhile, were scrambling not only to cooperate with each other and OWI on a joint release, but had to do so without allowing their long-standing interservice rivalry to turn the event into a race for recognition. Yet perhaps in that regard, it was too late. Once the ban had been lifted, the corollary question now facing all of the involved parties was how best to facilitate the release of the individual atrocity stories in an appropriate manner. There was now the Dyess–*Chicago Tribune* story and also a McCoy-Mellnik story that had been prepared under the auspices of the Navy Office of Public Relations with the help of an officer named Lt. Welbourn Kelley. The existence of the latter story suggests that McCoy had been at least somewhat successful in calling the Navy's bluff. In all likelihood, the Navy had acquiesced to McCoy's demands and assigned Kelley to take down his story before McCoy was transferred— tucked away, really—to a posting in the Bremerton Shipyards in Washington state.

The Army finally began reading the Dyess story on January 21—while several sets of eyes would pore over the material, General Marshall had declared that he himself would be responsible for the final edit—but the McCoy-Mellnik collaboration had not yet been sold. At this date, *Collier's* reportedly held the leading bid of $20,000, but *The Saturday Evening Post* and *Reader's Digest*, as well as *Life*, were still in the running.

A flurry of phone calls and messages was exchanged between OWI, the Army, the Navy, and the *Chicago Tribune*—these mainly involved Navy personnel who were trying to keep the Army and the *Tribune* from releasing the story in advance of McCoy and Mellnik's piece—but the Navy was operating at a distinct disadvantage because the McCoy-Mellnik story was Navy-produced and -controlled, whereas the Dyess story was controlled by a civilian entity and ostensibly outside the military's reach. Fortunately for the Navy, other circumstances and influences, both internal and external, would buy additional time.

Bissell had told Grogan during their conversation on January 21 that he had heard that "G-1 [Personnel] and Service Commands both suggest delay in implimentation [*sic*] of the President's order. . . . They have good reasons for suggesting delay, but they're not questioning the ultimate decision. They think that certain things should be brought about which would bring about a rather appreciable delay if it were carried out—for certainly about three months."

"Well, of course they may," Grogan replied. "In the meantime the Dyess story may be broken."

"They understand that," replied Bissell, "but they feel that that's one of the things you have to take a chance on."

Grogan's assumption, that the *Chicago Tribune* would likely exhaust its patience in the event of another delay, was probably correct. Elmer Davis, addressing the external factors that had recently come into play in a January 22 memorandum distributed to Surles, Healy, Lattimore, and others within OWI, warned of such a possibility:

> Steve Early telephoned me tonight and said that the British and the State Department had protested to the President against the release of the Dyess-McCoy story on Monday morning, January 24. The President accordingly had determined to give the British another week to prepare any simultaneous release of their own which they might desire. They are to be advised that we shall release in any event in morning papers of January 31. In the meantime if the

Dyess story should be broken in Congress or elsewhere we shall release the joint Army-Navy statement immediately.

Once again, undertakings in Europe would have a direct bearing on,
or exercise a degree of control over, an aspect of the Pacific war. The remaining escapees were not out of the jungle, be it the politicized, bureaucratic one in Washington or the real one on Mindanao, just yet.

SATURDAY, JANUARY 22–TUESDAY, JANUARY 25, 1944
Baroy, Lanao Province, Mindanao

Perhaps Leo Boelens thought it was another false alarm—the bamboo
telegraph, after all, seemingly never stopped buzzing with reports of Japanese activity in the area. Perhaps he thought he could reassure his men
by appearing confident. Or maybe Boelens was just in need of some excitement. As his diary attested, the "pickens" had hardly been good. There
was ample evidence of a dull life dominated by bouts of boredom, chronic
illness, and, despite allusions to a romantic relationship with a mysterious
woman named Miguela, persistent loneliness.

In any event, Sgt. Wenceslao "Ben" del Mundo had been right.
Boelens and the others had moved to the evacuation area shortly after
the first shots were heard in the direction of Maranding at 0715. That
afternoon, del Mundo, Sam Grashio's old bodyguard, had suggested to
Boelens that he stay put. Though the Japanese had probably moved on,
there was no reason to take chances, argued del Mundo. But Boelens
shrugged off the advice, grabbing his carbine and five magazines of ammunition before heading back toward the airfield—*his* airfield. Evidently,
he intended to return soon. "Before moving out," del Mundo would write,
"he gave me his last word that if anything was lost among his things he
would find my dead body right beside them."

Following orders, del Mundo did not leave his post, not even when he
heard gunfire less than one hour later. When Boelens did not return the
following morning, del Mundo went to investigate. He found no sign of
the American nor the Japanese at the airfield, but the latter nearly discovered him sleeping in Boelens's quarters the next morning. Slipping away
undetected, he watched from a distance as Japanese soldiers ransacked
Boelens's billet, destroying a safe and several drums of crude and coconut

oil that had been buried nearby. When he finally made his way back to the evacuation area, a shaken del Mundo learned that the losses were greater than he had imagined.

A civilian led him to the edge of the airfield, where he found the mutilated body of Boelens; the Japanese had finally reclaimed one of the Dapecol escapees and their punishment had been severe. Sam Grashio was later told that Boelens had been shot by a hidden sniper and recaptured before being "put to death cruelly." From the descriptions in del Mundo's after-action report, there is evidence that Boelens may have been tortured before his execution. After a close examination of the body, del Mundo said that the corpse contained "two wounds at the back, a bayonet thrust behind the left ear and several knife wounds at the back of the head."

The next morning, del Mundo and several others burned Boelens's body and respectfully buried the remains in a four-foot grave. Even in death, Leo Boelens continued to inspire: "His personal belongings are still intact in my hands and have not been touched," wrote del Mundo.

Chances are, Boelens did not know of Ed Dyess's shocking death exactly one month earlier, much less the circumstances that precipitated it, but his own tragic end was jarringly similar in that it might have been prevented by some patience, or perhaps better judgment. As it was, Boelens would be the only American escapee not to return to the United States.

For some men, legacy trumps survival, and so it was with Leo Boelens. His legacy, however, would not be tangible: when he died, so did Farm Project No. 1 and his dream of building an airfield out of the Mindanao wilderness. Boelens's enduring legacy, as time would reveal, would not be what he did, but what he convinced others to do.

CHAPTER 21

Conditional Victory

Our faith is in the blood of weary men
Who take the coral beaches back again . . .
My country—Oh, my country—well we know
That final victory will be your part . . .

FRIDAY, JANUARY 28–MONDAY, FEBRUARY 7, 1944
Washington, District of Columbia

After months of interminable intragovernmental feuding, interservice rivalry, indecision, intrigue and executive esoterica, the official Army-Navy statement regarding atrocities committed by the Japanese military against American prisoners of war was finally released to the nation's media with military precision at exactly 12 A.M., Eastern War Time, on Friday, January 28, 1944.

Later that morning, General Strong called General Surles to assess the initial reaction. "You've got to give [the newspapers] 24-hours to get their editorials running," answered Surles.

It would not take that long. In cities and towns large and small from Long Island to Los Angeles, Americans were startled and stunned by black, blaring banner headlines such as the one appearing on the front page of the *New York Times*: "5,200 AMERICANS, MANY MORE FILIPINOS DIE OF STARVATION, TORTURE AFTER BATAAN." Sensational subheads such as the *Times*'s "AMERICANS BURIED ALIVE" and "Men Worked to Death—All 'Boiled' in Sun—12,000 Kept Without Food 7 Days" invariably led to "a horror story," proclaimed the Associated Press, "scarcely paralleled in the annals of modern war," eleven pages

319

of "factual and official" testimony from Dyess, McCoy, and Mellnik that spanned the fall of Bataan to the murder of a Dapecol POW. As per official orders, no details were provided about the method and route of escape, nor was there any mention of the guerrillas who aided the escapees. But in the midst of the resulting national furor, the absence of such details went largely unnoticed.

Radio, jammed telephone exchanges, and word of mouth relayed the shocking news of the Bataan Death March, the existence of charnel houses of horrors called O'Donnell and Cabanatuan, and the appalling stories of systemized starvation, slave labor, burial details, torture, and calculated enemy brutality to every corner of the country. The news traveled all across America; it was like nothing the nation had known before.

That Sunday, the first installment of the Dyess story ran on the front page of the *Chicago Tribune*, as well as in 100 associated newspapers. There would be twenty-four total installments, one appearing each day for the better part of the next month. To the public, it must have seemed as though the deceased pilot was daring them to close their eyes and imagine the horrors he and his comrades had endured. "To my commanding officers I repeated the story of what I had seen and experienced in the Philippines after the fall of Bataan," Dyess had opened. "And from each of my superiors came the warning: 'The Public won't believe it.' Perhaps the public will not. But the story I am about to tell is true." Though what they would read seemed beyond belief, believe it they did. *Newsweek* would later claim that the revelation was a bombshell more explosive even than Pearl Harbor: "The American emotion . . . was a fury such as had never before gripped the nation in this war."

Washington was the epicenter of the outrage. "According to the reports of cruelty and inhumanity," said Secretary of State Cordell Hull, "it would be necessary to summon . . . all the demons available from anywhere and combine the fiendishness which all of them embody to describe the conduct of those who inflicted these unthinkable tortures on Americans and Filipinos as the report recites."

"Neither you nor I can express our reaction in words," America's ambassador to Japan, Joseph C. Grew, told a reporter from the North American Newspaper Alliance. "I have used the words 'fiery rage,' but my feeling is far too deep to try to express in language. My anger against those responsible for these dastardly acts is inexpressible."

The most vociferous reaction emanated from Capitol Hill. Texas representative Eugene Worley, a Navy officer who had spent four months on active duty in the Pacific in 1942, attacked the Europe First policy, asserting that, if they did not know so already, "the American people now know their number one enemy—the inhuman, despicable Jap."

Members of Congress, blind with rage, demanded immediate retribution. While Missouri senator Bennett Clark wanted to "bomb Japan out of existence," Alabama senator Lister Hill desired to "gut the heart of Japan with fire." Andrew J. May, a Kentucky Democrat and chair of the House Military Affairs Committee, wanted the Pacific fleet immediately dispatched to Tokyo to "blow it to Hades." Calls for the hanging of Hirohito as a war criminal were widespread.

Assigning blame was a natural, secondary reaction. "Mr. Roosevelt and Harry Hopkins," charged Indiana representative Gerald W. Landis, identifying Hopkins's role as the major policymaker behind Lend-Lease, "are directly responsible for not getting supplies to Gen. Douglas MacArthur that would have saved these men." As for the perpetrators of the crimes, "let these Japanese know in plain and no uncertain terms that we're going to hold them responsible for this nasty, damnable, despicable business," railed New York representative Sol Bloom, chair of the House Foreign Affairs Committee. "We'll hold the rats—from the Emperor down to the lowest ditch-digger—responsible for a million years if necessary."

In the ensuing week, the shockwaves rippled out from the nation's capital. Americans of all ages, stripes, and stations expressed their shared outrage in their own ways. New York mayor Fiorello La Guardia suggested that if the Mikado is the "true type of Japanese gentleman, let him, in keeping with the custom of his country, commit hara-kiri to prove it." One of La Guardia's constituents, a Bronx housewife, could manage only a few teeth-gritting words when asked her opinion of the Japanese: "They're stinkers."

At the Brooklyn Navy Yard on January 29, nineteen-year-old Margaret Truman smashed a bottle of champagne off the bow of the newly completed USS *Missouri*. As the 45,000-ton battleship slid into the East River, her father, Missouri senator and future president Harry S. Truman, told the crowd of 26,000 that the "christening and launching of this greatest warship of all time illustrates the decisive answer which the democracies of the world are making to the challenge of the aggressor nations. May this great ship be an avenger to the barbarians who wantonly slaughtered the heroes of Bataan."

Herby Funston, a young boy from Keota, Iowa, wrote General Marshall to tell him that he wanted to do more for the war effort than "selling and buying bonds and stamps and salvaging." The Army chief of staff was evidently so moved that he took time to respond to Funston's missive on February 2: "My dear Herby, I like your letter, the fact that you want to do your full part in licking these Japs . . . [but] these things must be done, so somebody must do them and that seems to be your duty at the present time. But I sympathize with you in your desire to avenge the 'nice kid' from your town who became a prisoner in the Philippines."

Security was added to the internment camps scattered throughout the West, a precautionary measure to prevent angry mobs from seeking retaliatory action. The threat, believed Western Defense Command chief Gen. Delos C. Emmons, was very real. After all, a forty-year-old Los Angeles hotel clerk was almost consumed by his burning hatred of the Japanese—literally. The man, who had confessed during an arrest in January to setting more than 200 fires in "cheap Jap flop houses" since Pearl Harbor, was booked again on suspicion of arson after two fires had broken out in his own hotel following the release of the atrocities story.

The news quickly went global. The *Chicago Tribune* was successful in arranging with the Associated Press for the distribution of the Dyess story to Cuban and South American newspapers, and by the first week of February two British newspaper groups, along with publications in Canada, were said to be bidding for the rights. The Soviets, though not at war with the Japanese, publicized the American atrocities stories.

In London, British foreign secretary Anthony Eden related tales of atrocities committed against Commonwealth citizens and military personnel to an enraged House of Commons. The most notable of these stories included the sinking of the unmarked hellship *Lisbon Maru*, which had been carrying 1,800 British POWs from Hong Kong to Shanghai in October 1942. Nearly 850 of the prisoners had died in the disaster, many belowdecks after the Japanese had locked the hatches to prevent their escape. "The Japanese have violated not only the principles of international law but all canons of decent civilized conduct," Eden said.

The Japanese responded to the Allied accusations by claiming through the official news agency, Domei, that the charges were "a mere reoccurrence of the enemy's vicious propaganda." And then, abruptly abandoning the denials, Japan launched an inflammatory, if not self-incriminating, propaganda assault. "If the American and British leaders are so ready to raise a hue and cry over the 'maltreatment' of their war prisoners, why don't they teach their men to stand up and fight to the finish?" prodded Tokyo radio. "The way the Americans threw up their hands at Corregidor and the way the British gave up at Singapore . . . surely shows that these men must have carried on their backs a pretty wide streak of yellow."

The ultimate significance of the escape was yet to be determined, but one thing was for certain: the secret was out. Somewhere, Ed Dyess was smiling.

Americans, riveted to and revolted by the Dyess story, received another sickening shock when the February 7 issue of *Life* hit newsstands. The issue, which contained an exclusive feature entitled "Death Was a Part of Our Life" authored by Cmdr. Melvyn McCoy, Lt. Col. Steve Mellnik, and Lt. Welbourn Kelley, included photographs of all ten escapees plus artists' conceptions of events related by the authors. The fifteen-page exposé was a sensation that at once rivaled and complemented the Dyess story by adding fuel to an already massive conflagration.

The indignation was not limited to the atrocities. Angered that Congress had been kept in the dark, Chairman Elbert D. Thomas of the Senate Military Affairs subcommittee announced that Army and Navy intelligence officers would be summoned to hearings. "My committee is going to get all the information it can through the proper channels," said the Utah Democrat.

In the meantime, exclamations turned into question marks and Americans—public officials, the press, and the public alike—began to speculate as to the reason for the strangely sudden announcement. Why had the story been released now, almost a full year after the escape, and six months since the escapees' homecoming? There is no single answer to that question. An examination of both concrete and circumstantial evidence suggests that the story was released when it was for multiple reasons, or, at the very least, multiple, credible hypotheses.

President Roosevelt said at his February 1 press conference that his "first impulse" was to make the atrocities known to the public immediately after the escaped POWs returned to the United States, but that discussions with Britain and China resulted in withholding the stories for "humanitarian" reasons. Interestingly, when meeting with reporters following the release, Press Secretary Steve Early would call this the "on-the-record" reason. Early did not elucidate upon any "off-the-record" reasons for the suppression of the story, but the implication that there was one or perhaps more "off-the-record" reasons, as previously suggested, is noteworthy. Despite the doublespeak coming from the White House, the motive of protecting the *Gripsholm*'s mission—the main "humanitarian" reason—remains, in all likelihood, partially legitimate.

The second reason, or piece of the political puzzle, had been strategically set in place before the release. Just as one could not walk down the street, open a newspaper, or view a newsreel without being reminded of Japanese atrocities, it was no coincidence that the release appeared at the time of the Fourth War Loan Drive.

The War Finance Committee had been tasked with the purpose of engaging the American public to purchase bonds that would help the U.S. government finance the conflict. The first of what would be eight War Loan Drives began in November 1942; the Fourth War Loan Drive, with a target sales goal of $14 billion, had commenced on the 18th of January, barely ten days before the release of the atrocities story. While Elmer Davis and Palmer Hoyt would argue that the timing of the release with the Fourth War Loan Drive was "purely coincidental," a close examination arouses suspicion to the contrary.

Soviet successes on the Eastern Front, coupled with the surrender of Italy in early September 1943, brought clarity to a picture that had been muddled for the better part of two years: the European war would be ending in the foreseeable future, perhaps sooner than anyone had imagined. As Davis would note, this belief gave birth to a sense of complacency—stagnant bond sales and increased absenteeism in war plants served as solid indicators—during this pivotal period of the war. And it was none other than Hoyt who had claimed in 1943 that the responsibility of OWI was to provide accurate news information so that the public and industry could cooperate in war programs and drives. It should be as plainly obvious to any contemporary observer as it was to the powers-that-were at the time that some kind of perfect sales pitch, a reason for Americans to reach for their wallets, was needed.

Treasury Secretary Henry Morgenthau's men had been working on the problem for some time. "The men on the Treasury's bond staff, committed to advancing sales in 1943 . . . utilized market research to develop improvements in their program," wrote historian John Morton Blum. What the Treasury Department discovered was that Americans' motivations for buying bonds had little to do with "enthusiasm for the New Deal or the Four Freedoms, or even from a sense of national peril . . . consumers' preferences . . . called emphatically for an appeal to hatred." It is not difficult to comprehend how the sudden appearance of several POWs with a blockbuster story that was all but guaranteed to arouse a slumbering nation must have seemed heaven-sent to a cash-strapped government waging an ultra-expensive global war. The release of the atrocity stories to coincide with the Fourth War Loan Drive was perhaps the perfect manifestation of an "appeal to hatred" and cannot be dismissed as coincidence.

Across the country, War Bond sales soared. In New York State, sales of Series E bonds, the type favored by most citizens and small investors, exceeded $8 million, twice the daily average, on the day of the atrocity story's release. Sales of other types of bonds, like Series F and G, to wealthy individuals and companies skyrocketed, too, with sales of Series F securities quadrupling. Treasury Department officials reported increases of nearly 100 percent in individual sales in New Jersey, Pennsylvania, and Washington, D.C., and a national gain of $156 million in a twenty-four-hour period from February 1 to 2 that was attributable to "mounting indignation over the Japanese atrocity reports." In Maywood, Illinois, the suburban community twelve miles west of Chicago that was the home of the American Bataan Club, long lines of angry Americans waited for the bond sales office to open; when doors closed that evening, sales had increased 50 percent over the previous day's total. In Indianapolis, Melvyn McCoy's hometown, long lines were reported at downtown banks and post offices. Total sales on the day after the story's release reportedly reached $2.6 million, more than $1 million above average. In Utah, nearly $900,000 worth of bonds were sold the day of the release, more than double any previous day's total in the Beehive State. "The more figures we receive and the more people we talk to," said Nevil Ford, executive manager of the New York State War Finance Committee, "the stronger is our substantiation of the fact that vastly stimulated bond buying is resulting from the Bataan disclosures." These nationwide trends would continue throughout the remainder of the drive.

It was a team effort. After an impassioned address by Lt. Gen. Alexander A. Vandegrift, commandant of the Marine Corps, on the floor of the New York Stock Exchange, Wall Street ponied up nearly $104 million for war bonds. Fifty thousand Boy Scouts and Cub Scouts in the greater New York area were deputized by the Treasury Department to commence a doorbell-ringing sales drive. Singer Kate Smith kicked off a special around-the-clock bond sale broadcast on the CBS nationwide radio network at 8 A.M. on February 1. Sixty volunteers working four-hour shifts fielded an average of five calls per minute. By the time Smith signed off after her last appeal, a record-breaking total of more than $100 million in bonds had been sold. Albert Einstein participated, too, by donating two manuscripts—one of which was his treatise on the theory of relativity—which would be auctioned off and the proceeds added to the drive.

The biggest celebrity presence during the Fourth War Loan and subsequent drives, which remains to be discussed in detail, were those men responsible for the revelation itself. In a staggering succession of events, the stateside escapees had their gag orders removed and were prodded onto the national stage. During the first weekend of the announcement, for example, Sam Grashio was in high demand for newspaper interviews and made several national radio appearances on the Mutual and NBC networks. McCoy, too, was drafted by the Treasury Department. In a giant, full-page advertisement in the January 31 edition of the *New York Herald Tribune*, McCoy implored Americans to support the Fourth War Loan Drive. Beneath a large photograph of a grim-faced McCoy, there was a title that read, "Japanese Barbarism Speaks to the American People."

> Jap brutality is beyond description. . . . I urge all of you—those with brothers, sons and fathers who are seeing action in the Pacific Theater—to back them up by buying Bonds so that they would have the necessary supplies to avenge our men who have suffered at the hands of the Japs. There is no way we who stay at home can avenge this revolting cruelty. What we can do is pathetically little. If all of us put every cent we can into War Bonds, it would still be only the humblest gesture to the boys who are doing the fighting, the suffering, the dying.

It remains unknown whether the words were actually McCoy's, but full-page advertisements complete with photographs and government-approved copy do not appear in large metropolitan newspapers overnight. A significant amount of time, undoubtedly several weeks' worth, would have been necessary to coordinate numerous government agencies, to concentrate resources and to organize, publicize, and ultimately capitalize on such a situation. It was no wonder then that Gen. Clayton

Bissell had told Col. Stanley Grogan that the personnel commands desired a "delay in the implementation" of the presidential order to release the atrocities story.

Some saw through the government's transparent attempt at channeling the nation's hatred of its Pacific enemy, as well as capitalizing on the misery of its captive POWs. New Mexico senator Dennis Chavez told the AP that the only plausible explanation he had heard "for the release of the account last week was Secretary Morgenthau's assertion it would mean the sale of more war bonds." Dr. V. H. Spensley of the Bataan Relief Organization concurred: "I can't understand why such information should be brought out now . . . except to sell bonds. For that purpose it's absolutely rotten. If the morality of America has sunk so low it required this kind of propaganda to sell bonds, we wonder what the boys are fighting for." The Port Clinton (Ohio) Bataan Clan sent telegrams to FDR and Stimson echoing Spensley's sentiments: "It has been a grievous error to wait for a 'psychological moment' before unloosening the screws on the lid of censorship. We gave our boys and we had a right to know what was happening to them then, not 21 months later. We are tired of red tape and promises—we want action."

The U.S. State Department had issued a stern, strongly worded promise to both the American people and the Japanese leadership: "The American Government will hold personally and officially responsible all officers of the Japanese Government who have participated [in these crimes], and with the inevitable and inexorable conclusion of the war will visit upon such Japanese officers the punishment they deserve for their uncivilized and inhuman acts." In an appended statement, a representative of the Judge Advocate General's division suggested that those Japanese deemed responsible would be liable to postwar punishment handed down from an American military commission, including the death penalty, thus foreshadowing the probability of war crimes trials in a conquered Japan. But a seething American public wanted more than promises of postwar justice.

On the 10th of February, representatives from the Pacific theater and POW relief clubs convened in Washington, D.C., to decide on a unified course of action. "We intend to make our feelings known—and those are to get the necessary ships, men and material to General MacArthur as soon as possible to get our sons and husbands back," announced Spensley. But would MacArthur, as well as Nimitz and other Pacific commanders, be provided with the resources needed to sate America's thirst for vengeance? Would the Pacific war be elevated by Allied war planners to equal status with the European war? Hanson W. Baldwin, the military correspondent of the *New York Times*, whose dispatches from the Pacific had won him the Pulitzer Prize in 1943, predicted that the atrocities revelation would certainly "have an effect on the Pacific war." However, that effect on the military prosecution of the war would not be immediately nor completely quantifiable.

The president had added during his February 1 press conference that the atrocity revelations had only steeled America's resolve to punish the perpetrators. "We are moving against them as rapidly as humanly possible," he had declared. Shortly thereafter, Admiral King announced: "1944, our year of attack, has just begun. Plans have been made and are being made for the most extensive and important naval operations ever undertaken." News from the forward areas certainly seemed to back up that statement. During the first week of February, a long-anticipated Pacific offensive, one centered around an invasion of the Japanese-held Marshall Islands, commenced. The two-pronged attack, which called for the forces of MacArthur and Nimitz to advance simultaneously in the Central and Southwest Pacific areas, respectively, was a follow-up to the Gilbert Islands operation that had resulted in the capture of Tarawa the previous fall.

Baldwin also believed that the revelation would arouse Britons, as well as "serve rather definite notice to those Americans who have doubted Britain's official interest in the Pacific war that Britain is in it until the end." And there were positive signs that progress was being made in terms of the Allied prosecution of the Pacific war: fresh British operations in Burma; the buildup of forces in India; the "recent tour of the so-called 'Lethbridge Mission' of twenty-six Allied officers, who have been studying Pacific warfare with a view to recommending industrial, technical and tactical adjustments in Britain's war machine to fit the needs of the Pacific."

Despite the highly agitated state of the American public, it nevertheless remained unlikely that there would be any comprehensive overhaul of Allied grand strategy, especially with the invasion of Europe looming. But when one takes into consideration these developments, as well as the fact that Admiral King would eventually succeed in securing a larger percentage of America's war production output and troops for the Pacific conflict, there is evidence that the release of the atrocities story was the catalyst responsible for altering, however slightly, the course of the war during this critical time period.

Only time would tell, though, whether these developments and operations were only political feints, limited thrusts undertaken to satisfy the demands of irate Americans. In the meantime, however, Americans would have to be satisfied with the Central Pacific offensive and a steady increase in the number of so-called revenge operations. "Angry Airmen Hit Jap Bases: Anger over Jap Atrocities Against Prisoners Is Credited with Increase" was the headline of a story describing one such operation on enemy installations on Rabaul, New Britain, New Guinea, and the Marshall Islands that appeared in the January 30 edition of the *Fort Worth Star-Telegram*.

The fact that the release of the Dyess story had coincided with the commencement of a Pacific offensive had not gone unnoticed, either. "On the day that Washington revealed details of the sickening Japanese treatment of captured troops in the Philippines and in lost British bastions of the China Sea," wrote longtime Washington AP staffer Kirke Simpson in his column, "Wide World War," "there were strong hints that the double-thrust from the south and east to clear a thousand-mile-wide pathway through Japanese central and South Pacific island outposts is gaining momentum." Just as the timing of the release with the Fourth War Loan Drive hardly seemed a chance occurrence, it would not be out of the realm of possibility to suggest that the release was also deliberately followed by a new offensive in order to provide immediate proof that the retaliatory blow that America was demanding had been in some way delivered.

There were, however, several absolute certainties concerning the stories' effect on America's prosecution of the war. For one, there was no chance now that Americans would settle for anything but Japan's unconditional surrender. "You can answer every sleazy item of the 'Peace Now' program with one word," wrote columnist Walter Winchell: "Bataan."

U.S. military personnel in the Pacific were filled with a new resolve, too. Those close to the fighting fronts, having read and heard of the atrocities committed against their comrades in the Philippines, would not dream of surrendering. "Like the Indian fighters of the West, each planned to save a bullet for himself," declared *Newsweek*. They were also equally against the taking of prisoners. As a result of the revelation, the Pacific war—already a conflict filled with more base barbarism than perhaps any other modern clash—had taken a darker, more sinister turn. The dehumanization of the enemy by both sides would result in a virulent escalation of unparalleled carnage. With the January 28 release, the Pacific war had become, in the words of one Navy Department observer, "a knockdown, drag-out, no-quarter war."

Though there would be instances of atrocities committed against the Japanese by American military personnel during the war, an overwhelming majority of American troops would continue to adhere to the rules of engagement of the era. The demarcation line between soldier and surrendered prisoner was observed in the majority of situations, even by the first U.S. troops to enter combat with knowledge of the atrocities. According to one correspondent with the 7th Infantry Division during the invasion of the Marshall Islands, "The troops were enraged. There were ominous predictions as to the fate of any little yellow men who might survive to fall into our hands at Kwajalein." The correspondent followed a small group of rare Japanese prisoners, some of whom were wounded, taken on that atoll and seemed almost surprised to report that "there was no long march in choking dust, harried by bayonet-wielding guards" for these men. Instead, the enemy POWs were given clothes and K rations. "The worst thing that befell them was a series of verbal reflections, delivered in a language they did not understand anyway, upon the legitimacy of their honorable ancestors." Enemy combatants, on the other hand, remained fair game. "We see a lot of soldiers who have come back from Europe and the Pacific," one War Department observer told the *New York Times*. "The boys from Europe speak impersonally of the enemy. Those from the Pacific do not. They all want to go back and kill more Japs."

With an understanding of that prevailing mind-set, it is useful to consider the role played by the atrocities story in influencing the way in which the Pacific war was concluded. The revelation in late January 1944 had been only the beginning of the bad news. Throughout the war's final eighteen months and even beyond, Americans would receive a steady diet of stomach-wrenching stories. There were tales of Allied POWs being forced to build the Burma–Siam Railroad and toil in Japanese factories, mines, and docks as slave laborers. The U.S. military discovered that downed American airmen were beheaded, chained naked in cages in Japanese zoos, and vivisected by sadists masquerading as doctors. America thirsted for revenge, to settle a blood debt for Pearl Harbor, Bataan and other events. Even as late as December 1945, three months after the formal cessation of hostilities, a *Fortune* magazine survey reported that a surprising number of Americans, 22.7 percent, lamented that more atomic bombs had not been employed against Japan.

It was no surprise then that FDR's successor, Harry Truman, understood that the atomic bomb presented a double opportunity for ending the war and exacting some amount of revenge. But the closest glimpse one has into Truman's mind is his diary, in the pages of which he called the Japanese "savages, ruthless, merciless and fanatic," so any supposition that Truman allowed personal or national malice to factor into his decision will remain forever a subject of historical speculation.

Some high-ranking brass and officials, on the other hand, openly shared the sentiments of regular Americans. After hearing news of the successful completion on August 6, 1945, of the mission of the *Enola Gay*—the B-29 Superfortress that dropped the first atomic bomb, Little Boy, on the Japanese city of Hiroshima—Maj. Gen. Leslie Groves, the Army officer who had supervised the top secret Manhattan Project that developed the bomb, was jubilant. Even in this pre–politically correct era, General Marshall cautioned Groves about rejoicing in the large loss of civilian life. "I was not thinking about those casualties," Groves would say. "I was thinking about all of our boys who were murdered by the Japs on the Bataan Death March!"

Perhaps the most important consequence of the escape and the resulting revelations was the effect on the home front. Columnist Samuel Grafton believed that the revelation would serve as a wake-up call, "a kind of second Pearl Harbor" for America. It did.

Editorial cartoons lamented the Pacific theater's stepchild status. "I guess the European Front is the most important," sighed a weary, disheveled POW in a cartoon drawn by the *Chicago Tribune*'s Carey Orr entitled "The Heroes of Bataan." Columns noted that Dyess's account mentioned that the Battle of Bataan began with only nine planes and urged all Americans, from citizens to lawmakers, to atone for that sin. "Our force in the Philippines was the victim of 'too little, too late,' before it was exposed to Japanese barbarity," editorialized the *Fort Worth Star-Telegram*. "Certainly our people are outraged by the revelation of Japanese atrocity [*sic*] against war prisoners, but indignation cannot be confined to the Japs alone. We should be angry at ourselves for having betrayed our fighting men into the hands of a ruthless enemy. Indignation aroused by Japanese atrocities should steel our people into an all-out war effort. The home front has an obligation to do justice toward our men now on the war fronts and to make amends for our betrayal of those on Bataan."

"We've got to have the nature of this war drilled in on us day after day before we sense the full horror of it, the demands of it, the danger of it. We haven't won it by a long shot, and we don't know it," wrote Palmer Hoyt in an *American* magazine article published one week after the release. "This war has not yet become personal with us at home. It can never be personal without the searing flame of battle and the cry of wounded in our ears. But if we hear the truth day by day, by radio, read it in our newspapers and magazines, hear it from the rostrum and the housetops, we'll silence the babble, sober the feather-minded, and fight like hell."

From January 28 forward, the nature of the war would be drilled into the minds of all Americans. A well-devised propaganda campaign—one that tapped into America's hatred and employed racial undertones—coordinated with ensuing War Bond drives ensured that Americans' memories did not lapse. There was a postage stamp for the Federated Organizations for Bataan Relief that featured wounded POWs suffering behind barbed wire—"We will not let them down," read the tagline. Among the many posters designed to incite Americans was one that featured a solemn soldier holding his doughboy-style helmet while asking, "Do you remember me? I was at Bataan." A line at the bottom reminded the reader to "BUY WAR BONDS." Another poster used the Death March as a way to implore Americans to stay focused on their jobs. Above an artist's depiction of prisoners being led into captivity, a question asked, "What are YOU going to do about it?" Below a foreground illustration of a sneering Japanese soldier beating a POW with a rifle butt and a reprint of one of the earliest Death March headlines came a direct command: "Stay on the job until every MURDERING JAP is wiped out!"

The message, by and large, would be received. Thanks to the efforts of the escapees, the war had finally become personal. January 28 would prove the antidote to the complacency epidemic that had infected much of the nation. Whether it was buying more War Bonds, donating more blood, combating absenteeism in war plants, scrimping and saving a little more, and complaining about rationing and other sacrifices a little less, Americans seemed more aware of what was demanded of them and better prepared for the long road ahead. And it would be long.

The victories at Coral Sea, Midway, and Guadalcanal had enabled the United States to blunt Japanese advances, and the advantage held by the United States in resources and industrial capability would assure its armed forces strategic dominance in the Pacific. Nevertheless the nation seemed a long way from total victory. "Let us face the facts and admit that after two years of war Japan is the victor," Carlos Romulo told the Hearst newspapers. "Out of 1,366,000 square miles of land she has grabbed we have only recaptured 160,150 square miles. We have been fighting 3,000 miles from the Japanese mainland, have advanced only 200 miles and have taken only 377 Jap prisoners." Using his January 26 birthday as a marker, *Newsweek* noted the sluggish progress being made by MacArthur: on the occasion of his sixty-third birthday on January 26, 1943, MacArthur's forces were heavily invested in Eastern New Guinea, some 2,500 miles from Manila; one year later, they had advanced only 240 miles closer to his stated objective. In 1944, one newspaperman examined the distances involved, and the logistical and political constraints facing U.S. forces in the Pacific, and remarked that "at this pace, we won't get to Tokyo until 1960."

Good news or bad, Americans would now know where they stood. The *Detroit Free Press* would hail the atrocities story as "the most important piece of journalism to come out of this war." And perhaps it was. As Hoyt explained in *American* magazine, the release of the atrocities story was a pivotal victory for the Fourth Estate and the First Amendment over the oppression of officialdom. After Pearl Harbor, a "precedent" had been set "for withholding and delaying all kinds of information, which could, if continued, make of us—the best informed people on earth—the least informed. . . . That kind of censorship lulls us into indifference and may, if we put up with it, destroy our freedom."

Instead, thanks to the Dapecol escapees and a handful of dedicated journalists, a new precedent had been established. War news for the most part would no longer be suppressed or else parceled out in portions at the whim of the government or powerful officials. "The breaking of the Bataan story was tremendously important," Hoyt later declared to a fellow editor in his private correspondence, "because it opened the way for other stories."

In the war-torn Pacific, news of the Dapecol escape and release of the atrocities story affected the fighting men. "In this theatre there is no doubt what is the most widely read and best remembered story ever to appear in *Life*," remembered photographer Carl Mydans. Whether it was the *Life* or the Dyess version of the atrocities, the story traveled throughout the Pacific theater of operations and China-Burma-India theaters, from South Pacific islands to Australia and mainland China—where there were Americans, there was the story.

Perhaps no nation needed a bigger boost than the occupied Philippines. For months, one copy of the February issue of *Life*, brought in by submarine, traversed Mindanao. Like the escapees, it traveled by banca and over jungle trails. In barrios, remote outposts, and large towns, Filipinos recognized the photos of the escaped POWs and beamed with pride and shared accomplishment. Each morning, the guerrilla padre, Father Edward Haggerty, would take the tattered issue to mass; in the afternoons it was circulated at market. When eager crowds assembled at the cockpits, a sergeant was assigned to turn the pages while soldiers kept the masses from pressing too close. Still, the worn periodical, often damp with jungle rain, always returned to him "with more loose pages, more tears, more dirty fingerprints."

Two men, recalled Haggerty, were permitted to peruse the magazine at their leisure: Paul Marshall and Bob Spielman. "They both expressed satisfaction at knowing now that the people back home had learned about the Jap treatment of our people," Haggerty wrote. As one Spyron operative claimed, the ragged copy of *Life* was "a symbol, of joy to many, and a satisfaction to others . . . a tangible 1944 link with the U.S.A.; the first most of them here had had since 1942." It would prove not only a tangible link to America, but a bridge to future victories.

And what of those fighting a day-to-day battle for their lives, the prisoners of war still held captive by the Japanese? Would the revelation have any positive effect, as believed by Ed Dyess and the other escapees, on their plight? Hanson Baldwin, for one, was not optimistic. "Whether or not this course will be effective in relieving our prisoners of some of their misery is doubtful," wrote Baldwin in the *New York Times*. "But it is certain that the policy of 'suffer in silence' has ended." That much was true. The escapees had at the very least successfully accomplished part of their mission: lifting the curtain of silence that the Japanese had closed across the Philippines in 1942.

As time would reveal, there would be consequences. It was probably with great satisfaction in the spring of 1944 that Melvyn McCoy made a broadcast via shortwave radio that he hoped would reach his former comrades in captivity. "Be of good cheer," McCoy's message read. "Your hour of deliverance will not be long delayed. Meanwhile, I have reason to believe your stay in prison camps is to be made more bearable. The Japanese government recently announced that it was preparing to permit International Red Cross and Y.M.C.A. to alleviate the horrible conditions that prevailed in Japanese camps in the past."

Feeling the weight of world opinion, the Japanese had been forced into action. In March 1944, the Imperial vice minister of war sent the following edict to all POW camp commanders:

> In light of the recent intensified enemy propaganda warfare, if the present condition continues to exist, it will needlessly add to the hostile feelings of the enemy and it will also be impossible for us to expect the world opinion to be what we wish it to be. Such will cause an obstacle to our prosecution of moral warfare. Not only that, it is absolutely necessary to improve the health condition of POW's from the standpoint of using them satisfactorily to increase our fighting strength.

POW historian E. Bartlett Kerr added that "this admonition was followed by instructions to be sure that the prisoners were given their full allowance of food and clothing and that efforts were made to improve medical care." As the decree indicated, Japan's decision to improve the lives of its prisoners was not entirely motivated by shame nor by a desire to right past wrongs. Japan's leadership was more preoccupied with propaganda and tapping the deep labor pool of prisoners to prop up the crumbling war effort. So mistreatment continued, as did the deaths. All the same, the escapees had, to a certain extent, correctly gauged Japanese psychology. They had forced their former captors into demonstrating at least some semblance of humane treatment, resulting in the saving of lives. While a shocking percentage of Allied prisoners—37 percent—would ultimately perish at the hands of the Japanese it was probably due in part to the Dapecol escapees that the number was not significantly higher. (In comparison, only one percent of Allied POWs—excluding Russian prisoners—held by Germany died during the period of their confinement.)

Though the remaining imprisoned defenders of the Philippines could not have known it at the time, the relief columns that they had dreamed of in 1942 had finally arrived, albeit the relief, in the most indirect way, had arrived in the form of newspaper columns, syndicated stories, magazine features, and editorial cartoons. The escape from the Davao Penal Colony had proved that not only was the American pen mightier than the Japanese samurai sword, but that perhaps the most important weapons in America's arsenal were its typewriters, printing presses, microphones, radios, and calls of corner newsboys, as well as the most powerful weapon of all, an infuriated, well-informed, and galvanized civilian population.

Even so, an overwhelming number of the American prisoners still in Japanese hands, most of whom had nearly two more years of captivity awaiting them, would not learn of the Dapecol escape nor have any inkling of what it meant to them, their country, and the war. And though many of these captives would perish, the escape and the story of the escape was nevertheless a victory—one of the most important if least known of the entire war. A victory won by twelve extraordinary men who dreamed, then dared to attempt, and then ultimately accomplished what had seemed impossible.

Epilogue

We'll have our small white crosses by and by
Our cool, green lawns, our well-spaced, well-cared trees
Our antique cannons, muzzles to the sky,
Our statues and our flowers and our wreaths.

The release of the atrocities story was significant for many reasons, but above all it signaled the successful conclusion to the escapees' epic quest. "I felt very satisfied," Jack Hawkins would say, "because I knew the story was worldwide. I felt very good that we had done all we could do."

Yet in early 1944, there was still plenty of war left. The paths that each escapee took to V-J—"Victory over Japan"—Day were extensions of their escape odyssey, divergent, yet sometimes intersecting, and filled with adventures gratifying and depressing, bewildering and banal, but in the end, enduring.

Sam Grashio had been Ed Dyess's understudy, and after Dyess's death, his replacement: upon Dyess's death, Grashio's orders were changed again, transforming him from squadron leader to Treasury Department spokesman.

For much of the next two years, he traveled the country on the War Bond circuit, speaking everywhere from Spokane to Jersey City, where he gave fifteen speeches in one exhausting day. He spoke in churches, schools, theaters, factories, mills, and shipyards, before Rotary and Kiwanis clubs, chambers of commerce, the Red Cross, the Veterans of Foreign Wars, the YMCA, and, of course, the Bataan Relief Organization. No audience was too small or too large—he addressed a crowd of 50,000 that had gathered at Forest Lawn Memorial Park in Los Angeles to jointly commemorate Easter and Bataan Day—and, according to Grashio, "no publicity gimmick was left unused." At one munitions plant he posed for a photograph next to a 400-pound bomb to which he had affixed his signature and a message for General Tojo: "In appreciation of your hospitality."

While the size of the crowd or the location might change, Grashio's speech was the same. He condemned the Japanese loudly and vehemently—one of his favorite, crowd-pleasing lines, which had been written for him by Colonel Frank Capra, the director who was then making training films for the Signal Corps, was "I can't tell you very much about the education or the training of the Japs, but I can tell you what the result is. The finished product is a lying, rotten, bullying son-of-a-bitch!" He would then exhort his audience to do their part, lest his long-suffering comrades "will all perish miserably at the hands of the cruelest captors in the world." The results varied as little as the speeches. "Large crowds attended the war bond rallies everywhere, accounts of the Death March invariably left many listeners crying, and bond sales skyrocketed," he remembered.

Fawned over by politicians, corporate sponsors and military brass, Grashio rubbed elbows with people like Gen. Hap Arnold, financier Bernard Baruch, actress Brenda Marshall, actor Pat O'Brien, singer Bing Crosby, boxer Jack Dempsey, and other celebrities. It was all too mind-boggling. Scarcely months earlier, Grashio had been a starving, shivering, suffering slave laborer in rags. Now he had his own plane and personal secretary. He was even the subject of an adventure comic strip. "Everywhere I went I was treated as a hero, given awards, asked to speak, taken to expensive nightclubs, fed steaks, plied with drinks, introduced to famous people, and photographed endlessly," he recalled. But Grashio would not allow himself to be blinded by the glare of the klieg lights or the flashbulbs. "Despite it all, the sense of frustration never left me. Every time I ate another steak in another plush night club with another Big Name I thought of the starving prisoners left behind to a fate still unknown."

Much to the dismay of his handlers, Grashio began to devote more time to the inquiries he continued to receive from those hoping to learn something about the fate of their loved ones in the Philippines. Many waited in long lines for Grashio to complete his speeches; others rushed him with photographs and questions, pleading for answers. Grashio considered the bond tour rewarding, but felt trying to answer the innumerable requests was "the most permanently satisfying thing I did during the remainder of the war."

But that did not mean it was easy. He sat for hours scanning photographs, trying to recall faces and names. It was painfully difficult for him when he was unable to identify an individual or provide some piece of information to an anxious mother or wife. But there were moments that made it all worthwhile. Once, in Seattle, a line of information seekers stretched from the entrance of Grashio's hotel down the block. He had not had much luck on this day until the parents of John Arthur Davis, an enlisted man in the 21st Pursuit, presented him with a picture of their son. "I want you to wait here," Grashio told them. "I want to talk to you after everyone has gone through." Later, Grashio told the Davis family that he had seen their son being beaten with an ax handle and dragged into a burial shack at one of the Luzon POW camps. But, Grashio recalled, the next day Davis crawled out alive and was still alive as far as he knew. The news buoyed Davis's parents until the day their son returned home.

The best news of the war, however, was not Grashio's to deliver. That honor went to Bert Bank, who was reunited with Grashio in San Francisco in early 1945. Bank, along with 500 others, had been liberated from Cabanatuan by Army Rangers in a daring January raid. The two friends caught each other up on everything that had happened since the escapees had disappeared into the jungle that Sunday morning nearly two years earlier. Grashio was relieved to learn that none of the Dapecol prisoners had been executed by Major Maeda. "That news lifted a cloud that had hung over me," Grashio would write.

At war's end, Grashio would find himself back at Hamilton Field, welcoming home prisoners of war from the Pacific theater. He retired from the Air Force in 1965, reaching the rank of colonel, and then served as the assistant to the president of Gonzaga University until 1977. In the 1980s, Grashio would meet and befriend the man who almost shot him out of the sky on the first day of the war, Japanese fighter legend Saburo Sakai. Grashio passed away in 1999.

In early 1944, the Marines discovered that evading their fame was a challenge that rivaled evading the Japanese on Mindanao. Each was given two months' leave, but the time was largely spent speaking at bond rallies, dodging reporters, and answering the letters and calls from prisoners' relatives that invariably found them at their residences. Mike Dobervich and Jack Hawkins agonized over lengthy, sugarcoated replies to these relatives, but Austin Shofner remained his usual, blunt self. "If I knew about it, I said, 'yes, your son was killed.' . . . I told it straight," he would say. "Nobody ever suggested I play ring around the rosie."

One task that Shofner relished was reconnecting with University of Tennessee football coach Robert Neyland. Shofner told Neyland that it was the coach's training and maxims that had enabled him to return home alive. He reportedly caused the tough old coach's eyes to well up when he told him, "You always taught us to play for the breaks, and when one comes your way, score. That's what I did."

Jack Hawkins found his new fame flattering, yet ultimately a nuisance. Hawkins had married his fiancée, Rhea, in Annapolis just after Christmas 1943 and was inundated with so many media and information requests that the newlyweds were forced to flee Fort Worth for Detroit in hopes of enjoying some semblance of a honeymoon. But it was not until the couple relocated to Quantico, where Hawkins was reunited with Dobervich and Shofner at the USMC staff and command officers school, that they were able to enjoy a somewhat normal life. Even then, the reprieve, not to mention the Marines' reunion, was abridged.

Upon graduation, Hawkins received a most peculiar assignment: Hollywood. He was assigned to be a military adviser to Col. Frank Capra. Hawkins spent several weeks working on what he called "the film business," as well as hobnobbing with some of Hollywood's biggest stars. Capra invited Hawkins to cocktail parties and even included him in late-night bull sessions during which time Capra and his colleagues kicked around scripts. None of those stories, of course, could compare with what Hawkins had just lived through. He recalled Capra and the other "Hollywood-types" being riveted by his account of the Dapecol escape. "A movie should be made out of this," Capra told Hawkins.

After hearing Hawkins tell the story over lunch at the Brown Derby, Darryl Zanuck, head of Twentieth Century–Fox studios, agreed. Zanuck drew up a contract: Hawkins would receive a $10,000 option payment and then $75,000 when the full manuscript was approved by military censors. Hawkins returned to Quantico and spent many a late night formulating his story. Despite his efforts, the War Department refused to clear the 377-page work, ostensibly for fear of compromising guerrilla operations on Mindanao.

At least Hawkins could keep his $10,000 option, which he dutifully divided among the escapees. The escape was proving to be a lucrative venture. In addition to receiving equal installments from *Life* amounting to $5,000 per man, there were payments from book deals negotiated by Dyess, McCoy, and Mellnik. The *Chicago Tribune* series later became *The Dyess Story,* and the *Life* article *Ten Escape from Tojo* in book form. Both became bestsellers. McCoy reportedly sold the movie rights to *Ten Escape from Tojo* to Republic Pictures and Dyess's estate settled on an agreement with another studio, but no motion picture on the Dapecol escape was ever made.

While getting rich had certainly never been a goal, getting revenge on their captors had been. Among the Marines, Dobervich and Shofner would have the earliest opportunity. Fighting with the 1st Marine Division, both participated in the Battle of Peleliu in September 1944, which had the highest casualty rate of any battle in the Pacific war. Shofner, now a lieutenant colonel, would win his second Purple Heart leading an assault battalion ashore. When the battle entered its closing stages, the Marines were charged with flushing obstinate Japanese from caves and fortifications. "I would say a lie if I said I didn't enjoy this," Dobervich told a war correspondent. "I am not a cruel man. I would treat them kindly if they surrendered to me. But I am glad they want to fight it out."

After stints aboard the carrier *Philippine Sea* and the battleship *New Jersey,* Dobervich would command the 1st Amphibian Tractor Battalion during the Korean War. Retiring from the Marine Corps in 1954, Beaver Dobervich kept busy by running a food processing business, working at the Fargo, North Dakota, YMCA, and teaching Sunday school until his death in 1997.

Shofner retired as a brigadier general in 1959 and returned to Shelbyville, Tennessee, where he raised five sons and managed finance and insurance businesses. Just as Shofner kept the escape party from fracturing in the swamp, he did his best to keep the group together in the decades following the escape by calling many of the participants on the April 4 anniversary of their breakout. Shofner's passing in 1999 was noted in a *New York Times* obituary.

• • •

"When we escaped, well, our story was really just beginning," Paul Marshall believed. Marshall and Bob Spielman, newly minted guerrilla officers, wasted little time using the Surigao-based 114th Infantry Regiment as a vehicle for revenge. "We went around and gathered up anybody that had the same feeling about the Japanese that we did," said Spielman. In between assaults and ambushes—which he planned aboard his mobile command post, a launch called the *So What*—Marshall also continued to wage his paper war, trading incendiary notes and leaflets with the local Japanese commander who repeatedly requested his surrender.

"Bob Spielman basically took over combat operations when [the 114th] got so big," said Marshall. "I had a lot to do. [Clyde Childress] wrote and told me to get my ass off my boat and quit chasing Japs and start running my operation." That operation was intelligence gathering, the guerrillas' primary mission as assigned by GHQ. Spielman admitted that his and Marshall's early actions were "not significant militarily. It did great things for my ego, but MacArthur wanted information." So, at the time, Childress's pleas fell on deaf ears. "Like all the other orders we got that we didn't like, we didn't pay any attention to it," he added.

And then they heard from Steve Mellnik. Mellnik had been running the Philippine Section of G-2 for GHQ, an assignment that tasked him with coordinating espionage nets and gathering information on Japanese troop strengths and dispositions everywhere from Aparri to Zamboanga. In late 1943 and early 1944, however, Mellnik would spend an excessive amount of time on a pet project that had taken on a life of its own: the breakout of POWs from Dapecol.

The plan was structured around Capt. Harold Rosenquist, a MIS-X (Military Intelligence Service, X-section) officer in his late twenties who had been trained in the latest escape and evasion techniques. Rosenquist would be inserted into the Philippines on what was essentially a fact-finding mission, to make contact with both the guerrillas and the POWs in order to ascertain the best way to liberate the camp. It naturally fell to Marshall and Spielman to provide the latest intelligence. Though he would not be able to steal any chickens from the poultry farm, Spielman would get close enough to map the penal colony and Japanese defensive positions, as well as leave cigarettes and chocolate bars carrying the message "I Shall Return" for the POWs.

Rosenquist was to depart in February, but internal discord in GHQ held up the mission. "Colonel Whitney's influence too strong," Rosenquist would write in his diary. Regrettably, Rosenquist did not set foot on Mindanao until June 1. He made his way to Kapungagan, where he met with the escapees' old friend Claro Laureta, now a major. Rosenquist gave Laureta a cigarette lighter from Mellnik, as well as President Quezon's pardons for Ben de la Cruz and Victor Jumarong. With building anticipation, Mellnik traced Rosenquist's progress through garbled radio messages. Rosenquist easily infiltrated Dapecol—but that was because the camp was deserted. "Walked around Penal Colony," read the deflating communiqué. "Found no, repeat no PWs. Happy convicts say PWs evacuated ten days ago, probably to Manila."

As Mellnik, Marshall, and Spielman learned, approximately 1,250 American prisoners had been blindfolded, tethered to each other, and marched out of Dapecol on June 6, 1944. Arriving at the Lasang Pier, these men were packed aboard the merchant vessel *Yashu Maru*, which would take them to Cebu City. The prisoners would then board the *Singoto Maru* for the remainder of their journey to Manila, where they would then be redistributed to Bilibid Prison, Cabanatuan, and other prison camps scattered throughout Japan's shrinking empire. But not all of the Dapecol POWs left Mindanao.

In March, nearly 700-odd prisoners had been selected for a work detail to build an airfield near Lasang. After finishing their labors in August, this last shipment of Dapecol POWs was herded aboard a familiar vessel, the *Erie Maru*, for the short haul to Zamboanga, where they would board the hellship that was supposed to take them to Manila: the *Shinyo Maru*. "Seems that more POW have left Davao area . . . guess I won't get the chance to do what I really came here for," lamented Rosenquist in his diary. He would not be the only one with regrets.

None of the final Dapecol POWs would ever reach Manila. In fact, fewer than 100 would survive the final voyage of the *Shinyo Maru*. It was to be an all too common occurrence in the war's latter stages: according to author Gregory Michno, more than 126,000 Allied POWs were transported in 156 voyages on 134 Japanese vessels that also carried supplies or arms. Since the Japanese steadfastly refused to mark these vessels as POW transports, some 21,000 POWs were killed or injured on the ships as a result of attacks from American planes or submarines.

The commander of the submarine *Paddle* had no idea that the merchant ship he sighted in the enemy convoy zigzagging north along the western coast of Mindanao on the afternoon of September 7, 1944, was carrying American prisoners of war. Seconds after the *Paddle* fired a spread of torpedoes at the slow-moving *Shinyo Maru*, the fish slammed into the hull of the antiquated freighter, rocking the ship with a series of explosions. Water poured into the holds and panicked POWs clambered up to the decks, only to be beaten back by rifle butts. It would take less than ten minutes for the 2,600-ton vessel to break apart and sink, and in that time, only a handful of Americans would make it abovedecks and jump overboard. Though most of POWs would experience horrible deaths trapped inside the flooded holds, many of those who made it into the water would suffer equally worse fates. As launches arrived to pluck Japanese survivors from the water, the handful of weak Americans struggling to stay afloat were fired upon, beaten with oars, and drowned. By the time darkness fell, only eighty-two washed up on the shore alive. Guerrillas would spirit away the survivors and nurse them back to health before another American submarine, the *Narwhal*, was dispatched to retrieve them.

The failure to reach the Lasang-Dapecol prisoners in time, and the subsequent *Shinyo Maru* tragedy, would remain a point of contention among the Mindanao guerrillas for years. "I thought it [a prison break] could [work] and Bob thought it could," Marshall would say. "But the powers-that-be didn't want anything to do with it." Marshall believed that Wendell Fertig's refusal to cooperate with Rosenquist limited the latter's ability to coordinate and execute the mission. That certainly was likely. Clyde Childress explained that Rosenquist's attitude toward Fertig and the guerrillas was generally cold and condescending, thus creating an adversarial relationship. Fertig probably believed that such an operation was logistically impossible, and that it might have led to a massive Japanese counterinsurgency that could have destroyed the guerrilla movement on Mindanao.

Historical hindsight shows that Mellnik's mission faced almost insurmountable odds. While a raid on Dapecol or any other local POW compound would have been easy to execute due to the guerrillas' numerical advantage over any guard detail, the main problem was arranging the transportation of hundreds of sickly, emaciated POWs to an extraction point. It is also highly unlikely that the guerrillas in the Davao sector, however numerous and spirited, could have held off the large, well-equipped Imperial Army garrison that would undoubtedly have been dispatched from Davao City to recover the prisoners.

Still, in view of what happened to the men aboard the *Shinyo Maru*, Marshall thought the attempt should have been made: "I often wondered if it would have been worthwhile, but that's just supposition. Could we have pulled it off and what would we have done with them after we got them out of there?" Childress would be loath to credit Fertig for much during the war, but he would insist that the decision—whoever made it—to scrub the Dapecol rescue mission was the correct one. Of course, as Marshall would counter, "but then we'll never know, will we?"

Marshall and Spielman would henceforth devote their time into building what was perhaps the most successful guerrilla province on the island, a model outfit complete with an extensive intelligence network, a strong civil government and school system, and a hard-hitting army that kept the Japanese bottled up. Ironically, it was by toeing the line and fulfilling their mission for GHQ that the two former POWs were finally able to get some revenge. In fact, they'd get more.

A few months after the *Shinyo Maru* sinking, with MacArthur's forces rapidly approaching, Marshall's coast watchers had noticed that the local Japanese forces—commanded by Marshall's Japanese pen pal—were preparing to bug out. "The Japs had about 14 or 15 small inter-island boats and they were going to move all these troops in Surigao someplace else," he remembered. The report was relayed to GHQ and Marshall received a strange reply. "I got a message saying, 'in the morning, get up on your hilltop.' That is all it said."

As ordered, Marshall, Spielman, and some others ascended his hilltop observation post at approximately 0800. Marshall's ears soon perked up; he heard what sounded like a giant swarm of bees approaching: the humming of the engines of several dozen American fighter planes, probably F4U Corsairs, which had been dispatched from a Navy carrier task force. The guerrillas watched as the planes roared in over the water with their machine guns blazing. The Japanese flotilla did not have a chance. "[The planes] came in and when they left there wasn't a stick big enough to float," said Marshall. To conclude the one-sided battle, Filipinos on the shore grabbed their bolos and paddled out in barotos to finish off the survivors. The ensuing scene was wild, bloody mayhem, the result of nearly three years of pent-up humiliation. Marshall could not have stopped it had he tried. "[The Filipinos] hated the Japs," he said. "I think we all did at the time."

Marshall's fire would fade after the war but would never be fully extinguished. Like most of the escapees, he refused to drive Japanese cars, a decision attributable to both his memories of his treatment as a POW and his lifelong attachment to Chrysler. When Marshall came home, he returned to a promised brand-new black Chrysler sedan, the first of its kind in Pueblo. He also found a check from *Life* and three years' back pay waiting for him. Marshall would marry, raise three sons, and work in the meat and real estate industries. He stayed in the Army Reserve, retiring as a lieutenant colonel in 1963, and was instrumental in helping to craft POW SERE—Survival, Evasion, Resistance, and Escape—training as recently as 1996. Marshall passed away in 2006.

Spielman did not rush home upon his separation from the Army in 1946. He worked as the manager of a lumber company in Surigao before returning to Texas with his wife and young family in 1948. Receiving a degree from the University of Texas, he settled in Austin and embarked on a career in education as a teacher at the Texas School for the Deaf. Like Marshall, Spielman stayed in the Army Reserve, retiring a colonel. He died in 2008.

For Melvyn McCoy and Steve Mellnik, the war came full circle in February 1945 at the most appropriate location: Corregidor.

Returning to the Philippines with MacArthur's forces in October 1944, Mellnik found himself in Subic Bay on Valentine's Day 1945 answering questions on Corregidor's topography and tunnels posed by the leaders of the assault teams that had been assigned to retake the Rock.

Mellnik's war ended a few weeks later. Plagued by malaria, he packed his travel orders, his razor, and a toothbrush into the same musette bag that he had carried out of Dapecol and headed off to Pier One to board the Navy oiler that would take him home. Mellnik's postwar résumé included General Staff and command assignments in the United States and Europe. The erstwhile enlisted man retired with the rank of brigadier general in 1963. He died in 1994.

Though Melvyn McCoy would often joke in early 1944 that the only sea duty he had had during the war was the twelve-day journey to Mindanao aboard the *Erie Maru*, he stressed that he had a "score to settle" with the Japanese. "When the Philippines are invaded, I expect to be there," he told the *Indianapolis Times*. Like MacArthur, McCoy made good on his promise: he was the executive officer on one of the cruisers in Manila Bay providing fire support for the invasion of Corregidor. McCoy and Mellnik reunited on the Rock several days after the island was secured and posed for a celebratory picture, photographic proof that they had come, both literally and figuratively, a long way together from the muddy rice fields of Mactan.

McCoy would also participate in the last major land battle of the war, Okinawa. One of his most memorable contributions to the fight was hosting a hungry Marine visitor aboard his cruiser—Shifty Shofner. McCoy would command two ships in the postwar period, the oiler *Severn* and the destroyer tender *Markab*. He retired from the Navy in 1951 with the rank of rear admiral and continued to live the itinerant lifestyle characteristic of a sailor. Late in his life, McCoy would frequently relive his famous escape by temporarily breaking out of an assisted-living facility in El Paso—he was always tracked down at his favorite watering hole a few blocks away. He died in 1988, his body cremated and his ashes scattered at sea.

Okinawa would be Jack Hawkins's last shot at combat. Promoted to lieutenant colonel, he was assigned the role of assistant operations officer in the 1st Marine Division. "I got my revenge on the Japs that way. Not with a gun in my hand, but with operations orders, writing them every day. I can remember when we would confer with everybody before writing the order of the day and it always started out, 'The First Marine Division attacks.' Every one that way. Every day."

After Okinawa, Hawkins was assigned to an industrial incentive tour. He would spend the war's final months much like Sam Grashio, giving pep talks to factory workers and bond buyers whose efforts were needed to keep America's assembly lines rolling as the invasion of Japan loomed. Hawkins had the routine down pat. He was caught off guard, though, just before taking the stage in a crowded theater in Baltimore on August 15, 1945. Japan, he was just told, had surrendered; the war was over. Hawkins would have to discard his prepared script and make his final speech off-the-cuff. He announced the surrender news and thanked his audience for its hard work and help in winning the conflict. As the audience streamed out to join in the massive public celebration unfolding across a triumphant nation, Hawkins must have felt much like Ed Dyess had, standing alone in the Texas night in November 1943 with everything and nothing to say.

The war might have been over, but history, as well as fate, was not finished with Hawkins. In the Korean War, he commanded the 1st Battalion, 1st Marines at the Inchon landing, the capture of Seoul, and operations in North Korea. His next assignment—as a military adviser to the CIA—placed him in the middle of tactical planning for the ill-fated Bay of Pigs invasion of Cuba in 1961. Upon learning that the site of the invasion had been changed and that there was no solid commitment for air cover for the paramilitary landing forces, Hawkins informed Richard Bissell, CIA deputy planning director, that Fidel Castro's fighter aircraft (if not destroyed), would sink the invasion fleet and the operation would end in disaster. Bissell did not relay to President John F. Kennedy Hawkins's recommendation. Instead, he urged Kennedy to go ahead even as the president further cut by half the already inadequate air operations plan. The result was exactly as Hawkins predicted. Involvement in the Bay of Pigs fiasco may have cost Hawkins a general's star, since the president and secretary of defense, Robert McNamara, used Hawkins as a scapegoat. Hawkins retired from the Marine Corps in 1965. The last surviving Dapecol escapee, Hawkins, ninety-four, lives in Fredericksburg, Virginia.

Although he had been recommended for the Congressional Medal of Honor, Ed Dyess instead received the Soldier's Medal for committing a heroic act not involving an armed enemy. On December 1, 1956, Abilene (Texas) Air Force Base was officially renamed Dyess Air Force Base in his honor. "If Ed was watching in the Great Beyond he probably would have laughed," Sam Grashio would write, "for it was a bomber base while he was a fighter pilot."

Thanks to the efforts of Madge Miguela Martin, the remains of an American serviceman were found buried in a shelter near Balingbing, Lanao, in early 1947. A makeshift dog tag—a 50-centavo coin on which the individual's name and Army serial number had been engraved—found among the skeletal remnants identified them as those of Leo Boelens. Boelens's body was temporarily interred at the U.S. Armed Forces Cemetery Leyte No. 1 before being transferred to the Manila American

Cemetery, where it remains today. His small white cross can be found in plot F, row 2, grave 97.

The remaining Dapecol POWs had been shipped back to Luzon shortly before MacArthur's landing on Leyte in the fall of 1944, with the majority continuing via hellships to POW camps in China, Formosa, or Japan. After being rescued in Cabanatuan in January 1945, Bert Bank regained his eyesight. Bank eventually operated two radio stations in his hometown of Tuscaloosa and was responsible for forming the University of Alabama football radio network. Bank would serve twelve years in the Alabama Senate and House of Representatives in the late 1960s and early 1970s, during which time he introduced legislation requiring that patriotism be taught in all state schools. Decades after their first encounter, Bank would marry Emma Minkowitz, the 1939 Miss Georgia, whom he had known while stationed in Savannah. Bank passed away in 2009.

Juan Acenas, the Filipino agricultural supervisor who literally showed the escapees the way out of Dapecol, was promoted to superintendent after the war.

After attending the July 4, 1946, ceremonies marking Philippine independence, Steve Mellnik visited Candido "Pop" Abrina, the man whose guile and guts contributed to the success of the escape. Mellnik was pleased to discover that the raconteur was still telling tall tales. "Pop," Mellnik told Abrina, "when I asked you to help us escape, I told you our reports would make history. They did: they shocked the whole world with the news of Japanese atrocities. And they made the words Corregidor, Bataan Death March familiar to every household in America. Your country and mine owe you a great debt." Abrina died in 1956.

Perhaps the most capable guerrilla leader on Mindanao, Clyde Childress, retired from the U.S. Army Reserve as a lieutenant colonel and worked as a sales representative in the heavy-equipment industry. He passed away in 2007.

Casiano de Juan, Big Boy, reportedly received a battlefield promotion to lieutenant at the end of the war. Little is known of his postwar life.

For the remainder of the war, Benigno de la Cruz served honorably in B Company, 6th Medical Battaltion, 110th Infantry Division on Mindanao. After the war, de la Cruz managed a pineapple farm and worked as a driver for the Joint United States Military Assistance Group in Manila before his death in 1980.

With the passage of the Immigration and Naturalization Act, scores of Filipino World War II veterans were permitted to receive U.S. citizenship in the early 1990s. For Magdaleno Dueñas, it seemed the fulfillment of a lifelong dream. Instead, it was a nightmare. Dueñas and more than a dozen other elderly veterans moved to the United States and were in effect held in captivity by an abusive landlord who fed them dog food and cashed their Social Security checks for himself. Fortunately for Dueñas, exactly fifty years after he helped a handful of American POWs evade their captors, a group of community activists freed him from his own imprisonment ordeal in 1993. Dueñas passed away in San Francisco at the age of ninety in 2005.

Wendell Fertig received the Distinguished Service Cross and was promoted by MacArthur after the war to colonel. Fertig's leadership of the Mindanao guerrillas would be more fully appreciated by the U.S. Army in the postwar period—Fertig was instrumental in the creation of the Special Warfare School, home of U.S. Special Forces training, at Fort Bragg, North Carolina. He died in 1975.

By all accounts, Victorio Jumarong served with the Mindanao guerrillas until the end of the war. His subsequent life remains a mystery.

Claro Laureta ended the war with the rank of lieutenant colonel.

Col. Ernest McClish passed away in 1993.

After retiring from the Navy Reserve in 1948 with the rank of commander, two Navy Crosses, a Distinguished Service Cross, the Bronze Star, and the Philippine Medal of Valor, Charles "Chick" Parsons set about rebuilding his businesses and his adopted homeland of the Philippines. Parsons passed away in 1988 and is buried in the Metro Manila Memorial Park.

Jose Tuvilla would receive the Bronze Star in 1947 for escorting the American POWs to Medina. Retiring as a captain, Tuvilla became a farmer. He passed away in 2008.

Fely Yap (née Campo), the nurse known as the "Florence Nightingale of Dapecol," married a doctor and continued fighting the Japanese after the penal colony was closed. Much like the escapees, she owed a debt of gratitude to Casiano de Juan and his guerrillas for spiriting her and her husband into the hills during the war's latter stages. She lives in Davao City.

With victory came the justice that an outraged America had demanded and that American diplomats, politicians, and military leaders had promised in early 1944. After research conducted by the office of the Supreme Commander of the Allied Powers—MacArthur's occupation command would be known as SCAP—the International Military Tribunal for the Far East (IMTFE) convened in Tokyo in May 1946 to try the leaders and functionaries of the defeated Japanese empire. A panel of judges was selected to include representatives from each of the victorious Allied powers and a classification system was used to identify, group, and prosecute different varieties of war criminals. Those charged with crimes against peace, mostly politicians, war ministers, and other government officials, were designated Class A defendants, while those facing charges of war crimes and crimes against humanity were assigned B and C designations. Most military officers charged with committing war crimes in the field were classified as C criminals. As Japanese atrocities were widespread, there were trials held in several cities throughout the Far East in addition to Tokyo.

When the tribunal wrapped up proceedings in November 1948, twenty-three Class A war criminals had been convicted. Seven—including former Prime Minister General Hideki Tojo—were put to death and sixteen given life sentences. Elsewhere in Asia, more than 5,700 Class B and C criminals were brought to trial. Of that number, 3,000 were convicted and sentenced; 920 were executed. Most notably, Emperor Hirohito and all other members of the royal family were given immunity from prosecution on the order of MacArthur. Those Japanese military personnel and civilians specifically linked to atrocities committed against American prisoners of war in the Philippines received a variety of sentences ranging from satisfactory to shocking.

Masanobu Tsuji, the man perhaps responsible for the most excessive displays of brutality on the Death March, was never indicted for war crimes and reportedly passed away in 1968.

Yoshio Tsuneyoshi, the sadistic commandant of Camp O'Donnell, received life imprisonment. Though he was undoubtedly responsible for the deaths of thousands of Americans and Filipinos, Tsuneyoshi would reportedly serve only ten years of that sentence.

The commandant of Cabanatuan, Shigeji Mori, was also reportedly sentenced to life at hard labor.

Kazuo Maeda was relieved as commandant of the Davao Penal Colony on March 1, 1944, and served in Korea until the end of the war. He was taken into custody by U.S. forces on February 15, 1946, and tried by the IMTFE. Though there were no executions or widespread atrocities committed during the period of his command, the tribunal did find Maeda guilty of starving the Dapecol prisoners and permitting an environment of mistreatment and general brutality to exist in the camp. The fifty-eight-year-old officer was sentenced to twenty-five years at hard labor.

Yoshimasa Hozumi reportedly returned to Japan in September 1943. Hozumi was interrogated by SCAP personnel in November 1947, but was never charged with any war crimes.

After the war, Kempei Yuki lived with his family in Ibaraki Prefecture on Honshu, where he was employed as a clerk in the prefectural Crop Reporting Office of the Forestry Bureau.

Shusuke Wada, the diminuitive and despicable civilian interpreter known as Running Wada, was sentenced to life in prison for his role in the deaths of several hundred American POWs who perished when the hellship transporting them to Formosa, the *Oryoku Maru*, was sunk by U.S. Navy dive-bombers off Subic Bay in December 1944.

It remains unknown if the other civilian interpreter employed by the Japanese at Dapecol, the hated Mr. Nishamura, Simon Legree, was ever brought to justice.

For Americans, the name of one man, General Masaharu Homma, would become synonymous with the most notorious war crime in U.S. military history, the Bataan Death March. The controversy surrounding that perception, as well as the circumstances of Homma's death, continues to this day. Forced into retirement in 1943, the "Poet General" returned to Japan and lived out the rest of the war in virtual seclusion. After the surrender, he was taken into custody and extradited to the Philippines for the Manila war crimes trials. Unlike the other trials, which were coordinated under the auspices of the IMTFE, the Manila proceedings were coordinated by the U.S. Army, creating controversy and claims that the verdict was all but preordained. "As the Allied Commander of the Pacific Theater, Douglas MacArthur was responsible for selecting the venue, the defense, the prosecution, the jury, and the rules of evidence in the trial of a man who beaten him on the battlefield," wrote author Hampton Sides.

Nevertheless, someone had to be held responsible. Though Homma pled not guilty to the charges levied against him, he was doomed by testimony from Death March survivors. According to Sides, Homma was sentenced to death on the "slippery concept of command responsibility." It was Homma's duty as commander of the Japanese 14th Army to know what his officers and men were doing. Ignorance was not a believable or acceptable plea. "The death penalty does not mean I'm guilty," a defiant Homma wrote his children in a final letter, "it means, rather, that the United States had avenged itself to its satisfaction."

Shortly before 1 A.M. on April 3, 1946, in the town of Los Banos, Homma was executed by firing squad.

Unlike Camp O'Donnell or Cabanatuan, the Davao Penal Colony was not a death camp in the sense that substantial numbers of American prisoners of war perished within its barbed wire boundaries. In fact, only sixteen American POWs are believed to have died in Dapecol. But the effects of one's incarceration at Dapecol would be revealed by time. Call it the curse of Dapecol: of the 2,009 estimated total number of POWs held in Dapecol during the period of its existence from October 1942 to June 1944, only 805 would survive the war, a mortality rate almost 25 percent higher than the total average of Allied POWs thought to have died in Japanese hands. Before the official surrender ceremony on September 2, 1945, nearly 60 percent of Dapecol prisoners were destined to die—most when the hellships they were traveling on were bombed or sunk by friendly fire, but many in subsequent Japanese prison camps due to their debilitated conditions.

After the war, Dapecol reverted to the control of the Philippine Bureau of Prisons. Today, the rechristened Davao Penal Farm continues to serve as a rehabilitation complex for violent criminal offenders. The notorious swamp that once bordered the camp, however, has long since been drained and the land transformed. Banana trees now stretch as far as the eye can see. Although none of the original structures remains, the camp layout remains virtually unchanged from its wartime configuration; when a building rotted away or collapsed, a replacement was constructed on nearly the same spot.

Preservation, in all regards, seems both a challenging and a worthy task. Just as the seemingly insignificant wartime date of April 4, 1943, and the escape that took place on that day are only dim memories, like a curio box in a trunk left in the cobwebbed attic of American military history, there is little at the penal farm to indicate the historical significance of the location. The only tangible evidence that American prisoners of war had once been incarcerated there is a small, weather-beaten bronze memorial plaque affixed to a petrified kapok tree stump anchored near the baseball field.

Acknowledgments

Telling an epic World War II escape story, like attempting to break out from an escape-proof prison camp, requires meticulous planning, patience, dedication, a bit of luck, and, most important, a team effort. Accordingly, I am indebted to dozens of individuals and organizations without whose assistance this book would not have been possible.

I am grateful to the late Mario Tonelli, because it all started with Motts. If not for him, I would not have known of the Dapecol escape, nor commenced an amazing journey in search of the full story of that adventure.

In keeping with my firm belief that to truly know an individual means to walk the very same earth, I found myself in places such as Albany, Texas, and Shelbyville, Tennessee, and later, following an inevitable progression, more distant locales such as Mariveles, Bataan, and Lungaog, Davao del Norte, Philippines. I felt as though I was treading on common ground with my main characters and indeed I was—in more ways than I immediately understood. I soon sensed that I was both physically and spiritually following in their footsteps, that I was being conducted from one town, one phone call, one e-mail, one handwritten letter, one clue to the next by some inexplicable, guiding force.

At each stop—be it a street address or an e-mail address in cyberspace—I was greeted by archivists both amateur and professional, storytellers, sons, daughters, spouses, veterans, friends, and researchers who had dutifully preserved the diaries, letters, telegrams, yellowed newspaper clippings, photographs, yarns, and anecdotes entrusted to them, in some cases for decades, as if in anticipation of my—or someone's—long-awaited arrival. These individuals graciously opened their hard drives, attics, address books, and basements to me, fed me, put me up, and put up with me; and then, in ways both direct and indirect, pointed me forward.

My most cherished stateside stops were Fredericksburg, Virginia; Lake Oswego, Oregon; and Austin, Texas—the hometowns of Jack Hawkins,

Paul Marshall, and Robert Spielman, the three surviving escapees I had the privilege of befriending throughout the course of my research. Heroes all, these men welcomed me into their their lives and patiently endured what must have seemed like a never-ending interrogation—several years of interviews, questions, phone calls, and letters—with nary a complaint. They gave freely of their time, thoughts, emotions, and support, and for that I am eternally grateful. It was an honor to tell their story.

I am also beholden to the multitude of other World War II veterans, privates and generals alike, many of whose names do not appear in this narrative and who have since mustered out of this world. All of these men had retired from military service many decades before I commenced my research; many, too, had long since retired their painful memories of that period. And yet they unhesitatingly reenlisted in my cause, dredging up memories, stories, documents, and photographs, as well as providing me with insight, suggestions, phone numbers, and addresses. They include Abie Abraham, Malcolm Amos, Charles Ankerbery, Bill Azbell, Tony Bilek, Ramon Buhay, Clyde Childress, John Cowgill, Jack Donahoe, I. B. Donalson, Magdaleno Dueñas, Ben Farrens, Dick Francies, Val Gavito, Richard Gordon, Ray Heimbuch, John Kinney, Lou Kolger, Joe Merritt, Joe Moore, Carl Nordin, Robin Olds, John Olson, Father Bob Phillips, Louis Read, Everett Reamer, Walt Regehr, Jose Tuvilla, Don Versaw, and Edgar Whitcomb.

The late Bert Bank deserves special commendation for his time, his remarkable powers of recollection, and also for his consummate generosity.

Shortly before his death, Motts Tonelli told me to call Mrs. Devonia Grashio. I thank her for picking up the phone and giving me Jack Hawkins's phone number—a pivotal event—but also for trusting me with family keepsakes ranging from photographs to phonograph records. I also appreciated the unfettered access to her husband's personal papers, scrapbooks, and records, the terrific hospitality I received from the Grashio family during my visit to Spokane, and the prompt replies to my numerous queries. The insight and encouragement I received from Grashio's son, Sam, a Vietnam veteran who followed in his father's footsteps in more ways than one, were deeply appreciated.

I'll never forget the warm welcome I received from the Shofner family during my trips to Tennessee and the generosity and support I continued to receive throughout the duration of my work on this project. In so many ways, Dr. Stewart Shofner helped me see this project and his father with clarity, as did Michael Shofner. Wes Shofner's basement yielded a treasure trove of documents, including perhaps the last surviving copy of the 400-page film treatment that Jack Hawkins had prepared for 20th Century–Fox in 1944. It was that document—the only raw, uncensored account of the escape story written so shortly after the event, while the memories were still vivid and fresh—that enabled me to accurately reconstruct dialogue and re-create many of the dramatic events featured in this book.

Nor will I forget the outstanding hospitality I enjoyed during my visit to Lake Jackson, Texas, to visit Elizabeth "Nell" Denman, Ed Dyess's sister. I want to thank Nell for her crucial help in supplying me with vital information and source materials, for patiently and thoughtfully replying to each e-mail, and, finally, for introducing me—in a manner of speaking—to her brother.

In Towson, Maryland, Kyle Richards catalogued a wealth of materials on his grandfather Steve Mellnik. Mellnik's daughter, Thelma Basham, contributed a significant amount of personal insight and information.

I traveled to Fargo, North Dakota, to meet Lois Dobervich and left with newspaper clippings, photographs, and, most important, a better understanding of her husband.

I thank Paul Marshall's sons—Bob, Scott, and Tim—for the practical assistance they rendered after their father's passing, as well as their encouragement.

Lucy Spielman's hospitality during my visit to Austin was greatly appreciated, as was Margaret Spielman's help in scanning and copying images of her father.

Thelma Kost, Leo Boelens's niece, was one of the most dedicated and enthusiastic supporters of this project. I owe Thelma a debt of gratitude for sending me copies of her uncle's diary and sharing her personal recollections. The same goes for Jeanie Peterson, who provided me with rare family photographs.

I'm grateful to Winsor Soule for sharing information and materials concerning his former father-in-law, Melvyn McCoy, and also for introducing me to McCoy's niece, Julie Witkoff, who supplied me with McCoy's surviving papers and documents, vital materials that immeasurably improved this book.

• • •

I am profoundly grateful for the many knowledgeable and talented archivists, curators, historians, and researchers whose assistance in locating and procuring primary source materials proved invaluable.

At the MacArthur Memorial in Norfolk, Virginia, the incomparable James Zobel worked tirelessly on my behalf locating many of the obscure orders, affidavits, after-action reports, records, and radio messages that became the bones of this book. I owe Jim a cold San Miguel—several.

There's perhaps no more proficient and personable archivist than Bob Parks at the Franklin D. Roosevelt Library in Hyde Park, New York.

At the National Archives in College Park, Maryland, Ken Schlessinger and Barry Zerby found important needles in quite a few paper haystacks for me.

The assistance of Alan Aimone at the U.S. Military Academy Library in West Point, New York, and Marilee Meyer of the West Point Alumni Archives was greatly appreciated.

In Annapolis, Maryland, Beverly Lyall at the U.S. Naval Academy Special Collections and Archives and Paul Stillwell at the Naval Institute provided essential help.

Kudos to Dr. James Kitchens and Jeffrey Saihaida at the U.S. Air Force Historical Research Agency at Maxwell Air Force Base, Alabama.

Dick Long, formerly of the Marine Corps Historical Center at the Navy Yard, Washington, D.C., was a fount of information.

I'm thankful for the help of Jim Ginther at the Marine Corps Research University Archives, Quantico, Virginia, and the late Col. John Ripley, USMC (Ret.) of the Marine Corps Historical Division.

Gary Johnson and Stephen Bye at the Center for Military History at Carlisle Barracks, Pennsylvania, deserve high praise.

I'm extremely grateful for the passion and professionalism that Richard "Doc" Warner, curator at the Dyess Heritage Center at Dyess Air Force Base in Abilene, Texas, brings to his job—it made mine so much easier. In Doc, Ed Dyess has a good man keeping an eye on his personal belongings and his legacy.

Randy Vance and Connie Aguilar of the Southwest Collection, Special Collections Department at Texas Tech University, Lubbock, Texas, were a huge help.

JoAnna Chrisco mined some terrific research material for me at the Denver Public Library with the help of archivists Ann Brown and Ellen Zazzarino.

I'd be remiss if I didn't thank Bob Conte at the Greenbrier Resort in White Sulphur Springs, West Virginia.

And they don't call Tennessee the Volunteer State for nothing: the staffs at both the Nashville Public Library and the Tennessee State Library and Archives were extremely helpful. I'd also like to thank Harris D. "Bud" Ford, the Associate Athletic Director for Media Relations at the University of Tennessee, plus Dr. Bob Bullen and Ken Byers at Middle Tennessee State University in Murfreesboro for providing me with video of Bullen's interview with Austin Shofner.

No research concerning American prisoners of the Japanese during World War II can be undertaken without the assistance of the American Defenders of Bataan and Corregidor, the Battling Bastards of Bataan, and AX-POW (American Ex-Prisoners of War). Roger Mansell's Center for Research, Allied POWs Under the Japanese, is an indispensable Internet resource.

Yuka Ibuki and Kinue Tokudome, the founder of U.S.-Japan Dialogue on POWs, Inc., deserve my thanks for their help in providing translations, as well as assisting me in my attempts (which were ultimately unsuccessful) to reach surviving Japanese participants. In that regard, Chris Laycock, U.S. Consul for Public Affairs in Osaka, Japan, and Justin Taylan and Alfred Weinzierl of Pacific Ghosts, deserve thanks, too.

Authors Bill Bartsch, Bill Smallwood, and Stanley Falk shared their time, thoughts, and the fruits of their many years of research with me, for which I am extremely grateful.

The escapees could not have succeeded without the help of their Filipino friends and neither could I. Earlier renderings of this story were largely incomplete because of a lack of information regarding most of the Filipino participants. These oversights, however, were not intentional: the exigencies of the war prevented the escapees from learning about their friends and allies in great detail during their brief period of comradeship in the guerrilla movement. Wartime censorship restrictions in the United States necessitated the purging of many names that were included in published accounts. Through the wonder of the Internet and the help of certain individuals, I was able to develop some of these largely unknown yet vital characters in greater depth. Most notably, Mercedes Brolagda and her brother, Eduardo Gardé, provided essential information concerning their father, Benigno de la Cruz. I'd also like to thank Angelica Abrina for marshaling members of her family in order to provide me with information concerning her grandfather Candido "Pop" Abrina.

During my research trip to the Philippines in 2005, I learned that the bamboo telegraph still functions extraordinarily well. A call went out and many individuals and organizations answered, helping make the trip a success. They include Myleen Abrigo, Peregrino Andres, Edna Binkowski, Art Boncato, Francis Ledesma and the staff at the Davao Marco Polo Hotel, Fé Campo, Lita de los Reyes, Alma Focolare, Alma Alesna, Dr. Ricardo Trota José of the University of the Philippines, Lt. Col. Art Matibag of the Corregidor Foundation, Rizalina Mitra-Pangan and the staff at the Davao Museum, Evelina Noroña-Togle, Josie San Pedro, and Fely Yap.

I'm especially grateful to Davao's historian emeritus, Ernesto I. Corcino, whose in-depth knowledge of the story from the previously undocumented guerrilla viewpoint enhanced this book.

Eddie Rojo, the executive assistant to the governor of Davao del Norte Province, was the catalyst who made possible my visit to the former Dapecol, the intersection where the escapees were united and the physical terminus of my own research odyssey. I'd also like to thank Superintendent Rodolfo V. Bagaoisan and his administrative officer, Efren S. Varabe, my tour guide Mario Asunción, plus the two police detectives who served as my bodyguards, Jose Colegado and Geriman Manos. My thanks to General Dionisio R. Santiago, the former director of the Philippine Bureau of Prisons, for his interest in this story, as well as his correspondence and contributions.

My friend Jim Litton arranged an unforgettable land-sea tour of the Bataan Peninsula. Capt. Nestor Saladero of Southstar Aviation provided me with a sensational bird's-eye view of the terrain surrounding the former Davao Penal Colony, the Libuganon River, and southern Agusan Province—and, most important, returned me safely and softly to terra firma.

I would also like to acknowledge the generous support of Carlos "Sonny" Dominguez, "The One" in the Philippines who made it all happen. Sonny immediately understood the historical significance of this story and put his time and resources in both Manila and Davao at my disposal.

Both in the States and in the Philippines, Lou Jurika selflessly served this project in a variety of capacities: editor; PR man; negotiator; travel agent; translator; research assistant; copilot; sailor; wingman; drinking partner. This book would have been a lesser work without his help.

Peter Parsons, the son of Charles "Chick" Parsons, deserves special recognition not only for his material contributions—documents, maps, and photographs from his family's archives—but also for sharing his firsthand experiences and memories of his father, for serving as a soundboard for my thoughts and ideas, as well as for his unwavering support. Banzai, Pete.

Other individuals who assisted me in various ways include Richard Burns, Jane Cambus, Cheryl Cerbone, Rowena Crow, Jeff Davis, Mauree Donalson, Jim Erickson, John Foreman of the *Champaign* (Illinois) *News-Gazette*, Duane Heisinger, Chad Hill, Wes Hoyt, Larry Gundrum, John Gunn, Mirana Medina, Rick Meixsel, Rick Rocamora, Richard Roper, Bruce Smith, Michael Sweeney, and Allan Winkler.

I'd also like to thank Brian Gallagher, Matt Griffith, Rich and Jessica Oskin, Christy Reese, Brad Spier, Mike Talmadge, and James Torrance for their couches, cars, and consideration as I Kerouacked across the country on research trips.

I am indebted to the Grashio family for permission to quote at length from Grashio's memoirs, *Return to Freedom*; the Shofner family for permission to quote from Austin Shofner's diary and other accounts; and Jack Hawkins to quote from his book, *Never Say Die*, and his unpublished film treatment. I'd also like to thank Bill Nugent and the Marajen Stevick Chinigo Estate for permission to quote extensively from *The Dyess Story*. In instances where I was unable to locate copyright holders, every effort will be made to provide proper credit in future editions.

If not for my agent, Gail Ross, this story would likely never have been told. Jenna Free, formerly of the Gail Ross Literary Agency, deserves a substantial amount of credit for helping sculpt an abstract idea into this book.

If intrepidity in editing leadership were a valorous action, my editor, Bob Bender, would deserve to be decorated. His understanding, talent, and patience are remarkable. Without Bob, I would not have made it out of the swamp.

I'd also like to thank Johanna Li of Simon & Schuster for her assistance, and Fred Chase for superb copyediting.

And while I credit all of the aforementioned for their help, any errors found in this work, factual or otherwise, are my responsibility.

John D. Lukacs
The Royal Hawaiian Hotel
Honolulu, Hawaii
December 6, 2009

Notes

PROLOGUE

PAGE

2 *WILL ARRIVE CHICAGO:* Western Union telegram from Dyess to wife Marajen Stevick Dyess, August 12, 1943, Dyess Papers, Southwest Collection, Special Collections Library, Texas Tech University Library, Lubbock, TX.

2 *"little more than a glimpse":* *Abilene Reporter-News* (Texas), November 8, 1943.

2 *But mystery had surrounded:* *Albany News,* July 29, 1943; *Fort Worth Star-Telegram,* July 24, 1943; *Esquire,* May 1943.

3 *"One-Man Scourge of the Japs":* *New York Times,* July 26, 1942.

3 *when a brief, cryptic message:* *Fort Worth Star-Telegram,* July 24, 1943.

3 *MacArthur, the first to hear:* Colonel Allison Ind, *Allied Intelligence Bureau: Our Secret Weapon in the War Against Japan* (New York: David McKay, 1958), 180.

3 *"the greatest story of the war in the Pacific":* *Fort Worth Star-Telegram,* January 29, 1944.

1. TEN PESOS

PAGE

7 *"Soldierman, sailorman and pioneer":* Henry Lee, "Manila," *Nothing but Praise* (Pasadena, CA.: Philippine Arts Council, Pacific Asia Museum, 1985), 12.

7 *from all corners of the United States:* William H. Bartsch, *Doomed at the Start: American Pursuit Pilots in the Philippines, 1941–1942* (College Station: Texas A&M University Press, 1992), 436–40.

7 *1939 Hollywood blockbuster:* I. B. "Jack" Donalson, author's interview.

7 *With crossed arms:* Lt. Col. Wm. E. Dyess, *The Dyess Story,* edited, with a biographical introduction, by Charles Leavelle (New York: G. P. Putnam's Sons, 1944), 27.

8 *"Men, you are not a suicide squadron yet:"* Ibid., 27.

8 *Pursuit George, as was his way:* Lt. Col. Allison Ind, *Bataan: The Judgment Seat* (New York, Macmillan, 1944), 3.

8 *George paused:* Dyess, *The Dyess Story,* 27.

8 *had watched the winds of war whip:* Letter from Lt. Col. Ray Hunt, USAF (Ret.), to the Commander, American Defenders of Bataan and Corregidor, 1981.

8 *According to Japan's militarists:* Willis Lamott, *Nippon: The Crime and Punishment of Japan* (New York: John Day, 1944), 92–93; John Dower, *War Without Mercy* (New York: Pantheon, 1986), 273–74.

8 *The annexations of Formosa, Korea, and Manchuria:* Brig. Gen. Steve Mellnik, *Philippine Diary: 1939–1945* (New York: Van Nostrand Reinhold, 1969), 4.

8 *By the summer of 1941:* Louis Morton, *U.S. Army in World War II: The War in the Pacific: The Fall of the Philippines* (Washington, D.C.: Center of Military History, United States Army, 1989), 17–18.

9 *The relentless climate:* Gen. Douglas MacArthur, *Reminiscences* (New York: McGraw-Hill, 1964), 84; "Transcript of Interview with Brig. Gen. Stephen Michael Mellnik, U.S.A., Retired"—Conducted at Fort Bliss, TX, December 13, 1983, by Charles E. Kirkpatrick (cited hereafter as Kirkpatrick interview).

9 *in a universal lethargy:* Duane Schultz, *Hero of Bataan: The Story of General Jonathan M. Wainwright* (New York: St. Martin's, 1981), 43; John W. Whitman, *Bataan: Our Last Ditch* (New York: Hippocrene, 1990), 25.

9 *An exchange rate:* Malcolm Amos, author's interview; e-mail correspondence from Louis B. Read, to the author, October 20, 2004.

9 *bunks neat and their shoes shined:* E-mail correspondence from Louis B. Read, October 20, 2004; Anton Bilek; author's interview; e-mail correspondence from Joe Merritt to the author, October 26, 2004.

9 *most were energetic young officers:* E-mail correspondence from Joe Merritt, October 26, 2004; Samuel C. Grashio and Bernand Norling, *Return to Freedom* (Spokane: Gonzaga University Press, 1982), 33.

9 *Poker, baseball, and air-conditioned double features:* Anton Bilek, in collaboration with Gene O'Connell, *No Uncle Sam: The Forgotten of Bataan* (Kent, OH: Kent State University Press, 2003), 4; Anton Bilek, author's interview.

9 *Clark Field and Fort Stotsenburg:* E-mail correspondence from Richard B. Meixsel to the author, February 1, 2005.

9 *slugged ice-cold bottles:* Bilek, *No Uncle Sam*, 4.

9 *The real action, however:* E-mail correspondence from Clyde Childress to the author, December 13, 2004.

9 *Santa Ana Cabaret:* E-mail correspondence from Louis Read to the author, October 23, 2004.

9 *sailors drank at the Silver Dollar:* "The Cruiser Houston," online exhibit hosted by the University of Houston, Special Collections Library, http://info.lib.uh.edu/sca/digital/cruiser/onboard.htm.

9 *air redolent of jasmine, sewage:* Mellnik, *Philippine Diary*, 5.

9 *Officers mingled:* E-mail correspondence from Clyde Childress to the author, December 13, 2004.

10 *MacArthur also suffered:* The Japanese had perhaps as many as six million troops, many of which were veterans of the China war, under arms; William Manchester, *American Caesar* (New York: Dell, 1978), 211–12; Morton, *The Fall of the Philippines*, 24.

10 *Ten Philippine Army reserve divisions:* Quoted from Col. Clifford Bluemel, 31st

Division, Philippine Army, Report of Operations, in Morton, *The Fall of the Philippines*, 30.

10 *The American and Filipino soldiers:* MacArthur, *Reminiscences*, 110.

10 *Glaringly, there were no tanks:* According to Morton, *The Fall of the Philippines*, 33, the first armored units, the 192nd and 194th Tank Battalions, each consisting of fifty-four M-3 Stuart light tanks, arrived in November 1941.

10 *Hangars throughout the archipelago:* Morton, *The Fall of the Philippines*, 23; Bartsch, *Doomed at the Start*, 2.

10 *The Asiatic Fleet was still anchored:* Morton, *The Fall of the Philippines*, 46.

10 *"a little stick which the United States":* Clark Lee, *They Call it Pacific: An Eye-witness Story of Our War Against Japan* (New York: Viking, 1943), 121.

10 *He deemed War Plan Orange:* Manchester, *American Caesar*, 213

10 *Envisioning the Philippines:* Morton, *The Fall of the Philippines*, 31–50, 64–65.

11 *Stimson and Marshall:* Henry L. Stimson and McGeorge Bundy, *On Active Service in Peace and War* (New York: Harper Brothers, 1947, 1948), 388–89.

11 *A shortage of transports:* Louis Morton, *U.S. Army in World War II: The War in the Pacific: Strategy and Command: The First Two Years* (Washington, D.C.: Office of the Chief of Military History, Department of the Army, 1962), 99; *Time*, December 15, 1941.

11 *Lieutenant Dyess, for example:* William H. Bartsch, *December 8, 1941: MacArthur's Pearl Harbor* (College Station: Texas A&M University Press, 2003), 246–47.

11 *There was hardly any engine coolant:* Ind, *Bataan*, 18.

11 *"The inability of an enemy":* Ibid., 193.

12 *Imperial General Headquarters:* Ibid., 422.

12 *An unidentified plane:* Ibid., 235–37.

12 *Since the blips meshed:* Bartsch, *December 8, 1941*, 194.

12 *MacArthur ordered his B-17s:* MacArthur, *Reminiscences*, 113. The B-17s that did fly 500 miles to the south on the island of Mindanao landed at Del Monte Field, which was originally a fairway of a golf course hacked from the vast pineapple fields of the Del Monte Corporation. Karl C. Dod, *The Corps of Engineers: The War Against Japan* (Washington, D.C.: Official Center for Military History, 1966), 65.

12 *a bustling, multicultural historical intersection:* Mellnik, *Philippine Diary*, 5, 35; Schultz, *Hero of Bataan*, 45–46.

12 *John Dyess, a Welshman:* Dyess, *The Dyess Story*, 13.

12 *a position he would hold:* Elizabeth Nell Denman, author's interview.

12 *Hallie and Richard Dyess:* E-mail correspondence from Elizabeth Nell Denman to the author, April 4, 2004.

12 *Doc Holliday and Wyatt Earp: Texas Monthly*, June 2003, 92.

12 *Father and son were inseparable:* Ibid.

13 *a fascination with flight: Abilene Reporter-News* (Texas), September 9, 1956.

13 *he worked several jobs:* Elizabeth Nell Denman, author's interview.

13   *Dyess was the school's ranking:* Ibid; *J-Tac*, student publication of John Tarleton Agricultural College, February 15, 1944.

13   *intending to enroll in the law school:* Dyess, *The Dyess Story*, 15–16; e-mail correspondence from Elizabeth Nell Denman to the author, July 23, 2004.

13   *"Son," Judge Dyess promised:* Dyess, *The Dyess Story*, 16.

13   *A Presbyterian who had embraced:* E-mail correspondence from Elizabeth Nell Denman to the author, July 23, 2004.

13   *"Mother," he would reply:* Hallie Dyess, quoted in *Abilene Reporter-News* (Texas), April 23, 1974.

13   *he stood six foot one:* E-mail correspondence from Elizabeth Nell Denman to the author, October 15, 2005.

13   *At Hamilton Field:* Letter from Ray Hunt to the Commander, American Defenders of Bataan and Corregidor, 1981.

13   *"You look like":* Ibid.

14   *"He was intelligent":* Grashio, *Return to Freedom*, 7.

14   *"PLUM":* Ibid., 2.

14   *Jack Donohoe:* Jack Donohoe, author's interview.

14   *At Pearl Harbor, the Coolidge:* Walter D. Edmonds, *They Fought with What They Had: The Story of the Army Air Forces in the Southwest Pacific, 1941–1942* (Boston: Little, Brown, 1951), 49–50.

14   *The Japanese, declared the officers:* Grashio, *Return to Freedom*, 2; *Fortune*, February 1942, 53; Ind, *Bataan*, 3. The most famous manifestation of this national hubris, however, was the declaration of Secretary of the Navy Frank Knox, who, while puffing on an after-dinner cigar just three days before the attack on Pearl Harbor, reportedly announced that a conflict with Japan "won't take too long . . . say about a six-months' war." See Bruce Catton, *The Warlords of Washington* (New York: Harcourt, Brace & World, 1948), 9.

15   *He concluded with an estimate:* Dyess, *The Dyess Story*, 27.

15   *"I'll bet you five pesos":* Grashio, *Return to Freedom*, 2.

15   *Grashio had just fallen back asleep:* Ibid., 3–4.

15   *Four, in fact:* Dyess, *The Dyess Story*, 29.

16   *For the ABCD powers:* Morton, *The Fall of the Philippines*, 77.

16   *Word of the Pearl Harbor attack:* Ibid., 79–83.

16   *It has been speculated:* Manchester, *American Caesar*, 230–35; Bartsch, *December 8, 1941*, 282.

16   *Shortly after receiving:* Bartsch, *December 8, 1941*, 282–83.

16   *At 1015 Formosa time:* Morton, *The Fall of the Philippines*, 84.

17   *At 1145:* Bartsch, *December 8, 1941*, 301.

17   *"Tally ho, Clark Field!":* Dyess, *The Dyess Story*, 30.

17   *While Dyess led:* Grashio, *Return to Freedom*, 4–5.

17   *Growing up, Grashio was competitive:* Devonia Grashio and Samuel E. Grashio, author's interview.

17   *"119 pounds of condensed dynamite":* *Spokane Spokesman-Review*, date unknown.

18 *Nevertheless, much like his father:* Devonia Grashio, author's interview; Grashio, *Return to Freedom*, 1.

18 *"Ed . . . took me right under his wing":* Chicago Tribune, January 29, 1944.

18 *"as smooth as glass":* Grashio, *Return to Freedom*, 5.

18 *until 1220 hours:* Ibid.

18 *"All P-40s return to Clark Field":* Ibid.

18 *It was about 1230:* Bartsch, *December 8, 1941*, 318–20.

18 *The Japanese bombardiers:* Morton, *The Fall of the Philippines*, 86; Manchester, *American Caesar*, 237–38; Saburo Sakai, *Samurai!* (New York: Bantam, 1978), 47.

19 *"how utterly and abysmally wrong":* Grashio, *Return to Freedom*, 5–6.

19 *In seconds, the hunters had become:* Ibid., 6; Sakai, *Samurai!*, 50.

20 *"I was sure I was going to die:"* Sakai, *Samurai!*, 6; Bartsch, *December 8, 1941*, 328.

20 *"Never try to outmaneuver a Zero":* Sakai, *Samurai!*, 6.

20 *When Grashio touched down:* Bartsch, *December 8, 1941*, 375.

20 *"By God, they ain't shootin' spitballs":* Dyess, *The Dyess Story*, 30.

20 *the order came in to abandon Nichols Field:* Bartsch, *December 8, 1941*, 393.

20 *"eerie glow":* Dyess, *The Dyess Story*, 30.

20 *"We got kicked in the teeth":* Joe Moore, author's interview.

20 *Despite sufficient advance warning:* Bartsch, *December 8, 1941*, 409.

21 *"Oh, God help us":* Lt. Cmdr. Charles "Chick" Parsons, Oral History, U.S. Naval Institute, Annapolis, MD, 128. Surprisingly, there would be scarcely a murmur of inquiry from Washington regarding the disastrous events of December 8, 1941, on Luzon. Brereton received only a dressing-down from Arnold and Marshall refrained from discussing the calamity with MacArthur, though weeks later he did wonder aloud in the presence of a reporter: "I just don't know how MacArthur happened to let his planes get caught on the ground." Unlike what transpired following the attack on Pearl Harbor, there would be no scapegoats, no official inquiries. Responsibility for the catastrophe would never be assigned. For a more detailed examination of these crucial events, see Bartsch, *December 8, 1941*, 410–24, and Morton, *The Fall of the Philippines*, 88–90.

2. A LONG WAR

PAGE

22 *"No time to falter or catch":* Henry Lee, "Abucay Withdrawal (Pilar Bagac Road)," *Nothing but Praise*, 15.

22 *McCoy had graduated from Annapolis:* Col. Jack Hawkins, USMC (Ret.), author's interview.

22 *Through orders and scuttlebutt:* Morton, *The Fall of the Philippines*, 161.

22 *With no air force, no navy:* Ibid., 90–97; MacArthur, *Reminiscences*, 121–26.

23 *The landing of Gen. Masaharu Homma's 14th Army:* Morton, *The Fall of the Philippines*, 98–114.

23   *Just barely ahead of them:* Ibid., 165–89; John Toland, *The Rising Sun: The Decline and Fall of the Japanese Empire, 1936–1945*, Volume 1 (New York: Random House, 1970), 314.

23   *All around him:* Edward Dissette and H. C. Adamson, *Guerrilla Submarines* (New York: Ballantine, 1972), 42; John Toland, *But Not in Shame: The Six Months After Pearl Harbor* (New York: Random House, 1961), 115; Ind, *Bataan*, 188; Lee, *They Call It Pacific*, 135; Mellnik, *Philippine Diary*, 50; Morton, *The Fall of the Philippines*, 165, 179, 234.

23   *Fired tanks containing millions of gallons:* Morton, *The Fall of the Pacific*, 164; Lee, *They Call It Pacific*, 153; Toland, *But Not in Shame*, 142.

23   *A rising tide of terror:* Morton, *The Fall of the Philippines*, 116, 232; Toland, *The Rising Sun*, 315.

23   *a gifted prodigy:* Biography of Rear Admiral Melvyn H. McCoy, U.S.N. (Ret.), Navy Office of Information, Internal Relations Division, March 27, 1968, 1.

24   *"It was as the Czar of Math":* *The Lucky Bag*, 1928, Nimitz Library, U.S. Naval Academy, Special Collections and Archives Division.

24   *Though he could be coldly cerebral:* Jack Hawkins, author's interview.

24   *After assignments in Nicaragua:* Biography of McCoy, 1.

24   *These lonely forays:* Lt. Commander Melvyn H. McCoy, Letters home from Canlaon, September 17, 1941, and Banahao, Philippines, November 6, 1941, Personal Papers.

24   *"It doesn't do her much justice":* *Evening Sun* (Baltimore), January 28, 1944.

24   *The hands of 1st Lt. Austin Shofner's wristwatch:* Lt. Austin C. Shofner, "Diary: 1941–1943" (unpublished), 160.

25   *Ordinarily, the Marine did not smoke:* Austin Shofner told Bill Smallwood that "I started smoking on Corregidor; you can't believe the starvation we went through."

25   *He had brought that infectious optimism:* Shofner, "Diary: 1941–1943," 160; Kenneth W. Condit and Edwin T. Turnbladh, *Hold High the Torch: A History of the 4th Marines* (Washington, D.C.: Historical Branch, G-3 Division, Headquarters, U.S. Marine Corps, 1960), 204.

25   *It was not long after that:* Austin Shofner, Smallwood interview.

25   *Located at the maw of Manila Bay:* Ibid., 206; Mellnik, *Philippine Diary*, 5–11; *Marine Corps Gazette*, November 1946; Morton, *The Fall of the Philippines*, 471–78.

25   *"Corregidor was indeed a mighty fortress":* Clark Lee, "Everybody Knew When the Planes Were Coming," in Samuel Hynes and Anne Matthews et al., *Reporting World War II: Part One: American Journalism, 1938–1944* (New York: Literary Classics of the United States Penguin, 1995), 303.

25   *Most of the Marines:* J. Michael Miller, *From Shanghai to Corregidor: Marines in the Defense of the Philippines* (Washington, D.C., Marines in World War II Commemorative Series, Marine Corps Historical Center, 1997), 18.

25   *Lieutenant Shofner jumped to his feet:* Shofner, "Diary: 1941–1943," 160.

25   *Corregidor's "antiquity" up close:* Austin Shofner, Smallwood interview.

25 *The soles of his spit-shined:* E-mail correspondence from Donald Versaw to the author, September 11, 2005.

26 *"I wanted to go out and see":* Shofner, "Guerrilla Diary" (unpublished), 2.

26 *Eighteen bombers:* Morton, *The Fall of the Philippines,* 480.

26 *men and machine guns chattered away:* Shofner, "Guerrilla Diary," 2.

26 *The twinkling of the metal bombs:* Shofner, "Diary: 1941–1943," 160.

26 *"I couldn't tell what their targets were":* Austin Shofner, Smallwood interview.

26 *His father had always told him:* Shofner, *Nashville Banner,* May 28, 1984.

26 *Shofner learned the values:* Ibid.; Stewart Shofner, author's interview. Austin Shofner, Smallwood interview.

26 *His gridiron prowess:* Austin Shofner, Smallwood interview.

26 *"Football Maxims":* As Austin Shofner and any Tennessee football player who played under legendary coach Robert Neyland would attest, Neyland's famed "Football Maxims" were not just the foundation of Neyland's highly successful eighteen-year coaching career in Knoxville, they were also an essential part of his plan for educating his charges to be successful in their endeavors away from the gridiron. According to the research of one of Neyland's former players, 1950s fullback Andy Kozar, Neyland's thirty-eight total maxims were derived from the six original axioms of another West Pointer who had a major impact on Neyland's life and career, the Army football coach known as the "Godfather of West Point Football," Charles Daly. Daly's axioms were divided into two categories, "Football Axioms" and "Game Axioms." Daly's "Football Axioms" were as follows: "1) Football is a battle. Go out to fight and keep it up all afternoon. 2) A man's value to his team varies inversely as his distance from the ball. 3) If the line goes forward the team wins; if the line comes backward the team loses." Daly's "Game Axioms": "1) Make and play for the breaks. When one comes your way, score. 2) If the game or a break goes against you, don't lie down—put on more steam. 3) Don't save yourself. Go the limit. There are good men on the side line, when you are exhausted." For more information, see Robert Reese Neyland and Dr. Andrew Kozar, *Football as a War Game: The Annotated Journals of General R. R. Neyland* (Knoxville, TN: Falcon 2002); Andy Kozar, "Neyland's Maxims," *College Football Historical Society* 16, no. 2 (February 2003).

26 *"There aren't many like Neyland":* Shofner, *Nashville Banner,* May 28, 1984.

27 *His uncanny ability to motivate:* Stewart Shofner, author's interview.

27 *supposedly bombproof Middleside Barracks:* Condit and Turnbladh, *Hold High the Torch,* 204.

27 *Shofner ordered a dentist:* Shofner, "Diary: 1941–1943," 161.

27 *"Suddenly," Shofner would say:* Shofner, "Guerrilla Diary," 2.

27 *Twenty-five miles in length:* Morton, *The Fall of the Philippines,* 245; Manchester, *American Caesar,* 267.

27 *nearly 80,000 American and Filipino troops:* Toland, *But Not in Shame,* 124–25.

27 *They came from all corners:* Ibid., 124; Ind, *Bataan,* 183;

28 *swollen cataracts of men, animals, and machines:* Ind, *Bataan,* 179.

28 *Following closely behind:* Toland, *But Not in Shame*, 118.

28 *"small Dunkirk":* Lt. John Posten of the 17th Pursuit Squadron, as quoted in Bartsch, *Doomed at the Start*, 197.

28 *carrying with it large stores:* Whitman, *Bataan*, 49.

28 *The abandonment of 5,000 tons of rice:* Despite the dire situation, overzealous Filipino officials adhered to commonwealth regulations that forbade the transfer of rice between provinces, ibid., 46. Even more shockingly, nearly 2,000 cases of canned fish and corned beef were not confiscated from Japanese wholesalers because USAFFE had placed a prohibition on such seizures, ibid., 46–47.

28 *MacArthur had also ordered:* Morton, *The Fall of the Philippines*, 255.

28 *The madness of the retreat:* Ibid., 254.

29 *On January 5, 1942:* Ibid., 257.

29 *loaded with suspect ammunition:* William B. Breuer, *The Great Raid: Rescuing the Doomed Ghosts of Bataan and Corregidor* (New York: Hyperion, 2002), 10, 26.

29 *waiting . . . for help from the States:* Ibid., 238–42.

3. THE RAID

PAGE

30 *"We only know our candle":* Henry Lee, "Prison Camp Reverie (Three Years from Home)," *Nothing but Praise*, 45.

30 *German forces controlled territory:* John Mosier, *Cross of Iron* (New York: Henry Holt, 2006), 180–81; Winston Groom, *1942: The Year that Tried Men's Souls* (New York: Atlantic Monthly Press, 2005), 157.

30 *it was feared that:* James K. Eyre, Jr., *The Roosevelt-MacArthur Conflict* (Chambersburg, PA: Craft Press, 1950), 68; David Brinkley, *Washington Goes to War: The Extraordinary, Story of the Transformation of a City, and a Nation* (New York: Ballantine, 1988), 91–92.

30 *gave way to mass hysteria:* William B. Breuer, *The Air-Raid Warden Was a Spy, and Other Tales from Home-Front America in World War II* (Edison, NJ: Castle, 2005), 14–16.

30 *Japanese submarines sank merchant vessels:* Ibid., 8; Richard Lingeman, *Don't You Know There's a War On?: The American Homefront, 1941–1945* (New York: Thunder's Mouth Press/Nation Books, 2003), 44, 63, 169.

30 *One elected official:* Toland, *The Rising Sun*, 297.

30 *The original copies:* Groom, *1942*.

31 *Roosevelt signed Executive Order 9066:* Lingeman, *Don't You Know There's a War On?*, 337–42; Dower, *War Without Mercy*, 79–81.

31 *America's romantic fascination:* Condit and Turnbladh, *Hold High the Torch*, 195.

31 *In an April panegyric:* Life, April 13, 1942.

31 *war celebrities:* New York Times, January 30, 1942; 105; Life, March 16, 1942; Time, February, 23, 1942.

31 *seemed heaven-sent to a nation:* Eyre, *The Roosevelt-MacArthur Conflict*, 60.

31 *Streets in large cities and small towns: Life*, March 30, 1942.

31 *Buoyed by messages from Washington:* Manchester, *American Caesar*, 270–71; Morton, *Strategy and Command*, 151; MacArthur, *Reminiscences*, 127.

32 *"Help is on the way":* MacArthur's typed communiqué, issued by Col. Carl H. Seals, adjutant general, was distributed to all USAFFE commanders on Bataan on January 15, 1942. College Park, MD: National Archives and Records Administration (cited hereafter as NARA), RG 407, Philippine Archives Collection, Box 12.

32 *And so the defenders:* Ray C. Hunt and Bernard Norling, *Behind Japanese Lines: An American Guerrilla in the Philippines* (New York Pocket, 1988), 25; Whitman, *Bataan*, 452.

32 *FDR had cabled President Quezon:* Manchester, *American Caesar*, 272.

32 *With the German and Italian declarations of war:* Morton, *Strategy and Command*, 143.

32 *America's ill-prepared military: The World Almanac and Book of Facts* (New York: New York World-Telegram, 1939), 948.

32 *According to Field Marshal Sir John Dill:* Field Marshal Alan Brooke (1st Viscount Alanbrooke), *Diaries* (London: Collins, 1957–1958), 292–93.

32 *At the end of the three-week Arcadia Conference:* Morton, *Strategy and Command*, 158–59.

32 *In his fireside chat:* President Franklin D. Roosevelt, "On Progress of the War," February 23, 1942, President Franklin D. Roosevelt Library, Hyde Park, NY.

33 *He was not told, however, that the convoys were not intended for the Philippines:* As Manchester explains in *American Caesar*, 275, "the White House and War Department were raising false hopes in the doomed Philippines, but they weren't guilty of malice." The most notable instance of this strategy regarding the Philippines concerns the *Pensacola* convoy, one of several American convoys that would sail from the United States for the Pacific in the early weeks of the war, but were instead destined for Australia or other outposts. The large convoy led by the heavy cruiser *Pensacola* was originally scheduled to arrive in the Philippines in the second week of December, but had been diverted to Brisbane shortly after the commencement of hostilities. The ships had been loaded with nearly 5,000 men, 9,000 gallons of aviation fuel, hundreds of trucks and jeeps, four dozen 75-millimeter guns, almost four million rounds of machine gun ammunition, 600 tons of bombs, fifty-two A-24 dive-bombers, and eighteen P-40s. Although this matériel would serve a vital role in the establishment of an operating base in Australia, one can only imagine what such a force could have meant in turning the tide of battle in the Philippines.

33 *pullout from the Philippines:* Eyre, *The Roosevelt-MacArthur Conflict*, 60, 66; a man who spent a considerable amount of time in the Philippines as MacArthur's aide, General Dwight D. Eisenhower, concurred, stating that the peoples of the Far East "will be watching us. They may excuse failure but they will

not excuse abandonment." Eisenhower, *Crusade in Europe: A Personal Account of World War II* (Garden City, NY: Doubleday, 1948), 22.

33 *"There are times"*: Manchester, *American Caesar*, 274.

33 *As mechanics on Bataan scrounged*: Lend-Lease records, NARA, Records of the Office of War Information, RG 208, Box 968.

33 *In March, exports to the Soviet Union*: *Chicago Tribune*, February 14, 1944.

33 *"following an intensive and well-planned campaign"*: FDR, quoted in *Time*, January 5, 1942.

33 *On Christmas Day 1941*: Toland, *The Rising Sun*, 318.

33 *"American war supplies were speeded"*: *Chicago Tribune*, February 14, 1944; Eyre, *The Roosevelt-MacArthur Conflict*, 79.

34 *A vociferous campaign for a greater effort*: Ibid., 67.

34 *In January, Senator James E. Murray*: *New York Times*, January 29, 1942.

34 *That someone was an obscure*: Eisenhower, *Crusade in Europe*, 12.

34 *The two men met on December 14*: Ibid., 16–22.

34 *"a problem that defied solution"*: Ibid., 22.

34 *Submarines brought in some supplies*: Ibid., 24–25.

34 *"I've been insisting"*: Ibid., 22, 31.

34 *One Japanese general*: Gen. Susumu Morioka, commanding officer of the Japanese 16th Division, quoted in Morton, *The Fall of the Philippines*, 218.

34 *"battle-hardened, vicious"*: Unknown officer quoted in Thaddeus Holt, "King of Bataan," in Robert Cowley, ed., *No End Save Victory: Perspectives on World War II* (New York: Putnam, 2001), 159.

34 *The once maligned "dogfaces"*: Lou Kolger, in an e-mail to the author on November 28, 2004, affirmed that the term "dogface" was a derivative of the discriminatory signs that adorned many business establishments in the prewar United States that read "No Dogs or Soldiers Allowed." "Hence soldiers affectionately called one another Dog-Face," explained Kolger. Although the term "GI," which stems from the phrase "government issue" and came to describe anything such as clothing or equipment issued to military personnel, was reportedly in Army use since circa 1935, its meaning in terms of being a descriptor for an enlisted soldier or member of the armed forces "did not really take hold until the last half of the war." See Harold Wentworth and Stuart Berg Flexner, *Dictionary of American Slang* (New York: Thomas Y. Crowell, 1975), 213; Paul Dickson, *War Slang: American Fighting Words and Phrases from the Civil War to the Gulf War* (New York: Pocket, 1994), 163.

35 *So high was their morale*: *New York Times*, March 2, 1942.

35 *They took immense pride*: Henry Lee, "Vindication," *Nothing but Praise*, 49.

35 *When General Homma attempted to land*: For detailed information on the Battle of the Points, the Battle of Trail 2, and the Battle of the Pockets, see Morton, *The Fall of the Philippines*, 296–332.

35 *Homma would request reinforcements*: Ibid., 332; MacArthur, *Reminiscences*, 132; e-mail correspondence from Louis Read to the author, December 16, 2004.

35 *As MacArthur would later exclaim*: Morton, *The Fall of the Philippines*, 291.

35 *Unscrupulous quartermasters:* Ibid., 372–73; Juanita Redmond, *I Served on Bataan* (Philadelphia: J. B. Lippincott, 1943), 80.

35 *As the daily ration dwindled:* Luzon Force surgeon Lt. Col. Harold W. Glattly estimated that defense of line required an expenditure of energy of at least 3,500 to 4,000 calories a day for each man, Morton, *The Fall of the Phillippines*, 377; Dyess, *The Dyess Story*, 48.

35 *In March, Wainwright:* Schultz, *Hero of Bataan*, 194–95; Gavan Daws, *Prisoners of the Japanese: POWs of World War II in the Pacific* (New York: William Morrow, 1994), 68.

35 *The ravenous troops:* Grashio, *Return to Freedom*, 18. Dyess, *The Dyess Story*, 39–40.

36 *Doctors, nurses, and medics:* Morton, *The Fall of the Philippines*, 376–84; Whitman, *Bataan*, 394, 397–99; Condit and Turnbladh, *Hold High the Torch*, 226; Redmond, *I Served on Bataan*; 56.

36 *Between bombings:* Groom, *1942*, 147–48; John Hersey, *Men on Bataan* (New York: Alfred A. Knopf, 1942), 283.

36 *One note—an attempt at alleviating:* Letter from Dyess to parents, March 10, 1942, Texas Tech University Library, Lubbock.

37 *They also tuned in music:* Mallonée, *The Naked Flagpole*, 108; Redmond, *I Served on Bataan*, 102.

37 *It was on Bataan that the famous:* Richard S. Roper, *Brothers of Paul: Activities of Prisoner of War Chaplains in the Philippines During World War II* (Odenton, MD: Revere, 2003), 90.

37 *The thunder bursts of sea storms:* E-mail correspondence from Louis Read to the author, December 16, 2004; Morton, *The Fall of the Philippines*, 387.

37 *despite the best Japanese efforts:* Toland, *But Not in Shame*, 267; Morton, *The Fall of the Philippines*, 384–85; Redmond, *I Served on Bataan*, 86–89.

37 *After reporting on the losing battle:* Morton, *The Fall of the Philippines*, 367.

37 *"The truth":* Hersey, *Men on Bataan*, 257.

37 *Edgy troops on Bataan:* Schultz, *Hero of Bataan*, 159.

37 *Many were displeased:* Ibid., 163.

37 *"Where the devil":* Lee, *They Call It Pacific*, 224.

37 *Lt. John Burns of the 21st Pursuit:* Burns diary entry (unpublished), February 15, 1942.

38 *While they never completely gave up hope:* Toland, *But Not in Shame*, 186; Mallonée, *The Naked Flagpole*, 111, Ind, *Bataan*, 303.

38 *On Corregidor, Quezon became combustible:* MacArthur, *Reminiscences*, 138.

38 *They also resented MacArthur:* Whitman, *Bataan*, 389; Breuer, *The Great Raid*, 19.

38 *After the arrival of a newborn:* Schultz, *Hero of Bataan*, 164.

38 *Some soldiers attempted to raise money:* New York Times, February 25, 1942.

38 *Months earlier, some soldiers:* Toland, *The Rising Sun*, 387.

38 *At 1125 hours, a mysterious voice:* Ind, *Bataan*, 306–7.

39 *While en route to George's quarters:* Dyess, *The Dyess Story*, 51–52.

39 *Dyess bounded up onto the porch*: Ibid., 52; Ind, *Bataan*, 307.

40 *Lt. John Posten commenced the mission*: Bartsch, *Doomed at the Start*, 329.

40 *At 1350, a crowd gathered*: Ibid., 329–30; Ind, *Bataan*, 309–10.

40 *Thirty air miles*: Dyess, *The Dyess Story*, 52–59; Bartsch, *Doomed at the Start*, 330.

41 *Safely on the ground at Bataan Field*: Ind, *Bataan*, 310–11; Dyess, *The Dyess Story*, 52–59.

41 *Twilight was fast approaching and Dyess*: Ibid., 312–13; Bartsch, *Doomed at the Start*, 332.

42 *George was hesitant*: Dyess, *The Dyess Story*, 55.

42 *Entering his dive at sundown*: Ibid., 55–58; Bartsch, *Doomed at the Start*, 332–34.

43 *"It was like flying down Broadway"*: Dyess, *The Dyess Story*, 58.

43 *"It was stuff much too strong"*: Ind, *Bataan*, 317.

43 *including Lt. Sam Grashio*: Ibid., 314.

43 *Dyess's individual exploits were staggering*: Dyess, *The Dyess Story*, 58.

43 *Radio Tokyo reported*: Ind, *Bataan*, 323.

43 *cement Dyess's legend*: For more information on Dyess's exploits as an infantry commander on Bataan, see *The Dyess Story*, 40–45; Morton, *The Fall of the Philippines*, 310–12; and Bartsch, *Doomed at the Start*, 295–302.

43 *The price of the victory*: Ibid., 335.

43 *Crellin's death*: Dyess, *The Dyess Story*, 59.

44 *"At least the death of our little air force"*: Ind, *Bataan*, 322.

44 *It was later discovered that George*: Ibid., 320–22.

44 *George wasted little time*: Dyess, *The Dyess Story*, 50.

44 *That evening, a silvery tropical moon*: Ibid., 50–51; Bartsch, *Doomed at the Start*, 336.

44 *"Had forgotten"*: Burns diary entry.

44 *By Dyess's accounting*: Dyess, *The Dyess Story*, 60.

44 *"Jesus Christ"*: Anton Bilek, author's interview.

44 *Surveying the scene*: Bilek, *No Uncle Sam*, 40.

4. GOD HELP THEM

PAGE

46 *"I felt my way with weary"*: Henry Lee, "Awakening," *Nothing but Praise*, 37.

46 *"How are things going over there?"*: At the request of 20th Century–Fox studio chief Darryl Zanuck in early 1944, Jack Hawkins prepared a 377-page treatment of the story of his capture, captivity, and escape from the Japanese in the Philippines in anticipation of making a feature film. The project, however, was never greenlighted. Nearly two decades later, the unpublished, uncensored film treatment became the basis for Hawkins's 1961 memoir, *Never Say Die*. The cornerstone of this narrative, this unedited source was discovered by the author in the personal papers of Austin Shofner in Nashville, Tennessee, and will be cited

hereafter as Jack Hawkins, film treatment. The material that corresponds to this particular notation is found on page 6.

46 *Unlike most of the 4th Marines:* Condit and Turnbladh, *Hold High the Torch*, 201; Miller, *From Shanghai to Corregidor*, 11–14.

46 *"It looks kind of bad, Jack":* Hawkins, film treatment, 6–8.

47 *twenty-five-year-old, straight-shooting Texan:* Ibid., 2.

47 *For an Annapolis plebe:* Jack Hawkins, author's interview.

47 *While growing up in the northeastern Texas:* Ibid.

48 *For Mike Dobervich:* Lois Dobervich and Robert Dobervich, author's interviews.

48 *"Minnesota Yankee":* Hawkins, film treatment, 4–5.

48 *"He talked":* Ibid.

48 *They would be roommates:* Jack Hawkins, author's interview.

48 *since the late 1920s: Marine Corps Gazette*, November 1946.

48 *By late 1941, the Japanese had encircled:* William R. Evans, *Soochow and the 4th Marines* (Rogue River, OR: Atwood, 1987), 35; *The Marine Corps Gazette*, November 1946; Jack Hawkins, author's interview; Austin Shofner, Smallwood interview.

49 *"Gee, that was good":* Hawkins, film treatment, 8–9.

49 *As the chief mechanic:* Leo Boelens, "Diary" 18.

49 *It would not be Boelens's first:* Dyess, *The Dyess Story*, 60; Bartsch, *Doomed at the Start*, 338.

50 *"I predict the beginning of the end":* Boelens, "Diary," 18.

50 *Sunk in January off Mariveles:* Bartsch, *Doomed at the Start*, 338, 348; Dyess, *The Dyess Story*, 46–48; Grashio, *Return to Freedom*, 30.

50 *The Duck, though, had delivered:* Bartsch, *Doomed at the Start*, 366–67.

50 *Leo Boelens, the youngest:* Thelma Kost, author's interview; e-mail correspondence from Thelma Kost to the author, November 21, 2004; J. Tom Davis, *Glimpses of Greybull's Past: A History of a Wyoming Railroad Town from 1867 to 1967* (Baltimore: Gateway, 2004), 15, 151, 154, 167, 305.

50 *At five foot seven and a half:* "Individual Deceased Personal File, Leo Boelens," Identification Data, Identification Section, Memorial Division, National Personnel Records Center, St. Louis, MO; Jonathan Davis, author's interview.

51 *No sooner had Boelens ducked:* E-mail correspondence from Thelma Kost to the author, March 7, 2005.

51 *Boelens and his crew:* Dyess, *The Dyess Story*, 64; Bartsch, *Doomed at the Start*, 367.

51 *Dyess then continued:* Dyess, *The Dyess Story*, 63–64; Bartsch, *Doomed at the Start*, 363; Grashio, *Return to Freedom*, 35.

52 *Not long after Dyess's convoy:* Carlos Romulo, *I Saw the Fall of the Philippines* (London: George G. Harrap, 1943), 178–82; Boelens, "Diary", 18; Bartsch, *Doomed at the Start*, 368–69; Schultz, *Hero of Bataan*, 241.

52 *"Never did a 4th of July display":* Dyess, *The Dyess Story*, 65; Morton, *The Fall of the Philippines*, 460.

53 *Surrender orders had begun to trickle down:* Morton, *The Fall of the Philippines,* 459–60.

53 *Lt. Sam Grashio had never:* Grashio, *Return to Freedom,* 35–37.

53 *Dyess had created a cult of personality:* Dyess, *The Dyess Story,* 61. Bartsch, *Doomed at the Start,* 341; MacArthur, *Reminiscences,* 145.

54 *But whereas MacArthur's pledge:* Dyess, *The Dyess Story,* 61.

54 *His pilots barely had enough strength:* Bartsch, *Doomed at the Start,* 343–44; Joe Moore, author's interview.

54 *In late March, the brass:* Dyess, *The Dyess Story,* 61–62.

54 *Dyess's convoy motored into Mariveles:* Ibid., 65; Grashio, *Return to Freedom,* 39; Bartsch, *Doomed at the Start,* 375.

55 *As his two-jeep caravan:* Holt, "King of Bataan," 155–73; Morton, *The Fall of the Philippines,* 463–64.

55 *On April 3, Japanese guns:* Morton, *The Fall of the Philippines,* 421–53; Toland, *But Not in Shame,* 292.

56 *King arrived at the town of Lamao:* Ibid., 303–5; Morton, *The Fall of the Philippines,* 464–66.

56 *Ed Dyess was seeing otherwise:* Dyess, *The Dyess Story,* 66–68; Grashio, *Return to Freedom,* 39.

57 *Luckily for the passengers:* Romulo, *I Saw the Fall of the Philippines,* 183–86.

58 *"God help them":* Boelens, Diary, 19

5. THE HIKE

PAGE

61 *"There was a blazing road:* Lee, "Awakening," *Nothing but Praise,* 38.

61 *According to a witness:* Dyess, *The Dyess Story,* 70–71.

62 *"A Philippines Times Square":* Ralph Levenberg, quoted in Donald Knox, *Death March: The Survivors of Bataan* (New York: Harcourt Brace, 1981), 119; Jack Donohoe, author's interview.

62 *Some Japanese soldiers, similarly exhausted:* Knox, *Death March,* 114.

62 *They had not conquered Bataan quickly:* Lawrence Taylor, *A Trial of Generals: Homma, Yamashita, MacArthur* (South Bend, IN: Icarus, 1981), 96; Stanley L. Falk, *Bataan: The March of Death* (New York: Jove, 1983), 64–66, 233.

62 *And though they despised their adversaries:* Falk, *Bataan,* 230.

62 *According to the code of* Bushido: Ibid., 230–32; Lamott, *Nippon,* 180; Grashio, *Return to Freedom,* 58.

62 *In the oppressive heat:* Dyess, EXPERIENCES and OBSERVATIONS as a P.O.W. in the P.I., Sworn statement of Major William E. Dyess, August 16, 1943 (Air Force Historical Research Agency, Maxwell Air Force Base, AL, 1; Daws, *Prisoners of the Japanese,* 74; Bert Bank, *Back from the Living Dead* (Tuscaloosa, AL: Self-published, 1945), 19; Falk, *Bataan,* 127–30.

62 *Determined not to let his Randolph Field ring:* Grashio, *Return to Freedom,* 40.

63 *"There still was plenty of fight":* Dyess, *The Dyess Story,* 68.

63 *Flanked by soldiers:* Manny Lawton, *Some Survived: An Eyewitness Account of the Bataan Death March and the Men Who Lived Through It* (Chapel Hill, NC: Algonquin, 1984), 18. Mario Tonelli, author's interview; Dyess, *The Dyess Story*, 73; John Olson, author's interview; Toland, *But Not in Shame*, 315–16; Falk, *Bataan*, 131–32.

63 *But it was no sightseeing tour:* Jack Donohoe, author's interview; Grashio, *Return to Freedom*, 48; Hunt, *Behind Japanese Lines*, 37; Mario Tonelli, author's interview; Knox, *Death March*, 130; Daws, *Prisoners of the Japanese*, 78.

63 *Even rest breaks:* Lawton, *Some Survived*, 19; Dyess, *The Dyess Story*, 76; Grashio, *Return to Freedom*, 49, Falk, *Bataan*, 133. The best description of the all-pervading heat on the Death March, in the author's opinion, comes from Pvt. Leon Beck in Knox, *Death March*, 133: "And the weather was hot, hot, hot. The sun comes up hot, and it goes down hot, and it stays hot all night. It was just plain hell hot."

64 *The passing motorized processions:* Toland, *But Not in Shame*, 312; Dyess, *The Dyess Story*, 73, 75; Grashio, *Return to Freedom*, 48; Bert Bank, author's interview.

64 *While most of these hapless prisoners:* Daws, *Prisoners of the Japanese*, 77; Knox, *Death March*, 121.

64 *One prisoner:* Mario Tonelli, author's interview.

64 *While their minds struggled to process:* Daws, *Prisoners of the Japanese*, 77; Grashio, *Return to Freedom*, 49; Dyess, *The Dyess Story*, 76.

65 *The demoralized, dehydrated prisoners:* Grashio, *Return to Freedom*, 46, 48; Mario Tonelli, author's interview; Knox, *Death March*, 130–31; Bank, *Back from the Living Dead*, 21.

65 *As morning melted into afternoon:* Dyess, *The Dyess Story*, 71, 13–14.

65 *they had been separated hours earlier:* Grashio, *Return to Freedom*, 47, 50.

65 *Though there was no logical explanation:* Ibid., 46–47, 52, 57.

66 *Since it certainly seemed:* Jack Donohoe, author's interview; Grashio, *Return to Freedom*, 48.

66 *There were, however, no absolute certainties:* Grashio, *Return to Freedom*, 47–48.

66 *Before the Japanese segregated the prisoners:* John Olson, author's interview; Jack Donohoe, author's interview; Bank, *Back from the Living Dead*, 20; Knox, *Death March*, 127; Dyess, *The Dyess Story*, 71; Daws, *Prisoners of the Japanese*, 76–77; John Cowgill, author's interview.

67 *At least they could count on:* James Litton, author's interview; Hampton Sides, *Ghost Soldiers: The Forgotten Epic Story of World War II's Most Dramatic Mission* (New York: Doubleday, 2001), 95; Bank, *Back from the Living Dead*, 23–24; Bert Bank, author's interview; Grashio, *Return to Freedom*, 52–53.

67 *Often, the aid came:* Daws, *Prisoners of the Japanese*, 76; Bank, author's interview; Grashio, *Return to Freedom*, 52–53, 56; Groom, *1942*, 134; Taylor, *A Trial of Generals*, 100.

67 *At midnight, after an exhausting:* EXPERIENCES OF 1st LT. SAMUEL C. GRASHIO WHILE A PRISONER OF WAR OF THE JAPANESE FROM APRIL

9, 1942, to APRIL 4, 1943, October 26, 1943, MacArthur Memorial and Archives, Norfolk, VA, RG 53, Box 9, Folder 14, 2; Dyess, *The Dyess Story*, 78–79.

68 *a catastrophic* masakozi: Falk, *Bataan*; John Gunther, *The Riddle of MacArthur* (New York: Harper & Brothers, 1951), 100.

68 *As a military plan:* Taylor, *A Trial of Generals*, 92–95; Lord Russell of Liverpool, *The Knights of Bushido* (New York: Berkley, 1959), 45–46; Falk, *Bataan*, 47–55; Grashio, *Return to Freedom*, 58. For additional detailed reading on the Imperial Japanese Army's written code of conduct (the *Senjin-kun*, or "Code of the Battlefield") or the *Rikutatsu* ("Army Instruction") concerning Japanese rules for the humane treatment of prisoners of war, see Falk, *Bataan*, 235–46.

68 *Homma's intentions:* Grashio, *Return to Freedom*, 56; Taylor, *A Trial of Generals*, 40–49; Falk, *Bataan*, 224–25; Arthur Swinson, *Four Samurai: A Quartet of Japanese Army Commanders in the Second World War* (London: Hutchinson, 1968), 36–44.

69 *That flaw:* Falk, *Bataan*, 40, 46, 56–66. As Falk indicates, after the war, Homma himself admitted that in April 1942 his primary focus was not on the prisoners of war: "My first and last concern was how I could assault the impregnable fortress [of Corregidor] in the shortest time possible" (p. 46).

69 *And despite the vaunted Japanese notions:* Ibid., 227–29; Maj. Eugene A. Wright, "The Jap Fighting Man," *Infantry Journal*, February 1945.

69 *Certainly, beheading:* Grashio, *Return to Freedom*, 59–60; Taylor, *A Trial of Generals*, 97; Toland, *The Rising Sun*, 367; Edwin P. Hoyt, *Japan's War: the Great Pacific Conflict* (New York: Cooper Square, 2001), 269.

69 *A final rationalization:* As Lord Russell of Liverpool states in *The Knights of Bushido*, 56, "those who committed these crimes had never expected that retribution would follow for, as one of them said 'we shall be the victors and will not have to answer questions.'"

70 *And whether by impulse or design:* EXPERIENCES OF MAJOR S.M. MELLNIK FROM THE FALL OF CORREGIDOR, MAY 6, 1942 TO ESCAPE FROM A JAPANESE PRISON CAMP, APRIL 4, 1943, MAC, RG 30, Box 3, Folder 5, 10.

70 *On April 24, a rancorous editorial:* Toland, *The Rising Sun*, 376.

70 *For hours, Ed Dyess had stumbled:* Dyess, *The Dyess Story*, 78–80.

70 *One American had started counting:* Toland, *The Rising Sun*, 371.

70 *"The bloodthirsty devils":* Dyess, *The Dyess Story*, p. 78.

70 *"the imaginations":* Grashio, *Return to Freedom*, 49.

70 *For Dyess, the worst part:* Dyess, *The Dyess Story*, 80–86; Mallonée, *The Naked Flagpole*, 151; Lawton, *Some Survived*, 21–22; Dyess, EXPERIENCES, 3.

71 *Finally, after being fed:* Dyess, *The Dyess Story*, 87.

71 *There, the train depot buzzed:* Falk, *Bataan*, 184–90; Grashio, *Return to Freedom*, 54–55.

72 *The train panted to a stop:* Dyess, *The Dyess Story*, 90–97; Falk, *Bataan*, 197.

6. GOODBYE AND GOOD LUCK

PAGE

74 *"Then came the bitter day"*: Lee, "Awakening," *Nothing but Praise*, 38.

74 *"Our flag still flies on this beleaguered"*: Jonathan Wainwright, *General Wainwright's Story: The Account of Four Years of Humiliating Defeat, Surrender and Captivity* (New York: Doubleday, 1946), 85.

74 *And, as Hawkins had also seen*: Hawkins, film treatment, 9–11.

74 *The resilient garrison*: Mellnik, *Philippine Diary*, 118; Morton, *The Fall of the Philippines*, 492, 535; Evans, *Soochow and the 4th Marines*, 59; Austin Shofner, Smallwood interview.

75 *Hawkins, who rarely left his dugout*: Jack Hawkins, author's interview.

75 *Continuing to surveil*: Hawkins, film treatment, 10.

75 *Not a single prisoner*: Michiel Dobervich, DESCRIPTION OF LIFE IN JAPANESE PRISON CAMPS, ENCLOSURE "A," Marine Corps Historical Center, Washington, D.C., 2.

75 *Rumbling in a slow convoy*: Ibid., 2–3.

76 *"The infuriating, obtuse guards"*: Mariano Villarin, *We Remember Bataan and Corregidor* (Self-published, 1990), 154.

76 *Dobervich was one of the first*: Dobervich, DESCRIPTION, ENCLOSURE "A," 3.

76 *After a long wait*: Jack Donohoe, author's interview; Dyess, *The Dyess Story*, 98–99; John Olson, *O'Donnell: Andersonville of the Pacific* (Self-published, 1985), 44–47; Grashio, *Return to Freedom*, 65.

76 *"The captain, he say Nippon"*: Dyess, *The Dyess Story*, 99; Dobervich, DESCRIPTION, ENCLOSURE "A," 3.

77 *"Words cannot describe"*: Dobervich, DESCRIPTION, ENCLOSURE "A," 5.

77 *The Japanese would attempt to cram*: Olson, *O'Donnell*, 8–9, 93–94, 97; E. Bartlett Kerr, *Surrender and Survival: The Experience of American POWs in the Pacific, 1941–1945* (New York: William Morrow, 1985), 62; Dobervich, DESCRIPTION, ENCLOSURE "A," 3–4; Dyess, *The Dyess Story*, 100; Knox, *Death March*, 159.

77 *The prisoners were fed tiny portions*: Dyess, *The Dyess Story*, 101–2; Grashio, *Return to Freedom*, 70; Lawton, *Some Survived*, 28–29.

77 *The starvation diet*: Dyess, *The Dyess Story*, 102–5; Olson, *O'Donnell*, 53, 117–19; Grashio, *Return to Freedom*, 72–76.

78 *Not content to let starvation*: Dobervich, DESCRIPTION, ENCLOSURE "A," 5; Lawton, *Some Survived*, 26–27; Breuer, *The Great Raid*, 55; Dyess, *The Dyess Story*, 100–101.

78 *It was not long before the corpses*: Dyess, *The Dyess Story*, 101; Knox, *Death March*, 165, 169; Bank, *Back from the Living Dead*, 28–29; Olson, *O'Donnell*, 132.

78 *The burial details*: Olson, *O'Donnell*, 139–45; Bank, *Back from the Living Dead*, 34; Grashio, *Return to Freedom*, 77; Mario Tonelli, author's interview.

79 *Tales of men being buried alive:* Dobervich, DESCRIPTION, ENCLOSURE "A," 5.

79 *Dogs and buzzards:* Bert Bank, *Back from the Living Dead*, 29; Olson, *O'Donnell*, 142, 145; Knox, *Death March*, 165.

79 *The whole affair looked:* Knox, *Death March*, 116, 156; John Olson, author's interview; Dobervich, DESCRIPTION, ENCLOSURE "A," 5–7.

79 *"Many Nippon die Bataan":* Haggerty, Edward, *Guerrilla Padre in Mindanao*, New York (Longmans Green, 1946), 116.

80 *Inanition, the word scrawled:* Olson, *Death March*, 159; Dobervich, DESCRIPTION, ENCLOSURE "A," 5; Miller, *From Shanghai to Corregidor*, 43; e-mail correspondence from Jane Cambus to the author, January 8, 2007; Dr. Ricardo T. José, "Civilians in Bataan and the Death March," Speech on the Occasion of the Battle of Bataan, April 9, 2008, Capas, Tarlac, Philippines (http://battlingbastardsbataan.com/rico.htm). As the above sources indicate, Dobervich's survival was yet another example of his amazing luck, or perhaps more accurately, the misfortune of others. In December 1941, fourteen Czech nationals living in Manila volunteered their services to the U.S. Army, eventually serving on Bataan in a variety of noncombat capacities such as truck drivers and salvagers. Though citizens of a German protectorate and thus technically Axis allies under the auspices of the Tripartite Pact, the Japanese nevertheless confined the Czechs in Camp O'Donnell alongside the surrendered Americans and Filipinos.

80 *The Japanese had mostly forbidden:* Dyess, *The Dyess Story*, 107–9; Mario Tonelli, author's interview.

80 *Each night, as the searchlights:* Olson, *O'Donnell*, 95; Mario Tonelli, author's interview.

80 *Many prisoners, likewise whirling:* Bert Bank, author's interview.

81 *As the reality of the surrender:* Grashio, *Return to Freedom*, 66, 85; Dyess, *The Dyess Story*, 120.

81 *It had once been inconceivable:* Bank, *Back from the Living Dead*, 25.

81 *Bert Bank's enlistment:* Bert Bank, author's interview.

82 *Bank had befriended Ed Dyess:* Bank, *Back from the Living Dead*, 21, 24; Dyess, *The Dyess Story*, 91.

82 *The Death March had proven:* John Olson, author's interview; Dyess, *The Dyess Story*, 102; Grashio, *Return to Freedom*, 76, 85.

82 *One man had been discovered:* Grashio, *Return to Freedom*, 87.

82 *Though more dark days:* Dyess, *The Dyess Story*, 111.

83 *Mellnik, a onetime USAFFE staffer:* Mellnik, *Philippine Diary*, 116, 130;

84 *Hello, darling:* Letter from Steve Mellnik to wife Thelma, May 3, 1942.

84 *An estimated 1.8 million pounds:* Jack Hawkins, author's interview; Morton, *The Fall of the Philippines*, 547, 549.

84 *Yet Mellnik was still there:* Mellnik, *Philippine Diary*, 50–51, 3–4.

84 *The ship carrying Tekla Mellnick:* Stephen M. Mellnik, "Personal History Info

on Stephen M. Mellnik" (unpublished), June 7, 1975, 1; Thelma Basham, family history (unpublished), 1.

85 *An ambitious private:* Thelma Basham, author's interview.

85 *It was during difficult times:* Stephen Mellnik, Kirkpatrick interview; letter from Steve Mellnik to wife Thelma, May 3, 1942.

86 *It took General Wainwright:* Schultz, *Hero of Bataan*, 285–87.

86 *The Marines, upon hearing:* Evans, *Soochow and the 4th Marines*, 80; Condit and Turnbladh, *Hold High the Torch*, 240; Hawkins film treatment, 17b–c.

86 *The surrender was doubly painful: Leatherneck,* June 1976; Shofner, "Guerrilla Diary," 7–8.

87 *History, as well as:* Frederick D. Parker, *Pearl Harbor Revisited: United States Navy Communications Intelligence, 1924–1941* (Washington, D.C.: Center for Cryptological History, National Security Agency, 1994), 7.

87 *McCoy had had several opportunities:* Melvyn McCoy, "Yankee Guerrillas" (unpublished) Personal Papers of Melvyn H. McCoy, 6.

87 *Having already supervised the destruction: Battle Report: Pearl Harbor to Coral Sea,* Prepared from Official Sources by Commander Walter Karig, USNR, and Lieutenant Welbourn Kelley, USNR (New York: Farrar & Rinehart, 1944), 324.

87 *The misty morning air:* Hawkins, film treatment, 28.

87 *Any place would seem to be better:* Ibid., 22–25; Edgar Whitcomb, *Escape from Corregidor* (New York: Paperback Library, 1971), 102–4; Cmdr. Melvyn H. McCoy and Lt. Col. S. M. Mellnik, as told to Lt. Welbourn Kelley, USNR *Ten Escape from Tojo* (New York: Farrar & Rinehart, 1944), 20–21; Mellnik, *Philippine Diary,* 155–61; Hawkins, film treatment, 22–25; Jack Hawkins, author's interview; Melvyn H. McCoy, ESCAPE OF LT. COMDR. MELVYN H. MCCOY, USN FROM A JAPANESE PRISON CAMP IN THE PHILIPPINES (Personal Papers of Melvyn H. McCoy, 5–6.

88 *The conquerors had enlisted:* Shofner, "Diary 1941–1943," 131; Shofner, "Guerrilla Diary," 8–9.

88 *Both Shofner and Hawkins:* Edgar Whitcomb, author's interview; Jack Hawkins, author's interview; Hawkins, film treatment, 25–28; Austin Shofner, Smallwood interview; Whitcomb, *Escape from Corregidor,* 106–13.

88 *"Where do you think they":* Hawkins, film treatment, 29–31.

89 *A modern-day Jonah:* Mellnik, *Philippine Diary,* 161–62.

89 *To Melvyn McCoy:* McCoy, ESCAPE, 6.

89 *"Shof, I wonder if":* Hawkins, film treatment, 32.

90 *The march soon proved:* Ibid., 33; McCoy, ESCAPE, 6.

90 *Nonplussed, the Japanese endeavored:* McCoy and Mellnik, *Ten Escape from Tojo,* 23–24.

90 *In so many ways:* E-mail correspondence from Peter Parsons to the author, July 24, 2005, October 6, 2005; William Wise, *Secret Mission to the Philippines: The Story of "Spyron" and the American-Filipino Guerrillas of World War II* (New York: E. P. Dutton, 1968), 140; Louis Jurika, author's interview.

90 *Officially, Parsons was not:* E-mail correspondence from Peter Parsons to the author, April 7, 2004, July 24, 2005.

91 *He embellished the ruse:* E-mail correspondence from Peter Parsons to the author, July 24, 2005; Travis Ingham, *Rendezvous by Submarine: The Story of Charles Parsons and the Guerrilla-Soldiers in the Philippines* (Garden City, NY: Doubleday, Doran, 1945), 20–39; Wise, *Secret Mission to the Philippines,* 36–38.

91 *With the help of his wife:* Wise, *Secret Mission,* 39–47; C. Parsons, MEMORANDUM AS TO CONDITIONS IN THE PHILIPPINES DURING PERIOD OF JAPANESE OCCUPATION, On Board M/S Gripsholm, August 23, 1942, Personal Papers of Charles Parsons, Baguio, Philippines, 28.

92 *The deception worked:* Wise, *Secret Mission to the Philippines,* 51–52; e-mail correspondence from Peter Parsons to the author, July 24, 2005.

7. A RUMOR

PAGE

93 *"We saw an open grave":* Lee, "An Execution," *Nothing but Praise,* 41.

93 *Steve Mellnik thought:* Mellnik, *Philippine Diary,* 167; Grashio, *Return to Freedom,* 69; McCoy and Mellnik, *Ten Escape from Tojo,* 34–35.

93 *Jack Hawkins, unable to find:* Jack Hawkins, author's interview; Hawkins, film treatment, 53–57.

94 *He was severely underweight:* Hawkins, film treatment, 53–64.

95 *"You won't like it here":* McCoy and Mellnik, *Ten Escape from Tojo,* 37–38, 44.

95 *"Those things don't happen to Americans":* Ibid., 42.

95 *That much was true:* Lawton, *Some Survived,* xviii.

95 *Located seventy-five miles north:* McCoy, ESCAPE, 8–9.

96 *"We used to say in Shanghai":* Jack Hawkins, author's interview; Evans, *Soochow and the 4th Marines,* 97; Dyess, *The Dyess Story,* 106–7; Hawkins, film treatment, 66; Grashio, *Return to Freedom,* 71.

96 *Dysentery prevented them:* Mellnik, *Philippine Diary,* 168; Hawkins, film treatment, 66, 70; Grashio, *Return to Freedom,* 72–73; Dyess, *The Dyess Story,* 129.

97 *Many ultimately ended up:* Calvin Chunn, *Of Rice and Men* (Los Angeles: Veterans Publishing Company, 1946), 40; Mellnik, *Philippine Diary,* 167–69; Jack Hawkins, author's interview.

97 *When Hawkins was stricken:* Hawkins, film treatment, 72–74, 76.

97 *Ed Dyess felt he had someone:* Dyess, *The Dyess Story,* 108.

98 *Mellnik noticed that the prisoners reacted:* Mellnik, *Philippine Diary,* 170; Shofner, "Guerrilla Diary," 24–25.

98 *Sam Grashio had made up his mind:* Grashio, *Return to Freedom,* 88–89, 93.

99 *War had, at the very least:* Ibid., 84; John Cowgill, author's interview; Shofner, "Guerrilla Diary," 24.

99 *Their Yankee humor and ingenuity:* Mellnik, EXPERIENCES, 4; Shofner, "Diary; 1941–1943," 174 (supp.).

99 *The mucky roads and alleys:* Dyess, *The Dyess Story,* 122.

99   *And there was a hustler:* Bank, *Back from the Living Dead*, 43.

99   *Prisoners produced shows:* Dyess, *The Dyess Story*, 127; Chunn, *Of Rice and Men*, 63–77; Hawkins, film treatment, 83, 90–91; McCoy and Mellnik, *Ten Escape from Tojo*, 60–61.

100   *Some prisoners taught classes:* Jack Hawkins, author's interview; Hawkins, film treatment, 69, 75; Knox, *Death March*, 264; Grashio, *Return to Freedom*, 90–91; Shofner, "Diary: 1941–1943," 97 (supp.).

100   *Germany's surrender:* Chunn, *Of Rice and Men*, 106–9; Alan McCracken, *Very Soon Now, Joe* (New York: Hobson, 1947), 29; Dyess, *The Dyess Story*, 113; Duane Heisinger, *Father Found: Life and Death as a Prisoner of the Japanese in World War II* (Xulon, 2003), 292–93; Grashio, *Return to Freedom*, 89–90.

100   *Since Cabanatuan was almost:* Chunn, *Of Rice and Men*, 106–7; Hawkins, film treatment, 67–69; Kerr, *Surrender and Survival*, 100–101.

101   *One sure sign:* Kempei Yuki, AFFIDAVIT OF KEMPEI YUKI, Kazuo Maeda, Case Docket 232, Vol. II, Records of Allied and Operational and Occupation Headquarters, NARA, RG 331, Box 9525, 1; Kempei Yuki, Lt. Kempei Yuki, 1942–1944, Records of Allied Operational and Occupation Headquarters, World War II, NARA, RG 331, Box 1911, 1.

101   *The Americans observed:* Dyess, *The Dyess Story*, 139–40.

102   *Guarding prisoners was not honorable:* Daws, *Prisoners of the Japanese*, 99; Grashio, *Return to Freedom*, 79; Dyess, *The Dyess Story*, 130; Robert S. LaForte, Ronald E. Marcello, and Richard L. Himmel, *With Only the Will to Live: Accounts of Americans in Japanese Prison Camps* (Wilmington, DE: Scholarly Resources, 1994), 21.

102   *The guards beat the prisoners:* Grashio, *Return to Freedom*, 79; Bert Bank, author's interview; Mario Tonelli, author's interview; Dyess, *The Dyess Story*, 126.

102   *For the Americans watching:* Statements from American POWs, Report, Prison Camp at Davao Penal Colony, 1945–1948, Records of Allied and Operational Headquarters, World War II, NARA, RG 331, Box 1290; Statement of Sgt. Joseph R. Stanford, Records of Allied Operational and Occupation Headquarters, World War II, NARA, Prisoner of War File, RG 331, Box 1903, Grashio, *Return to Freedom*, 96; 1st Lt. Yoshimasa Hozumi, 1945–1949, Records of Allied and Operational Headquarters, World War II, NARA, RG 331, Box 1893.

102   *After a guard had been killed:* Jack Donohoe, author's interview; Bank, *Back from the Living Dead*, 40–41; Bert Bank, author's interview; Jack Hawkins, film treatment, 88; Alan McCracken, *Very Soon Now, Joe*, 27.

103   *As if the wanton cruelty:* Hawkins, film treatment, 78–79; Grashio, *Return to Freedom*, 84; Lawton, *Some Survived*, 38–43; Dyess, *The Dyess Story*, 123.

103   *Though the entertainment value:* McCoy and Mellnik, *Ten Escape from Tojo*, 61–62.

104   *A hush fell over the audience:* Dyess, *The Dyess Story*, 131; Hawkins, film treatment, 82, 94–97.

105   *Escape may not have been:* Heisinger, *Father Found*, 245–46; Knox, *Death*

March, 269; Mellnik, *Philippine Diary,* 172; Hawkins, film treatment, 80; Daws, *Prisoners of the Japanese,* 99–101; Office of the Commander, Nipponese Headquarters, Records of Allied Operational and Occupation Headquarters, World War II, NARA, RG 331, Box 1116, 80; U.S. Department of State, Multilateral Agreements, 1918–1930, 938–57.

105 *Nevertheless, there were escapes:* Bank, *Back from the Living Dead,* 39–42; Mellnik, EXPERIENCES, 4–5; Dobervich, DESCRIPTION, ENCLOSURE "B," 1–2; Hawkins, film treatment, 79.

105 *The inconsistency:* Grashio, *Return to Freedom,* 80–81; Dyess, EXPERIENCES, 7; Jack Hawkins, author's interview; Mario Tonelli, author's interview; Jack Donohoe, author's interview; Richard Gordon, author's interview.

106 *It was so dark:* Mario Tonelli, author's interview; Mellnik, *Philippine Diary,* 173–74; Hawkins, film treatment, 97–99; McCoy, ESCAPE, 12–13.

106 *The next morning, Hawkins:* Hawkins, film treatment, 100–105; Grashio, *Return to Freedom,* 81; Dyess, *The Dyess Story,* 132–36; Richard Gordon, author's interview.

108 *Twenty-four hours would pass:* McCoy, ESCAPE, 14; Dyess, *The Dyess Story,* 136; Dyess, EXPERIENCES, 14.

108 *After the storm of the preceding week:* Shofner, "Guerrilla Diary," 16–17; Hawkins, film treatment, 108–9; Jack Hawkins, *Never Say Die* (Philadelphia: Dorrance, 1961), 12; Jack Hawkins, author's interview.

109 *Steve Mellnik waited:* Mellnik, *Philippine Diary,* 175; Dyess, *The Dyess Story,* 148; Sam Grashio, *Return to Freedom,* 96; Bert Bank, author's interview.

109 *Examining the manifest:* Hawkins, film treatment, 111; Jack Hawkins, author's interview; McCoy and Mellnik, *Ten Escape from Tojo,* 72.

8. THE *ERIE MARU*

PAGE

110 *"Death is a quiet room":* Henry Lee, "TO—(CAUSE OF DEATH—INANITION)," *Nothing but Praise,* 42.

110 *They had converged into Cabanatuan:* Grashio, *Return to Freedom,* 96; Hawkins, *Never Say Die,* 13.

110 *Under a steady gray drizzle:* Hawkins, film treatment, 113;

110 *The movement was:* Hawkins, *Never Say Die,* 116–17.

111 *Prodded into the port area:* Grashio, EXPERIENCES, 9.

111 *Sam Grashio had not expected:* Grashio, *Return to Freedom,* 97.

111 *There were several catches:* Ibid., 97; Mellnik, EXPERIENCES, 7; Dyess, EXPERIENCES, 12.

111 *The environment belowdecks:* Shofner, "Diary: 1941–1943," 134.

112 *While most prisoners were forced to remain:* Hawkins, *Never Say Die,* 20–22; Jack Hawkins, author's interview.

113 *The* Erie Maru *certainly:* Mellnik, *Philippine Diary,* 176; McCoy, ESCAPE, 15; Grashio, *Return to Freedom,* 98.

113 *The generous portions:* Hawkins, film treatment, 126.

113 *Other than the guards:* The POW was Alan McCracken, *Very Soon Now, Joe,* 39–41.

113 *This officer regained use:* Dyess, *The Dyess Story,* 152.

114 *The three Marines:* Hawkins, film treatment, 132–35; Hawkins, *Never Say Die,* 24; Dyess, *The Dyess Story,* 152–53; Grashio, *Return to Freedom,* 99.

115 *Much to the prisoners' dismay:* Jack Donohoe, author's interview; Bert Bank, author's interview; Jack Hawkins, film treatment, 136; Mellnik, *Philippine Diary,* 176.

116 *The announcement came:* Jack Donohoe, author's interview; Jack Hawkins, author's interview; Hawkins, *Never Say Die,* 28.

116 *After several hours:* McCoy and Mellnik, *Ten Escape from Tojo,* 73.

116 *The light of civilization dimmed:* Hawkins, *Never Say Die,* 28–29; Jack Hawkins, author's interview; Ed Dyess, *The Dyess Story,* 153.

116 *A brief pelting of raindrops:* Grashio, EXPERIENCES, 11; Jack Hawkins, author's interview; Shofner, "Diary: 1941–1943," 134; Grashio; *Return to Freedom,* 100; Brig. Gen. John Hugh McGee, U.S. Army (Ret.) *Rice and Salt: A History of the Defense and Occupation of Mindanao During World War II* (San Antonio: Naylor, 1962), 72; Hawkins, film treatment, 146–50.

9. A CHRISTMAS DREAM

PAGE

119 *"Across one brutal, endless year":* Lee, "To Our Country (Given to Chaplain Talbot, Christmas, 1942), *Nothing but Praise,* 36.

119 *Though more than six months:* Grashio, *Return to Freedom,* 101.

119 *Not Maj. Kazuo Maeda:* McCoy and Mellnik, *Ten Escape from Tojo,* 74–75; McCoy, ESCAPE, 15–16, Hawkins, film treatment, 153–55.

119 *The welcome:* Grashio, *Return to Freedom,* 102; Mellnik, *Philippine Diary,* 180; Carl Nordin, author's interview; Yuki, AFFIDAVIT, 2–3; McCracken, *Very Soon Now, Joe,* 45; Betty B. Jones, *The December Ship: A Story of Lt. Col. Arden R. Boellner's Capture in the Philippines, Imprisonment, and Death on a World War II Japanese Hellship* (Jefferson, NC: McFarland, 1992), 77; Victor Mapes, *The Butchers, the Baker: The World War II War Memoir of a United States Air Corps Soldier Captured by the Japanese in the Philippines* (Jefferson, NC: McFarland, 2000), 174.

122 *Only a man who had been through:* Boelens, "Diary," 26, 34, 37.

122 *The benefits of hewing:* A Brief History of the Philippine Prison System, Republic of the Philippines, Department of Justice, Bureau of Corrections, 19; Ernesto Corcino, author's interview; Fely Yap, author's interview; Fé Campo, author's interview.

123 *Much of the colony's substantial acreage:* Heisinger, *Father Found,* 314; Austin RECORD OF EVENTS AS A JAPANESE PRISONER OF WAR: 6 May, 1942 to 4 April, 1943, ENCLOSURE "A," MCHC, 7; Ernesto Corcino, author's in-

terview; Fely Yap, author's interview; Fé Campo, author's interview; Carl Nordin, *We Were Next to Nothing: An American POW's Account of Japanese Prison Camps and Deliverance in World War II* (Jefferson, NC, McFarland, 1997), 74; Knox, *Death March*, 251.

123   *The war, however, brought about:* Ernesto Corcino, author's interview; Fely Yap, author's interview; Fé Campo, author's interview; Juan Acenas, *Silver Jubilee Book—1957*, Philippines Bureau of Corrections, 32–33; *A Brief History of the Philippine Prison System*, 20.

123   *Forcing POWs to labor: Record of Proceedings of the International Military Tribunal for the Far East, 1946–1948* (The Tribunal, 1948), 73, 1076–77.

124   *There was perhaps no better place:* Mellnik, *Philippine Diary*, 176.

124   *And yet, despite Dapecol's seclusion:* Hawkins, film treatment, 151–52; McGee, *Rice and Salt*, 73.

124   *Dapecol was an open:* Jack Hawkins, author's interview; Hawkins, film treatment, 167–69; Fely Yap, author's interview; Fé Campo, author's interview; Nordin, *We Were Next to Nothing*, 75.

125   *Conditions were spartan:* Grashio, EXPERIENCES, 11; Jack Hawkins, author's interview; McGee, *Rice and Salt*, 72; Hawkins, *Never Say Die*, 33–34.

125   *"How ya doin'?":* Hawkins, film treatment, 156–58.

126   *Before dawn, brassy bugle calls:* Ibid., 158–59; McCoy, ESCAPE, 16; Dyess, EXPERIENCES, 12.

126   *Once a detail reached:* Shofner, Smallwood interview; Shofner, "Guerrilla Diary," 19; McCoy, ESCAPE, 16; Mellnik, EXPERIENCES, 8; McGee, *Rice and Salt*, 80; Hawkins, film treatment, 158–61; Jack Hawkins, author's interview; Jones, *The December Ship*, 79; Knox, *Death March*, 253–60.

127   *Just beyond Mactan:* Hawkins, *Never Say Die*, 36–39; Jack Hawkins, author's interview.

127   *The prisoners, in turn, exploited:* Hawkins, film treatment, 162–66.

128   *Relationships with the Filipinos:* McCracken, *Very Soon Now, Joe*, 50; Dyess, *The Dyess Story*, 156–57.

128   *Though all civilians:* Fely Yap, author's interview; Fé Campo, author's interview; McGee, *Rice and Salt*, 83.

128   *Not all of the aid:* Hawkins, film treatment, 178–79.

129   *Their itinerant labors:* John J. Morrett, *Soldier-Priest* (Roswell, GA: Old Rugged Cross Press, 1993), 80–82.

129   *The prisoners rarely saw Major Maeda:* Jack Hawkins, author's interview; Statement of Cpl. Michael B. Scopa, Records of Allied Operational and Occupation Headquarters, World War II, NARA, Prisoner of War File, RG 331, Box 1104, PERSONAL DATA SHEET RE ACCUSED, K. Maeda, Case Docket 232, Records of Allied Operational and Occupation Headquarters, NARA, RG 331, Box 9696; AFFIDAVIT of Austin J. Montgomery, Lt. Col, QMC: Names, descriptions, and personal history of the Japanese Staff at Davao Penal Colony, P.I., from 10 December 1942 until 3 June 1944, Records of Allied Operational and Occupation Headquarters, World War II, NARA, RG 331, Box 1911, 1; Carl

Nordin, author's interview; Statement of Sgt. Robert J. Endres, World War II, NARA, Prisoner of War File, RG 331, Box 1891.

129 *Maeda's nefarious subordinate, Hozumi:* McCoy and Mellnik, *Ten Escape from Tojo*, 76; Hawkins, *Never Say Die*, 14; Grashio, *Return to Freedom*, 104–5; Heisinger, *Father Found*, 324.

129 *Some Formosans shared:* Hawkins, film treatment, 175–77; La Forte et al., *With Only the Will to Live*, 53; Heisinger, *Father Found*, 324.

130 *The only way the prisoners:* McCoy and Mellnik, *Ten Escape from Tojo*, 76; McGee, *Rice and Salt*, 87–88; Dyess, *The Dyess Story*, 165; AFFIDAVIT of Austin J. Montgomery, NARA, RG 331, Box 1911, 1–8; Carl Nordin, author's interview; Nordin, *We Were Next to Nothing*, 78.

130 *But the guards:* Dyess, *The Dyess Story*, 156; Heisinger, *Father Found*, 356; McCracken, *Very Soon Now, Joe*, 46–47.

131 *To put their consumption:* Daws, *Prisoners of the Japanese*, 111; Shiraji (Lt), 1945–1947, NARA, P-201, Perpetrators and Suspected War Criminals, RG 331, Box 1083.

131 *They had lived with hunger:* McGee, *Rice and Salt*, 77; Bank, *Return from the Living Dead*, 72–73.

131 *As the battle of nutritional attrition:* Mellnik, EXPERIENCES, 8; Davao Penal Colony, Records of the Office of the Provost Marshal General, American Prisoner of War Information Bureau (ca. 1942—09/18/1947), NARA, RG 389, Box 2135, 112.

131 *Unsanitary living conditions:* Nordin, *We Were Next to Nothing*, 81; McCoy and Mellnik, *Ten Escape from Tojo*, 77; Mario Tonelli, author's interview.

131 *Some men awoke to find:* Bert Bank, author's interview; Bank, *Return from the Living Dead*, 75–76; La Forte et al., *With Only the Will to Live*, 182–83; Davao Penal Colony, NARA, RG 389, Box 2135, 115.

132 *Such a policy looked to spell:* Bert Bank, author's interview; McCracken, *Very Soon Now, Joe*, 50–51; Knox, *Death March*, 262.

132 *Melvyn McCoy angrily plunged:* Mellnik, *Philippine Diary*, 180–82.

133 *It would not take long:* Ibid., 183–84.

134 *Getting close to Abrina:* Ibid., 184.

134 *In reality, the fifty-five-year-old Abrina:* E-mail correspondence from Angelica Abrina to the author, January 12 and January 15, 2007; Mellnik, *Philippine Diary*, 184.

134 *Each day brought McCoy:* Mellnik, *Philippine Diary*, 185.

135 *One morning after the rice harvest:* Ibid., 186–89.

136 *This time, it was Paul Marshall:* Ibid., 190.

136 *It began on Corregidor:* Paul Marshall, author's interview; Robert Spielman, author's interview.

136 *Case in point:* Paul Marshall, Smallwood interview; Paul Marshall, author's interview.

137 *A static life was no life:* Paul Marshall, Smallwood interview.

137 *Bob Spielman had enlisted:* Robert Spielman, Smallwood interview.

138 *In Manila, while working:* Mellnik, *Philippine Diary*, 24; Paul Marshall, Smallwood interview.

138 *In Cabanatuan, when:* Paul Marshall, author's interview.

138 *Though no stranger to rackets:* Robert Spielman, Smallwood interview.

139 *After the brief reunion:* Mellnik, *Philippine Diary*, 190–91.

139 *"You can trust Bob and Paul":* Ibid., 191–92.

139 *They practiced their roles:* Ibid., 192–93.

140 *Unlike superintendent Pascual Robin:* McCoy, ESCAPE, 18; Mellnik, *Philippine Diary*, 193–94.

140 *Back in the compound:* Mellnik, *Philippine Diary*, 194–95.

141 *To celebrate the Christmas season:* Jack Hawkins, author's interview; Hawkins, film treatment, 192–97; Fely Yap, author's interview; Fé Campo, author's interview; McCracken, *Very Soon Now, Joe*, 53–54.

142 *"The difference between friend and foe:"* Maria Virginia Yap Morales, *Diary of the War: WWII Memoirs of Lt. Col. Anastacio Campo* (Manila, Philippines: Ateneo de Manila Press, 2006), 120; Fely Yap, author's interview.

142 *Upon exiting:* McCracken, *Very Soon Now, Joe*, 54.

142 *In Barracks Five:* Hawkins, *Never Say Die*, 54.

10. A BIG CROWD

PAGE

143 *"I probed the whirling darkness":* Lee, "Anniversary of Parting," *Nothing but Praise*, 27.

143 *Crankcase oil and powdered lime:* McCracken, *Very Soon Now, Joe*, 43.

143 *Generally, the reports just smelled funny:* Heisinger, *Father Found*, 320; Knox, *Death March*, 261; Calvin G. Jackson, *Diary of Col. Calvin G. Jackson, M.D.* (Ada: Ohio Northern University Press, 1992), 94–96; Hawkins, film treatment, 211; McCracken, *Very Soon Now, Joe*, 56–64.

143 *"It's Christmas, Commander McCoy!":* McCoy and Mellnik, *Ten Escape from Tojo*, 80; McCracken, *Very Soon Now, Joe*, 64.

144 *Each POW received approximately:* Jack Hawkins, author's interview; Dyess, *The Dyess Story*, 160–61; Hawkins, film treatment, 212–13; American Red Cross Prisoner of War Invalid Food Package No. 1, NARA, RG 407, Records of the Adjutant General's Office, 1905–1981, Box 144, 2–4; McCoy and Mellnik, *Ten Escape from Tojo*, 81–82.

144 *The rejuvenating effect:* Grashio, *Return to Freedom*, 107–8.

144 *The belated Christmas gifts:* Dyess, *The Dyess Story*, 157, 163–64; Grashio, *Return to Freedom*, 103.

144 *On the heels:* McCracken, *Very Soon Now, Joe*, 66–68; Boelens, "Diary," 42; Dyess, *The Dyess Story*, 166.

145 *Nineteen forty-three, by all early indications:* Hawkins, *Never Say Die*, 45; Grashio, *Return to Freedom*, 112; Dyess, *The Dyess Story*, 163–65.

146 *the appeal to Major Maeda's pocketbook:* Mellnik, *Philippine Diary*, 197–200;

McCoy and Mellnik, *Ten Escape from Tojo*, 84; Paul Marshall, author's interview; Robert Spielman, author's interview.

148 *Confounded, the Japanese:* La Forte et al., *With Only the Will to Live*, 158; Jack Hawkins, author's interview; Paul Marshall, author's interview; Grashio, *Return to Freedom*, 112; Mellnik, *Philippine Diary*, 202.

148 *The plotters decided:* Mellnik, *Philippine Diary*, 210.

149 *Abrina's support was a major coup:* Daws, *Prisoners of the Japanese*, 99–101; Diary of Major William J. Priestly, NARA, RG 407, Box 1482 (the time period for these escape attempts, as compiled by Priestly, spans the camp's inception in June 1942 through the culmination of America's reconquest of the Philippines in early 1945); McCracken, *Very Soon Now, Joe*, 48. For American military personnel in World War II, the question of whether to attempt to escape was a decision not only influenced by one's own unique circumstances of captivity, but also certain moral and legal obligations, both real and perceived. Some American officers, more so senior officers than junior ones, were aware that they were expected to escape in the event of being captured by an enemy. This topic had reportedly been addressed in their commissioning oaths and other regulations. Most enlisted men, however, were ignorant of any such regulations. The topic was not fully and officially addressed until the standardized U.S. Armed Forces Code of Conduct was issued in 1955.

150 *Geography was perhaps:* Robert Spielman, Smallwood interview; Paul Marshall, author's interview; Mellnik, *Philippine Diary*, 209–12.

151 *Thanks to Shofner:* Jack Hawkins, author's interview; Hawkins, film treatment, 180–91, 203–4; Mellnik, *Philippine Diary*, 203; Grashio, *Return to Freedom*, 103.

151 *Even so, there was an ominous sign:* Jack Hawkins, author's interview; Hawkins, film treatment, 215–19; Shofner, "Guerrilla Diary," 20–21.

151 *Austin Shofner was doing more:* Dyess, *The Dyess Story*, 166.

152 *"When do we go?":* Ibid., 167; Grashio, *Return to Freedom*, 118.

152 *Hawkins and Dobervich:* Jack Hawkins, author's interview; Hawkins, film treatment, 219–20; Hawkins quoted in *Abilene Reporter-News* (Texas), May 25, 2003.

152 *At nightfall, the Marines:* Jack Hawkins, author's interview; Hawkins, film treatment, 220–26; Hawkins, *Never Say Die*, 66; Shofner, "Guerrilla Diary," 20–22; Dyess, *The Dyess Story*, 167.

155 *The Japanese had challenged:* Hawkins, film treatment, 227–34; Grashio, *Return to Freedom*, 109.

156 *The conspirators could not dwell:* Jack Hawkins, author's interview; Hawkins, film treatment, 235–37; Hawkins, *Never Say Die*, 69–71; Grashio, *Return to Freedom*, 120.

11. THE PLAN

PAGE

158 *"All night in endless circles"*: Lee, "Awakening," *Nothing but Praise*, 37.

158 *In spite of their iron resolve*: Grashio, *Return to Freedom*, 123.

158 *They soon realized*: Ibid., 120, 124; Jack Hawkins, author's interview.

158 *They began formulating*: Hawkins, film treatment, 238–39; Grashio, *Return to Freedom*, 124; Paul Marshall, author's interview; Dyess, *The Dyess Story*, 170.

159 *A Sunday, they then decided*: Jack Hawkins, author's interview; Mellnik, *Philippine Diary*, 206; Grashio, *Return to Freedom*, 124–25.

159 *Unfortunately, there was*: Mellnik, *Philippine Diary*, 217; Hawkins, *Never Say Die*, 83–84; Hawkins, film treatment, 240.

160 *As plans progressed*: Grashio, *Return to Freedom*, 133; Roper, *Brothers of Paul*, 73–78.

160 *They then decided*: Shofner, Smallwood interview; Grashio, *Return to Freedom*, 103, 118; Dyess, *The Dyess Story*, 168.

161 *They were also looking out*: Knox, *Death March*, 264; Hawkins, *Never Say Die*, 71–72; Mellnik, *Philippine Diary*, 212.

161 *After compiling a list*: Jack Hawkins, author's interview; Hawkins, film treatment, 241–45; Austin Shofner, Smallwood interview.

161 *When he wasn't pilfering tools*: McCoy, *Ten Escape from Tojo*, 86; Mellnik, *Philippine Diary*, 214–15; Jack Hawkins, author's interview; Grashio, *Return to Freedom*, 126; Hawkins, film treatment, 243–47.

162 *After so many other nerve-racking effects*: Austin Shofner, Smallwood interview.

162 *McCoy and Spielman were anxious*: Mellnik, *Philippine Diary*, 214–18; Hawkins, film treatment, 247.

163 *Sam Grashio, always*: Hawkins, film treatment, 247–49; Hawkins, *Never Say Die*, 91–93; Jack Hawkins, author's interview; Grashio, *Return to Freedom*, 127–28. Although Hawkins feels strongly on the matter, Grashio declined full credit for the recruitment of de la Cruz and Jumarong. He later speculated that the colonos had in all probability already been selected by Pop Abrina—as the latter had promised to McCoy and Mellnik he would do—and steered to Grashio, a natural intermediary because his current work assignment at the dispensary facilitated an ease of communication between the two parties.

163 *Six feet tall*: Mercedes Brolagda, author's interview; Eduardo Gardé, author's interview.

164 *Despite the portentous significance*: Grashio, *Return to Freedom*, 124–25; Hawkins, film treatment, 250–52.

165 *What little free time*: Robert Spielman, Smallwood interview; Davao Penal Colony, NARA, RG 389, Box 2135, 113; Shofner, RECORD, 8; Dyess, EXPERIENCES, 12–13.

165 *Dyess daringly exacted*: Dyess, *The Dyess Story*, 159–60; Acenas, *Silver Jubilee Book—1957*, 32–33.

166 *Austin Shofner was determined*: Jack Hawkins, author's interview; Hawkins,

Never Say Die, 94–97; Hawkins, film treatment, 252–56; Mellnik, *Philippine Diary*, 216–17; McCoy and Mellnik, *Ten Escape from Tojo*, 88; Shofner, "Guerrilla Diary," 23.

12. CAT-AND-MOUSE

PAGE

168 *"All night I lie with eyes"*: Lee, "Awakening," *Nothing but Praise*, 37.

168 *The POWs, so deeply immersed*: Hawkins, film treatment, 257–63; Jack Hawkins, author's interview; Hawkins, *Never Say Die*, 80–81.

170 *Nonsense—that was Melvyn McCoy's response*: Hawkins, film treatment, 264–65; Jack Hawkins, author's interview; Shofner, "Guerrilla Diary," 23–24.

171 *On March 17*: Hawkins, film treatment, 265–66; Jack Hawkins, author's interview; Dobervich, DESCRIPTION, ENCLOSURE "B," 2; McCracken, *Very Soon Now, Joe*, 57; Boelens, "Diary," 44.

172 *On some level*: Dyess, *The Dyess Story*, 169–70; Mellnik, *Philippine Diary*, 219–21; McCoy and Mellnik, *Ten Escape from Tojo*, 88–89.

174 *Returning to the coffee patch*: Mellnik, *Philippine Diary*, 221; Hawkins, film treatment, 266–67; Jack Hawkins, author's interview.

175 *Visibly shaken*: Hawkins, film treatment, 268–69; Jack Hawkins, author's interview; Shofner, "Guerrilla Diary," 24–26; Grashio, *Return to Freedom*, 129.

176 *Once darkness fell*: Hawkins, film treatment, 270–73; Hawkins, *Never Say Die*, 101–2; Dyess, *The Dyess Story*, 170.

177 *The day began*: Hawkins, film treatment, 273–76.

178 *Toiling in the rain*: Mellnik, *Philippine Diary*, 222; McCoy, ESCAPE, 23; Boelens, "Diary," 45; McCoy and Mellnik, *Ten Escape from Tojo*, 28; Hawkins, film treatment, 278; McCoy and Mellnik, *Ten Escape from Tojo*, 91–92; Grashio, *Return to Freedom*, 129.

179 *Dyess, Grashio, and Boelens*: Grashio, *Return to Freedom*, 129; Dyess, *The Dyess Story*, 170; Jack Hawkins, author's interview.

180 *But that did not mean*: Hawkins, film treatment, 269–70; Hawkins, *Never Say Die*, 101–2; Shofner, RECORD, 8; McCoy and Mellnik, *Ten Escape from Tojo*, 93–95; Dyess, EXPERIENCES, 14.

181 *By the time the compound*: Shofner, "Guerrilla Diary," 26.

13. A MIRACLE

PAGE

185 *"I am awake"*: Lee, "Awakening," *Nothing but Praise*, 39.

185 *Just before dawn*: Mellnik, *Philippine Diary*, 225; Hawkins, film treatment, 280.

185 *In their barracks*: McCoy and Mellnik, *Ten Escape from Tojo*, 95–96; Shofner, "Guerrilla Diary," 32–33.

186 *Thanks to Mike Dobervich*: Jack Hawkins, author's interview; Hawkins, film treatment, 281.

186 *Paul Marshall was perhaps:* Paul Marshall, author's interview.

186 *In Barracks Eight:* Mellnik, *Philippine Diary*, 225; McCoy and Mellnik, *Ten Escape from Tojo*, 96.

186 *Back in Barracks Five:* Bert Bank, author's interview.

187 *It was almost 0800:* Grashio, *Return to Freedom*, 133; Roper, *Brothers of Paul*, 81–82.

187 *On his way back:* Grashio, *Return to Freedom*, 133–34.

187 *Pop Abrina, in all probability:* Affidavit of Candido Abrina (sent to U.S. secretary of war through the American high commissioner), February 16, 1946, Abrina family records, 21.

187 *With McCoy out front:* Hawkins, film treatment, 281–83; Jack Hawkins, author's interview; Paul Marshall, author's interview; Robert Spielman, author's interview.

188 *"I knew that the next":* Dyess, *The Dyess Story*, 171; Hawkins, *Never Say Die*, 109; Mellnik, *Philippine Diary*, 226.

189 *Abrina had a jaunt:* Affidavit of Candido Abrina, 21.

189 *Their first hurdle cleared:* Mellnik, *Philippine Diary*, 226; Dyess, *The Dyess Story*, 172.

189 *If ever there was:* Marshall, author's interview; Mellnik, *Philippine Diary*, 227; McCoy, ESCAPE, 21, 24; McCoy and Mellnik, *Ten Escape from Tojo*, 98;

190 *In the span of several minutes:* Dyess, *The Dyess Story*, 172–73; McCoy, ESCAPE, 25; Hawkins, film treatment, 285.

191 *The escapees sat silently:* Mellnik, *Philippine Diary*, 227–28; McCoy, ESCAPE, 25; Hawkins, film treatment, 286.

191 *The escape party:* Hawkins, film treatment, 287–89; Paul Marshall, author's interview.

192 *The afternoon sun:* Mellnik, *Philippine Diary*, 229; Hawkins, film treatment, 289–92; Paul Marshall, author's interview; Austin Shofner, Smallwood interview; Grashio, *Return to Freedom*, 135–36; Hawkins, *Never Say Die*, 116.

194 *Hawkins, though:* Jack Hawkins, author's interview; Hawkins, film treatment, 292–94; Shofner, "Guerrilla Diary," 41; Austin Shofner, Smallwood interview; Mellnik, *Philippine Diary*, 230; Dyess, *The Dyess Story*, 175–76.

194 *They finished their beds:* Shofner, "Guerrilla Diary," 42–43; Dyess, *The Dyess Story*, 175.

195 *Bert Bank had experienced:* Bert Bank, author's interview; Fely Yap, author's interview.

195 *"The Japanese were beside themselves":* Carl Nordin, author's interview.

196 *But the Japanese promptly:* Lawton, *Some Survived*, 72–73.

196 *This revelatory pronouncement:* Jack Hawkins, author's interview; Jack Donohoe, author's interview; Paul Marshall, author's interview.

196 *Nobody knew:* Bert Bank, author's interview; McCracken, *Very Soon Now, Joe*, 76; Jack Donohoe, author's interview; Bank, *Back from the Living Dead*, 81.

196 *There was plenty of blame:* Affidavit of Candido Abrina, 21–22,

197 *While the fuming Japanese:* McCracken, *Very Soon Now, Joe,* 76; McGee, *Rice and Salt,* 104; Lawton, *Some Survived,* 73.

197 *Bert Bank had no idea:* Bert Bank, author's interview; Bank, *Back from the Living Dead,* 82.

198 *At dawn:* Statement of Brown, Oscar Burton (Pfc.), NARA, RG 331, Box 1090, 2.

198 *Nearly two dozen trees:* Grashio, *Return to Freedom,* 137.

198 *Jumarong and de la Cruz:* Hawkins, film treatment, 294–95; Dyess, *The Dyess Story,* 176; Grashio, *Return to Freedom,* 137.

199 *An occasional grassy hillock:* Dyess, *The Dyess Story,* 176.

199 *They staggered in silence:* Jack Hawkins, author's interview; Hawkins, film treatment, 295–97; Shofner, "Guerrilla Diary," 40–41.

200 *Making the mission more difficult:* Dyess, *The Dyess Story,* 176.

200 *Thankfully, they had not:* Austin Shofner, Smallwood interview; Dobervich, DESCRIPTION, ENCLOSURE "B," 3.

200 *By noon, several crises:* McCoy, ESCAPE, 26; Mellnik, *Philippine Diary,* 231.

201 *McCoy stumbled upon:* Hawkins, film treatment, 297; Mellnik, *Philippine Diary,* 232; Paul Marshall, author's interview; Shofner, "Guerrilla Diary," 44.

202 *As they lay gulping:* Hawkins, film treatment, 297–98; Dyess, *The Dyess Story,* 177; Grashio, *Return to Freedom,* 138–39.

202 *"The pain of the stings":* Dyess, *The Dyess Story,* 177; Hawkins, film treatment, 299; Hawkins, *Never Say Die,* 120; Jack Hawkins, author's interview; Paul Marshall, author's interview.

203 *Dyess concurred:* Dyess, *The Dyess Story,* 177–78; Mellnik, *Philippine Diary,* 133.

203 *That, however, was where:* Hawkins, film treatment, 299–300; Jack Hawkins, author's interview; Austin Shofner, Smallwood interview; Stewart Shofner, author's interview.

204 *There was little doubt:* Hawkins, *film treatment,* 300; Jack Hawkins, author's interview; Paul Marshall, author's interview; Grashio, *Return to Freedom,* 139.

205 *But their luck was about to change:* Grashio, *Return to Freedom,* 139–40; Mellnik, *Philippine Diary,* 233–34; Hawkins, film treatment, 301; Dyess, EXPERIENCES, 17; Jack Hawkins, author's interview; Paul Marshall, author's interview; Robert Spielman, Smallwood interview; Shofner, "Guerrilla Diary," 45.

206 *No sooner had night fallen:* Dyess, *The Dyess Story,* 178–79; Austin Shofner, Smallwood interview; Jack Hawkins, author's interview; Hawkins, film treatment, 302; Grashio, *Return to Freedom,* viii, 140.

14. ANOTHER GAMBLE

PAGE

208 *"Thus hunger, thirst":* Lee, "Prisoners' March (Death of a Friend)," *Nothing but Praise,* 31.

208 *Melvyn McCoy did not know:* McCoy, ESCAPE, 27; Dyess, *The Dyess Story,* 179.

208 *The scene in the swamp:* Grashio, *Return to Freedom,* 140.

208 *Every few hundred yards:* Hawkins, film treatment, 304–5; Grashio, *Return to Freedom*, 140; Mellnik, *Philippine Diary*, 235–36.

209 *It was an oddly anticlimactic triumph:* Shofner, "Guerrilla Diary," 47; Dyess, *The Dyess Story*, 180; Jack Hawkins, author's interview; Paul Marshall, author's interview.

210 *At the Marines' suggestion:* Jack Hawkins, author's interview; Shofner, "Guerrilla Diary," 47–48; Hawkins, film treatment, 309–11; McCoy, "Yankee Guerrillas," 12.

211 *They marched about two kilometers:* Hawkins, *Never Say Die*, 127–29; McCoy, "Yankee Guerrillas," 12; McCoy, ESCAPE, 28; Grashio, *Return to Freedom*, 142.

212 *Frozen and frightened stiff:* McCoy, ESCAPE, 28; Jack Hawkins, author's interview; Mellnik, *Philippine Diary*, 238–41; McCoy, "Yankee Guerrillas," 13.

214 *"Look, Major":* Mellnik, *Philippine Diary*, 241–42; Hawkins, film treatment, 313–14; Shofner, "Guerrilla Diary," 49–51; Dobervich, DESCRIPTION, ENCLOSURE "B," 3; Ernesto Corcino, author's interview; McCoy, ESCAPE, 29; McCoy, "Yankee Guerrillas," 15–16; Jack Hawkins, author's interview; Paul Marshall, author's interview.

216 *Approaching Ed Dyess:* Grashio, *Return to Freedom*, 143; Hawkins, *Never Say Die*, 129; Ernesto Corcino, author's interview.

217 *The distance between hell and paradise:* McCoy, ESCAPE, 28–29; Hawkins, film treatment, 316–19, Austin Shofner, Smallwood interview; Grashio, *Return to Freedom*, 143; McCoy, "Yankee Guerrillas," 12–17; Shofner "Guerrilla Diary," 52–53; Jack Hawkins, author's interview; Paul Marshall, author's interview; Paul Marshall, Smallwood interview; Robert Spielman, Smallwood interview.

218 *The escapees, however:* Hawkins, film treatment, 320–24; Jack Hawkins, author's interview; Shofner, "Diary: 1941–1943," 65–66; McCoy, "Yankee Guerrillas," 17; McCoy, ESCAPE, 29.

219 *The fun-loving Filipinos:* McCoy, "Yankee Guerrillas," 19–20; Mellnik, *Philippine Diary*, 242–43; Shofner, "Guerrilla Diary," 55–57; Shofner, "Diary: 1941–1943," 69; Paul Marshall, author's interview; Grashio, *Return to Freedom*, 143–44.

221 *Tears welled in the eyes:* Bank, *Back from the Living Dead*, 82–83; Bert Bank, author's interview; McCracken, *Very Soon Now, Joe*, 76–80; Lawton, *Some Survived*, 74; Nordin, *We Were Next to Nothing*, 104–5; Heisinger, *Father Found*, 338; Jack Donohoe, author's interview.

224 *Despite their improved circumstances:* McCoy, "Yankee Guerrillas," 39; Grashio, *Return to Freedom*, 141; Mellnik, *Philippine Diary*, 243–44; Jose Tuvilla, author's interview; Hawkins, film treatment, 325–27; Austin Shofner, Smallwood interview; Shofner, "Guerrilla Diary," 58.

225 *The escapees had little choice:* Hawkins, *Never Say Die*, 134–35; Shofner, "Guerrilla Diary," 58–60; McCoy, ESCAPE, 30–31; Mellnik, *Philippine Diary*, 244–45; Jack Hawkins, author's interview; Hawkins, film treatment, 326–27, 333–34; McCoy, "Yankee Guerrillas," 23; Grashio, *Return to Freedom*, 144.

15. UNEXPLORED

PAGE

229 *"There was no trail"*: Lee, "Awakening," *Nothing but Praise*, 38.

229 *The flotilla glided*: Hawkins, film treatment, 335–37; Jack Hawkins, author's interview; McCoy, *Yankee Guerrillas*, 24; Grashio, *Return to Freedom*, 145; Mellnik, *Philippine Diary*, 246–47; McCoy, ESCAPE, 31–32.

230 *While roughly ten*: Jack Hawkins, author's interview; Hawkins, film treatment, 338–40; Magdaleno Dueñas, author's interview; Shofner, "Guerrilla Diary," 61–62; McCoy, "Yankee Guerrillas," 25; Hawkins, *Never Say Die*, 139–40.

230 *At 1730, the party*: McCoy, ESCAPE, 32–33; Hawkins, film treatment, 340–43; Jack Hawkins, author's interview; Shofner, "Guerrilla Diary," 65–66; Grashio, *Return to Freedom*, 146.

232 *Their lesson learned*: Shofner, "Guerrilla Diary," 65–67; Shofner, "Diary: 1941–1943," 74; McCoy, ESCAPE, 33–34; McCoy, "Yankee Guerrillas," 27–28; Hawkins, film treatment, 345–46.

233 *Regardless of the fact*: Mellnik, *Philippine Diary*, 247–50; Grashio, *Return to Freedom*, 146–47; Paul Marshall, author's interview; Robert Spielman, author's interview; McCoy, ESCAPE, 35–36; Hawkins, film treatment, 346–48; Jack Hawkins, author's interview; McCoy, "Yankee Guerrillas," 28–30.

234 *"Seldom in my life"*: Grashio, *Return to Freedom*, 147.

234 *Save for a surprise appearance*: McCoy, ESCAPE, 38–39; McCoy, "Yankee Guerrillas," 32–33; Shofner, "Guerrilla Diary," 64, 70–73; Mellnik, *Philippine Diary*, 251–52; Jack Hawkins, author's interview.

236 *Barrio Buenavista*: Shofner, "Guerrilla Diary," 74–84; McCoy, ESCAPE, 40; McCoy, "Yankee Guerrillas," 35–37; Jose Tuvilla, author's interview; Austin Shofner, Smallwood interview.

239 *With refreshments in hand*: McCoy, ESCAPE, 41; Shofner, "Guerrilla Diary," 84–87; Clyde Childress, author's interview; e-mail correspondence from Clyde Childress to the author, December 9, 2004; Thomas Mitsos, *AGOM: American Guerrillas of Mindanao* (Self-published, date unknown), Chapter 4, 1–6; GUERRILLA ORGANIZATION OF THE 110th DIVISION, TENTH MILITARY DISTRICT, NARA, RG 407, BOX 481, 1–8; ANALYSIS OF STRENGTH AND EQUIPMENT 10th MILITARY DISTRICT, NARA, RG 407, BOX 481, 13–16; Dyess, EXPERIENCES, 20–21; Paul Marshall, author's interview; Robert Spielman, author's interview; Paul Marshall, Smallwood interview; Robert Spielman, Smallwood interview; Grashio, *Return to Freedom*, 150–52.

243 *Just past noon*: McCoy, "Yankee Guerrillas," 40–44; Shofner, "Guerrilla Diary," 89–91; Shofner, "Diary: 1941–1943," 87–90; Austin Shofner, Smallwood interview; Mitsos, *AGOM*, Chapters 1, 3; McCoy, ESCAPE, 42, 45–46.

16. LITTLE TIME TO REST

PAGE

246 *"I find my way"*: Lee, "Awakening," *Nothing but Praise*, 38.

246 *It was 0520 when*: Mellnik, *Philippine Diary*, 252–53; Gerald Chapman, author's interview; Jack Hawkins, author's interview; Hawkins, *Never Say Die*, 155–56; Shofner, "Guerrilla Diary," 91–93; Shofner, "Diary: 1941–1943," 91; Austin Shofner, Smallwood interview; Paul Marshall, author's interview; Grashio, *Return to Freedom*, 153–54; McCoy, "Yankee Guerrillas," 48–49; McCoy, ESCAPE, 43.

247 *McCoy knew that*: McCoy, ESCAPE, 43–44; McCoy, "Yankee Guerrillas," 49–51; Mellnik, *Philippine Diary*, 255–58.

249 *The message reached*: Edward Haggerty, *Guerrilla Padre in Mindanao* (New York: Longmans, Green, 1946), 113–15; McCoy, ESCAPE, 45; Mellnik, *Philippine Diary*, 259–60; Edward Dissette and H. C. Adamson, *Guerrilla Submarines* (New York: Ballantine, 1972), 32–37; Wise, *Secret Mission to the Philippines*, 56–70; Peter Parsons, author's interview.

251 *In Medina, it was hard to tell*: Boelens, "Diary," 49; Hawkins, *Never Say Die*, 156–57; Jack Hawkins, author's interview; Hawkins, film treatment, 352–54; Paul Marshall, author's interview.

252 *Dawn had just broken*: Mellnik, *Philippine Diary*, 261–62; McCoy, ESCAPE, 45–46; Message from General Wendell Fertig to GHQ, MacArthur Memorial and Archives, Norfolk, VA, RG 16, Box 17, Folder Fertig Select Messages, Feb.–May 1944; Fertig diary entry, May 30, 1943, Fertig Diary, 1943, MAC, RG 53, Box 8, Folder 2, 81; Fertig manuscript (unpublished), MacArthur Archives, RG 53, Box 10, Folder 4, 201–2; Clyde Childress, author's interview.

256 *The bolt of lightning*: Mellnik, *Philippine Diary*, 263–65; Clyde Childress, author's interview; Fertig diary entry, June 10, 1943, Fertig Diary, MAC, RG 53, Box 8, Folder 2, 86; Individual files, Ball, Robert V, MAC, RG 53, Box 9, Folder 98; Ind, *Allied Intelligence Bureau*, 174–75; Boelens, "Diary," 51; Miscellaneous messages, Fertig to GHQ, June 10–20, 1943, Fertig Messages, Feb.–Aug., 1943, MAC, RG 16, Box 29, Folder 11; McCoy, "Yankee Guerrillas," 55–57.

259 *Shofner knocked on the door*: Hawkins, *Never Say Die*, 160–63; Jack Hawkins, author's interview; Shofner, "Guerrilla Diary," 101–2; McCoy "Yankee Guerrillas," 57, 78–79; Ira Wolfert, *American Guerrilla in the Philippines* (New York: Simon & Schuster, 1945), 127–32; Ind, *Allied Intelligence Bureau*, 175.

261 *Early on the morning of June 26*: Letter from Fertig to General Hugh Casey, July 1, 1943, Individual Files, Wendell Fertig, MAC, RG 16, Box 11, Folder 24; Folder 1, 4; Boelens, "Diary," 52; Ingham, *Rendezvous by Submarine*, 102–4; Dyess, EXPERIENCES, 17–18.

17. A STORY THAT SHOULD BE TOLD

PAGE

263 *"Westward we came"*: Lee, "Under the Southern Cross," *Nothing but Praise*, 31.

263 *The raindrops pattered*: Letter from Ed Dyess to Sam Grashio, July 2, 1943, Dyess archives, Public Affairs, Dyess Air Force Base; Haggerty, *Guerrilla Padre*, 116.

264 *Entering Fertig's mobile headquarters*: John Keats, *They Fought Alone: A True Story of a Modern American Hero* (Philadelphia: J. B. Lippincott, 1963), 242; Dyess, EXPERIENCES, 17–18; Ind, *Allied Intelligence Bureau*, 176.

265 *Parsons's plan*: Keats, *They Fought Alone*, 243–46; Mellnik, *Philippine Diary*, 271; Wise, *Secret Mission to the Philippines*, 118; Ingham, *Rendezvous by Submarine*, 114; MEMORANDUM for Lt. S. Jamelerin from Lt. Commander Chick Parsons, July 8, 1943, Personal Papers of Charles Parsons, Baguio, Philippines.

266 *The expedition commenced*: McCoy, "Yankee Guerrillas," 80–81; McCoy, ESCAPE, 47; Wise, *Secret Mission to the Philippines*, 119–25; Ingham, *Rendezvous by Submarine*, 115–23; Mellnik, *Philippine Diary*, 272–73; Peter Parsons, "Special Mission Subs in the Philippines: The Chick Parsons Connection," *Bulletin of the American Historical Collection* 31, no. 1 (January–March 2003).

269 *It was the Dinas*: Miscellaneous maps, Parsons Papers; Wise, *Secret Mission to the Philippines*, 126–30; Ingham, *Rendezvous by Submarine*, 124–25; McCoy, "Yankee Guerrillas," 82–83; Mellnik, *Philippine Diary*, 274.

270 *It was there that they found*: Mellnik, *Philippine Diary*, 275–76; Wise, *Secret Mission to the Philippines*, 131–34; Ingham, *Guerrilla Submarines*, 126–27; McCoy, "Yankee Guerrillas," 83–84; *Dictionary of American Naval Fighting Ships* (Washington, D.C.: United States Department of Defense, 1969), 304; Dissette and Adamson, *Guerrilla Submarines*, 16–17; A. H. Clark, Annex Able to CTF 71 Operation Order No. 16-43 of May 14, 1943, NARA, RG 38, Records of the Office of the Chief of Naval Operations, 1875–1989, Box 1482, 1–2.

273 *Squinting through the bright sunlight*: Mellnik, *Philippine Diary*, 279.

274 *The rapidly unfolding series of events*: Ind, *Allied Intelligence Bureau*, 180; Minutes of Conference held in Room 803, A.M.P. Building, Brisbane, Australia, approximately 10:00 A.M., July 26th 1943, NARA, RG 407, BOX 478, 1–16; NOTES FOR MEMORANDUM: Conference in G-3 Planning Section 1700K/16, August 1943, Subject: Guerrilla Activities in MINDANAO, NARA, RG 407, Box 478, 1–4; Mellnik, *Philippine Diary*, 279–80; McCoy, ESCAPE, 65.

18. DUTY

PAGE

277 *"You say I'm jesting"*: Lee, "An Answer to the Inevitable Question," *Nothing but Praise*, 14.

277 *A cargo plane had*: Mellnik, *Philippine Diary*, 281.

278 *His only outlet*: Dyess, EXPERIENCES, 1, 17.

278 *Ashford was the perfect place:* Louis E. Keefer, *Shangri-La for Wounded Soldiers* (Reston, VA: COTU, 1995); 1–14; Dr. Robert Conte, author's interview.

278 *Although one needed a special pass: Chicago Tribune,* 1951; Dyess, *The Dyess Story,* 18–19.

278 *He had the* Associated Press: *New York Times,* July 26, 1942; Dyess, *The Dyess Story,* 3.

278 *Some of his visitors: Chicago Tribune,* February 2, 1944; Dyess, *The Dyess Story,* 3–4.

280 *MEMORANDUM FOR:* MEMORANDUM FOR: The Secretary of War; The Secretary of the Navy. Subject: Japanese Atrocities Reports of by Escaped Prisoners, NARA, Records of the Office of War Information, RG 208, Box 2.

280 *Trohan, in turn, dialed:* Transcript of telephone conversation between Trohan and Surles, September 9, 1943, NARA, RG 107, Records of the Office of the Secretary of War, 1791–1948, transcripts of the director's telephone conversations, compiled 08/1941–12/1945, Box 1–4.

281 *On the home front during:* Presidential Executive Order No. 9182, NARA, Federal Register page and date: 7 FR 4468, June 16, 1942.

282 *The mission of OWI chief:* Allan M. Winkler, *The Politics of Propaganda: The Office of War Information, 1942–1945* (New Haven: Yale University Press, 1978), 1–7, 31–37; *Life,* September 20, 1943; Breuer, *The Air-Raid Warden Was a Spy,* 135–36.

282 *It was not long after the fall: New York Times,* April 13, April 19, April 11, 1942; *Bataan,* July 1943, Franklin D. Roosevelt Library, Hyde Park, NY; Dorothy Cave, *Beyond Courage* (Las Cruces, NM: Yucca Tree, 1992), 266; *Chicago Tribune,* January 31, 1944.

283 *In a telephone conversation:* Transcript of telephone conversation between Major Greenwood and Surles, September 14, 1943, NARA, RG 107, Box 1–4; Kerr, *Surrender and Survival,* 158; e-mail correspondence from Stanley Falk to the author, May 6, 2004; Morton, *Strategy and Command,* 537; Thomas B. Buell, *Master of Sea Power: A Biography of Fleet Admiral Ernest J. King* (Boston: Little, Brown, 1980), 399.

284 *MacArthur believed himself to be fighting:* SECOND DRAFT, "P.R.S. Admin, March–July 1943," MacArthur Archives, RG 16, Box 63, Folder 4, 4; MacArthur, *Reminiscences,* 146–47.

285 *War correspondent Raymond Clapper:* Winkler, *The Politics of Propaganda,* 53.

285 *No matter what their government:* Iris Chang, *The Rape of Nanking: The Forgotten Holocaust of World War II* (New York: Penguin, 1997), 144–45; Dower, *War Without Mercy,* 49–50.

285 *Why was Dyess encountering:* Michael S. Sweeney, *Secrets of Victory: The Office of Censorship and the American Press and Radio in World War II* (Chapel Hill: University of North Carolina Press, 2001), 79–81.

286 *The fact that it was:* Transcript of telephone conversation between General Strong and General Surles, September 13, 1943, NARA, RG 107, Box 1–4, 4–8.

286 *McCoy's situation:* Letter from Fertig to Gen. Hugh Casey, 1 July 1943, Indi-

vidual Files, Wendell Fertig, MAC, RG 16, Box 11, Folder 24, 6; Jack Hawkins, author's interview.

287 *Mellnik, too, was obsessed:* Miscellaneous newspaper reports, 1944; Mellnik, *Philippine Diary*, 282.

287 *By mid-September:* Dyess, *The Dyess Story*, 11, 12, 17; *Chicago Tribune*, February 2, 1944.

288 *At last, Sam Grashio's hands:* Grashio, *Return to Freedom*, 162–66, 168–69, 239; McCoy, "Yankee Guerrillas," 107–8.

19. GREATER LOVE HATH NO MAN

PAGE

291 *"I kneel to thee":* Lee, "Prayer Before Battle (To Mars) (December 8, 1941)," *Nothing but Praise*, 14.

291 *The arrival of autumn:* *New York Times*, October 6, 1943; Larry I. Bland and Sharon Ritenour Stevens, eds., *The Papers of George Catlett Marshall*, Volume 4, *"Aggressive and Determined Leadership," June 1, 1943–December 31, 1944* (Baltimore: Johns Hopkins University Press, 1996), 149.

292 *That policy greeted Sam Grashio:* Grashio, *Return to Freedom*, 177–82; Grashio, EXPERIENCES, MacArthur Archives, RG 53, Box 9, Folder 14, 12; *Los Angeles Evening Herald-Express*, January 28, 1944.

293 *Dyess, however, was temporarily placated:* Grashio, *Return to Freedom*, 183.

293 *Ed Dyess no sooner rose:* *Albany News* (Texas), November 11, 1943; *Fort Worth Star-Telegram*, November 6, 1943; *Abilene Reporter-News* (Texas), November 6, 1943; *Dallas Morning News*, November 6, 1943; e-mail correspondence from Chad Hill to the author, March 6, 2006.

296 *It was almost 1600 hours:* Hawkins, *Never Say Die*, 190–96; Hawkins, film treatment, 355–64; Jack Hawkins, author's interview; Shofner, "Guerrilla Diary," 137–44; Shofner, "Diary: 1941–1945," 143; McCoy, "Yankee Guerrillas," 123–26; Paul Marshall, author's interview; Robert Spielman, author's interview; Lucy Spielman, author's interview; *Saturday Evening Post*, June 23, 1945.

299 *The Pan Am Clipper:* Jack Hawkins, author's interview; Hawkins, film treatment, 368–70.

300 *No one could accuse Ed Dyess:* *Fort Worth Star-Telegram*, February 6, 1944; *Chicago Tribune*, February 2, 1944; letter from Dyess to Grashio, December 21, 1943, Dyess Air Force Base.

302 *Just before Dyess's arrival:* Robin Olds, author's interview.

302 *After Olds hopped down:* USAAF investigative board report no. 44-12-22-22, Air Force Historical Research Agency, Maxwell Air Force Base, AL; Olds, author's interview.

303 *Dyess must have arrived:* Olds, author's interview; USAAF investigative board report no. 44-12-22-22, Air Force Historical Research Agency.

304 *By the time an ambulance:* *World War II*, July 2002, 8; Bert Bank, author's interview; Austin Shofner, Smallwood interview; *Chicago Tribune*, February 1944.

305 *Sam Grashio recognized:* Grashio, *Return to Freedom*, 183–84, *Spokane Spokesman-Review*, December 28, 1943; *Fort Worth Star-Telegram*, December 23, December 27, December 28, 1943; *Abilene Reporter-News* (Texas), December 23, December 28, 1943; *Dallas Morning News*, December 28, 1943; Elizabeth Nell Denman, author's interview.

20. LEGACIES

PAGE

308 *"We want no unearned plaudits":* Lee, "Letters from Home (February, 1944)," *Nothing but Praise*, 41.

308 *Ed Dyess had been laid to rest:* Spokane *Spokesman-Review*, December 28, 1943.

309 *So skillfully, however, had the story:* Memorandum on telephone call from War Department to Jack Lockhart, November 17, 1943, NARA, RG 216, Office of Censorship—Press Division, Day File, Jan. 19, 1942–Dec. 31, 1944, Box 1414; Memorandum of telephone call to Jack Lockhart from W. H. Mylander, December 24, 1943, NARA, RG 216, Box 1414.

309 *To OWI chief Elmer Davis:* Letter from Elmer Davis to Admiral William D. Leahy, December 24, 1943, NARA, RG 208, Box 2, 1–3.

310 *A carbon copy:* Letter from Palmer Hoyt to Bert Andrews (Chief, New York Herald Tribune Bureau), January 31, 1944, Hoyt Papers, Denver Public Library, WH 1226, Box 2. In its February 7, 1944, issue, *Newsweek* credited "Owen Lattimore, authority on Oriental psychology now in charge of OWI Pacific operations," with helping his bosses sway the Joints Chiefs and the Oval Office. Lattimore "argued that exposure and warning impress the Japs, while continued suppression of the atrocity stories might give them a feeling of impunity. To this dominant motive was added a desire to stiffen home-front morale, boost War Bond sales, blood bank donations, etc."

310 *Gen. George Strong of the Secret:* Letter from General George Strong to Elmer Davis, December 24, 1943, NARA, RG 208, Box 2; Letter from Elmer Davis to General Strong, December 27, 1943, NARA, RG 208, Box 2; *Chicago Tribune*, February 2, 1944.

311 *Strong must have thought:* Transcript of telephone conversation between General Surles and General Strong, December 29, 1943, NARA, RG 107, Box 1–4; Transcript of telephone conversation between General Surles and Byron Price, December 29, 1943, NARA, RG 107, Box 1–4.

313 *Nineteen forty-four was slightly less than a week old:* Letter from Cordell Hull to Elmer Davis, January 8, 1944, NARA, RG 208, Box 2.

313 *"Two things," Price began:* Transcript of telephone conversation between General Surles and Byron Price, January 8, 1944, NARA, RG 107, Box 1–4.

314 *The two-week moratorium:* Memorandum by Jack Lockhart, Subject: Dyess Story for *Chicago Tribune*, January 19, 1944, NARA, RG 216, Office of Censorship—Press File, Day File, January 1944, Box, 1416; Transcript of telephone

conversation between Steve Early and Colonel Stanley Grogan, January 24, 1944, NARA, RG 107, Box 1–4.

315 *A subsequent conversation:* Transcript of conversation between General Clayton Bissell and Colonel Stanley Grogan, January 21, 1944, NARA, RG 107, Box 1–4.

315 *Via Early, Davis had been directed:* NOTES OF CONVERSATION WITH STEVE EARLY VIA TELEPHONE, January 20, 1944, NARA, RG 208, BOX 2; MAJOR GENERAL CLAYTON BISSELL, RELEASE OF INFORMATION ON ATROCITIES, January 21, 1944, NARA, RG 107, Box 1–4; MEMORANDUM, From: Jack Lockhart, To: W. H. Mylander, Subject: Navy Asks Simultaneous Release Dyess-McCoy Stories, January 21, 1944, NARA, RG 216, Office of Censorship—Press File, Day File, January 1944, Box 1416.

316 *Elmer Davis, addressing the external factors:* MEMORANDUM, January 22, 1944, NARA, RG 208, Box 2.

317 *Perhaps Leo Boelens:* Boelens, *Diary*, 64–65; My name is WENCESLAO DEL MUNDO (Sgt., USFIP), 26 Jan 44, MacArthur Memorial and Archives, Norfolk, VA, RG 16, "Checksheets forwarding documents, May 1942–June 1944," Box 6, Folder 7.

21. CONDITIONAL VICTORY

PAGE

319 *"Our faith is in the blood":* Lee, "Prison Camp Reverie (Three Years from Home)," *Nothing but Praise*, 45.

319 *After months of interminable:* JOINT ARMY-NAVY RELEASE, January 28, 1944, Marine Corps Historical Center, Washington, D.C., 1–11.

319 *Later that morning:* Transcript of telephone conversation between General Strong and General Surles, RE: REACTION ON ATROCITY STORY, January 28, 1944, NARA, RG 107, Box 1–4.

319 *It would not take that long:* Associated Press, in *New York Times*, January 28, 1944.

320 *"To my commanding officers":* Chicago Tribune, January 30, 1944; *Newsweek*, February 7, 1944.

320 *Washington was the epicenter:* New York Times, January 28, 1944; *Fort Worth Star-Telegram*, February 5, 1944.

320 *The most vociferous reaction:* Fort Worth Star-Telegram, January 30, 1944; *New York Times*, January 29, 1944; *New York Herald Tribune*, January 31, 1944.

321 *At the Brooklyn Navy Yard:* Associated Press, January 30, 1944.

322 *Herby Funston:* Bland and Stevens, eds., *The Papers of George Catlett Marshall*, 261.

322 *Security was added:* United Press International, January 30, 1944; Associated Press, January 31, 1944.

322 *The news quickly went global:* Chicago Tribune, February 2, 1944; United Press International, January 29, 1944; *New York Times*, January 29, January 30, 1944.

323 *Americans, riveted to and revolted by:* Life, February 7, 1944.

323 *The indignation was not limited:* United Press International, January 30, 1944.

323 *President Roosevelt said: The Complete Presidential Press Conferences of Franklin D. Roosevelt* (New York: Da Capo, 1972), 11–12.

324 *The War Finance Committee:* Letter from Palmer Hoyt to Steve Monchak (news editor of *Editor & Publisher*), date unknown, Hoyt Papers, Denver Public Library, WH 1226, Box 2.

324 *Soviet successes on the Eastern Front:* Letter from Elmer Davis to Admiral William D. Leahy, December 24, 1943, NARA, RG 208, Box 2, 1–3.

324 *Treasury Secretary Henry Morgenthau's men:* John Morton Blum, *V Was for Victory: Politics and American Culture During World War II* (New York: Harcourt Brace Jovanovich, 1976), 20.

325 *Across the country, War Bond sales: New York Times,* January 29, January 30, 1944; (Nashville) *Tennessean,* January 30, 1944; *Fort Worth Star-Telegram,* February 3, 1944.

326 *The biggest celebrity presence: New York Herald Tribune,* January 31, 1944.

327 *Some saw through: Fort Worth Star-Telegram,* February 1, 1944, February 10, 1944; (Nashville) *Tennessean,* February 4, 1944.

327 *The U.S. State Department: New York Times,* January 29, 1944.

327 *On the 10th of February: Fort Worth Star-Telegram,* February 1, 1944; *New York Times,* January 30, 1944.

328 *The president had added: New York Times,* January 30, 1944; (Nashville) *Tennessean,* February 2, 1944; *Fort Worth Star-Telegram,* January 30, 1944.

329 *"You can answer every sleazy":* (Nashville) *Tennessean,* February 4, 1944.

329 *U.S. military personnel in the Pacific: Newsweek,* February 7, 1944; *New York Times,* January 30, 1944.

330 *Though there would be instances: New York Times,* January 30, 1944; Falk, *Bataan,* 210–211.

330 *Even as late as December 1945: Fortune,* December 1945.

331 *It was no surprise then:* Robert H. Ferrell, *Off the Record: The Personal Papers of Harry S. Truman* (New York: Harper & Row, 1980), 55.

331 *After hearing news:* Breuer, *The Air-Raid Warden Was a Spy,* 207.

331 *Perhaps the most important consequence:* (Nashville) *Tennessean,* February 1, 1944; *Chicago Tribune,* January 29, 1944; *Fort Worth Star-Telegram,* February 2, 1944.

332 *We've got to have the nature:* Palmer Hoyt, "What the Public Must Be Told," *The American,* February 1944.

333 *"Let us face the facts": Philippines Mail,* February 25, 1944; *Newsweek,* February 7, 1944;

333 *Good news or bad: Editor and Publisher,* February 1944; Palmer Hoyt, "What the Public Must Be Told," *The American,* February 1944.

333 *Instead, thanks to the Dapecol escapees:* Letter from Palmer Hoyt to Wilbur Forrest (associate editor, *New York Herald Tribune*), February 19, 1944, Hoyt Papers, Denver Public Library, WH 1226, Box 2.

333 *In the war-torn Pacific:* Letter from Carl Mydans, "I Know of Nothing Out Here That Has Done More Good," *Life*, January 8, 1945.

334 *"with more loose pages":* Haggerty, *Guerrilla Padre in Mindanao,* 113; Mydans, "I know of nothing."

334 *And what of those fighting: New York Times,* January 30, 1944.

335 *"Be of good cheer:"* Copy of Commander McCoy's message to prisoners, U.S. Naval Academy Special Collections Library, Annapolis, MD.

335 *Feeling the weight of world opinion:* Kerr, *Surrender and Survival,* 163–64.

EPILOGUE

PAGE

337 *"We'll have our small":* Lee, " 'Group Four, November 11, 1943 (Cabanatuan Camp Cemetery)," *Nothing but Praise,* 32.

337 *The release of the atrocities story:* Jack Hawkins, author's interview.

337 *Sam Grashio had been:* Grashio, *Return to Freedom,* 184–90; e-mail correspondence from Jeff Davis to the author, September 26, 2005; Devonia Grashio, author's interview.

339 *In early 1944, the Marines discovered:* Austin Shofner, Smallwood interview; Jack Hawkins, author's interview; Paul Marshall, author's interview; Obituary of Melvyn H. McCoy, *San Diego Union-Tribune,* January 19, 1989.

341 *When the battle entered: Honolulu Star-Bulletin,* January 12, 1944; *Brainerd Daily Dispatch* (Minnesota), August 10; 1997; Stewart Shofner, author's interview; *New York Times,* November 17, 1999.

342 *"When we escaped":* Paul Marshall, author's interview; Robert Spielman, author's interview; Robert Spielman, Smallwood interview.

342 *In late 1943 and early 1944:* Mellnik, *Philippine Diary,* 283–90; Rosenquist Diary #3, Fertig Papers, Mac, RG 83, Box 9, Folder 32; Jack Donohoe, author's interview; Gregory Michno, *Death on the Hellships: Prisoners at Sea in the Pacific War* (Annapolis: U.S. Naval Institute Press, 2001), 173–76, 225–31; Clyde Childress, author's interview; Paul Marshall, author's interview; Paul Marshall, Smallwood interview; Robert Spielman, Smallwood interview; Peter Parsons, author's interview. Parsons believed that, if estimates were reasonably accurate, Laureta's forces possessed only about 200 rifles, meaning that only one-fifth of his force would be armed.

346 *For Melvyn McCoy and Steve Mellnik:* Mellnik, *Philippine Diary,* 302–12; McCoy biography, 2–3; *Indianapolis Times,* February 1, 1944; Winsor Soule, author's interview; Julie Witkoff, author's interview.

347 *Okinawa would be Jack Hawkins's last shot:* Jack Hawkins, author's interview.

348 *"If Ed was watching":* Grashio, *Return to Freedom,* 184.

348 *Thanks to the efforts:* "Individual Deceased Personal File, Leo Boelens," National Personnel Records Center, St. Louis, Missouri.

349 *The remaining Dapecol POWs:* Bert Bank, author's interview.

349 *Juan Acenas:* Ernesto Corcino, author's interview.

349 *After attending the July 4, 1946, ceremonies:* Mellnik, *Philippine Diary*, 316.

349 *Perhaps the most capable:* Dee Childress, author's interview.

349 *Casiano de Juan:* Ernesto Corcino, author's interview.

349 *For the remainder of the war:* Mercedes Brolagda, author's interview; miscellaneous e-mail correspondence between Mercedes Broladga and the author, 2004–2006.

350 *With the passage of:* Obituary of Magdaleno Dueñas, *San Francisco Chronicle*, March 6, 2005.

350 *By all accounts, Victorio Jumarong:* Ernesto Corcino, author's interview.

350 *Colonel Ernest McClish:* Clyde Childress, author's interview.

350 *After retiring from the Navy Reserve:* Peter Parsons, author's interview; miscellaneous e-mail correspondence between Peter Parsons and the author, 2004–2009.

351 *International Military Tribunal:* "Record of Proceedings of the International Military Tribunal for the Far East, 1946–1948;" 1145–1211; sides, *Ghost Soldier*, 333–34; Judgment IMFTE, Part 3, Chapter VII, The Pacific War, 1940–1948. Supreme Commander for Allied Powers, MAC, RG 331, Box 1333; *American Heritage*, February/March 2007.

353 *Unlike Camp O'Donnell or Cabanatuan:* E-mail correspondence from Duane Heisinger to the author, June 12, 2004; Dapecol camp roster (as of April 15, 1944), NARA, RG 407, Box 95; Pablo Asuncion, author's interview.

Bibliography

INTERVIEWS BY AUTHOR

Malcolm Amos

Pablo Asuncion

Bert Bank

Thelma Basham

Anton Bilek

Mercedes Brolagda

Ramon Buhay

Gerald Chapman

Clyde Childress

Dee Childress

Fé Campo

Dr. Robert Conte

Carroll H. Cook

Ernesto Corcino

John Cowgill

Jonathan Davis

Elizabeth Nell Denman

Lois Dobervich

Robert Dobervich

I. B. "Jack" Donalson

Jack Donohoe

Magdaleno Dueñas

Dick Francies

Eduardo Gardé

Devonia Grashio and Samuel E. Grashio

Jack Hawkins

Louis Jurika

Thelma Kost

James Litton

Paul Marshall

Joe Moore

Carl Nordin

Robin Olds

John Olson

Peter Parsons

Walt Regehr

Stewart Shofner

Winsor Soule

Lucy Spielman

Robert Spielman

Mario Tonelli

Jose Tuvilla

Edgar Whitcomb

Julie Witkoff

Fely Yap

INTERVIEWS BY BILL SMALLWOOD

Paul Marshall

Austin Shofner

Robert Spielman

UNPUBLISHED SOURCES

Boelens, Leo. "Diary." Courtesy of Thelma Kost.

Burns, John. Diary. Burns family papers.

Dobervich, Michiel. DESCRIPTION OF LIFE IN JAPANESE PRISON CAMPS, EN-CLOSURE "A." Marine Corps Historical Center, Washington, D.C., 2.

Dyess, William. EXPERIENCES and OBSERVATIONS as a P.O.W. in the P.I., Sworn statement of Major William E. Dyess. August 16, 1943. Air Force Historical Research Agency, Maxwell Air Force Base, AL.

Grashio, Samuel. EXPERIENCES OF 1st LT. SAMUEL C. GRASHIO WHILE A PRISONER OF WAR OF THE JAPANESE FROM APRIL 9, 1942, to APRIL 4, 1943, October 26, 1943. MacArthur Memorial and Archives, Norfolk, VA, 14.

Hawkins, Jack. Film treatment, 1944. Personal Papers of Austin C. Shofner.

McCoy, Melvyn H. ESCAPE OF LT. COMDR. MELVYN H. MCCOY, USN FROM A JAPANESE PRISON CAMP IN THE PHILIPPINES. Personal Papers of Melvyn H. McCoy.

McCoy, Melvyn. "Yankee Guerrillas," 1945. Personal Papers of Melvyn H. McCoy.

Mellnik, Stephen. EXPERIENCES OF MAJOR S.M. MELLNIK FROM THE FALL OF CORREGIDOR, MAY 6, 1942 TO ESCAPE FROM A JAPANESE PRISON CAMP, APRIL 4, 1943. Marine Corps Historical Center, Washington, D.C.

Shofner, Austin. "Diary: 1941–1943." Tennessee State Library and Archives, Nashville, TN.

Shofner, Austin. "Guerrilla Diary," 1944. Tennessee State Library and Archives, Nashville, TN.

Shofner, Austin. RECORD OF EVENTS AS A JAPANESE PRISONER OF WAR: 6 May, 1942 to 4 April, 1943, ENCLOSURE "A," Enclosure "B." Marine Corps Historical Center, Washington, D.C.

ORAL HISTORY TRANSCRIPTS

Mellnik, Stephen. Conducted at Fort Bliss, TX, December 13, 1983, by Charles E. Kirkpatrick.

Parsons, Charles "Chick." The United States Naval Institute, Annapolis, MD.

LIBRARY AND ARCHIVAL SOURCES

Denver Public Library, Denver, CO

Duke University Library, Special Collections, Durham, NC

Library of Congress, Washington, D.C.

MacArthur Memorial and Archives, Norfolk, VA

Marine Corps Historical Center, Quantico, VA

National Archives and Records Administration (NARA), College Park, MD

New York Times Archive, New York, New York, NY

Franklin D. Roosevelt Presidential Library, Hyde Park, NY

John Tarleton State University Library, Stephenville, TX
Tennessee State Library and Archives, Nashville, TN
Texas Tech University Special Collections Library, Lubbock, TX
U.S. Army Military History Institute, Carlisle, PA
U.S. Military Academy Special Collections Library, West Point, NY
U.S. Naval Academy Special Collections Library, Annapolis, MD

BOOKS

Bank, Bertram. *Back from the Living Dead.* Tuscaloosa, AL: Self-published, 1945.

Barlow, Keith. *Bunker's War: The World War II Diary of Col. Paul D. Bunker.* Novato, CA: Presidio, 1996.

Bartsch, William H. *December 8, 1941: MacArthur's Pearl Harbor.* College Station: Texas A&M University Press, 2003.

———. *Doomed at the Start: American Pursuit Pilots in the Philippines, 1941–1942.* College Station: Texas A&M University Press, 1992.

Bilek, Anton, in collaboration with Gene O'Connell. *No Uncle Sam: The Forgotten of Bataan.* Kent, OH: Kent State University Press, 2003.

Bland, Larry I., and Sharon Ritenour Stevens, eds. *The Papers of George Catlett Marshall,* Volume 4, "*Aggressive and Determined Leadership,*" June 1, 1943–December 31, 1944. Baltimore: Johns Hopkins University Press, 1996.

Blum, John Martin. *V Was for Victory: Politics and American Culture During World War II.* New York: Harcourt Brace Jovanovich, 1976.

Bocksel, Arnold A. *Rice, Men and Barbed Wire: A True Epic of Americans as Japanese POW's.* Hauppauge, NY: Michael B. Glass, 1991.

Braverman, Jordan. *To Hasten the Homecoming: How Americans Fought World War II Through the Media.* Lanham, MD: Madison, 1996.

Breuer, William B. *The Air-Raid Warden Was a Spy: And Other Tales from Home-Front America in World War II.* Edison, NJ: Castle, 2005.

———. *The Great Raid: Rescuing the Doomed Ghosts of Bataan and Corregidor.* New York: Hyperion, 2002.

Brinkley, David. *Washington Goes to War: The Extraordinary Story of the Transformation of a City and a Nation.* New York: Ballantine, 1988.

Buell, Thomas B. *Master of Sea Power: A Biography of Fleet Admiral Ernest J. King.* Boston: Little, Brown, 1980.

Catton, Bruce. *The Warlords of Washington.* New York: Harcourt, Brace & World, 1949.

Cave, Dorothy. *Beyond Courage: One Regiment Against Japan, 1941–1945.* Las Cruces, NM: Yucca Tree, 1996.

Chang, Iris. *The Rape of Nanking: The Forgotten Holocaust of World War II.* New York: Penguin, 1997.

Chunn, Calvin E. *Of Rice and Men.* Los Angeles: Veterans Publishing Company, 1946.

Condit, Kenneth W., and Edwin T. Turnbladh. *Hold High the Torch: A History of the*

4th Marines. Washington, D.C.: Historical Branch, G-3 Division, Headquarters, U.S. Marine Corps, 1960.

Corcino, Ernesto I. *Davao History.* Davao City, Philippines: Philippine Centennial Movement, 1998.

Cowley, Robert, ed. *No End Save Victory: Perspectives on World War II.* New York: Putnam, 2001.

———. *What If? Eminent Historians Imagine What Might Have Been.* New York: Putnam, 2001.

Davis, Elmer, and Byron Price. *War Information and Censorship.* Washington, D.C.: American Council on Public Affairs, 1943.

Davis, J. Tom. *Glimpses of Greybull's Past: A History of a Wyoming Railroad Town from 1887 to 1967.* Baltimore: Gateway, 2004.

Daws, Gavan. *Prisoners of the Japanese: POWs of World War II in the Pacific.* New York: William Morrow, 1994.

Dissette, Edward, and H. C. Adamson. *Guerrilla Submarines.* New York: Ballantine, 1972.

Dod, Karl C. *The Corps of Engineers: The War Against Japan.* Washington, D.C.: Official Center for Military History, 1966.

Dong, Stella. *Shanghai: The Rise and Fall of a Decadent City.* New York: Perennial, 2000.

Dower, John W. *War Without Mercy: Race and Power in the Pacific War.* New York: Pantheon, 1986.

Dyess, William E, Edited, with a biographical introduction, by Charles Leavelle. *The Dyess Story: The Eye-Witness Account of the Death March from Bataan and the Narrative of Experiences in Japanese Prison Camps and of Eventual Escape.* New York: G. P. Putnam's Sons, 1944.

Edmonds, Walter D. *They Fought with What They Had: The Story of the Army Air Forces in the Southwest Pacific, 1941–1942.* Boston: Little, Brown, 1951.

Eisenhower, Dwight D. *Crusade in Europe: A Personal Account of World War II.* Garden City, NY: Doubleday, 1948.

Evans, William R. *Soochow and the 4th Marines.* Rogue River, OR: Atwood, 1987.

Eyre, James K., Jr. *The Roosevelt-MacArthur Conflict.* Chambersburg, PA: Craft Press, 1950.

Falk, Stanley L. *Bataan: The March of Death: A Shattering Saga of Horror and Heroism.* New York: Jove, 1983.

Ferrell, Robert H., ed. *Off the Record: The Private Papers of Harry S. Truman.* New York: Harper & Row, 1980.

Frank, Richard B. *Downfall: The End of the Imperial Japanese Empire.* New York: Penguin, 1999.

Gaskill, Col. Robert C. *Guests of the Son of Heaven.* New York: Vantage, 1976.

Glusman, John A. *Conduct Under Fire: Four American Doctors and Their Fight for Life as Prisoners of the Japanese, 1941–1945.* New York: Viking Penguin, 2005.

Grashio, Samuel C., and Bernard Norling. *Return to Freedom.* Spokane: Gonzaga University Press, 1982.

Grew, Joseph C. *Report from Tokyo*. New York: Simon & Schuster, 1942.

Groom, Winston. *1942: The Year That Tried Men's Souls*. New York: Atlantic Monthly Press, 2005.

Gunther, John. *The Riddle of MacArthur: Japan, Korea and the Far East*. New York: Harper & Brothers, 1951.

———. *Roosevelt in Retrospect: A Profile in History*. New York, Harper & Brothers, 1950.

Haggerty, Edward. *Guerrilla Padre in Mindanao*. New York: Longmans, Green, 1946.

Hawkins, Col. Jack, USMC. *Never Say Die*. Philadelphia: Dorrance, 1961.

Heimbuch, Raymond C. *I'm One of the Lucky Ones, I Came Home Alive*. Crete, NE: Dageforde, 2003.

Heisinger, Duane. *Father Found: Life and Death as a Prisoner of the Japanese*. Xulon, 2003.

Hersey, John. *Men on Bataan*. New York: Alfred A. Knopf, 1942.

Hoyt, Edwin P. *Bowfin: The True Story of a Fabled Fleet Submarine in World War II*. Short Hills, NJ: Burford, 1983.

———. *Japan's War: The Great Pacific Conflict*. New York: Cooper Square, 2001.

Hunt, Ray C., and Bernard Norling. *Behind Japanese Lines: An American Guerrilla in the Philippines*. New York: Pocket, 1988.

Hynes, Samuel and Anne Matthews, et al., eds. *Reporting World War II: Part One: American Journalism, 1938–1944*. New York: Library of America/Penguin, 1995.

Ind, Allison. *Allied Intelligence Bureau: Our Secret Weapon in the War Against Japan*. New York: David McKay, 1958.

———. *Bataan: The Judgment Seat—The Saga of the Philippine Command of the United States Army Air Force, May 1941–May 1942*. New York: Macmillan, 1944.

Ingham, Travis. *Rendezvous by Submarine: The Story of Charles Parsons and the Guerrilla-Soldiers in the Philippines*. Garden City, NY: Doubleday, Doran, 1945.

Jackson, Col. Calvin G. *Diary of Colonel Calvin G. Jackson, M.D.—Kept During World War II, 1941–1945*. Ada: Ohio Northern University Press, 1992.

Jones, Betty B. *The December Ship: A Story of Lt. Col. Arden R. Boellner's Capture in the Philippines, Imprisonment, and Death on a World War II Japanese Hellship*. Jefferson, NC: McFarland, 1992.

Jones, Wilbur D., Jr. *Football! Navy! War! How Military Lend-Lease Players Saved the College Game and Helped Win World War II*. Jefferson, NC: McFarland, 2009.

Karig, Cmdr. Walter, and Lt. Welbourn Kelley, USNR. *Battle Report: From Pearl Harbor to Coral Sea*. New York: Farrar & Rinehart, 1944.

Keats, John. *They Fought Alone: A True Story of a Modern American Hero*. Philadelphia: J. B. Lippincott 1963.

Keefer, Louis E. *Shangri-La for Wounded Soldiers*. Reston, VA: Coru, 1995.

Kerr, Bartlett E. *Surrender and Survival: The Experience of American POWs in the Pacific, 1941–1945*. New York: William Morrow, 1985.

Knox, Donald. *Death March: The Survivors of Bataan*. New York: Harcourt Brace, 1981.

LaForte, Robert S., Ronald E. Marcello, and Richard L. Himmel. *With Only the Will to Live: Accounts of Americans in Japanese Prison Camps, 1941–1945*. Wilmington, DE: Scholarly Resources, 1994.

Lamott, Willis. *Nippon: The Crime and Punishment of Japan*. New York: John Day, 1944.

Larrabee, Eric. *Commander in Chief*. New York: Touchstone, 1987.

Lawton, Manny. *Some Survived: An Eyewitness Account of the Bataan Death March and the Men Who Lived Through It*. Chapel Hill, NC: Algonquin, 1984.

Lee, Clark. *They Call It Pacific: An Eye-witness Story of Our War Against Japan from Bataan to the Solomons*. New York: Viking, 1943.

Lee, Henry. *Nothing but Praise*. Pasadena, CA: Philippines Arts Council, Pacific Asia Museum, 1985.

Lingeman, Richard. *Don't You Know There's a War On?: The American Homefront, 1941–1945*. New York: Thunder's Mouth Press/Nation Books, 2003.

MacArthur, Douglas. *Reminiscences*. New York: McGraw-Hill, 1964.

Maga, Tim. *Judgment at Tokyo: The Japanese War Crimes Trials*. Lexington: University Press of Kentucky, 2001.

Mallonée, Richard C. *The Naked Flagpole: Battle for Bataan*. San Rafael, CA: Presidio, 1980.

Manchester, William. *American Caesar: Douglas MacArthur, 1880–1964*. New York: Dell, 1978.

Mapes, Victor L., with Scott A. Mapes. *The Butchers, the Baker: The World War II Memoir of a United States Army Air Corps Soldier Captured by the Japanese in the Philippines*. Jefferson, NC: McFarland, 2000.

Maynard, Mary McKay. *My Faraway Home: An American Family's WWII Tale of Adventure and Survival in the Jungles of the Philippines*. Guilford, CT: Lyons, 2002.

McCoy, Cmdr. Melvyn H., and Lt. Col. S. M. Mellnik, as told to Lt. Welbourn Kelley, USNR. *Ten Escape from Tojo*. New York: Farrar & Rinehart, 1944.

McCracken, Alan. *Very Soon Now, Joe*. New York: Hobson, 1947.

McCullough, David. *Truman*. New York: Simon & Schuster, 1992.

McGee, Brig. Gen. John Hugh. *Rice and Salt*. San Antonio: Naylor, 1962.

Meixsel, Richard B. *Clark Field and the U.S. Army Air Corps in the Philippines, 1919–1942*. Quezon City, Philippines: New Day, 2002.

Mellnik, Brig. Gen. Steve. *Philippine Diary: 1939–1945*. New York: Van Nostrand Reinhold, 1969.

Michno, Gregory. *Death on the Hellships: Prisoners at Sea in the Pacific War*. Annapolis: U.S. Naval Institute Press, 2001.

Miller, J. Michael. *From Shanghai to Corregidor: Marines in the Defense of the Philippines*. Washington, D.C., 1997.

Mitsos, Thomas. *AGOM: American Guerrillas of Mindanao*. Self-published, date unknown. Courtesy of Clyde Childress.

Morales, Maria Virginia Yap. *Diary of the War: WWII Memoirs of Lt. Col. Anastacio Campo*. Manila, Philippines: Ateneo de Manila Press, 2006.

Morrett, John J. *Soldier Priest*. Roswell, GA: Old Rugged Cross Press, 1993.

Morton, Louis. *U.S. Army in World War II: The War in the Pacific—Strategy and Command: The First Two Years*. Washington, D.C.: Office of the Chief of Military History, Department of the Army, 1962.

———. *U.S. Army in World War II: The War in the Pacific—The Fall of the Philippines*. Washington, D.C.: Center of Military History, United States Army, 1989.

Mosier, John. *Cross of Iron*. New York: Henry Holt, 2006.

Neyland, Robert Reese, and Dr. Andrew Kozar. *Football as a War Game: The Annotated Journals of General R. R. Neyland*. Knoxville, TN: Falcon, 2002.

Nordin, Carl S. *We Were Next to Nothing: An American POW's Account of Japanese Prison Camps and Deliverance in World War II*. Jefferson, NC: McFarland, 1997.

Norman, Elizabeth: *We Band of Angels: The Untold Story of American Nurses Trapped on Bataan by the Japanese*. New York: Pocket, 1999.

Olson, John E. *O'Donnell: Andersonville of the Pacific*. Self-published, 1985.

Osgood, Charles. *Defending Baltimore Against Enemy Attack: A Boyhood Year During World War II*. New York: Hyperion, 2004.

Parker, Frederick D. *Pearl Harbor Revisited: United States Navy Communication Intelligence, 1924–1941*. Washington, D.C.: Center for Cryptological History, Nation Security Agency, 1994.

Philippines. Victoria, Australia: Lonely Planet Publications, 2003.

Quezon, Manuel Luis. *The Good Fight*. New York: D. Appleton-Century, 1946.

Redmond, Juanita. *I Served on Bataan*. Philadelphia: J. B. Lippincott, 1943.

Romulo, Carlos P. *I Saw the Fall of the Philippines*. London: George G. Harrap, 1943.

Roper, Richard. *Brothers of Paul: Activities of Prisoner of War Chaplains in the Philippines During World War II*. Odenton, MD: Revere, 2003.

Lord Russell of Liverpool. *The Knights of Bushido*. New York: Berkley, 1958.

Sakai, Saburo. *Samurai!* New York: Bantam, 1978.

Schultz, Duane. *Hero of Bataan: The Story of General Jonathan M. Wainwright*. New York: St. Martin's, 1981.

Sides, Hampton. *Ghost Soldiers: The Forgotten Epic Story of World War II's Most Dramatic Mission*. New York: Doubleday, 2001.

Souvenir Program of 40th Anniversary, Philippine Veterans Legion of Davao, Inc., Davao City—May 2, 1999, and Annual General Membership Assembly of Region XI, Veterans Federation of the Philippines, Davao City, Philippines, May 2, 1999.

Spielman, Robert B. "The History of the 114th Infantry Regiment, 118th Division, 10th Military District, United States Forces in the Philippines." MA diss., University of Texas, 1987.

Sweeney, Michael S. *Secrets of Victory: The Office of Censorship and the American Press and Radio in World War II*. Chapel Hill: University of North Carolina Press, 2001.

Swinson, Arthur. *Four Samurai: A Quartet of Japanese Army Commanders in the Second World War*. London: Hutchinson, 1968.

Steele, Richard W. *Free Speech in the Good War*. New York: St. Martin's, 1999.

Stewart, Sidney. *Give Us This Day*. New York: W. W. Norton, 1956.

Stimson, Henry L., and McGeorge Bundy. *On Active Service in Peace and War*. New York: Harper Brothers, 1948.

Tanaka, Yuki. *Hidden Horrors: Japanese War Crimes in World War II*. Boulder, CO: Westview, 1996.

Taylor, Lawrence. *A Trial of Generals: Homma, Yamashita, MacArthur*. South Bend, IN: Icarus, 1981.

Toland, John. *But Not in Shame: The Six Months After Pearl Harbor*. New York: Random House, 1961.

———. *The Rising Sun: The Decline and Fall of the Japanese Empire*, 1936–1945. Volume 1. New York: Random House, 1970.

Valencia, Jerry. *Knights of the Sky*. San Diego: Reed Enterprises, 1980.

van der Vat, Dan. *The Pacific Campaign: World War II, The U.S.-Japanese Naval War, 1941–1945*. New York: Simon & Schuster, 1991.

Voss, Frederick S. *Reporting the War: The Journalistic Coverage of World War II*. Washington, D.C.: Smithsonian Institution Press for the National Portrait Gallery, 1994.

Wainwright, Jonathan. *General Wainwright's Story: The Account of Four Years of Humiliating Defeat, Surrender and Captivity*. New York: Doubleday, 1946.

Walker, J. Samuel. *Prompt and Utter Destruction: Truman and the Use of Atomic Bombs Against Japan*. Chapel Hill: University of North Carolina Press, 1997.

Whitcomb, Edgar. *Escape from Corregidor*. New York, Paperback Library, 1967.

Whitman, John W. *Bataan: Our Last Ditch*. New York: Hippocrene, 1990.

Winkler, Allan M. *The Politics of Propaganda: The Office of War Information, 1942–1945*. New Haven: Yale University Press, 1978.

Winter, William. *Voice from America: A Broadcaster's Diary, 1941–1944*. Manila, Philippines: Anvil, 1994.

Wise, William. *Secret Mission to the Philippines: The Story of "Spyron" and the American-Filipino Guerrillas of World War II*. New York: E. P. Dutton, 1968.

Wolfert, Ira. *American Guerrilla in the Philippines*. New York: Simon & Schuster, 1945.

The World Almanac and Book of Facts. New York: New York World-Telegram, 1939.

NEWSPAPERS AND NEWS AGENCIES

Abilene (Texas) *Reporter-News*

Albany (Texas) *News*

Associated Press

Brainerd (Minnesota) *Daily Dispatch*

Chicago Tribune

Dallas Morning News Fort Worth Star-Telegram

Honolulu Star-Bulletin

Indianapolis Times

Los Angeles Herald-Express

Marine Corps Gazette

New York Herald Tribune

New York Times

Philippines (Salinas, CA) *Mail*

San Diego Union-Tribune

San Francisco Chronicle

Spokane Spokesman-Review

Stars and Stripes

(Nashville) *Tennessean*

United Press International

MAGAZINES, JOURNALS, OFFICIAL AND SEMI-OFFICIAL PUBLICATIONS

American
American Heritage
Bataan
Collier's
Editor & Publisher
Esquire
Fortune
The Grassburr
Harper's
The Howitzer
Infantry Journal
J-Jac

Leatherneck
Life
Naval History
Newsweek
New York Times Magazine
The Quan
Saturday Evening Post
The Shipmate
Texas Monthly
Time
World War II

WEB SITES

The American Defenders of Bataan and Corregidor: http://www.west-point.org/family/adbc/

The American Guerrillas of Mindanao: http://www.theagom.org/

The Battling Bastards of Bataan: http://home.pacbell.net/fbaldie/Battling_Bastards_of_Bataan.html

Center for Research, Allied POWs of the Japanese: http://www.mansell.com/

Corregidor.org: www.corregidor.org

Duke University Library, Special Collections: http://library.duke.edu/digitalcollections/

MacArthur Memorial: http://www.macarthurmemorial.org

Fourth Marines Band: http://www.lastchinaband.com

Franklin D. Roosevelt Library: http://www.fdrlibrary.marist.edu/

University of Houston, Special Collections Library: http://info.lib.uh.edu/sca/digital/cruiser/onboard.htm

PHOTOGRAPHIC ARCHIVAL SOURCES

Australian War Memorial
Bert Bank
Clyde Childress
Lois Dobervich
Dyess Air Force Base
Grashio family
Jack Hawkins
Thelma Kost
Leatherneck
MacArthur Memorial
Marshall family

National Archives and Records Administration
Evelina Noroña-Togle
Peter Parsons
Jeanne Peterson
Kyle Richards
Stewart Shofner
Winsor Soule
Spielman family
Submarine Force Museum

Index

Page numbers in *italics* refer to maps.